DEFORESTATION IN GHANA

Explaining the Chronic Failure of Forest Preservation Policies in a Developing Country

Michael S. Asante

University Press of America,® Inc.
Lanham · Boulder · New York · Toronto · Oxford

Copyright © 2005 by
University Press of America,® Inc.
4501 Forbes Boulevard
Suite 200
Lanham, Maryland 20706
UPA Acquisitions Department (301) 459-3366

PO Box 317
Oxford
OX2 9RU, UK

Library of Congress Cataloging-in-Publication Data

Asante, Michael S.
Deforestation in Ghana : explaining the chronic failure of forest
preservation policies in a developing country / Michael S. Asante.
p.   cm
Includes bibliographical references (p.).
1. Deforestation—Ghana. 2. Forest policy—Ghana. I. Title.

SD418.3.G4 A82 2002
333.75'137'09667—dc21   2002021485 CIP

ISBN 0-7618-2297-6 (clothbound : alk. ppr.)

To
"Asaase Yaa"
(Mother Earth)

Contents

List of Figures

List of Tables

Preface

For over a century, in particular, the past three decades or so, a great deal has been said and written about the looming havoc resulting from the unrelenting destruction of forests in sub-Saharan Africa. In spite of the numerous explanations and solutions, and the apparent commitment of effort and resources to halt the trend, with every passing year, new information reveals that the threat of serious environmental degradation through uncontrolled deforestation becomes more ominous. The imminent effects of rapid deforestation on the environment and, consequently, the quality of life of billions of people are well known. Clearly, the fact that actions to protect the forests of the developing countries have yielded little or no success leaves little doubt about the inherent shortcomings of the policies and actions that have been applied thus far.

This research provides answers to a critical question, using Ghana as a case study: Why has deforestation remained a problem in spite of the lengthy catalogue, spanning the colonial era to the present, of protective regulatory policies meant to address it? The answer to this question is highly critical because it provides the background and framework for the required new radical measures for practical effective solutions to the crisis.

This book establishes the foundation for a new comprehensive and decisive strategy for terminating the cycle of faulty policies, and provides a holistic, in-depth, and systematic analysis of the forestry policy process in Ghana. It explains the disconnection between deforestation policies and their intended outcomes, thus revealing the weaknesses of the traditional measures for solving the problem. It is a compendium of detailed historical, political, social, cultural, and economic information that clarify the agenda and modus operandi of the succession of key players in the forestry policy arena. The details presented herein reveal the conflicts, contradictions, and in some cases naivety and dishonesty that have helped paralyze the policy-making process as well as the institutions and individuals responsible for formulation and implementing deforestation policies.

This research points to one clear conclusion: without any exception, governments in Ghana, colonial and post-independence alike, lack a genuine desire and intent to protect existing forests and replenish those that have been, and continue to be destroyed. In all cases, regardless of expressed beliefs, immediate political and economic priorities have consistently superseded present or long-term threats to the environment. Consequently, policies deriving from, and driven by, genuine intent to protect forests have not yet been realized.

An explanatory model of the forestry policy process in Ghana is utilized as an analytical framework for a systematic explanation of the factors and structure of the process. The research shows that past, as well as present, policies to address deforestation were destined for failure. A complex of factors has produced two sets of contradictory policy outcomes: increased extraction driven by Ghana's economic circumstances, and failure to achieve forest conservation objectives. The foremost public policy challenge is how to reconcile these conflictual outcomes in order to achieve sustainability.

The research shows, in addition, that radical political, institutional, and economic actions are critical for reforming the forestry policy process. Realization of this need can only be precipitated on a realization on the part of the dominant forces in the policy arena - politicians, bureaucratic elites, and business interests – that the existing entrenched policy culture is not fashioned to succeed. Such a realization should be followed by an unflinching resolve to overhaul the policy environment and policy formulation and implementation process. There is a critical need to balance the present short-term benefits of uncontrolled, inefficient extraction of forest and land resources against the immeasurable future long-term gains from forest preservation.

A series of policy recommendations grounded in the above, have been advanced for addressing deforestation in Ghana. To reiterate an earlier statement, only radical and holistic policies will usher in a new era of sensible policies and actions.

The principal objective of this book, however, is to provide comprehensive information on the scope and policy aspects of deforestation in Ghana as an example of a complex problem existing in several developing countries, so as to initiate a discourse on this multi-faceted problem, and ultimately lead to pragmatic, practicable and effective policies, not only on deforestation, but, even more importantly, on the sustainable development of Ghana.

Michael S. Asante, Ph.D.

Acknowledgements

I was privileged to benefit from the immense support, insight, and encouragement of Dr. Joseph McCormick, II of the Department of Political Science, Howard University, Washington, D. C. His expertise in public policy analysis, as well as his critical reviews of my material and ideas provided the required guidance in this project.

Dr. John Cotman, Dr. Michael Frazier, and Dr. Richard Seltzer offered invaluable advice and suggestions that facilitated significant improvements in the work.

Credit for the high quality format goes to my wife, Barbara. Her exemplary skills, coupled with her fervent desire to assist, saved me from the demanding task of editing and tidying up the manuscript for publication.

Chapter 1

Introduction

This book is the outcome of a policy-oriented research on deforestation in Ghana. It is an example of the policy environment of countries in sub-Saharan Africa. It contains descriptive, explanatory, and prescriptive dimensions of a phenomenon, which, left unaddressed, would pose a serious threat to the very foundation of the livelihood of millions of Ghanaian citizens, both present and future. A major goal is to provide empirical knowledge and explanations about the political dimensions of the policy process in Ghana as it applies to the problem of deforestation.

Deforestation policies in Ghana have largely taken the form of protective regulatory policies.[1] Given this, the purpose of the research was to systematically examine Ghana's policy responses to deforestation, and provide a theoretical explanation as to why policy failures have occurred. This book contains explanations about the formulation and implementation of protective regulatory policy in Ghana, and the factors that have influenced both the stages and the outcomes of the deforestation policy process. Ultimately, the task of this research was to derive and assess potential alternatives to the prevailing untenable situation.

This chapter contains a discussion of the historical background to the problem of deforestation in Ghana, the policies adopted in connection with it, and the actions that have been taken to control it. Also included are the hypotheses, the objectives of the research, the methodology applied in the research.

The Problem: Persistent Deforestation in Ghana

In spite of the fact that for almost a century, since 1901, a series of policies has been adopted in Ghana to control deforestation, data show that the problem is getting worse. This problem is the basis of the central thesis of the research;

the disconnection between policy intentions and observed policy outcomes. The public policies for combating deforestation, and the institutions that have administered those policies, have not had the desired impact. The central research question therefore is: Why has the depletion of forests in Ghana continued even though a succession of political leaders has recognized it to be a serious environmental problem, and has put in place a number of protective regulatory policies designed to address it?

Background of the Problem

Several legitimate concerns have been raised about the environmental impact of extensive destruction of forests. In the past century, a consensus has emerged among scientists, economists and conservationists that the prevailing patterns of deforestation are bound to wreak serious havoc on the earth as the home of humankind and as the source of sustenance.[2] Without any doubt, deforestation remains a serious aspect of the environmental problem the world over.

Simply defined, deforestation is the "conversion of forests to non-forests."[3] It is closely associated with the biological, physical and chemical processes that result in the loss of the productive potential of natural resources. A multi-dimensional and organic problem, it is a particularly serious threat to the well being of humankind. Deforestation has intricate and far-reaching links with the quantity and diversity of vegetation cover as well as climates, soils, animal life, and water resources.

The elimination of forest cover sets in motion a chain of devastating ecological consequences that accelerate soil degradation and erosion, eliminate wildlife habitats, and lead to the loss of bio-diversity. It is associated with severe implications for local and regional climates and hydrological regimes.

Underlying the ecological crises of forest destruction is a complex of social, economic, and political issues that include rural poverty, rapid population growth, food and energy deficiency, foreign debt, territorial sovereignty, and misguided modernization policies.[4]

Deforestation in sub-Saharan Africa is by no means a recent phenomenon. As long ago as 450 B.C. Herodotus documented losses of forest resources in the region.[5] He described an active trans-Saharan trade that was based on precious stones, gold dust, and slaves; an activity that had adverse effects on the vegetation. For example, large areas along the trade routes were cleared of trees and shrubs, the *acacia radiana* in particular, for firewood and also for the production of charcoal. In the late eighteenth century, large caravans of up to 4,000 camels and 1,000 men are reported to have made stops at the desert margin of West Africa, where wood was cut to produce charcoal for sale and for cooking.[6]

The high rate of annual population growth in sub-Saharan Africa (currently 3.1%, and ranging from 2.3 % in Rwanda to 3.6% in Togo)[7], and its associated increased pressure on land for settlement and infrastructure, farmlands, timber for local use and for export, and game has resulted in the current widespread and intensive deforestation. The area occupied by forest in sub-Saharan Africa, estimated at 2.6 million square miles in 1980, has been diminishing at about 11,194 square miles per year, a rate that is accelerating.[8]

Deforestation in Ancient Ghana

Ghana has been no exception from the environmental destruction and degradation of forests in sub-Saharan Africa. Opinions, however, vary as to the earliest incidence of deforestation in the country. R. S. Rattray, for example, has said it started when the "original races gave up their primitive hunting habits and began to cultivate imported foods such as cassava, yams, etc".[9] He suggests that deforestation started after the earliest contacts with European explorers and traders in the mid-fifteenth century. However, early historical accounts of Ghana indicate that the population had largely settled down in farmsteads, villages, and small towns and had been practicing shifting cultivation, bush fallowing, and trading long before the first contacts with Europe.[10]

There is evidence that exploitation of forest resources occurred in very ancient times in the region presently occupied by Ghana. Radiocarbon data obtained from sites at Kintampo and Munute in the Brong-Ahafo Region, indicate that around the early-to-middle part of the Second Millennium B.C., food production was, at least, partially initiated in Ghana.[11] Also, extensive excavations have revealed ruins of stone-using village communities; and analyses of artifacts from various locations have suggested that farming was the life-blood of populations in the forest region of Ghana as long ago as the Second Millennium B.C.[12] Anquandah's analysis has shown that yams, oil palm, rice, millet, etc. were among the vital subsistence crops cultivated in Ghana prior to the introduction of other crops from the New World and Asia.

The prevalence of a trans-Saharan trade with the Arab world in the fifteenth century is confirmed by G. B. Kay[13] who considers the volume of transactions 'substantial." He regards the view that so-called traditional societies in southern Ghana were completely dominated by subsistence production as simple and uninformed.[14] Kay further produces credible evidence to show that the practice of exploiting local resources of the forest region of Ghana for export had prevailed long before the arrival of the first European traders in the mid-fifteenth century.

Other records confirm the existence of "a well established, complex trading infrastructure," and tribes of "skilful bargainers, premier traders, and venturesome entrepreneurs"[15] in Ghana prior to the arrival of the earliest Europeans in the region. The Akans, in antiquity, organized long-range trade with the middle Niger regions before turning southward toward the coastal areas. Bengo in North-western Brong Ahafo, for example, was well known for its trade and cultural links with the northern trading tribes.[16] The period from A.D. 1000 to A.D. 1400 seems to have witnessed the emergence of the earliest towns in the Akan areas. Trade had stimulated the process of urbanization and state formation.[17]

The foregoing indicate that farming, exploitation of forest resources, mining, and urbanism existed in the forest region of Ghana several centuries before contact with Europe was established. The rapid destruction of forests, however, began after the epoch of incessant inter-tribal warfare had passed, a time that approximately coincided with the introduction and initial stages of the timber and cocoa export industries in the late nineteenth century.[18]

Deforestation in Colonial Era Ghana

H. N. Thompson's *Report on Forests* is among the earliest most detailed written accounts of the nature and condition of forests, and the problem of deforestation in Ghana. In this report, Thompson, a specialist in tropical forestry, who had been invited to the Gold Coast by the British colonial authorities to examine and make recommendations on forestry in that territory, expressed serious concern about the "rampant destruction of forests."[19] While accepting the reality that forests needed to be cleared for the cultivation of cocoa, rubber-yielding plants, and cola, he added that "in doing so, it should not be overlooked that there is a limit to the amount of forest that can be destroyed with impunity for that purpose."[20]

Citing specific cases, Thompson catalogued the ecological relevance of forests in Ghana, and demonstrated how they are being threatened by the "wasteful system of farming practiced by the natives" and the "over-exploitation of forests for timber, fuel, and other produce such as gums, resins, rubber, etc."[21]

In 1922 Thomas F. Chipp, after having taken an extensive tour of the forest region, gave another detailed account of the distribution of forests in Ghana, and the incidence of deforestation.[22] Chipp projected that of the then 28,000 square miles of timber bearing forests, only 11,400 square miles would be left within a decade, given the pace of tree removal for food and cash crop cultivation, timber exploitation, and firewood for domestic use as well as fuel supplies for mines and railways. He concluded that "if the unrestrained exploitation went on unchecked, ultimately, the whole of the forests of the Gold Coast will disappear..."[23] He foresaw a "calamitous state of affairs" in the distant future because he had no doubt that the rate of forest destruction would naturally increase with growth of the population and the eventual adoption of increasingly intensive and extensive methods of agriculture.

A government publication in 1950 unequivocally confirmed the fears expressed by Thompson and Chipp. In *Wealth in Wood*, the Public Relations Department of the Gold Coast stated: "In another 35 years or so, the forest areas will, unless part of them are protected by reservation, have practically disappeared."[24]

The foregoing clearly indicates that deforestation and its short and long-term consequences were identified and catalogued about a century ago. However, in spite of a long series of policy declarations by a succession of governments, the establishment of various institutions, and allocations of large sums of money and resources, all with the intention of lessening its incidence, the problem has persisted, and has even gotten worse over the years. The goal in this research therefore was to advance an empirical explanation of this problem.

Such explanations are critically needed so as to avert the inevitable consequence of continued deforestation. From every indication, the forests of Ghana are destined for the "tragedy of the commons"[25] syndrome, unless timely, effective preventive action is taken.

Colonial Policies to Control Deforestation

Prior to the reports by Thompson (1910) and Chipp (1922), the British colonial authorities in the Gold Coast had instituted mechanisms for controlling the exploitation of forest resources and the incursion of farmers into forest areas. Those mechanisms were contained in four ordinances enacted by the British colonial governor. They were:

- The Forestry Ordinance #28 of 1901
- The Ashanti Administration Ordinance #1 of 1902
- The Ashanti Concessions Ordinance #3 of 1903
- The Forest Conservation and Timber Protection Ordinance of 1907

In 1948 the first comprehensive forest policy was published by the government. It defined the scope of the problem of deforestation, highlighted the threat it posed to the environment and economy of the then Gold Coast, and established a strategy for solving it. In addition to other measures, this document provided for the creation and management of forest estates and efficient exploitation of areas not dedicated to permanent forestry as a means of preserving and replenishing the forests. Prominent among the ordinances were:

- The Forest Ordinance #15 of 1911
- The Timber Export Duty Ordinance #7 of 1921
- The Forest Ordinance of March 30, 1927
- The Forest Ordinance (Cap 157) of 1951

These edicts bore, without exception, four main features: the intent to protect forests; detailed catalogues of rules; emphasis on government authority; and penalties for infringements. This public policy reveals a determination on the part of the authorities to assume complete control over forests throughout the colony. The key strategy was the creation of forest reserves - clearly marked forest areas where all activities are strictly controlled - and the establishment of the hierarchical Department of Forestry, a government agency that is staffed by forest officers whose main function was to police the reserves. The policy environment, especially, the process by which forest policies were formulated and implemented in the colonial era will be revisited and discussed in greater detail in Chapter Three.

Policies on Deforestation in Post Colonial Ghana

The large number of acts and decrees that have been enacted since 1957, when Ghana gained self-government, demonstrates the fact that the desire to control Ghana's forests and prevent their depletion has not weakened. If anything, that resolve appears to have gained strength.

Policies of the colonial era have prevailed in self-governing Ghana with few modifications. In addition, new laws have been introduced to establish institutions, re-organize existing ones, set fees and fines, control timber operations, prevent bush fires, etc. The following is a selection of the major post-independence edicts that were designed to curtail deforestation, among other things:

- Forest Improvement Fund Act (Act 12), 1960.
- Trees and Timber Regulations 1960 as amended by the Trees and Timber Regulation, 1976.
- Concessions Act (Act 124), 1962.
- Forest Improvement Fund (Amendment) Act, 1962
- Timber Operations (Government Participation) Decree, 1972.
- Forest Protection Decree (NRCD 243), 1974.
- Trees and Timber Decree (NRCD 273), 1974.
- Timber Operations (Amendment) Decree, 1974.
- Environmental Protection Council Decree, (NRCD 239), 1974.
- Trees and Timber (Amendment) Regulations, 1976.
- Forest Fees Regulations, 1976.
- Timber Industry and Ghana Timber Marketing Board (Amendment) Decree, 1977.
- Economic Plants Protection Decree, 1979
- Ghana Forestry Commission Act (Act 405), 1980.
- PNDC (Establishment) Proclamation Law, (Changing the Forestry Commission) 1982.
- Forest Protection (Amendment) Law, (PNDC Law 142), 1986.
- Control and Prevention of Bushfires Law (PNDC Law 229), 1990.
- Environmental Protection Agency Act (Act 490), 1994.

Article 34 of the constitution of the Third Republic of Ghana prescribed the establishment of a Forestry Commission with responsibilities that included: a "review of national practices relating to forests and forest resources, and the formulation of recommendations of national policy on forests..," and "ensuring that needless waste and destruction of forests and associated natural resources are avoided."[26] The commission was established in 1982.

The Fourth Republic Constitution of 1992 retained Article 34.[27] Article 241(3) of this constitution reiterates the country's commitment to sound environmental management. Article 36(9) also stipulates that "the State shall take appropriate measures needed to protect and safeguard the national environment for posterity......"[28] By implication, the state is authorized to take steps to enforce the laws on the environment. That it was deemed necessary to make environmental policy, and forest policy in particular, a constitutional item, suggests a strong concern for forest conservation in Ghana.

A Ghana Environmental Resource Management Project (GERMP) was launched in March 1993. It was designed as a vehicle for implementing a National Environmental Action Plan (NEAP). In addition to other goals, the NEAP is meant to bolster efforts at preserving forests.

In the same year (1993), a Ministry of Environment was established. It was later merged with the Ministry of Science and Technology to form the Ministry of Environment, Science and Technology (MEST). Alongside the MEST, a Ministry of Lands and Forestry, also headed by cabinet-rank minister, was established. On the whole, official documents and policy statements by high ranking government officials have suggested a recognition, on the part of the Ghanaian authorities, of the need to halt the destruction of Ghana's forests in particular, and to prevent environmental degradation in general.[29] The Executive Director of the Ghanaian Environmental Protection Agency (EPA),[30] in a statement that denotes the seriousness with which the government sees the problem, categorically called degradation of vegetation through deforestation and overuse the "most serious environmental problem facing the country"[31] in terms of their ecological impact and the area and number of people they affect.

Annual allocations of funds to the forestry sector have been consistently justified with reasons such as, "a need to pursue vigorously a re-forestation program underlain by the fact that the country's high quality timber species are being depleted,"[32] the need to tackle the "problem posed by the southward drift of the Sahara,"[33] and the "need to make up for the rapid rate of depletion of timber resources."[34] Under the Five-Year Development Plan (1975/76-1979/80) C55.6 million (approximately \$41.7 million) was allocated to the Forestry Department, of which C44.3 million (approx. \$33.2 million) was for plantation programs.[35] More recently, the 1995 Ghana Budget included an allocation of C16.7 billion (approx. \$13.9 million) to the Ministry of Environment, Science and Technology, and C12.4 billion (approx. \$10.4 million) to the Ministry of Lands and Forestry.[36]

In 1993 the Ministry of Lands and Forestry[37] issued a Draft National Forest Policy which, among other things, precisely defined the aim of Ghana's current forest policy as: "The conservation and sustainable development of the forest resources for maintenance of environmental quality and the most possible benefit to society."[38]

A new Forest and Wildlife Policy, a revised version of the Forest Policy of 1948, was published in November 1994. This new policy affirms Ghana's forest policy and draws its guiding principles from the Constitution of the Fourth

Republic, Ghana's Environmental Action Plan (formulated in 1991), and international agreements. The most prominent among its five objectives is "to manage and enhance Ghana's permanent state of forest and wildlife resources for preservation of vital soil and water resources, conservation of biological diversity and the environment, and sustainable development of domestic and commercial produce."[39]

The foregoing bears testimony that both the colonial and post-colonial governments in Ghana have recognized the problem of deforestation. There is also evidence that they have paid considerable attention to controlling deforestation. The public policies that have been introduced, the number of institutions established, the resources expended, and the different sets of actions taken, suggest a persistent drive to address the problem.

Outcomes of Policies on Deforestation

In spite of all the measures to conserve forests, evidence shows that deforestation in Ghana has not declined. Rather, the area of land occupied by forest has consistently reduced over the years.[40] By implication, government policies and the actions of institutions and agencies that have been assigned to address the problem have not been effective.

There are variations in the earliest estimates of the area of forest in Ghana. The first available data, published in 1922, indicate that 38,110 square miles of Ghana's total land area of 80,000 square miles (47.6 percent) was forest-covered land.[41] Later, in 1950, an official government publication stipulated forest reserves in Ghana at 5,913 square miles, and forests outside the reserves at 10,423 square miles, making a total of 16,336 square miles,[42] 20.4 percent of the total land area. This document gave the first specific indication of the pace of deforestation; 300 square miles per year.[43] In 1951 a government committee confirmed this rate of deforestation in a report that identified the spread of farming as the cause and reiterated the threat to Ghana's forests.[44] The report declared Ghana's forests as "doomed to imminent destruction"[45] by farming activities.

In 1984, thirty-three years after the committee's report was released, Gruppe and Ofosu-Amaah[46] sounded the same alarm. Considering that some 30,000 square miles of forest that existed in Ghana in 1900 had been reduced to 10,000 square miles by 1981, they projected a grim picture that suggested that all forests in Ghana would disappear by the year 2,000.

Data from the United Nations Food and Agricultural Organization (UNFAO), an institution that has been a major source of information on forest resources in Ghana for the past three decades or so, indicate that forests and woodlands in Ghana consistently declined at 0.8 percent per year, from 34,392 square miles in 1978 to 33,041 square miles in 1983, 31,690 square miles in 1988, and further to 30,494 square miles in 1993.[47]

Additional data from the FAO indicate that forests and woodland occupied 32,424 square miles and 30,880 square miles, (1,544 square miles less) in 1986 and 1991 respectively.[48] This means that the annual spatial average of deforestation for the period (1986 through 1991) was 532 square miles, a rate of 1.3 percent per year. This rate of deforestation is confirmed in two other FAO publications.[49]

Further concern about the severity of Ghana's deforestation was raised in a 1984[50] article from a team led by Caroline Sargeant, an authority on forestry in Ghana. The authors maintained that, there was "virtually no significant area of closed forest" outside the forest reserves. They provided evidence to show that even forest reserves are not exempt from the assault. The reserves were described as "variable" and "deteriorating" with under 50 percent in good condition due to "disturbances." While some species were being exploited at near sustainable levels, others had reached "economic extinction."[51]

A recent document from Ghana's Department of Forestry[52] estimates the "high forest zone" of Ghana at 13,590 square miles, and categorically concludes that outside this permanently protected area, "there is very little remaining intact forest." In 1994 it was estimated that 80 percent of the total timber harvest came from areas outside of the reserves, from farms and fallow lands.[53] This meant that non-forest areas were being further cleared of trees in the absence of easily accessible forests.

Another dimension of the deforestation problem lies in the fact that the "current installed capacity (the amount of wood that can be processed if the existing equipment and machinery within Ghana are operated at full capability) of the timber industry is about twice the annual allowable cut (the total amount of trees that can be legally felled within a year), and it is still expanding."[54]

Hypotheses

Three hypotheses have been constructed to help answer the central research question, which is, why policies designed to address the problem of deforestation in Ghana have failed to achieve the desired effects. They are:

a.   The policy environment for the formulation and implementation of coherent, long-term policies to combat deforestation requires a certain level of political stability that is peaceful and involves predictable transitions of authority over time. Because such political stability has been absent in Ghana, the formulation and implementation of coherent, long-term policies has been impossible.

b.   Because Ghana lacks a legislative tradition of policy-making, other governmental actors such as heads of state, bureaucrats, or the two in combination, have tended to dominate the policy-making process. Hence, forestry policies have reflected the priorities of these actors.

c.   In the policy environment of Ghana, given the conditions stated in (a) and (b) above, and where two sets of bureaucratic institutions[55] operate at cross-purposes around the same product/resource (timber and woodlands), the priority given to the policy outputs of the bureaucratic institutions will reflect the decisions of heads of state, which, in turn, will reflect the demands that have been made on the state. Inconsistent forest policies have resulted from the pressure felt by the state authorities to generate revenue from the forest resources.

These hypotheses suggest that the disconnection between deforestation policies and their outcome can be explained by a combination of a number of "internal" and "external" factors. The internal environment refers to the principal actors, the structure and operational processes of the principal institutions, the contents of policies, and the actions taken to pursue those policies. The external environment, on the other hand, refers to the overall circumstances under which the policy process takes place. It comprises political instability, structure of the economy, the high rate of population growth and its associated increasing demand for resources, external demand for Ghana's forest products, Ghana's external debt obligations, and the influence of the World Bank/ International Monetary Fund over Ghana's economic policies.

Objectives of the Research

The main interests of the study were: (a) the origin, form, and extent of the deforestation problem in Ghana; (b) the state's responses to the problem and their outcomes; (c) the political and economic implications of forest policies in Ghana; and, (d) formulation of policy recommendations for solving the problem. The research was conducted with two timeframes in mind: the colonial era (1900-1957), and the post-colonial era (1957-1997). The colonial era was included in the research because the policies introduced in that era remain relevant at present. Because forest policies in Ghana have been developed in an incremental fashion, knowledge about the background and content of earlier policies would help explain the context and content of latter ones.

Aspects of the state's responses to the problem that were considered include; the contents of policies, the manner in which such responses to deforestation emerged and evolved, and the key actors in the deforestation policy process. The behavior and relationships among these actors, the amount of influence they command, and the consequences of such influence were also examined.

Another dimension of this research dealt with bureaucratic institutions. The research covered: how the institutions responsible for administering forest policy originated, expanded and evolved; the mandates of those institutions; and their actual activities. Possible areas of conflict between the various institutions, and their shortcomings were also identified and examined.

Significance of the Research

As has been shown in this introduction, deforestation in Ghana has persisted even though it was identified as a problem almost two centuries ago. The problem is becoming more extensive and intensive with time, in spite of the fact that successive governments have adopted a series of policies with the aim of controlling it. Through the various institutions that have been charged with dealing with it, large amounts of resources, financial, human, etc., have been expended in the process. This suggests that there is an urgent need to reexamine this phenomenon and the past responses to it in order to explain the failure, and advance alternative solutions to the problem.

A workable resolution of the deforestation problem will reduce, and ultimately terminate, the very serious short and long-term adverse consequences on vegetation, soil, drainage, climate, etc. Furthermore, the threat posed by deforestation to Ghana's long-term sustainable development, given the critical importance of forests,[56] will be significantly reduced if the overall circumstances are clearly understood and effective answers found.

Trends in the evolving new world economic order suggest that, until new avenues for generating external income are discovered, Ghana's participation in international trade will become increasingly restricted to the production and export of primary produce. The already high ranking of timber and wood products among Ghana's exports is likely to receive a boost if the present trend continues.[57] There is, hence, a critical need to preserve Ghana's forests as a future source of revenue.

This study was therefore considered a significant contribution towards providing an in-depth understanding of the factors and processes that have produced the past and present ineffective deforestation policies in Ghana. Such understanding was deemed to be a pre-condition for advancing more effective alternative policies and solutions to the problem.

Since deforestation is a common problem in sub-Saharan Africa, the findings of this research and the strategies it proposes can be of benefit to other countries in the region. This research was intended to provide the basis for a subsequent comparative study that will enable scholars to determine the extent to which the public policy process in a developing country such as Ghana conforms to or deviates from the mainstream theories that are derived from western policy-making environments.

The findings from this research are a contribution towards the construction of policy theory that is specifically tailored to the Ghanaian scenario.

Research Methodology and the Database

A policy process oriented approach, as suggested by the work of Randall Ripley,[58] was modified to fit the realities of the Ghanaian setting, and utilized in this study. While studying the history of forest policy formulation and implementation in Ghana, the researcher gathered information to test the hypotheses advanced earlier.

This research entailed reconstructing a series of events that reflect how Ghana has developed a policy response towards the problem of deforestation. This reconstruction included a description and analysis of key events so as to explain the content of policies, the instruments for pursuing those policies, and the outcomes of specific policies concerning deforestation.

An explanatory model of the forest policy process in Ghana (Fig. 1) was constructed to facilitate an analysis of factors within the external and internal environments of the process. An exploratory survey on the attitudes of the grassroots population towards forests and deforestation was also conducted. The database consists of the following:

Library Research: The information in this research was obtained mainly from secondary sources. The researcher used library facilities in the Washington, DC metropolitan area, e.g., the Library of the United States Congress, those of the Consortium of Universities, and The World Bank. In addition, research was conducted at the library of the Environmental Protection Agency (EPA), and the World Resources Institute.

Major libraries in Ghana, especially those at the University of Ghana, Legon, the Forest Research Institute at Kumasi, the Planning Division of the Department of Forestry, Kumasi, and the Environmental Protection Agency in Accra were visited for additional information. Government archives and reports, principally those on the Ghanaian Department of Forestry and other institutions that have been involved in forestry policy, were also studied.

Among the first tasks in this study was a preliminary research involving two main activities: a review of literature on deforestation in Ghana; and, interviews with selected individuals who possess insight into the forestry sector as a whole and forest policy in particular.

Interviews: The interviews were conducted in June and July of 1996. Respondents included the Deputy Minister of Forestry, the Chief Conservator of Forests, and an official of the Forestry Commission of Ghana. A schedule of open-ended questions was followed (See Appendix 1), and the responses were recorded on audiotape.

The researcher sought after specific information from these respondents about the scope of deforestation in Ghana, causes of the problem, past and current government policies for addressing the problem, and reasons why deforestation has remained a continuing problem. In addition to answering the specific questions, the respondents were encouraged to discuss the issues at length, to express opinions, and to volunteer other related information.

During the preliminary library research, statistical information on the area of forest lands in Ghana since the late nineteenth century was collected. Also, bills, decrees, and regulations on the creation and management of forest reserves, the exploitation and export of timber, saw milling, farming, charcoal production and other activities that depend on forest resources were analyzed for information on the objectives and contents of the Ghanaian government's policies on forest resources. This information was to help determine the extent of forest loss in Ghana and to demonstrate the motives and the series of activities for combating the problem.

Official government statements, addresses, conference papers, and the pronouncements of high level politicians and bureaucrats who play important roles in the policy process were also analyzed. This information, and those obtained during the preliminary research, helped in constructing the hypotheses for this research.

The follow-up research had greater scope and depth. In August 1996, additional interviews were conducted with the three government officials contacted during the preliminary research. The purpose was to seek clarifications of some information obtained during the research, obtain greater details, and fill in the gaps in the information gathered. Another objective of the follow-up research was to verify the economic importance of forest resources to Ghana. Statistics on the amounts of timber extracted from Ghana's forests, the receipts from timber exports, and the volume of locally consumed forest resources were compiled.

Other data on the structure and condition of Ghana's economy that are relevant to this research (such as the status of forest resources, the rate of population growth, the rate of urbanization, increasing demand for food, firewood, charcoal and other fuels, the size of Ghana's foreign debts, composition of Ghana's exports, etc.) were also compiled. These data have been used to verify the associations between the rate of deforestation on the one hand, and revenues acquired from timber exports, population growth, increase in farming lands, expansions in the road network, on the other hand.

Other sources of secondary information were scholarly books, research reports, government archives and publications, and seminar papers. Publications of international institutions such as The World Bank, the United Nations Food and Agricultural Organization, and the International Timber Trade Organization were studied.

Explanatory Model of the Deforestation Policy Process in Ghana

The purpose of constructing an explanatory model of the deforestation policy process in Ghana was to provide an analytical framework for guiding this research by establishing a systematic basis for performing a comprehensive explanation of its structure and operation. The model (shown in Fig 1, page 14) was intended to be a systematic, logical illustration that could assist the researcher in identifying and analyzing the relevant factors in the forest policy process in Ghana so as to determine their significance to the research question. The model was also designed to assist the reader in understanding the relationships between the various components of the forest policy environment. It would show how those components function to create the disconnection between deforestation policies and their intended outcomes.

For the purposes of this research, Randall Ripley's conceptualization of the public policy environment was utilized.[59] In line with this conceptualization, the Ghanaian policy environment was examined from two perspectives: internal and external. The model therefore illustrates the configuration of the two environments within which the deforestation policy process in Ghana occurs.

The internal environment refers to the overall circumstances within the government establishment. Its components include the characteristics of the principal actors involved, and the structure and pattern of inter-relationships between governmental institutions and non-governmental actors. Participants in the policy process within the internal environment include the head of state, ministers of state, other leading politicians, and high-level bureaucrats from the extractive and protective regulatory institutions.

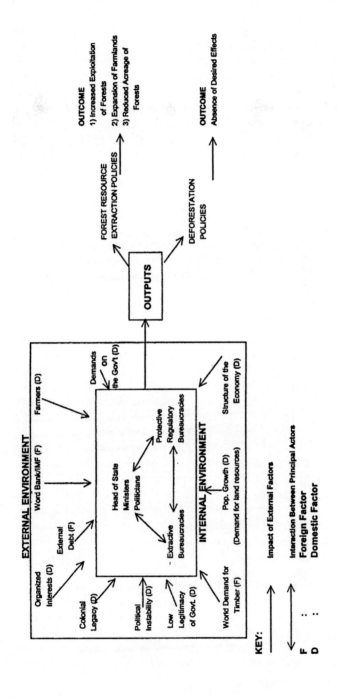

FIGURE 1: AN EXPLANATORY MODEL OF THE FOREST POLICY PROCESS IN GHANA

The internal environment also involves the operative processes of the institutions that are involved in policy-making and implementation. A second dimension of the internal environment includes government policy statements and declarations of the intent to pursue given directions, and the actions the government has actually taken to implement those declared intents.

The logic behind the concept of external environment was that what has happened within the internal environment of the public policy process has been influenced by factors that are outside of the governmental apparatus. Two categories of the external environment of the public policy process in Ghana were identified: local and foreign. The first (local) is related to the historical, economic, political, and cultural events within Ghana that have some relevance to forest policies.

The second category (foreign) includes the largely economic influences that originate outside the country, the most important being Ghana's external debt obligations, external markets for timber and other forest commodities from Ghana, and, in connection with that, the content of Ghana's exports, and the influence of international institutions such as the International Monetary Fund (IMF) and World Bank over Ghana's economic policies. The elements within the model will be analyzed in greater detail in chapters four, six, and seven.

A proposition made by this researcher was that the operation of this complex process produced two categories of contradictory outputs: i) forest resource extraction policies, and ii) policies intended to combat deforestation. The first category of policy outputs generates increased exploitation of forests and the expansion of farmlands; developments that cause a depletion in the acreage of forests in Ghana. Because of the political and economic priorities of Ghanaian political leaders and the other key actors in the policy process as well as the sustenance needs of the citizens, forest resources extraction policies have had greater effect than protective regulatory ones.

The result has been that in spite of policy statements, legislation, and activities of institutions charged with protecting and regenerating forests, anti-deforestation policies have not had the desired effects in Ghana. This argument is the central theme of this book.

Exploratory Survey on Attitudes of the Grassroots Population
Towards Forests and Deforestation

An important aspect of this research was the investigation of the attitudes of the grassroots population in the forest region towards the forests, the incidence of deforestation, and the government's policies and actions to combat it. The purpose was to determine whether these attitudes generally coincide with or are in conflict with the official government position, and to determine whether the grassroots population is likely to cooperate with or undermine the government's efforts at controlling deforestation.

Although a full-blown opinion survey was necessary to obtain complete and reliable information on those attitudes, it was not possible to undertake a survey on that scale, due to a lack of resources. In addition, the preliminary information obtained suggested that the opinions of the grassroots population have not been important factors in the government's forest policies.

Research indicates that high-level politicians and bureaucrats have dominated the policy process. As such, instead of a comprehensive survey, an exploratory survey was conducted in a selected forest district in August 1996.

It is important to emphasize that this exploratory survey was not intended to produce a complete picture that is representative of the attitudes of the population in Ghana's forest area. Instead, it availed the researcher with a cursory idea about the situation in a small area. Details about the operationalization of this survey; selection of the venue for the survey, selection of the sampling unit, categories of respondents, and the actual respondents can be found in Appendix 2.

Limitations of the Research

As has been noted, the full-blown opinion survey that is necessary to produce a complete picture that is representative of the attitudes of the grassroots population in Ghana's forest area towards deforestation and the government forestry policies was not conducted due to a lack of resources. For the same reason, only a few bureaucratic elites and politicians involved in the forestry sector were interviewed.

Although the exploratory surveys shed some light on the attitudes and positions of these groups and complemented the secondary data, more detailed research is recommended for more complete information.

Organization of the Book

This book consists of eight chapters including this Introduction. Chapter Two is a review of literature on policy formulation and implementation. Western mainstream theories are examined with particular attention to relevance to non-industrialized countries, especially those in sub-Saharan Africa. Other theories and literature that specifically deal with the policy process and public administration in Ghana, sub-Saharan Africa, and similar environments, are given special attention. The objectives of this literature review are to determine whether the established theories on protective regulatory policies apply to the deforestation policy process in Ghana, and to identify leads that can steer the research towards answers to the questions at hand.

The subject of chapter three is the environment of the forest policy process in the colonial era in Ghana. The policy process is examined with special attention to the activities of the key actors and institutions; political, bureaucratic and non-governmental. The objective of this chapter is to establish an overall synthesis on how the internal environmental factors; the institutions, and individuals, independently and/or in concert, operated to determine the contents and outcomes of colonial era forest policies.

Chapter Four contains a discussion of the external environment of the forest policy process as depicted in the explanatory model. The focus of the analysis is the contextual setting within which the formulation and implementation of policies for addressing deforestation in Ghana has been occurring - the external environment. Explanations for the disconnection between the policies and their outcomes are advanced.

In Chapter Five an analysis of policies for addressing deforestation in Ghana is performed. The content of legislation introduced since Ghana's political independence is examined so as to identify their objectives, and strategies for implementation. This is done within the context of the historical, political, and economic circumstances of Ghana. The purpose is to determine why those policies failed to achieve their intended results.

Chapter Six deals with an important aspect of the internal environment of the deforestation policy process in Ghana -- the executive arm of government. The status, motives, roles, actions, and interactions between the heads of government, ministers of state, and high -level politicians are analyzed. The objective is to determine the amount of influence they command, and in lieu of that, the extent to which they are accountable for the contents and outcomes of deforestation policies.

The subject of Chapter Seven is the role of bureaucratic and non-governmental institutions in the forest policy process of Ghana. The missions, authority, and activities of the institutions are described and analyzed so as to reveal the way in which policies emerge and get implemented. The analyses also demonstrate the leverage that individuals within those institutions have over the content and outcomes of policies, and the reasons for the non-achievement of the deforestation policy goals.

Chapter Eight treats the Department of Forestry, the lead institution within the forestry sector of Ghana. The mandates, organization, functional characteristics, and problems of the Department are examined. The analyses show that shortcomings of the department are accountable for the failure on the part of the Ghanaian government to achieve its deforestation policy objectives. The results and inferences drawn from the exploratory survey are also discussed.

The work will be capped with discussions of a set of policy recommendations for action towards a more effective policy to address the problem of deforestation in Ghana.

Chapter 2

Review of Related Literature

The purpose of this chapter is to examine public policy literature that focuses on policy-making and implementation. The primary objective is to determine how useful these theories are in describing and explaining the environment, process and outcomes of deforestation policies in Ghana. Even though this book is concerned with Ghana, most of the available literature on the subject deals with sub-Saharan Africa, and in some instances, the whole of the "Third World" as analytical units. In fact, few scholarly writings have been done on the policy process in Ghana. As such, this review will treat available literature on those regions, since they are likely to contain concepts that are relevant to the Ghanaian situation.

The researcher recognized that mainstream theories on the formulation and implementation stages of the public policy process have typically been based on the experiences of western parliamentary systems. As such, they are not perfectly applicable to the Ghanaian situation. Nevertheless, a selection of such theories has been examined in so far as they help to describe and explain the deforestation policy process in Ghana.

This chapter is organized in two parts. The first deals with behavioral and normative theories that are not specifically rooted in the Ghanaian experience, but nevertheless, are relevant to the theme of this book. The second part is a treatment of theories that are focused on sub-Saharan Africa.

This review is intended to help to refine the hypotheses and objectives, and expedite the establishment of more precise bearings for the investigation. In the process of this review, an effort will be made to identify concepts that may be useful in constructing a theoretical framework and in answering questions that are not adequately answered in the available literature.

Behavioral Theories on Policy Formulation

Behavioral theories are empirical ones that, while explaining policy-making, stress the actions of participants and the operations of the institutions involved in the process. Prominent among these them are Charles Easton's political systems theory,[60] Graham Allison's organizational process theory,[61] the group equilibrium theory, explained at length by David Truman,[62] and later developed by Charles Lindblom[63] and Thomas Dye,[64] among others, the bureaucratic politics theory,[65] and the elite preference theory.[66]

The dominant focus of these theories is the process by which public policies are formulated and implemented. They examine the relationships and interactions between participants in the policy process and the overall functioning of the institutions that are involved in such policies. Their scrutiny can therefore assist in explaining the Ghanaian forest policy process.

Easton's theory, for example, is a formulation of a "systems approach" which emphasizes the process as opposed to the structure of the policy machinery. In this theory, policy-making is conceptualized in terms of inputs (demands and claims made by individuals and groups on the political system), the conversion processes (policy-making, policy choices, and policy decisions), outputs (policy outcomes), and feedbacks (policy impact analysis; the effects of policies on the environment, subsequent demands, or on the character of the political system itself).

Systems theory has several merits. A key one is that it gives direction to inquirers into the process of policy formulation.[67] It also simplifies the policy milieu by isolating its components; thereby presenting the process in an orderly, interconnected arrangement that is easier to comprehend. Charles Jones maintains that in order to facilitate understanding of public policy, political scientists should limit their focus to the process that produces public policy.[68] Another important merit of this "process" theory is that it presents, in line with what obtains in reality, policy-making as an on-going process.

Systems theory has, nevertheless, been criticized for two major weaknesses: its narrow focus, and its static character. Its principal shortcoming, according to the critics, lies in its failure to adequately explain how policy decisions are made and developed, a task that has subsequently been undertaken by Jones[69] and Ripley.[70] Because of the aforementioned shortcomings, Hugh Helco, for example, condemns the system theory as being "a verbal accounting system, which is of little help in specific policy analysis."[71] Paul Sabatier also refers to it as a casual theory that has "outlived its usefulness."[72]

Systems theory can be a useful analytical model for explaining the Ghanaian forest policy environment. It is a tool with which a researcher can conceptualize the forest policy process in a structured way. Instead of delving into intricacies of the process at the beginning of a research, one can generate a holistic picture of the process and identify the key components and stages before treating the details. It is important, however, that certain unique features of the Ghanaian policy environment are given due consideration when applying the theory. For example, contrary to the process portrayed by the theory, policies in Ghana typically originate from the government rather than from the demands of the citizens. Ghanaian citizens usually get to know about policies at the implementation stage, the point at which those policies have an impact on their lives. Consequently, any demands, participation, representation or conflicts, and the resolution of such conflicts, typically take place at the implementation stage of the policy process.

In addition, important aspects of the Ghanaian policy environment, such as, the dominance of the political regime, the bureaucracy, and non-governmental elites, and the inadequacy of information and resources must not be overlooked when utilizing this theory. If applied in an appropriate manner, the systems theory can provide a distinct perspective of the broad political framework of the public policy process in Ghana. Because of the systematic conceptualization of the policy process, this theory was used as a heuristic devise to guide the research.   Similar to the systems theory, the organizational process theory deals with the broad framework of the policy process, but pays more attention to the processes and procedures of government institutions. Allison demonstrates, through his case study of the Cuban missile crisis, that policies are the outputs of established procedures and routines of organizations. He infers that large organizations function "according to standard patterns of behavior"[73] and rules of thumb that ensure concerted action.

In this connection, the organizational process theory reflects characteristics of the Ghanaian bureaucracy. Allison's perspective of policy institutions and their processes is expanded by J. A. Egonmwan who describes them as, "...established conglomerates of semi-independent organizations, each with its sphere of specialization, goals, and programs, and where change will be marginal and incremental and where long-range planning is disregarded and emphasis placed on matters of the moment. "[74]

In accordance with this, Allison depicts policy institutions as a "conglomerate of semi-feudal, loosely allied organizations, each with a substantial life of its own,"[75] with government leaders sitting at the top. This portrayal suggests that policy outputs are shaped by the self-interests of the principal actors, since such actors tend to behave in such a way as to protect their individual and organizational interests, and to minimize their risks. Public organizations maintain a typically strict adherence to standard processes, procedures and established routines, a practice presumed necessary because of the importance of coordination and predictability. Unquestionably, it will be difficult to explain the Ghanaian government's actions on deforestation without understanding the nature of the organizations that are involved in the sector.

Allison's theory indicates that the usually large size of government organizations affects the process, content, and outcomes of public policies. Size of organizations and the associated specialization of officials within them often prevent a single central authority from making all the important decisions or directing the important activities. Problems often get broken into fragments to permit specialized attention to particular aspects. Accompanying this disaggregation of functions is a dissipation of power to individual or group actors, a state of affairs that can foster organizational parochialism. Nevertheless, in Allison's scheme of things, public organizations tend to develop considerable stability in terms of their priorities, perceptions, issues and activities.

Given that the organizational process theory reflects the characteristics of the Ghanaian bureaucracies in the forestry sector, (Department of Forestry, Ministry of Lands and Forestry, Forestry Commission, etc.), the theory was applied to explain the structure, culture, operations, and effectiveness of those institutions. As is necessary with the application of all theories, certain factors were borne in mind as this researcher utilized this theory. For example, experiences during the Kwame Nkrumah regime show how the pre-eminence of a political party, the ruling Convention Peoples Party, enabled it to exert a strong influence over individual public servants and the bureaucracy as a whole. That era marked the beginning of the increased politicization of the Ghanaian bureaucracy, a characteristic that has survived to the present. Second, in the immediate post-independence era of Ghana, the urgency to provide infrastructural and social amenities was so great that innovative policies rather than incremental ones were pursued.[76] Consequently, the policy process in Ghana under Nkrumah appeared to be a departure from the standardized, minimal risk taking, restrained format propounded by this theory.

Furthermore, ethnic loyalties and tribalism, significant ingredients of politics and the policy process in Ghana, cannot be discounted in explaining the deforestation policy process. They have been identified as elements that usually dominate the mind-set and behavior of the principal actors in politics and public policy, often distorting the nature of the organizational process.

The group equilibrium theory does not explain policy decision-making per se. Rather, it attempts to analyze the relationships among those who show an interest and participate in the process. According to this theory, the activities of such groups determine the outcomes of policies. Analyses are not restricted to those within the internal environment of the policy process, (such as bureaucrats and politicians), but includes those in the external environment, (business people, workers' unions, ethnic associations, etc.). The equilibrium theory seeks to formulate a complete synthesis of the interactions between groups in a policy environment, and the consequences of such interaction on the process, content, and outcomes of policies.

According to the theory, these groups have special, often conflicting interests. They exist in a constant state of competition to translate their interests into policy. In the process of this competition, political power is so fragmented, amorphous, shifting, and tentative that, in the long run, no group can be said to have more power than others.

Dye suggests that the competition for influence creates a counteracting center of power which checks the influence of any single group and protects the weaker individuals and classes from exploitation.[77] By implication, public policies at any given time, therefore, are the equilibria reached during group struggles.[78] The kind of equilibrium envisaged by Dye, however is not feasible in the Ghanaian case. This is because the groups are not equally endowed. The political resources available to the competing groups (such as the strategy adopted, the amount of money spent, the skills and competence with which the group operates, internal cohesion, access to decision-makers, and organizational strength) determine their fate. Hence some would exert greater influence over policies than others. In the case of Ghana, it is the political leaders, bureaucrats, owners of big businesses, and elites who have this advantage. Policies, therefore, reflect the equilibria among these elite actors.

Apart from the politicians and bureaucrats, groups in Ghana that show some interest in deforestation policies include: a) timber merchants, charcoal manufacturers, sawmill operators, and other business people who, in pursuing profits, seek to exploit the forest resources to the fullest possible; b) religious groups and tribal associations who revere forests and the land, and, as such, object to the government's denial of their rights over certain forest areas; c) tribal leaders and elders who maintain a historical claim to certain lands and forests; d) environmental groups that are advocating conservation; and, e) the growing population of farmers whose livelihoods depend on the land.

There are divergent, in some cases, conflicting interests in the deforestation policy environment of the country. However, there is such an imbalance of power that, contrary to Dye's conjecture, the weaker groups such as the rural dwelling peasants appear excluded from the process. In addition, the dominance of the state in Ghana minimizes the leverage of those groups who lack the organization and connections to the centers of political power. Hence, certain individuals and groups appear to have exerted disproportionate amount of influence on forest policies.

Pluralism, as is assumed in the group equilibrium theory, can also be faulted on account of the unrepresentative nature of most governments in Ghana - military dictatorships at times, and autocratic civilian regimes at others,[79] an entrenched and powerful bureaucracy, and tribal leadership that often appears to pay more attention to personal prestige and wealth than the welfare of their subjects.

Viewed in the Ghanaian context therefore, this theory diminishes the power and influence of government office holders and bureaucrats on the shape and direction of public policy. In the Ghanaian environment, mediating structures such as environmental groups, strong opposition political parties, labor unions, and professional associations are in their embryonic stages, and subject to the manipulation of the authorities. They have, therefore, not been able to exert much influence in the pursuit of their particular interests.

In spite of the relative weakness of certain categories of groups, recent history reveals that, occasionally, tribes, clans, farmers associations, students, etc., can offer determined resistance to policies they do not favor.[80] There is a possible connection between the militancy of such interest groups, however limited, and (as will be pointed out in discussions on the series of forest policies) the tendency towards decision-making through small incremental moves instead of through comprehensive reform programs.

Given the circumstances that prevail in Ghana nevertheless, the group equilibrium theory remains a useful tool that sheds some light on an important aspect of the policy environment. The role different groups in Ghana have played in the forest policy process, and the amount of impact they have had on the process and outcome will be examined as explanations of the disconnection between deforestation policies and their outcomes are investigated. As denoted by its name, bureaucratic politics theory deals with the activities, relationships, and interactions among civil servants, and the consequences to pubic policies. An inference of this theory is that such activities and interactions - what Allison refers to as "bargaining games"[81] - have significant consequences to the content and outcomes of policies.

Allison's position is that governments perceive problems through organizational sensors. To better understand government policies, one must perceive them as "outputs of large, partially coordinated organizations that are functioning according to standard patterns of behavior."[82] Allison portrays bureaucracies as establishments within which individual office holders engage in intricate, often subtle, simultaneous, overlapping games. As part of the game, the actors actively engage in politics with the goal of influencing the allocation of resources. In the process, they jockey for positions and status, and negotiate with other actors to payback old debts and favors.[83]

His conclusion is that public decision-making is not a monolithic action of the government. Rather, it involves several individuals who are playing the dual role of civil servants engaged in the administration of policies and programs, and members of a class, an interest group, who are seeking to advance their own sectional benefits.

The level of influence bureaucrats exercise over policy outcomes depends on the amount of power they command; power in such terms as "bargaining advantages, formal authority and responsibility, control over resources and information, access to important persons within the government, and the will to use such bargaining advantages."[84] Their parochial priorities and perceptions of what qualifies as part of the national interest are key ingredients of their decisions and actions. Ultimately, the content and outcomes of policies derive from such perceptions and the decisions and actions that are taken in connection with them. According to the theory, public policy is the aftermath of compromise, coalition, competition, and confusion among government officials who see different faces of various issues.

The preliminary research as well as the literature indicates that, since the colonial era, the bureaucracy in Ghana has been a key institution within the policy process. It wields considerable power and remains indispensable.[85] The information also indicates that, the activities of Ghanaian bureaucrats reflect the picture portrayed in the bureaucratic politics theory. The political activities of bureaucrats will be given close attention in this study. Concepts from bureaucratic politics theory will set the tone and guide the study. A key objective will be to determine to what extent bureaucrats in the forestry sector influence the content and outcomes of forest policies, and how their influence explains the disconnection between policies and their outcomes.

Directly related to bureaucratic politics, elite preference theory concentrates on decision-makers, power holders, and aggregations of political actors, social forces, and variables such as status, power, influence, and authority. According to this theory, through bargaining and compromises reached by competing groups in pluralist societies, as portrayed in the group equilibrium theory, major power blocks eventually emerge in the form of distinct groups or coalitions of groups. Usually, the most dominant of these tends to be the elites; that small group of specialized leaders, within the government establishment or outside of it, who are able to dominate politics and the decision-making process. One effect of the dominance of these elites is the limitation it imposes on the scope of participation of the masses of the population.[86]

Two key assumptions of this theory match what prevails in Ghana. The first is that political systems are divided into two strata: the ruling minority and the ruled majority. The second is; policies reflect the preferences of the ruling minority who happen to be the elites in the society.[87] Considering the immense power possessed by the elites of Ghana,[88] it may seem that, even though millions of Ghanaians depend on the land and forests for their livelihood, it is the elites who determine forest policies. It has been suggested that elites in sub-Saharan Africa tend to equate their group objectives with those of their communities, or the communities from which they originated, and are able to mobilize others to fight their cause, beliefs, and interests as if those were their own cause, beliefs and interests.[89]

It has also been suggested that because of the desire of the elites to preserve, even enhance, their own interests, changes in policy tend to be slow and incremental. Also, because elites have greater control over information and the channels of communication, they are often able to manipulate mass sentiments and opinions, and propagate their own perspectives on issues.[90] This will determine the validity of these assertions in connection with deforestation policies in Ghana.

Some aspects of elite behavior as portrayed in the elite preference theory, however, appear inapplicable to the Ghanaian case. Contrary to the notion that elites routinely have a sense of solidarity and typically function as a unified group to protect their common interests, there have been cases in Ghana where individuals or groups of elites have engaged in "counter-elite" behavior, setting out to reshape rather than preserve the existing social order. For example, in the early twentieth century, educated Ghanaians unified to protest the colonial system of policy-making on the grounds that policies that did not derive from the demands of the population at large lacked legitimacy.[91] Later, from the 1940s until the 1960s, Dr. Kwame Nkrumah spearheaded a move to dismantle the elite-controlled governmental culture. He and his supporters advocated a rejection of the then established norms of politics and the procedures of government, and sought to assert their own philosophical and ideological ideals which sought to place the grassroots population at the center of the government's policy apparatus.[92]

Between 1979 and 1992 the Peoples National Development Council government of J. J. Rawlings flirted with the concept of establishing a populist form of democratic government; an endeavor that threatened to dismantle the established practices and institutions of government and replace them with a unique system that would curtail the central role of the key political and bureaucratic elites.[93]   In spite of such past attempts at transformation, the dominance of Ghanaian elites in politics and the policy process remains so significant that the term "ruling class" has been suggested as more appropriate than the term "elite".[94]   It is also important to note that, over the years, as a result of increased education and activism, the notion that the Ghanaian masses are a largely passive, apathetic, and ill-informed people who are often manipulated by the elites is rapidly becoming outmoded.[95]

Factors, such as cultural pluralism and kinship structures that tend to foster a high degree of communalism and parochialism appear to have rendered elites in Ghana a fragmented rather than cohesive class.[96]   There are, for example, the ethnic-based elites whose indirect impact on the policy process is significant due to their firm, albeit diminishing, hold on the majority traditional population.[97]   There are also the business elites and opinion leaders whose views must be sought before major decisions affecting their communities are taken, to ensure successful implementation.   Such differences imply that Ghanaian elites do not necessarily always have a consensus about the "rules of the game", or common goals.   It is, thus, unlikely that there can be no competition among them in spite the existence of certain common fundamental elitist attitudes and positions on issues.

At various points in this discussion, references have been made to the power and influence of the elites of Ghana, and the extent of their dominance of the public policy process.   It is evident that a critical condition for understanding the deforestation policy process in Ghana, particularly the disconnection between the policies and their outcomes, is to possess an in-depth understanding of the objectives and activities of these key actors in the process. The elite preference theory provides the framework for the necessary investigation of elite behavior in Ghana, as well as their impact on deforestation policies.

Normative Theories on Public Policy Formulation

In contrast with the behavioral theories, normative theories on public policy formulation deal with conceptualization; the description and explanation of what actually transpires as policy decisions are made.   Normative theories typically highlight the shortcomings of existing theories, and propose more reality-based explanations of the policy process, offering solutions to the problems identified. Two such theories reflect some aspects of the Ghanaian forest policy process. They are: *disjointed incrementalism* (sometimes referred to as "muddling through," and mixed scanning. Disjointed incrementalism, as proposed by Charles Lindblom, was a more practical alternative to the rational comprehensive theory.[98] This theory perceives public policy as ongoing; a continuation of past government activities.[99] The preliminary research and literature on the subject indicated that the Ghanaian forest policy process has been fashioned in line with the ideas propounded by this theory.

Information from available literature and other published reports suggest that in the forest policy process in Ghana, only a narrow range of possibilities are seriously considered, and selections appear to be made between the few policy alternatives that present themselves. This means that Ghanaian forest policy-makers do not question the legitimacy of previous policies; but rather build on them. (This fact will be demonstrated later on in chapter four, when the contents of past laws and decrees on the forest sector are analyzed.) Past investments in existing programs, and established routines of individual, institutional and political behavior (especially, the use of short-term budgeting as the major instrument of policy formulation and implementation),[100] tend to preclude radical changes in policies, thus resulting in a great deal of incrementalism.[101]

The forest policy process in Ghana, and the resulting policy content suggest that policies that connote major changes from the past, and which imply high risks, are scarcely adopted. Instead, the process is geared towards improving the existing situation through small, calculated actions.

One of the strongest endorsements of incremental policy-making has come from Yehezkel Dror. He considers it "fully geared to the actual experience of practicing public administrators..... A very valuable contribution..... more closely tied to reality, more sophisticated in theory and more adjusted to human nature."[102] Although Dror endorses the theory especially in terms of its applicability to reality, he is, at the same time, one of its most ardent critics. His concern, however, is not about its inherent validity, but its potential impact on actual policy-making practices. He expresses the fear that incrementalism's main impact on public decision-making may turn out to be "an ideological reinforcement of the pro-inertia and anti-innovation forces prevalent in all human organizations, administrative and policy-making",[103] and wonders whether the favorable evaluations do not constitute a "dangerous over-reaction"[104] and an endorsement of a policy of "no effort."

Specifically, Dror makes three assumptions for the "muddling through" thesis; conditions which imply a high degree of social, economic, and political stability, among other things. They are:

1. Past policies should be perceived as satisfactory so that what is required are improvements through small changes;
2. The nature of problems remain unchanged over time; and,
3. The available means of solving problems are unchanged over time.

These criteria apply to the Ghanaian deforestation policy environment. Analyses of a series of policy statements and related documents on deforestation have not revealed any evidence of censuring of past forest policies. Rather, the process, in large part, appears to be rooted on the assumption that past policies only need to be complemented with new ones. This situation seems to be related to the fact that the Ghanaian political culture appears to be resistant to sudden changes. In addition, the Ghanaian bureaucracy has consistently remained a key factor in the policy process. Given these realities, radical policies that would reverse or abandon existing ones do not seem likely.

Furthermore, it appears that Ghanaian leaders, mindful of the country's economic circumstances, have embraced a policy approach in which the gradual commitment to programs is preferred to radical, risk-laden policies. Also, considering the lack of adequate information for effective policy-making, it appears the leaders have deemed it "unwise to specify objectives in much detail when the means of attaining them are virtually unknown".[105] Besides, if the deforestation problem in Ghana has changed over the years, it has only been in terms of the scale. The main causes remain exploitation of timber, and clearance of forests for farming. Given the above, it is clear that Dror's criteria for the applicability of incrementalism have been met in the Ghanaian case.

There are still other criticisms of incrementalism. It has been characterized as descriptive and not permitting a determination of causal relationships or an explanation of phenomena.[106] Robert Gooding describes incrementalism as an "a-theoretical decision-making routine,"[107] and Amitai Etzioni calls the process "drifting - action without direction."[108] From Etzioni's point of view, the steps in incremental decision-making may be "circular - leading back to where they started, or dispersed - leading in many directions at once but leading nowhere."[109] Although such criticisms raise issues that deserve serious consideration, they do not question the validity of the theory. Rather, they are concerned with its utility in improving the policy process. But incrementalism is not designed for that purpose. Its goal is to describe what occurs in practice.

Given that this is concerned with both the behavioral and normative dimensions of the Ghanaian deforestation policy process, it is anticipated that answers to some of the questions posed by these critics will be provided in the form of explanations as to why the Ghanaian forest policy process has been incrementalist and conservative, promoting little or no change in past policies.

Amitai Etzioni reaches beyond criticizing incrementalism to propound "Mixed Scanning" as a more viable alternative for describing the policy process.[110] His solution to the shortcomings of incrementalism is to combine the strongest features of that theory with those of the rational theory.[111]

Mixed scanning requires two sets of mechanisms: logical policy-making processes which are directed towards achieving certain goals on the basis of complete analyses of readily available information, as assumed in the rational theory; and, processes geared towards making small additions or modifications to existing policies so as achieve newly determined goals, an assumption of the incremental theory. The format of mixed scanning therefore includes elements of both the rationalist and the incremental approaches. The procedure involves scanning the whole public area but not in great detail, assessing the identified problems against stated values, and then homing in on those aspects that need more in-depth consideration. Within this framework, decision-making proceeds incrementally in matters of detail.

Etzioni contends that each of the two components of mixed scanning helps to reduce the shortcomings of the other; incrementalism reducing the unrealistic aspects of rationalism by limiting the details required in fundamental decisions, and rationalism helping to "overcome the conservative slant of incrementalism by exploring longer-run alternatives."[112] A major appeal of mixed scanning therefore is its flexibility. It allows policies to be adjusted to suit changing circumstances during formulation and implementation. Decision-makers can emphasize either of the two aspects where necessary, given their purposes and the singular circumstances prevailing. Scanning gives consideration to the varying capacities of decision-makers; those with adequate skills and information, and those without either.

However, scanning, as outlined above, seems to be very abstract, and Etzioni does not show how it works in practice. Mixed scanning has also been criticized as being utopian, and failing to reconcile the conflicting principles of the rationalist and incremental theories.[113]

Such criticisms notwithstanding, mixed scanning has its adherents. Egonmwan, for example, suggests that some of the criticisms of the concept stem from a lack of adequate understanding of Etzioni's concepts. His own interpretation of the scheme is that, due to limitations on time, manpower, knowledge, etc., it is not possible to subject every policy area to a comprehensive analysis according to the rational model, but it is possible to identify a few of such areas every year where performance is not satisfactory, and subject them to a detailed scrutiny, and thereafter continue incremental change.[114]

This explanation suggests that, the important task is to determine policy objectives and the appropriate policy instruments for achieving them, by means of a comprehensive analysis. But when it comes to implementation, it is usually more feasible to pursue these objectives through incremental steps. This seems reasonable. Yet, the fact remains that mixed scanning does not explicitly specify an institutional framework necessary for its operationalization.

Merits of mixed scanning, when considered in the Ghanaian setting, derive from the fact that Ghanaian deforestation policy-makers are not devoid of information about the historical, social, cultural, political and economic factors surrounding the problem. Available information indicates that, in practice, scientific data serve as part of the grounds upon which political leaders and bureaucrats process policy decisions.[115] By implication, they utilize aspects of both incrementalism and rationalism. In view of this, mixed scanning deserves some attention in the quest for explanations of the Ghanaian deforestation policy process and the reasons why the policies have not had the intended effects.

So far, the theories dealt with in this discussion have shown that policy-making is a complex process. Through the behavioral theories it has been shown how the perceptions, goals, and activities of actors in the policy process can have far-reaching consequences for the contents and outcomes of policies. In connection with Ghana's deforestation policies - policies that, in most respects, belong to the protective regulatory category, and are intended to regulate the activities of particular groups of citizens - these theories have highlighted the possible far-reaching consequences various groups and institutions can have on the process, contents and outcomes of policies.

The organizational process theory has indicated that the functional characteristics of bureaucracies rank high among the determinants of the types of policies introduced as well as the outcomes of those policies. The group equilibrium theory has also drawn attention to the effects of politics, competition, and other forms of interaction among the various groups (politicians, bureaucrats, business people, tribal associations, farmers, environmentalists, trade unions, political parties, etc.) on the policy apparatus as well as the contents and outcomes of policies. This suggests that one cannot overlook powerful groups within the government or outside of it if one should explain the deforestation policy process of Ghana.

Because they both take a close look at the background, parochial priorities and behavior of bureaucrats and elites, the bureaucratic politics theory and the elite preference theory emphasize the significance of "bargaining games" played by those groups during the public policy process. The status and power of bureaucrats and elites in a developing country such as Ghana, particularly the fact that they remain a small minority who possess an inequitable share of expertise, and wealth implies that the institutions within which they operate deserve close study.

The normative theories that have been discussed have facilitated an overall look at the policy process, and shown the types of policy processes that can result from different policy environments. The two theories have been shown as directly related to what entails in the Ghanaian deforestation policy scenario. They help to establish a point of reference for this research. In the following section, literature that treats the public policy process in sub-Saharan Africa will be examined. The objective is to determine how relevant such theories are to explaining the disconnection between deforestation policies and their outcomes.

Theories on the Public Policy Process in Sub-Saharan Africa[116]

Published analyses of public administration in sub-Saharan African countries have been largely diagnostic in content. Literature on the subject routinely describes and analyzes the failures of public institutions, the reasons why attempted reforms have not materialized. In some instances, it examines the dichotomy between policy making and policy implementation.

This review will not emphasize descriptions of the policy-making systems. Rather, attention will be given to the literature that deals with aspects of the policy process that would help to explain the problem with which this book is concerned. Three subjects dictate the scope of this review: shortcomings of the policy process; weaknesses of the institutions involved; and attributes of the environment within which the process occurs.

Two major themes: bureaucratic ineffectiveness, and politics, consistently run through the literature on public policies in sub-Sahara Africa. History, economics, and ecology are discussed in several instances, yet the bureaucracy and consequences of politics are given substantial attention in describing and analyzing public policy goals, the process, the contents, and the outcomes. This review will be organized on the bases of four interconnected subjects: 1) effects of the indigenous cultural milieu, 2) politics, 3) the bureaucracy, and 4) administrative weaknesses.

The Effects of the Indigenous Cultural Milieu on Policy Effectiveness

In addition to the bureaucracy, the wider social, economic and cultural contexts within which the policy process occurs are also significant factors treated by Fred Riggs.[117] He suggests that public administrative systems in the Third World tend to operate ineffectively because the indigenous cultures are not congenial to the dictates of modern administrative machinery. His position is that organizations transplanted from industrialized societies, and which may appear to an observer as modern, are, in reality, penetrated by aspects of the indigenous social system. The outcome of this is a hybrid institution, many of whose features are dysfunctional. This socio-cultural hybrid Riggs refers to as "poly-normativism". He concludes that the inter-penetration of indigenous and foreign systems without their modification and adaptation to suit the prevailing public policy environment will continue to produce the non-rational, inconsistent and chaotic atmosphere that pervades the administrative systems in developing countries.

Literature abounds where the failures of public administrative systems are explained in terms of the manner in which foreign institutions and conventions were introduced in the sub-Saharan environment with barely any concessions to the values and culture of the indigenous people.[118] Those that focus on Ghana are being considered here. Robert Gardiner, for instance suggests that the administrative system that was handed over to newly independent Ghana was in no way designed to suit the socio-cultural setting. Consequently, it has "suffered from a paucity of personnel, lack of administrative resources, weak infrastructure, and potentially explosive relationships between bureaucrats and politicians."[119]

Over four decades after Ghana's independence, questions about the suitability and adaptability of the colonial established administrative system in the country remain relevant. This is because the system has remained largely alien. Even though administered by indigenous people, it has barely been adapted to the realities of the local culture. As such the prevailing system continues to function within a cultural setting whose characteristics and impact tend to undermine its effectiveness.

In a more recent review, Goran Hyden draws an inference that sustains the decade-old contentions of Gardiner and Eisenstad. She attributes much of the disorder in African management to the lack of congeniality between the demands of modern management and the African cultural milieu.[120] By implication, the two systems remain highly incompatible in spite of the length of time the have co-existed. It has not been possible to adequately adjust the administrative systems to the local cultures.[121]

A study by Robert Price depicts yet another dimension of the impact of the cultural milieu on administrative practices in Ghana. He shows that so much "social pressure" is placed on the Ghanaian civil servant that "organizationally dependable role behavior"[122] is unlikely. Furthermore, the values and reference groups to which commitment is socially rewarded are such that spontaneous innovation towards the accomplishment of organizational goals is diminished. Price argues that administrative performance in Ghana suffers from "institutional malintegration"[123] because the socio-cultural environment functions in a way that undermines the effectiveness of public organizations. The basis of the alleged malintegration, according to Price, is the nature of social organization in the Ghanaian society, and the fact that the prevailing orientation of social integration does not provide the cultural legitimacy for separation of personal and official roles.

While conceding that the "large functional loads carried by bureaucracies in these relatively new states, and the increase in this load as development proceeds,[124] are grounds for their inadequacies, Price points to the "phenomenon of administrative corruption, nepotism, ritualism, and mismanagement"[125] as the trade marks of those institutions and the main reason for their ineffectiveness. Peter H. Koehn corroborates the explanations offered by Price for this state of affairs, citing the "omnipresent social obligations"[126] to personal relations, and the personal interests of the higher bureaucrats[127] as part of the cause. Using Ghana as an illustration of the situation in sub-Saharan Africa, Price produces evidence to suggest that the performance of the public bureaucracy played "a direct part in alienating the citizens from their governments."[128] A consequence of this was that it squelched the positive, cooperative attitude the public might have had, or could have developed, concerning public policies.

Price's argument further suggests that it is difficult, from the point of view of social survival, for public servants to maintain the necessary "universalistic posture"[129] and the requisite commitment to institutional goals as they seek to achieve esteem and social approval.   Public servants thus violate organizational rules and standards of behavior, thereby rendering organizational goals unreachable.

The above review has delved into a question that belongs to the core of this, which is, the failure of policies to combat deforestation to achieve the desired impact. The analyses indicate that public administration in Ghana cannot be improved unless the institutions and the processes involved are effectively modified and adjusted to the prevalent cultural environment. With regards to Ghana's deforestation, a question that stems from this is; how can the deforestation policy process be made more effective given the impact of the indigenous culture? This question will be revisited in chapter six as the bureaucracies within the forest sector are treated.

Politics as a Factor in the Process, Content, and Outcomes of Public Policies in Sub-Saharan Africa

Literature on the policy process in sub-Saharan Africa has identified politics as a major factor in the process. The general consensus is that it is inevitable that the public policy process should be political.   Political instability, politicization of the bureaucracy, and competition between sectional interests have been identified as the factors that have significant effects on the process.[130]

Riggs's argument is that in sub-Saharan Africa, just as it is elsewhere, public policy decisions entail activities on the part of various individuals and groups who have an interest in those policies. In the case of political leaders and bureaucrats, such interests derive from their direct involvement in the formulation and implementation process, as well as the benefits they stand to gain from the policies. Other individuals and groups have an interest due to the fact that those policies that would be introduced are likely to affect them in a positive or negative way. The policy environment is therefore a competitive one in which groups and individuals vie for influence over the contents of policies, the manner of implementation, and ultimately the outcomes of the policies.

This competition serves as the root of the political activities and events that take place within the policy environment. There are other proponents of this argument. In one instance, J. O. Udoji alludes to the pervasive power-struggle between politicians and bureaucrats in African countries, each group seeking to maintain a dominant position in the political and public policy arena.[131] According to Udoji, valuable resources have been devoted to this competition to the detriment of the quality and outcomes of policies in sub-Saharan Africa.

Nelson Kafir considers the dominance of top-level politicians in the policy process as another reason for the deficient policy process in sub-Saharan

Africa.[132] The basis for this position is the trend in newly independent nations whereby political leaders revised constitutions, adopted one-party systems, and invariably had most authority concentrated in the hands of the chief executive. (This occurred in such countries as Ghana, Guinea, Zimbabwe, and Tanzania.)   Such centralization of power and policy-making authority, according to Kafir, over-politicized the process, resulting in a preponderance of heads of governments and small cliques of politicians in highly centralized policy apparatuses. Ben Amonoo, in a treatment of the relationships between political institutions and the civil service, indicates that Ghana is an outstanding example of this phenomenon.[133]

Given the continued prevalence of this arrangement, it is clear that explanations of the policy environments in sub-Saharan African nations that are devoid of adequate attention to the role of heads of state and their closest advisors, heads of government departments, and high ranking party activists will be inadequate.

Other writers refuse to isolate the various aspects of the factors underlying the administrative weakness that foment policy failures. Rather they consider the totality of the environment within which the public policy process occurs as part of a political malaise.[134]   A. H. Rweyemanu suggests that the policy process in sub-Saharan African countries can only be understood in terms of the totality of the social, economic, political and cultural forces in the societies. These forces, he posits, interact with each other and with external forces in a complex combination that produces the conditions that determine the patterns of behavior of politicians and bureaucrats, the principal actors in the policy process.[135]   An effect of the complexity of the policy scenario and the behavior of the policy actors, according to Rweyemanu, is a dichotomy between policy formulation and implementation due to a lack of realism in the setting of policy goals. In his opinion, this is the primary cause of policy failures in sub-Saharan Africa.

W. N. Wamalwa also maintains a focus on ecology, pointing to the pluralistic nature of the societies in sub-Saharan Africa. He identifies social pressure in the form of divergent claims, competing interests, and conflicting orientations"[136] as a factor that undermines efficiency and effectiveness in the policy process.   Clement Onyemelukwe describes this condition as "turbulence"; a turbulence in the political and administrative environment that bars policy effectiveness.[137] He makes an important point that directly helps to explain the disconnection between deforestation policies and their outcomes.   Given the keenness with which the early post-independence governments tried to eradicate poverty and disease, and transform the societies, institutional efficiency and conservation of resources were not priorities. Rather, in the then prevailing political and social atmosphere, it was how to exploit the resources needed to accomplish those goals.

Merilee Grindle[138] wrote yet another treatise that identified politics as a key explanatory factor of the public policy situation in sub-Saharan Africa. She argues that the most serious aspect of the problem occurs during implementation. This is because, since policies are usually aimed at introducing changes in social, political, and economic relationships, the implementation stage is subjected to influences from the various interests that stand to be affected by the programs. According to Grindle's theory, the fate of policies depends on the degree of behavioral change envisaged by the programs.

This theory has a direct bearing on the deforestation policy scenario in Ghana. Deforestation policies in Ghana, being of the protective regulatory category, have typically imposed restrictions on the activities of certain citizens - farmers, hunters, timber contractors, etc. At the same time, the policies appear to provide avenues for the government, businesses, and individuals to benefit from the forest resources to the exclusion of others. There is evidence that indicates that the mistrust and hostility towards the government that was generated during the colonial era persists. Tensions, strains and stresses still prevail between landless farmers, traditional rulers, timber merchants, and citizens who depend on the forest for their livelihood and the government. Inevitably, this situation complicates the process, with serious political consequences to the policy process and outcomes.[139]

In his discussion of the ecology theory, Gelase Mutahaba identifies the effective elimination of the otherwise significant role of legislatures in the policy-process as another explanation of the ineffectiveness of the policy process in sub-Saharan Africa. The absence of a legislative culture, he suggests, is a direct result of the incessant political crises, especially coups d'etat, and their resulting sporadic changes in government leadership.[140] Political instability, according to Mutahaba, has fomented discontinuity, frequent changes in the key decision-makers, and hence erratic changes in goals and policies. This has spawned unpredictability and inept policy actions.

Bureaucratic Power: Its Implications to Public Policy

Almost without exception, literature that deals with the power of bureaucracies in sub-Saharan Africa indicates that because of the policy-making tradition bequeathed by the colonial rulers, coupled with the virtual collapse of legislatures in sub-Saharan African nations, the bureaucracy has emerged as the only stable, enduring and important institution in policy-making and implementation. In the absence of consistent and active legislatures, the frequently changing military rulers and inexperienced civilian heads of governments and departments inevitably find the bureaucracy indispensable in running the affairs of the nation. The level of dependence on the bureaucracy has, over time, enhanced its power and status of the top and middle level civil servants. Their prominent role in the policy process also implies that they belong to a category of actors that deserves close scrutiny in explaining deforestation policies in Ghana.

Two themes have consistently emerged when attempts are made to explain the nature and shortcomings of the public policy process in sub-Saharan

Africa: excessive bureaucratic power and bureaucratic politics. Two to three decades ago, Riggs,[141] Udoji,[142] and Price[143] drew attention to the entrenchment of bureaucrats within the public policy arena and the control they possessed over information and events. More recently, this theme has been revisited and the point of earlier writers reiterated.

Koehn explains the clout bureaucrats possess in terms of the critical role they play as sources of expertise and hence, as indispensable agents of the government. As was mentioned earlier, he suggests that the level of bureaucratic power derives from the absence of political control over civil servants.

C. L. R. James' illustration of the endurance of Ghanaian bureaucrats shows the extent of resilience that group possesses.[144] From the 1940s until the 1960s, during Ghana's transition from a colony into a self-governing nation, Dr. Kwame Nkrumah spearheaded a move to dismantle the elite-controlled governmental culture.[145] He and his supporters advocated a rejection of the then established norms of the public policy process, and sought to place politicians and the grassroots population at the center of the government policy apparatus. In spite of Nkrumah's charisma and the enthusiasm of his followers, by the end of his regime in 1966 the bureaucrats and elites remained as indispensable participants in Ghana's policy process.

Amonoo delves into this era of Ghana's history and demonstrates how during the C.P.P. regime, action was taken to replace the old administrative regime because it was considered unresponsive to the demands for change. According to Amonoo, the new institutions created to replace the old non-responsive ones ended up being tailored to suit the political purposes of the party. Nevertheless, old administrative practices were not abandoned. The new institutions were "dissuaded from adopting the irregular and makeshift operational procedures for which the purposes of the regime called."[146] An outcome of this, according to Amonoo, was that the new politically inspired institutions ran parallel to the old institutions. In effect, there was no fusion of Ghana's political and administrative institutions, but a dual structure. Amonoo concludes that "much of the stuff of government and politics in Ghana between 1957 and 1966 was provided by problems in the interrelationships" between political and bureaucratic institutions.[147] This denotes a powerful and entrenched bureaucracy that was able to endure and defeat political pressure that was intent on dismantling it.

The continued prominence of bureaucrats in Ghana has been re-examined in other recent literature.[148] In one case, reference is made to the revolutionary era between 1979 and 1982 when Flight Lieutenant J. J. Rawlings, as leader of the Peoples National Development Council (PNDC), ventured to establish a populist form of democratic government. In pursuit of this, and for a brief period, Rawlings and his followers threatened to dismantle the established institutions of the government and replace them with a unique alternative that would replace bureaucrats with "Peoples" and "workers" committees.[149] In spite of the threat posed by such incidents, as well as the increasing education and political awareness of Ghanaians,[150] the dominance of Ghanaian bureaucrats and elites in politics and the policy process remains.[151]

Excessive bureaucratic power as prevails in sub-Saharan Africa generates questions about how such power is used.   It has been suggested that the stability and dominance of the bureaucracy in the policy process does not imply a sidelining of political leaders.   According to Koehn, the already complex policy environment of sub-Saharan Africa is further complicated by the fact that, despite the seeming absence of control over the bureaucrats, politicians still maintain the power to make important decisions and influence policy outcomes.[152]   He submits that although political leaders have the prerogative of the final say in policy-making, the bureaucrats are the ones who take the actions that translate into the physical manifestations of policies. Koehn mentions the possibility that the bureaucrats' interpretations of policies and their style of implementing them do not necessarily reflect the thinking of the political leaders.   It is reasonable to speculate that stability of the bureaucracy is the reason for the consistency of forest policies in Ghana. Yet there is no evidence that the actions of bureaucrats in the policy process do not reflect the thinking of the political leaders.

Shortcomings of the Public Administration Institutions
Paucity of administrative systems in sub-Saharan countries has been identified as one of the causes of ineffective public policies.[153]   Some writers, in making this point, have stressed the existence of some structural and operational characteristics of bureaucracies in sub-Saharan Africa, which, until they are rectified, will continue to preclude effective policy formulation and implementation.[154]

In one instance the problem is perceived in terms of the large responsibilities the bureaucracies in sub-Saharan Africa have had to bear.[155] In another, the ineffectiveness of bureaucracies is explained in terms of the relative youthfulness of the post-colonial public service and the excessive expectations of politicians and citizens that such bureaucracies can fulfill the administrative needs of their countries.[156]

Onyemelukwe points out that in the rush to Africanize before political independence, European-held positions were quickly filled with young people, some of whom lacked the prerequisite training and experience.   Such early bureaucrats relied more on politics than competence to maintain their positions, giving inadequate attention to productivity and management.   This argument suggests that the traditions established by the early bureaucrats through their activities under those circumstances have endured. Consequently, bureaucrats in sub-Saharan Africa pay more attention to politics than to competence and efficiency.

Tony Killick treats the case of Ghana in this regard and concludes that indifference, poor leadership, inadequate personnel policies, low morale, and weak motivation[157] are the roots of the weakness that has prevented the bureaucracy from becoming an instrument for the successful pursuit of public objectives.

James S. Larson highlights another dimension of the problem as he explains why policy failures are rampant in sub-Saharan Africa.[158] He suggests that bureaucracies in sub-Saharan Africa are engaged in three main activities: interpretation, organization, and application. In his opinion, these activities cannot be effectively undertaken in the prevalent excessively complex environment in which implementation of policies is so highly political, where many implementation problems are unpredictable, and where there is a need for co-operation among numerous people functioning within a host of complex organizations. Bardach[159]and Hargrove[160] have advanced similar arguments. Although some of the assumptions made by Gabriel Inglesias are debatable, he broadens the scope of the analyses by drawing attention to several other aspects of administrative organizations that affect their effectiveness. He concludes that effective administration of public policies depends on administrative capacity of the agency concerned.[161]

Central to his argument is the identification of certain factors that can increase or decrease the capacity of administrative organizations to formulate policies, implement programs successfully, and convert critical inputs of programs into pre-determined outputs. These factors include: resources (adequate skilled personnel, funding, plant and equipment, materials, etc.); structure (Organizational roles and relationships which are relevant to the program); technology (knowledge and behavior that are essential to the operation of the organization); support (the range of actual or potential roles and behaviors that tend to promote the attainment of certain organizational goals); and leadership (the ability to modify or alter the other critical inputs during the formulation and implementation process).

By isolating these inputs and analyzing the way they impact the effectiveness of institutions engaged in the policy process, this theory draws attention to the chronic problem of the inability of the bureaucratic and political leadership of developing countries to alter and modify critical inputs of programs so as to achieve policy goals. This idea helps to establish a premise for explaining the disconnection between policy objectives and outcomes.

Although Inglesias' theory is useful for clarifying the shortcomings of administrative organizations in the Third World, it is important to bear in mind its debatable assumptions so as to give due consideration to all relevant dimensions of the problem. Particularly important is the seeming visualization of the formulation and implementation processes as mechanical constructs that can be manipulated at will. He tends to downplay social, cultural, historical, and political factors; highly significant ingredients of the policy environment.

These critical components of the policy process, which usually determine the shape and direction of policies, sometimes surpassing logic and common sense, cannot be handled as if they are "mechanical" elements. Another implicit assumption made in this theory is that inputs such as technology, personnel, and support can be made readily available. But, it is a well-known fact that the economic realities of Ghana, and sub-Saharan Africa as a whole, include a predominance of rudimentary technology, shortage of trained personnel, a usually sporadic and half-hearted support for programs (especially where the anticipated political gains are limited), and highly unpredictable political climate, given the series of *coups d'etat* and rapid changes in governments. Lastly, the assumption that public policies in the Third World stem from the demands of the general population is erroneous.

Conclusions

The issues discussed in this review have shed some light on the factors that deter effectiveness of the public policy process in sub-Saharan Africa. It has been shown that even though the classical theories explain formulation and implementation of policies in the western democratic settings, they still treat several factors and issues that are relevant to the Ghanaian experience. The behavioral theories have been shown to shed light on the processes and procedures involved in the policy process. They also discuss the levels of influence, the types of activities, and interactions between the various actors and institutions responsible for government policies.

Though the literature on public policy in sub-Saharan Africa has paid more attention to implementation, it deals with a number of elements that have helped to clarify the deforestation policy scenario in Ghana. The impact of the congenial indigenous cultures and social norms has been emphasized as a factor that complicates, even undermines, the effectiveness of the policy process. Political instability, it has been shown, causes a high turnover among national leaders. Yet, politicians play a dominant role in the policy process, and this contributes towards rendering the policy process highly political.

The influence of politicians notwithstanding, the ineffectiveness of the policy process in sub-Saharan Africa has also been attributed to the lack of effective political control over the bureaucracy. Furthermore, it has been pointed out that competition among the various interest groups has helped to shape the policy process and, ultimately, its outcome. Other explanations offered in the literature for ineffectiveness of the policy process are the lack of realism in the setting of policy goals, pluralism and the social pressures generated by divergent claims and competing interests. It has also been suggested that the wholesale transplant of foreign institutions into the peculiar cultural environments of the region during the colonial era has precipitated in administrative systems that have not been conducive to the effective pursuit of policies.

Some of the literature deals with bureaucracies. It discusses the resiliency of bureaucracies in the region, and how they have maintained a consistently powerful, indispensable role in the policy process. The implication is that the background, objectives, and activities of bureaucrats deserve ample attention in this.

Another emerging theme is the structural and operational weaknesses of the administrative systems. The literature indicates that because of government involvement in virtually every sphere of the affairs of the countries, the responsibilities required of the relatively young, ill-equipped public administrative institutions are beyond their capabilities. The limited administrative capacity of the institutions, coupled with corruption, mismanagement, poor leadership, and low morale are accentuated by the highly complex social, cultural, and political environments within which the policy process occurs.

These will be verified in order to find explanations to the disconnection between deforestation policies and their expected outcomes in Ghana. Overall, the review has revealed that public policy formulation and implementation are very complicated stages of the policy process. The literature has shown that the unique historical, social, economic, cultural, and political circumstances of sub-Saharan African nations render policy formulation and implementation highly complicated. At the same time it helps to identify aspects of the Ghanaian deforestation policy process that should be examined in order to explain the disconnection between the policies and their outcomes.

From the various criticisms, it becomes evident that none of the theories and inferences deriving there-from perfectly describes the forest policy scenario in Ghana. The theories and inferences will therefore be selectively utilized, applied only where they are directly relevant to the unique circumstances of the deforestation policy process in Ghana. The next chapter deals with the forest policy process in colonial Ghana. The objective is to establish a synthesis of the internal and external environments of the process, and how the factors involved determined the contents and outcomes of colonial era forest policies.

Chapter 3

The Forest Policy Process in Colonial Ghana

The objective of this chapter is to examine the internal and external environments of the forest policy process in the colonial era of Ghana for the purpose of determining how they explain the prevailing disconnection between forest policies and their intended outcomes. This discussion is particularly critical for achieving the objectives of this research because the current policy-making structure in Ghana rests on the legacy of the colonial era; an era in which government policies on the forests had a purpose that was disconnected from the internal needs and concerns of Ghanaian society.

As will be pointed out here and in chapter seven, present day political and institutional structures in Ghana are derived from those that operated during the colonial era. After forty years of self-government in Ghana, the processes of public policy-making and implementation remain conditioned by the colonial era philosophy and strategy of government. Therefore, to better understand the current disconnection between deforestation policies and their outcomes, it is important to understand the nature of the forest policy process in colonial Ghana.

The relevant colonial institutions to be considered in this discussion include: the British Colonial Office, the governor, the executive council, provincial and district administrations, and business interests.

Two approaches will be used in this analysis. The first involves discussion about the principal actors, and the other, the stages of the policy process. The areas to be dealt with include the background and characteristics of institutions and individual actors within those institutions, the manner in which they functioned, the way they interacted with each other, their impact on forest policy contents and outcomes, and the overall process by which policies were formulated and implemented.

The first part of the discussion is an account that reveals that British commercial activity preceded public administration and public policies in Gold

Coast. This account of the earliest involvement of British business interests in the administration of the territory helps to clarify their participation and impact on the governance of the territory in later years. The evidence produced shows that by the early nineteenth century, British commercial interests had established such a dominant presence in the colony that their practices and business interests laid the basis for public policy, that is, colonialism and imperial rule. The influence of business interests in the public policy process provided the basis for Lord Luggard's "dual mandate" proposition.[162]

The Role of Business Interests in the Political Economy of Gold Coast

British mercantile activity in Gold Coast preceded official colonial rule by several decades. The first business venture in the territory, the Royal African Company, formed in 1672, held a monopoly over British trade in the territory until it was broken up in 1750. The Royal African Company was reconstituted into the African Company of Merchants. In return for a $26,000 subsidy from the British government, this company was required to maintain its forts and trading posts under the British flag. It was also required to carry out necessary diplomatic negotiations, maintain an army, and generally safeguard British interests.[163] The company was therefore simultaneously engaged in administration of the colony. This combination of political and commercial activities became the classic British pattern in Gold Coast until 1844 when the first administrative system; a governor with a council, having purely advisory powers, was established.[164]

That British colonial policy was hinged on trade is evident from the fact that in the earliest colonial times British merchants played a key role in the administration of the territory. In 1807 for example, when Asante forces reached Anomabu, a Council of Merchants, constituted by British merchants operating in the territory, was established to look after British interests in the coastal areas of the territory.[165] In 1821 the failure of the merchants to cope with this duty prompted the British government to abolish this council and place the territory under direct Crown rule. After two more clashes between Asante forces and the British troops, London, unwilling to incur the increased expenditure for governing the territory, returned it to merchant control in 1828. The reintroduction of merchant rule was particularly consequent to strong protests by British merchants who, in the face of the might of Asante military force, dreaded the idea of being left unprotected by Britain. Crown rule was reinstated in 1843, but consequent to this, there continued to be persistent calls by the parliamentary committee to abandon Gold Coast because of the perceived cost of its administration.[166]

It is important to note that political responsibility of administering the colony was assigned to the merchants because of the underlying interest Britain had in the economic potential of the territory.[167] Additional arguments substantiating the economic basis of British colonialism have been made by J. P. Cain and A. G. Hopkins who indicate that the industrialization process that was taking place in England, and Europe as a whole, and the associated intensified competition from other European colonists for markets and raw materials formed a good basis for an increased effort at colonization. Although D. C. M. Platt argued convincingly that, in the early days of colonialism, many of the colonies were not of central importance to the British economy, he proceeded to show how, after 1882, the traditional policy of the British Foreign Office to seek no special favor for British merchants changed when the shortcomings of laissez-faire began to be realized.[168] The result was that annexations for safeguarding markets played an important part in the scramble for Africa.[169] These developments established the foundation for the "dual mandate'" philosophy which guided future British colonial administrations on Gold Coast. They show the strong political influence British mercantile interests commanded in the colony prior to the establishment of formal colonial administration, and explain why this strong influence endured in later years. They also serve as the grounds for explaining the content and outcomes of policies to combat deforestation.

W. G. Hynes, in later studies, highlighted the degree to which after 1881, commercial interests, especially when panicked by bouts of severe recession, successfully lobbied for greater protection for trade and annexation of territory.[170] The foregoing facts provide the background for discussing the role of business interests in the formulation and implementation of policies in colonial Ghana.[171]

The following section demonstrates how merchants played a direct and prominent role in the policy process under the rule of governors in Gold Coast. During the colonial era, a small number of firms including Elder Dempster Shipping Lines, Bank of British West Africa, Barclays Bank, Royal West African Company, United Africa Company, and African and Eastern Trading Company were virtual monopolies in the colony. The prominence of merchants, especially with regard to the formulation of policies, was facilitated by the membership of agents of British firms operating in the colony on the executive as well as the legislative council beginning with their formation in 1850. The 1850 legislative council, for example, consisted of the governor, the judicial assessor (later Chief Justice), the collector of customs, and two merchants. The colonial officials were well aware of the huge wealth of the privately held British firms. The large revenues and profits they remitted to their investors in England were the basis of immense political clout both in Britain and in Gold Coast colony. The political stature of merchants was therefore strong at the outset and throughout British rule.[172] Hugh Clifford's views about Gold Coast legislative council shed additional light on the role that these merchants played in the colonial government. According to Clifford, the Europeans selected for the council were "ordinarily drawn from the best fitted to speak for the mercantile and mining interests respectively."[173]

Changes in latter years that increased the membership and status of "natives" did little to curtail this prominence of business interests. The most far-reaching among such changes under the 1948 constitution established a majority of "natives" in the legislative council. Yet the governor was given the prerogative of nominating thirteen members of the council -- six official members, six nominated members, and one extra-ordinary member - the last two categories making room for the merchant interests. The executive council (which also included agents of merchants) retained its sweeping powers.

The preceding discussions have been used to describe the internal environment of the colonial policy-making process and to show that colonial policy-making was highly influenced, if not dominated, by British business interests. The implication of the facts are that policies enacted and implemented in Gold Coast reflected the economic goals of the British establishment, highly influenced by the interests of British merchants. It is important to note that exploitation and shipping of timber were two of the key economic activities of British businesses in Gold Coast. The above discussions and the inferences drawn from them are particularly significant for answering the central research questions of this book as they apply to the colonial era. They help to establish the atmosphere within which forest policies were processed.

The discussions show that British business interests in Gold Coast played a conflicting and contradictory role in the government. On one hand, they were profit-seekers whose fortunes depended on exploitation of resources such as timber. Because the consequence of such exploitation was deforestation, British business activity contributed to the problem. On the other hand, agents of these same interests were members of a government that was seeking to control the problem.

The "dual mandate" philosophy of colonial administrations in Gold Coast together with the above demonstrated dual role of mercantile interests help to establish the goals of the administrations and the atmosphere within which the deforestation policies were formulated and implemented. Given the circumstances, it becomes clear why policies to combat deforestation failed to achieve the declared objectives. In the following section we take a closer look at the internal environment of the colonial policy process in Gold Coast.

The Policy Apparatus During the Colonial Era of Ghana

The Bond of 1844, a compact by which many of the chiefs in the coastal areas of the colony acknowledged British rule, marked the beginning of formal British authority over Gold Coast.[174] Gold Coast remained a British territory until 1957 when it gained political independence and was renamed Ghana. The British monarch was the sovereign and the territory was administered by the Colonial Office, an agency of the British government between 1844 and 1957, for a period of 113 years.

British Colonial Objectives in Gold Coast

A review of the objectives of the British government concerning the colony would help establish the basis for analyzing the policy environment of the colonial government as well as the nature of the colonial administrative system. It is important to note that trade between the coastal areas of Ghana and Britain began years before formal colonization.[175] The British government only established a presence in the territory at the urging of British business interests who needed military protection from the indigenous ethnic groups as well as other European competitors.   As such, the primary concern of the administrations that were set up within the colonies, a part of the dual mandate philosophy, was to "maintain order for the benefit of the expatriate firms."[176]

The dual mandate proposition provides an authoritative validation of the economic intentions of the British imperial government concerning the colony.[177] As a high-ranking official in the colonial administration, with several years of service as governor in Northern Nigeria and Gold Coast, Lord Luggard was an insider, fit to interpret and expound official policy. He affirmed that the concept of dual mandate meant that officials of the colonial administration were to govern in the interest of Britain and also of the colonized people. The logic behind dual mandate goes back to the 17th century when merchants administered Gold Coast Colony in the name of the British crown.   The economic aspect of the proposition, the exploitation and export of natural resources, was given most emphasis to the exclusion of the welfare of the indigenous people. This has left a lasting legacy to the political economy of Ghana.

As Ebere Nwambani explains, dual mandate was a philosophy of imperialism.[178] In theory, the practice aimed at achieving a presumed reciprocal relationship between the economy of the metropolis (Great Britain) and that of the periphery (the colony). It was intended to facilitate a symbiotic existence for the mutual benefit of both, based on the idea of a liberal international division of labor.   Although dual mandate was supposed to take advantage of the comparative advantages of Great Britain and her colonies, in practice, it was no more than a cheap masking of imperial objectives. The mandate required that each colony must finance its own administration, and more important, that each administration provide ideal conditions for the success of British business.

The much-acclaimed revolutionary development of the infrastructure of Gold Coast between 1919 and 1927, during the tenure of Governor Gordon Guggisburg, helps to validate this fact. It important to recall a caveat Guggisburg issued soon after he assumed office, that "too quick an advance at any period in the development of a race means delay in the end."[179] This idea demonstrated that he was not necessarily interested in the development of the colony or the advancement of the indigenous people. The program of infrastructure development he oversaw was limited to construction of a network of feeder roads and railways that, by design, were channels that connected the sources of cocoa, timber, and mineral resources to the coast. A harbor was also constructed at Takoradi to facilitate the export of those resources.[180] The design of this system portrays the ultimate intentions of the colonial government to promote the exploitation and export of the available resources. From every indication, those developments were nothing less than ventures that were intended to enhance the conditions for successful British business activity. Henrika Kuklick suggests that as an ingredient of this fundamentally commercial-grounded policy, the administrative interests of the colonial authorities were in "safeguarding African rural societies from rapid development," and an administrative convenience was served by a "conservative, custodial rule, in which resistance to modernization was a constant theme."[181]

British commercial intentions in Gold Coast were evident prior to the Bond of 1844. As was mentioned earlier, between 1828 and 1830, when the British terminated their political presence in the colony, it was the merchants who managed British assets. Although this policy changed in 1844, merchants continued to play a prominent role in the administration of the territory, eventually occupying seats on the highest policy-making bodies, the governors' executive council and the legislative council, until the introduction of the Coussey Constitution in 1950.[182] This was an indication of British economic objectives in Gold Coast. Prior to the establishment of formal administration, Britain marshaled the power of its well-established presence in the territory and the facilities of British business interests for the purpose of promoting what has been termed, the "civilization of Africa," and more important, "to foster new branches of legitimate and less harmful trade."[183]

Data on the export of cocoa and timber from Gold Coast in the first sixty years of the twentieth century indicate consistently increasing volumes (See Table 3.1 below). The volume of cocoa exports multiplied over the years, jumping by 750% from 2,500 tons in 1900 to 190,600 tons in 1930, and, and by a further 59% to 302,800 tons in 1960. The volumes of log exports, though not as consistent, still increased by 766% from 90,000 tons in 1900 to 780,000 tons in 1949. From 1950 onwards, log exports showed dramatic increases, rising by 179% from 104,000 tons up to 290,000 tons in 1960. There were no exports of sawn timber until 1950 when 2,100 cubic feet were exported. From then on, there were regular annual increases up to 8,300 cubic feet by 1960.

TABLE 3.1
GOLD COAST: EXPORTS OF COCOA AND TIMBER, 1900-1960

YEAR	COCOA (000 tons)	LOGS (000,000 tons)	SAWN TIMBER (,000 cu.f.t)
1900	05	0.9	-
1910	23.0	1.9	-
1920	124.8	2.7	-
1930	190.6	0.5	-
1940	223.9	1.3	-
1950	267.4	10.4	2.1
1960	302.8	29.0	8.3

Source: Barbara Ingham, Tropical Exports and Economic Development: New Perspectives on Producer Response in the Low Income Countries, (New York: St. Martins Press, 1981), p. 336.

These increases in exports of forest produce and crops that are cultivated in hitherto forest lands are indicators of intensified destruction of forest cover. They can be considered a reflection of British colonial economic policies and priorities. Such intensified production and export of resources and crops would not have occurred without the deliberate involvement of the colonial government.

Excerpts from *Wealth in Wood*, an official government publication on the timber industry of the colony, depict the government's policies, intentions and expectations on forest resources, and the consequences of those policies. Government policy was to encourage "the fullest use of the timber resources of the country, controlled in such a way as to supply for all time the needs of the people of Gold Coast and of a flourishing export trade."[184]   Because it considered the forests outside forest reserves as "doomed to be destroyed", the government insisted that tree felling should be concentrated outside reserves so as to remove valuable timber before their destruction to make way for farms. Because of this position, non-reserved forests, an area estimated at 10,200 square miles, 63% of the total estimated forest area, were declared open for exploitation, without any measures being taken to replace what was cut. It was estimated that the rate of forest destruction in the 1950s, was 300 square miles a year. On that basis, the government itself projected that all forests outside of reserves would disappear in thirty-five years, unless measures were taken to protect them.[185]

Structure of the Colonial Policy-Making System

Figure 2 depicts the hierarchical nature of the colonial administrative system of Gold Coast. This structure remained unchanged until the territory was granted political independence in 1957. This was a hierarchical system with a monarch at the top, and Gold Coast bureaucracy at the lowest level. The other principal institutions were the British House of Commons (the legislative body), the Colonial Office (the bureaucracy in charge of administering the colonies), the Governor, Gold Coast Executive Council, and Gold Coast Legislative Council. The status and role of these institutions will be examined in the following sections. The discussions on these institutions and the individual actors involved in the policy process are done in detail because the facts that will be presented establish the grounds for understanding the policy process, the content, and outcomes of the policies that were introduced.

Fig 2
HIERARCHY OF THE POLICY-MAKING INSTITUTIONS OF GOLD COAST

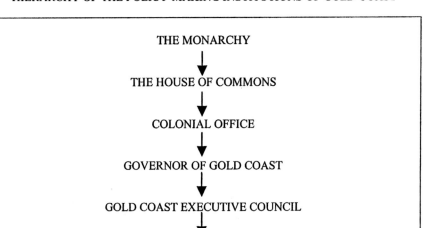

The Principal Institutions of the Policy Process in Gold Coast

The Monarchy

Although the monarch was the highest authority in the British colonial system, he played a very limited direct role in the policy-making and in the administrative process. Only the most important policies had to be approved by the monarch and his council.[186]   Royal instructions concerning the administration of the empire were clearly established, and the actual decision-making concerning the British government's goals regarding the colonies, and the mechanisms for achieving those goals rested with the House of Commons (the legislature) and the British Colonial Office.

The Colonial Office

Under the British colonial system, the administration of all territories and dependencies was the direct responsibility of the Colonial Office.[187] Established in 1812, the basic task of this office was to function with "as little trouble and expense to the home government as possible."[188]   Charters of justice and laws were drawn up at the Colonial Office in London, and after their approval of the Houses of Parliament, put into effect in the colonies. It was required that all laws, ordinances, and regulations that were proposed in the colonies should be sent to England for scrutiny and approval by the Secretary of State for the Colonies or the British House of Commons, where necessary.[189]

From every indication, the Colonial Office, was a typical bureaucracy.[190] Although it was only a minor department when compared with the several others in the British government, it bore the enormous responsibility of administering the numerous British colonies.[191]   Even though this agency was responsible for managing the colonies, in practice, the power of decision-making was divided among a number of different agencies.   Most colonial questions, whether they were concerned with administration or policy-making, had to be submitted to several other departments, boards, etc., for their input before final decisions could be made.

Paul Knaplund uses the clause "circulatory correspondence arising from a division of powers," to describe the way this system functioned.   As he describes it, policy-making and administration were circuitous and could "extend to more than half a dozen government agencies concerning a single question."[192]

At its inception, and for several decades afterwards, the Colonial Office was also responsible for military security in the colonies.   This combination of responsibilities in an era when Britain was actively engaged in the scramble for territories in Africa, Asia, and Latin America, an era in which the military was one of the most important, if not the most important instrument for pursuing British colonial ambitions, meant that administration of the already acquired colonies was given less prominence than it deserved.   Acquisition of more territories and protection of those already seized were the major priorities.

Sir Alan Burns' 1949 account of the structure and activities of the Colonial Office included a critique of that institution.   He stressed the need for an "adjustment" in the way the agency was organized, because, in his opinion, it was impossible for the secretary of state to "cope with the immense and increasing amount of work he might deal with if colonial questions were to receive the attention which is their due."[193]   This comment conveys three important concerns about the way the agency was organized: the immense amount of responsibility the agency had to bear, the inability of the individuals involved to cope with the requirements of their work, and the comparatively low importance of colonial affairs within the British government.

The Colonial Office was over-centralized, decision-making being strictly reserved to the highest officials in London.   Worse still, the staff was scattered in different buildings in different parts of London.   Furthermore, there existed a dual organization into geographical and subject departments, a system Burns describes as "illogical and unworkable."[194]

The Colonial Office was beset by a host of other organizational shortcomings that further undermined its capacity for the administration of the colonies. Some of these were related to the overall environment of the British government of which it was a part.   The office was a relatively minor agency that was assigned the massive and complex task of administering the wide array of territories that were scattered the world over.   This responsibility had to be performed in an administration that did not consider the management of the colonies to be a priority. The standing of the office was low before politicians as well as bureaucrats in the other government departments. Blakeley reports that regardless of the abilities of colonial secretaries, their influence in the cabinet "was never that great." British political leaders looked upon debates concerning colonial affairs in the cabinet or parliament as "burdens to be avoided if possible". Blakeley states further that when a colonial topic received consideration, it was usually "because it affected Britain's foreign or defense policy."[195]

The level of influence that was wielded by other agencies over colonial policies also undermined the effective administration of the colonies. The performance of such agencies when dealing with the colonies implied that officials within those agencies did not consider them as important enough to merit prompt attention. Because bureaucrats in other departments did not consider the colonial office as a critical arm of the government, they "offered little cooperation" to its personnel, and resented any efforts to procure necessary information or solicit prompt action on colonial affairs.[196] To most bureaucrats, the colonial office was "no more than a mere stepping stone to higher ministerial appointments."[197]

Knaplund makes special mention of the treasury department in this connection. That department had "the unamiable habit of taking not less than two months and often two years or more to answer a single query from the Colonial Office."[198] The influence of other agencies, the legislature and the monarch amounted to a "paralyzing control" of that department. Instead of helping to coordinate and promote administration of the colonies, they rather formed what has been described as "a major obstacle" to the adoption of a more effective colonial policy.[199]

Because most British colonies were in distant lands (Gold Coast, for example, being over five thousand miles away from England), an efficient system of communication to operate an effective administration was required. Yet, the only available facility at that time was transportation by sea, voyages typically taking three months or longer. A typical message to and from Gold Coast colony therefore took about six months. Such slow communication and transportation severely hindered the quick transmission of information up and down the hierarchy.

The nature of the responsibilities of the secretary of state for the colonies required that he should be very familiar with the territories, yet up till 1949, no colonial secretary, and very few high officials of the Colonial Office, had set foot in Gold Coast.[200] Distance and the reluctance to undertake a several weeks' voyage were the apparent reasons for this fact. Consequently, decision-makers in the British establishment had "no experience of the colonies."[201] Their attitudes towards the colonies were tainted with the sagas of adventure seekers and accounts of traders who had visited the territories or nearby ones. Their decisions were influenced overwhelmingly by reports and advice received from the governors and the few other colonial servicemen. This situation and the slow pace at which British departments generally dealt with colonial matters did not augur well for an effective policy making and administration for the colonies.

The Colonial Office was also handicapped by the reported overall low caliber of personnel in its service. On the whole, the staff especially those posted to the colonies, were not the most suited for effective policy formulation and implementation. This was because the personnel preferences of the office largely reflected colonial objectives in the era under consideration. Positions were typically filled by "patronage," and frequently, candidates were chosen for "reasons other than ability."[202] This state of affairs was evident even to certain citizens of the territories. Casely Hayford in his 1903 condemnation of the colonial system attacked this practice, declaring that: "patronage rules the day at Downing Street.... Consequently, there is a class of men who, as human nature goes, would be most obedient, humble, servants of the Colonial Office."[203] Administrative competence was discounted as a criterion, its place taken by political and personal connections. Elizabeth Isichei provides a portrait of the individuals within the colonial service: "Some were escaping from financial problems or personal unhappiness, some were demobilized soldiers after the World Wars, some saw it as the only choice during the depression years, some were attracted by the prospect of change, adventure and outdoor life."[204]

Henrika Kuklick corroborates this portrayal of the background of the colonial service personnel. She contends that for several of the men, service in the colonies "seemed to represent only one in a series of attempts to find exotic adventure." She states further that "many were obviously escaping from an untenable situation at home," some saw it as "the only avenue open to them," and still others made the choice as an "act of desperation, undertaken only after past failures."[205]

Additional indications of the caliber of colonial service personnel are provided by Sir Alan Burns, who recommended "drastic changes" in the colonial regulations that included principles that perpetuated the system of patronage.[206] He pronounced some officers "merely unsuited to colonial life either through temperament or because of indifferent health."[207] In spite of this, Burns pointed out that officers were never removed except when they were convicted of a criminal offense. Even chronic alcoholics remained on the job, and men who were "unfitted" for their appointments were routinely promoted.[208] Such action, Burns asserted, was due to the cumbersome formalities needed for a civil servant to be removed, and the tendency of the Colonial Office, Governors, and heads of departments to find excuses for the culprits.

The foregoing suggests that members of the colonial service were not the most suited for the demanding tasks involved in decision-making and administration of territories, some of which were larger and more complex that Britain itself. In all probability, the personnel qualities preferred by Colonial Office recruiters explain the prevalence of this caliber of individuals in the bureaucracy. For example, a diary entry made by C. E. Skeene then Acting Commissioner of the Central Province of Gold Coast Colony, reflected his position that "a young District Commissioner... should have ruling traditions behind him."[209] Kuklick provides some more insight into the human resources culture of the Colonial Office by describing it as an organization that judges its staff on the basis of "immeasurable skills rather than precise technical accomplishments... tending to put a premium on the social graces that the man from a privileged background would possess. "[210]

She produces evidence to suggest that officers who had a military background were more likely to get promoted to higher grades in the colonial service.[211] This probably was due to their unique authoritarian style of administration, a style that must have been preferred by their superiors. She infers that, in colonial service thinking, candidates whose schooling had emphasized "athletic character-building were considered to be capable of the visceral judgements and exemplary behavior," attributes considered necessary to lead "genuine primitives," while those whose training had emphasized the development of "mere brains were but confined to an office..."[212] This atmosphere must have made it easy for C. E. D. O. Rew, for example, to exchange his position as commander of Gold Coast Regiment, West African Frontier Force, for that of Provincial Commissioner in 1907.[213]

Besides the hindrances presented by other departments that had roles to play in colonial affairs, relationships between personnel within the Colonial Service itself reflected an absence of comradeship, a prevalence of sectionalism, and a class-culture within which officials who were posted to the colonies were perceived to be inferior to those in the home office. A private note written by Robert Meade, then Assistant Under Secretary in the Colonial Office, points to a scenario in which a wide gap existed between two main classes of bureaucrats. His note states that the Colonial Office regarded the officials in the colonies as "ignorant, untrustworthy, quarrelsome, and indiscreet".[214] The officials who were based in the colonies, on the other hand, regarded their superiors in London as "uninformed meddlers" who should refrain from exercising the unwarranted close control over the colonies.[215]

The impact of such an atmosphere on the functional efficiency of the Colonial Office was perhaps predictable. There is enough evidence to indicate that there was no mutual trust and respect; neither was there an attitude of cooperation among the individuals and agencies within the establishment. Under such circumstances, the Colonial Office could not have been an effective institution for the formulation of goals and objectives, and the efficient implementation of those goals.

The above overview of the environment within which the British colonial administration functioned portrays the general circumstances within which the individual actors in the policy process functioned. These actors will be discussed forthwith.

The Secretary of State for the Colonies: The Secretary of State for the Colonies was a member of the British cabinet and the topmost politician directly responsible for policies and administration of the affairs of Gold Coast. Every law or regulation passed by the colony's administration had to be transmitted by the governor to the secretary of state who had the powers to approve, disallow, or give other instructions. The secretary even had the power to advise the monarch to disallow any measure that has already been enacted.[216] But, as has been indicated, his status among his cabinet colleagues was relatively low. This low status of the head of the agency responsible for the colonies reflects the position of the British government concerning the colonies. It also adds validity to the assertion that the primary British colonial objective was purely economic. Consequently, it is reasonable to infer that so long as the colonies were secure from threats from other European competitors and from the native Africans, and so long as the proper atmosphere was maintained for British businesses to operate successfully, the responsibility of the Colonial Office was considered fulfilled. Administration of the colonies for other purposes did not appear to be high in the policy agenda of the government.

Sir Burns' already cited work provides an insider's account and critique of the Colonial Office as it existed in 1949.[217] He was an insider because of his forty-two years service in several colonies and in the Colonial Office, eight of them as the Governor of Gold Coast (1941 to 1948). The following comments and facts are largely derived from Burns' book, *The Colonial Civil Servant*.

There were rather frequent changes in the persons filling the office of secretary of state. Between 1905 and 1947 there were no less than twenty-three secretaries, three of whom lasted a total of twelve years. This means the remaining twenty served for thirty years, an average of one and a half years! Such frequent changes had serious consequences. The majority of the appointed heads of the agency did not last long enough to be able to establish themselves in their position, much less learn and understand the area for which they were responsible. It could not have been possible for them to acquire adequate knowledge of the colonies or offer the appropriate leadership for effective formulation and implementation of policies. In all probability, the frequency with which secretaries were transferred conditioned newly appointed ones to consider their jobs as temporary. They did not see the need to immerse themselves in their work and endeavor to confront long term, or even medium term, policies.

In any case, the scope and depth of the responsibilities of the secretary were so great that in practice, it was impossible for them to cope. In particular, it was not practicable for them to visit the colonies as often as was necessary to acquire the knowledge and experience required for successful policy making.

A number of recommendations made by Sir Burns shed additional light on the circumstances surrounding the position of Secretary of State for the Colonies. Sir Burns considered the job to be of "highest importance and interest," and in view of that, he emphasized that appointees to the post should possess a "profound knowledge of human nature and administrative capacity of a high degree." In his opinion, it was a post that should be filled by "one of the best men in the cabinet."[218] He recommended regular visits by the secretaries so as to keep themselves "up-to-date with changes," develop a "realistic outlook on the facts of life," and enhance their sensitivity to local public opinion on colonial affairs.[219]

It is possible to draw two critical inferences about the circumstances surrounding the post of secretary of state for the colonies from these comments. First, because the position was, from every indication, taken for granted, the occupants, in all probability, could not have been the most capable men. Second, the secretaries did not visit the territories and, as such, were unfamiliar with the political and administrative problems that existed, neither were they aware of the values and needs of the indigenous people or the possible conflict between British colonial goals and the aspirations of the indigenous people. It appears that the secretaries of state were not capable of making the best policy decisions. In effect, they could not but rely largely on their agents in the colonies, the governors and their supporting officials, for information and advise on how to administer the colonies. In spite of the deficiencies of the secretaries of state and of the colonial office as a whole, much of Gold Coast colonial policy originated from and was guided by that agency.[220]

The administration of Gold Coast was also affected by the fact that British policy maintained uniformity in the laws and administrative procedures throughout the West African territories (Gambia, Sierra Leone, Gold Coast, and Nigeria) and in territories as far away as Asia.[221] As a result, in Colonial Office policy-making, Gold Coast was not perceived as a unique separate entity that required specific attention to its particular historical, socio-cultural, environmental, economic, and other differences, problems and needs. It was simply considered as part of a collection of territories for which wholesale laws and policies could be applied. Policies, including those on forests, were therefore not always formulated specifically for Gold Coast, but for all British colonies. These facts help to explain why policies to combat deforestation in post-independence Ghana have not achieved the intended outcomes. Similar to those of the colonial era, most of which still remain in effect, such policies and the institutions that have produced them have been geared more towards exploitation of resources than conservation.

The Governor: The 1850 Constitution of Gold Coast introduced by a British House of Commons Charter appointed the first governor for the colony. From then until 1957, the governor administered Gold Coast on behalf of the British Crown. As seen in Figure 3.1, the colony's administration was subordinate to the Colonial Office, and the governor was responsible to the secretary of state for the colonies, who in turn, was responsible to the British parliament. Technically, the governor was simply an agent of the British Colonial Office. As described by Sir James Stephen,[222] the governor had, "properly speaking, no independent authority at all. All he does, he does on behalf of the Queen, whatever power he exercises are (sic) exercised of her Majesty's account."[223] The system of administration required that major policies originated from London, and the governor's standing instructions required that "all colonial bills, acts, ordinances and regulations should be sent home for review."[224] Yet in practice, he had considerable powers and the scope to rule almost completely unimpeded by his superiors in London. For example, he had "full powers and authority"[225] to make land grants to private persons, appoint and dismiss judges and other officials, and impose fines and penalties.

Given the distance, the state of transportation and communication between Gold Coast and Britain in the eighteenth and nineteenth centuries,[226] and the already discussed low significance of colonial affairs in the eyes of British politicians and bureaucrats, it became imperative that the governor, being the leader, makes important decisions even if they might contravene orders from home. The bulk of legislation therefore originated from the colonial government. Another factor that made this possible was the bankruptcy of first-hand knowledge about conditions in the territory in the colonial office.

Added to the foregoing, under the colonial system, the powers of supplementary legislation, issuing of orders, and administrative regulation making to implement ordinances were conferred on the governor-in-council.[227] The governor had the power to appoint the executive council, provincial and district commissioners, and extra-ordinary members to executive council sessions as deemed necessary. Of course, it was required that all laws, ordinances, and regulations, as well as all appointments should be approved by the colonial office, but, in practice, this did not mean that everything needed formal sanctioning by the authorities. The governor's decisions were almost invariably upheld.

The governor also possessed "reserved powers" of legislation. This amounted to veto powers with which he could reject or overrule any and all decisions taken by his executive council or the legislative councils that were formed later in the early twentieth century.[228] Although laws that were not reported to the colonial office were deemed to be technically invalid, they were allowed to operate because the high officials of the colonial office believed that disallowing them would cause "irremediable distress"[229] to their surrogates in the colonies. Thus, it was possible for the governor to evade imperial regulations and run the colony virtually unhindered by the home government.

Indeed, constitutional changes were introduced throughout the colonial era, allowing the indigenous people to play an increasing role in government, and eventually culminating in political independence for Ghana. Nevertheless, such reforms barely affected the authority of the governor, neither did they affect the scope of his powers,[230] as such powers were considered to be "critical to the proper conduct of their administration."[231] The governor appointed members of boards, and committees, as well as the executive and legislative councils. He or his nominees chaired all sessions. Even after 1925 when nine unofficial native members were elected to the legislative council, they formed a small minority, the other twenty-three members were the Governor's appointed officials or their nominees. The 1925 Board of Education, for example, was a statutory committee set up under the Education Ordinance. It had fifteen members: the governor, the colonial secretary, four nominated official members, the director of education, the principal of Achimota College, four nominated members to represent missionary and educational societies, and five nominated official members.[232] The governor could, in addition, appoint extra-ordinary members for any session.

The extensive powers of the governor under the colonial system suggest that the individual holders of the position should be highly competent in decision-making and administration. But, in line with the existing practice of the colonial office, no fixed policy or standard had been set up for gubernatorial selection, and the criteria used to make appointments did not necessarily emphasize the qualities required for the best performance. Governorships were often used as a means of "taking care of high-ranking, half-pay military and naval officers."[233] Added to this there existed a policy of deliberately protecting the governors from any challenges to their authority so as to enhance their standing as representatives of the British monarch.

The position taken by Sir Stephen concerning the status and role of governors helps to illustrate how this was achieved. Sir Stephen held that "mistakes by governors should not pass unnoticed," yet he, at the same time, opposed sending out scolding dispatches to them.[234] An outcome of this position was that rebukes of governors were very rare,[235] hence they had a free hand to administer the colonies in ways they deemed fit.

The Colonial Executive Council of Gold Coast: Gold Coast Constitution of 1850 also instituted an executive council. It was a non-representative body, yet served as the highest governing body, the equivalent of a cabinet.[236] It was an advisory body that aided the governor in decision-making. The Constitution authorized the governor to appoint to his executive council "such persons as may from time to time be named or designated by us,"[237] us being members of the British House of Commons. In practice, membership of this council was exclusive to the highest government officials. Under the 1925 constitution, for example, it was an all-British body that comprised the governor as chair, the colonial secretary, the chief commissioners for the Colony, Asante, the Northern Territories (the three administrative regions of Gold Coast), the attorney general, the financial secretary, the director of medical services, and the secretary for native affairs.

Technically, the council had very sweeping powers, but given the commanding authority of the governor, its standing was considerably reduced. It therefore operated merely as the governors' advisory committee. Until the 1951 Constitution which stipulated that the executive council should end its role as an advisory body and become a principal instrument of policy, it was nothing less than a collection of colonial office appointed officials, who, in lieu of their positions in the administration, were appointed to sit on the highest policy-making body and to help to enforce mandates that had been handed down from London.[238] In a critique of the council, Sir Hugh Clifford, Governor of Gold Coast in 1951, remarked that; "No-one of its members is usually possessed of any intimate knowledge of native affairs or first hand experience in local provincial administration... I do not think that this expedient works in a satisfactory manner when native affairs are under discussion."[239]

As a solution to this deficiency, Sir Clifford recommended that at least one member should be in a position to reflect the wishes and opinions of the native population, and advise the governor and the other members accordingly. Notwithstanding this recommendation, he still endorsed the British position on the status of the governor by recommending a perpetuation of the same system that allowed the governor to exercise virtually limitless powers. Among his recommendations were that the governor should maintain an official majority in the council for reasons that were "self evident," and that all unofficial members should continue to be nominated by the governor.[240]

The bulk of colonial legislation in Gold Coast originated from the executive council. After the Attorney General drafted a bill, it was sanctioned by the governor-in-council, and then became law. Included in the changes that took place in 1850 was the institution of a legislative council. From that time onward, legislation was sent to the legislative council for deliberation before becoming law.

In spite of the apparent importance of the executive council, its activities with regard to the consideration of bills were considered as having no constitutional basis beyond usage.[241] Members of the executive council sat on the legislative council as well, and formed the majority on all boards and committees of the governor. They were therefore available to be used as instruments to endorse the governor's, (and therefore Britain's) policies in the colony.

Even after some indigenous people had been appointed to the council in 1942, and after Mr. E. C. Quist (a lawyer and member of the legislative council elected by the Joint Provincial Council of Chiefs) had been appointed by the governor to be the first native president of the legislative council in October 1949, the executive council remained the highest policy authority.[242] Under the radical 1951 Coussey Constitution, the legislative council had an African majority (three ex-officio and eight others), yet, it continued to be dominated by the official members and remained responsible to the governor who, under the new system, retained his reserved powers.

The Gold Coast Colonial Legislative Council: The 1850 Constitution of Gold Coast prescribed a legislative council in addition to an executive council. Specifically, the provision established a "not less than a two-member" council, "empowered to establish such laws, institutions, and ordinances as may from time to time be necessary for the peace, order, and good government."[243] Although its name suggested that it was the law-making body empowered to deliberate on governance of the colony, the British House of Commons required that in performing these functions, Gold Coast legislature had to "conform to and observe all such rules and regulations as shall be given and prescribed in and by such institutions as we, with the advice of the Privy Council, shall from time to time make for their guidance therein."[244]

Consequently, for the next 100 years (until 1951), Gold Coast legislative council was subordinated to the Colonial Office, from where most policies originated.[245] As such Gold Coast legislative council was nothing less than an instrument for pursuing British imperial objectives in the colony.

Between 1850 and 1951 increased advocacy and protests by the educated indigenous elites and some traditional rulers forced the British authorities to introduce a series of constitutional reforms that altered the institutional framework of the policy process in Gold Coast.[246] Such changes barely affected the authority of the Colonial Office or that of the governor, however. The 1925 legislative council can be used to illustrate the composition of the typical colonial legislature. In addition, reports by Martin Wright on some deliberations of the legislative council of that era shed light on the background of the members and the impact various categories of members made on policies.[247]

The legislative council was retained in the 1925 constitution.[248] The same instrument that provided for the formation of this legislature stated that "it was lawful for the governor... to make laws for the peace, order, and good government of the colony."[249] By implication therefore, the authority for lawmaking remained vested in the governor in spite of the existence of the legislature. The legislative council had thirty members: the governor (as president), fifteen ex-officio members nominated by the governor, and fourteen unofficial members. The unofficial members were six chiefs, elected by the provincial councils (assemblies of the highest-ranking traditional rulers), three elected representatives from the municipalities of Accra, Cape Coast and Sekondi, and five Europeans (two of whom were elected; the other three representing merchant and mining interests). The governor appointed nominated members for four years, subject to renewal. In addition, the governor could also appoint any person as an extra-ordinary member.

Legislative council members had to meet certain qualifications. Between 1925 and 1939, for example, provincial members were to be elected by the provincial councils. This meant that they had to be traditional rulers who belonged to the provincial councils. Members had to be competent at spoken and written English. The municipal representatives had to show proof that they owned property of at least $500. Finally, representatives of the mercantile firms had to be European, British specifically, and resident in the colony for at least eighteen months.

A series of reforms slowly diminished the powers of the governor and eliminated the dominance of Europeans, ultimately culminating in the Constitution of 1954. For example, the Burns Constitution of 1946 provided for a legislative council which had a majority of elected members. The Coussey Constitution of 1950 provided for the first general elections and an executive council presided over by an indigenous person and having a majority of indigenous members. In 1954 all the 104 members of the legislature were directly elected, the executive council was replaced by a cabinet, and the responsibilities of the governor were limited to consular matters and external affairs only.

Even though these reforms suggest an increasing role for elected representatives of the indigenous people, their power of policy-making was extremely constrained because under the arrangements, the secretary of state for the colonies and the governor continued to retain their immense reserved powers. The British monarchs could also issue royal instructions on whatever policy they chose to impose. A case that illustrates this continued subordination of local government and policy-making to the Colonial Office involved the events surrounding the cocoa holdup of 1939. Gold Coast farmers stopped selling the cocoa in protest against an imperial government scheme under which the purchase of cocoa was monopolized by European purchasing firms. This scheme had been introduced despite the local government's opinion against it.[250]

The governor continued to retain his veto powers over legislation. He could also reserve any bill "for the signification of His Majesty's pleasure through the secretary of state for the colonies."[251] Every ordinance and every reserved bill had to be transmitted by the governor to the secretary of state for approval, disallowance or any other instruction. The secretary had the power to advise the monarch to disallow any measure, even if already enacted.[252]

There is evidence that the colonial legislative councils were effectively prevented from having any significant impact on policies. The governor and his bureaucrats succeeded in manipulating the legislative process in a way that sidelined the legislature. For example, bills were submitted so late prior to the council meetings that members were virtually prevented from scrutinizing them adequately.[253] In any case, until 1946, the official majority always enabled the governor to secure the desired approvals.

Demands from the indigenous members that the power to bring ordinances into force should lie with the legislative council and not the governor-in-council were greeted with a response that such a change would abrogate the power of the executive committee. Council member, Sir Ofori Attah's remarks during a debate on the Cocoa (Control of Exportation) Bill in 1938 serves as a good reflection of the circumstances under which colonial legislators functioned. Evidently out of frustration, he exclaimed: "We are being asked to approve a bill which will empower the Governor-in-Council to make certain regulations, but what the regulations are going to be, nobody knows."[254]

Virtually no legislation originated from unofficial sources, and those that were enacted characteristically endorsed or promoted the objectives of the colonial government. Popular opinion or the opinions of the provincial councils (councils of traditional rulers) were entertained only when they endorsed the policies of the colonial government. For example, in 1933 the Eastern Provincial Council passed a resolution in favor of encouraging food crop production. The Central Provincial Council also endorsed the Cocoa Inspection Bill of 1934, and in doing so expressed the wish that the colonial government would pass similar measures to safeguard palm oil, and cola. The colonial government supported these. A resolution of the Joint Provincial Council concerning the deportation of non-native agitators resulted in the Immigration Restriction Bill of 1937.[255] In 1934, however, the Provincial Councils rejected two government bills, the Waterworks Bill and the Sedition Bill,[256] yet the legislative council subsequently passed those bills.

The governor, with the advice of his executive council, and subject to the approval of the secretary of state for the colonies, was empowered to make orders and rules, which, in his opinion, were necessary for administering the colonial territory.[257] The local legislature remained a very minor body compared with other policy institutions that existed both in Britain and in the territory. In effect, it was reduced to a rubber stamp, a largely insignificant body, considering that the governor, the secretary of state for the colonies, the House of Commons, and the monarch could override any and all decisions that this body made.

In practice, the legislative procedure was consciously based on the model of the British House of Commons. Questions were not a prominent part of the proceedings although the Standing Orders and the Rules of the Committee provided for questions.[258] The outcome of this arrangement was that several sessions passed without any questions being asked.[259] In the eight years between 1933 and 1941, for example, only one hundred and seventy-eight questions were asked by the native members; none by the Europeans. These were the procedural circumstances under which forest policies were formulated during the colonial era. Only the policies supported by the colonial office or the governor were adopted.

The legislative process functioned in the interest of Great Britain and British businesses. No other interests were allowed to make any inputs to the policy-making process. However, the indigenous people, through their traditional rulers and the Aborigines Rights Protection Society were able to make an impact during the implementation phase of the process, as will be shown later in this chapter.

The Provincial and District Officers: In examining the powers and roles of the provincial and district officers in Gold Coast, it is important to bear in mind the background of personnel in the British Colonial Service as discussed earlier in this chapter. The lack of requisite qualifications on the part of officials in the colonial service appears to be a factor in understanding the disconnection between forest policies and their outcomes.

"Long-grade" officers, the junior members of the colonial administrative service, ruled the indigenous population in the provinces and the districts, at the lowest levels of the colonial bureaucracy. Originally, this category included only the assistant district commissioners, district commissioners, and provincial commissioners. But an even more junior rank, the cadet, was later added.[260] Although these officers were the most junior in the establishment, they wielded considerable powers and decision-making autonomy because of the prevalent poor communication facilities between their stations and the administrative headquarters where the higher officials were located.   Their discretionary latitude later declined as communications improved, yet they continued to possess significant amount of power.

The district officers performed a wide range of duties. They were the immediate agents of the governor in their districts, and their responsibilities extended to all departments of the administration, which did not have special representatives at their stations. Thus, in addition to their primary functions as magistrates and political officers (the officers responsible for the maintenance of satisfactory relationships between the natives and the central administration), they typically were in charge of detachments of police, the districts' financial accounts, prisons, road construction, waterway clearing, or any other public works.

Officers were expected to travel far and wide within their districts, in the course of which they inspected the outlying areas, transacted any necessary business with the native chiefs, settled disputes between individuals or communities, and generally dealt with all matters requiring the personal attention of the representative of the government.[261] There was virtually no limit to the responsibilities of the district officers. In addition to the above listed activities, they had to be able to perform the role of veterinarian, health care dispenser, botanist, and forester.[262]

When the legislative council's Select Committee on the Africanization of Gold Coast public service published its report in 1951, it could only describe the duties of the district officer in very vague terms. The report read: "The duties of an Administrative Officer are so wide and varied that they cannot be set out in detail."[263] It was absolutely impossible for these officers to perform all their duties and meet all their obligations.[264] This is because their most important function was to create strong bonds of sympathy and loyalty between the natives and the colonial rulers, and to persuade them to implement the government's policy objectives.[265] To facilitate this function, the bureaucratic structure of the colonial administration was organized in such a way as to alter the balance of power between the district officer and the chiefs, reducing the latter to a lower status in the eyes of the natives.[266]

The district officers were required to organize the natives into functional hierarchies so as to enhance their own status. By supporting and protecting the chiefs, the officers earned the chiefs' obligation to follow instructions of the government. This in turn helped secure and elevate the officials' positions.[267]

At the same time, pro-native officers who identified too closely with their subjects and who displayed personal sympathies with them ended up alienating the European community and their superiors. This could also cost them success in their careers.[268]

Although district officers occupied a comparatively low position in the colonial hierarchy, they were the principal agents for implementing its policies. These were the individuals on whom the success or failure of policies mainly depended.[269] According to the colonial organizational scheme, instructions on policy were transmitted from the governor through a secretariat at the headquarters to the provincial officers and then on to the district officers. The district officers, being at the grassroots of the administration, were in the best position to diagnose the outcomes of policies and give feedback to the higher levels of the hierarchy.

Although the established procedures of operation of the government implied that the district officers could not turn a blind eye to instructions from the top of the hierarchy, their mode of operation suggests that, to them, formal policy was almost inconsequential. Being on the spot, and having minimal supervision from their superiors, they commanded the power to interpret policies and enforce them using their own judgments and principles. In 1924, for example, the Chief Commissioner of Asante complained about his district officers' ignorance of the legal constraints on their own authority and their persistence in the practice of so-called "personal administration."[270]

The extent to which the district officers disregarded government directives drove Kuklick to label them "dictators" who adopted "whatever tactics seemed necessary to realize their objectives."[271] Their very broad mandates coupled with the inability of their superiors to adequately oversee their activities, availed them the freedom to exercise unlimited options in defining their work. At the very least, their job required establishing the security of colonial rule, maintaining order, and demonstrating British rule and control. In pursuing these, they had every opportunity to be arbitrary and authoritarian.[272] They were simply implementers with few restrictions on their scope of functions as well as their power to undertake those functions.

The Goals of Colonial Era Forestry Policies

Various related reasons were given for the series of forest policies in the colonial era. But it can be demonstrated that contrary to the declared objectives of the colonial authorities, the logic for the earliest regulatory forest policies in Gold Coast was not "protective" in the sense that Ripley uses the term. In fact, they can be given the label "pseudo-conservation" policies.

The following discussions will show that the policies introduced were primarily intended to achieve the specific objectives of taking control of land and conserving forest resources in order to secure the supply of timber for exploitation by British merchants for a long time.

The Crown Lands Bill of 1894, the first law that directly dealt with forests, was intended to vest all "waste and uncultivated forest lands"[273] in the colony to the British Crown. The stated purpose of that bill was to regulate the administration of public lands in the colony.[274] The Concessions Ordinance of 1900 sought to "regulate the concession of rights with respect to land by the natives."[275] The Forest Ordinance of 1927, a document that has remained relevant to forest policies in Ghana, was designed to be an ordinance for the "protection of forests and for the constitution and protection of forest reserves."[276] These laws simply dealt with the question of tenure. Their intent was to enable the colonial government to take control of lands and forests. Some statements made by Thompson, and Thomas Chipp, policy consultants on forestry issues, shed some light on the underlying, but unstated reasons for the perceived need to control the use of lands and forests. It is important to note that the opinions and advice of these two formed the thrust of colonial forest policies in Gold Coast.

In his 1910 *Report on Forests*, Thompson's expressed opinion was that the "extraction of major forest produce (timber) of Gold Coast wants regulating not so much on account of any danger threatening the forest vegetation as a whole, but with a view to ensuring a continuous and sustained yield of the produce."[277] While discussing Gold Coast forestry problem, Thomas Chipp referred to the "vast forests only ten days' voyage away, capable of supplying the heart of the Empire with forestry produce." He further estimated the value of the colony's forest in stressing that: "It is rarely realized that Gold Coast is the most central part of the Empire that has vast quantities of lumber, in addition to the fancy woods generally classed under the trade-name of "African mahogany."[278]

These statements from the two principal experts and key advisors to the colonial government provide enough grounds to conclude that the motivation of the colonial authorities for conservation was to promote the immediate and long-term economic benefits of the empire by taking control of land and forests, and preserving them in order to guarantee future supplies. Colonial forest policies were not aimed at conservation for the sake of the environment and the well being of the indigenous population, but rather, at preservation, the control and management of the resources therein so as to guarantee immediate and long-term supplies of timber to British industries.

This position is reiterated by Kolade Adeyoju who has suggested that the objectives of the colonial administrations were to intervene and regulate the activities of the then flourishing entrepreneurs and the rush of newcomers to the timber business.[279] Adeyoju concludes that their goal therefore was to ensure an industry that would guarantee the sustained supply of tropical woods to Britain and at the same time, collect revenues from the merchants. Within the logic of colonial rule, a sustainable forest policy simply meant conserving today's supply of timber, so that it could be gradually extracted for commercial purpose over time. Considering the fact that British merchants were active and influential participants in the policy process, it is clear why forestry policies of the colonial era of Gold Coast were fundamentally grounded in the economic concerns of the British private sector and the imperialist concerns of the British government.

Hence, beginning with that era, forest policy in Gold Coast amounted to an extractive policy. Not only was deforestation policy non-existent during that era, but its presence would have been illogical given the predatory logic of colonial rule. Herein lie the grounds for calling colonial forest policies pseudo-conservation policies.

Sources and Content of Colonial Forestry Policies in Gold Coast

Armed with these facts about the institutions and the principal actors in the policy arena of colonial Ghana, the forest policies that were introduced in that era will now be examined so as to determine their sources, content, method of their implementation, and their outcomes. The goal here is to establish why such policies failed to achieve their declared objectives. Table 3.2 contains a categorization of colonial era forest policies.

TABLE 3.2
CATEGORIES AND PRINCIPAL PURPOSES OF
COLONIAL ERA FOREST POLICIES IN GOLD COAST

POLICY	CATEGORY	PRINCIPAL PURPOSE
The Crown Lands Bill, 1894	Land Tenure Policy	Colonial control over lands and forests
The Land's Bill, 1897	Land Tenure and Pseudo-Conservation Policy	Colonial control over lands and forests
The Concessions Ordinance, 1900	Pseudo-Conservation Policy	Colonial administration of contracts between the government and British timber merchants
The Forestry Ordinance, 1901	Pseudo-Conservation and Extractive Policy	Appointment of forestry officers, constitution of reserve acquisition of lands, and appointment of reserve commissioner
Timber Protection Ordinance 1907	Pseudo-Conservation and Extractive Policy	Preventing cutting of immature timber for the purpose of guaranteeing future supplies of timber
The Undersized Trees Regulation, 1910	Pseudo-Conservation	Enforcement of the timber protection ordinance
The Forestry Ordinance, 1911	Pseudo-Conservation and Extractive Policy	Creation, control, and management of forest reserves
The Forest Ordinance, 1927	Pseudo-Conservation and Extractive Policy	Involvement of traditional rulers and enforcement of forestry laws and regulations

NOTE: Although eight out of the ten policies listed above have been classified as "pseudo-conservation" policies because their main purpose was to take control of timber resources in order to guarantee future extraction, like the first two policies, they are all tied to the fundamental question of ownership and right to use land (land tenure).

As was indicated in chapter one, forest policies in colonial Gold Coast were stipulated in the form of statutory laws, orders, rules and regulations. The first recorded legislation, the Crown Lands Bill of 1894, was framed in the form of a law that vested all "waste and uncultivated" forestland in the colony to the British Crown.[280] Bowing to pressure from the indigenous population, who argued that there were no lands in the colony that could be categorized as unsettled, the authorities withdrew this bill. Three years later, in 1897, another bill was enacted -- the Lands Bill of 1897 -- with the intent of regulating the administration of public lands. The key provision of this bill was the establishment of a Concessions Court with the main function of vetting contracts made between the government and private exploiters of forest resources, particularly timber merchants. Again, strong opposition from the indigenous population, who viewed this bill as an attempt by the colonial authorities to seize their lands, forced the abandonment of this bill.[281] An important outcome of the attempt to introduce the Lands Bill was the formation of Gold Coast Aborigines Rights Protection Society (ARPS), a political advocacy organization of the educated indigenous people to serve as a watchdog over the government's activities.[282] The activities of this indigenous interest group are notable because they indicate a significant attempt by African people to influence policy implementation in the colonial era. The activities of this group are revisited and discussed in greater detail later in this chapter.

Parts of the withdrawn Lands Bill of 1897 were, however, reconstituted into the Concessions Ordinance of 1900. The Forestry Ordinance of 1901 followed quickly. The Timber Protection Ordinance Number 20 of 1907, and the Undersize Trees Regulation of 1910 were enacted later.

Like their predecessors, these three laws were designed to control accessibility to reserved areas as well as terminate the rights of individuals to trees in non-reserved forests. It was apparent that the successes achieved by the indigenous people at forcing the withdrawal of the 1894 and 1897 bills inspired them to oppose any actions that, in their opinion, threatened to deprive them of their rights to access and utilize forest resources in their localities. Mindful of this fact, the colonial authorities endeavored to render future edicts more acceptable by excluding the sensitive subject of land ownership.

The autocratic tone and content of these earliest edicts demonstrate the authoritarian style the colonial government used to implement policies. The Forest Ordinance of 1911, for example, was a very detailed catalog that covered the power of the governor to appoint forestry officers and a reserve settlement commissioner, and the functions and authority of these officials. It also contained the procedures for creating forest reserves. A point of emphasis, however, was the governor's power to declare any land as reserved or unreserved. Also notable in this ordinance was a long list of prohibitions and rules that strictly restricted access to forests and controlled the exploitation of resources in the forest reserves.[283] These laws did not have the desired effects on the rate of deforestation, given the expanding production of cash and food crops as well as the increasing extraction of timber (See Table 3.1).

It was in an effort to find an appropriate and effective solution to colonial government inability to devise a workable forestry policy that H. N. Thompson, a forester with wide experience in India and Nigeria, was invited by the government to Gold Coast in 1908 to conduct a study and recommend steps to be taken for the conservation and protection of forests. Thompson's proposals for the enactment of strong legislation and intensified efforts at the creation of forest reserves were accepted and introduced in the legislative council as the Forest Bill of 1910.[284]

Even though this bill was passed as the Forest Ordinance of 1911, in spite of strong opposition from the Aborigines Rights Protection Society (ARPS), it was declined a royal assent because of the continued protests. The royal position on this ordinance demonstrates the impact the indigenous were able to make on forest policies. The Forest Ordinance of 1927 formally repealed the Forest Ordinance of 1911.

The 1927 Ordinance preceded an unsuccessful attempt to involve traditional rulers in the forest policy process, using them as proxies for the achievement of the colonial government's objectives. In a bid to disabuse the minds of the natives of the notion that forest reservation was a colonial means of appropriating their lands, draft by-laws were made in 1924, to serve as guides for chiefs, as custodians of tribal lands, to create and protect forest reserves.[285] This new strategy implied that reserved forests were to be managed by the people themselves. It could have marked the beginning of private forestry in the colony. Response to it, however, was hostile.[286]

Similarities between the 1927 Ordinance and the forest laws of India suggest that it was strongly influenced by Thompson's earlier report. Some aspects were also borrowed from Nigeria and other British colonies. It maintained the authoritarian tone of the 1911 Ordinance, and authorized employees of the Forestry Department to enter any land at any time for any purposes. This edict continues to serve as the core of Ghana's forestry laws at the present. There was an indication in this edict of an attempt to avoid the past mistake of disregarding the wishes of the natives. This was in terms of a provision that stipulated that ownership of lands within earmarked forest reserves was not affected even after the reserves had been formally constituted. However, the tone and the authoritarian approach to enforcing its provisions were no different from those of the 1901 Ordinance neither were the suspicions and hostility of the traditional rulers and their subjects.

In agreement with the earlier argument, the objective for colonial legislation on lands and forests was primarily pseudo-conservation, the conservation of the forest resources so that they can be gradually extracted over a long period of time. This being the case, attempts to include protective policies in the legislation resulted in various, sometimes conflicting, policy objectives being tied in the same legislation. This is the historical basis for the conflicting bureaucratic dichotomy described in chapter seven.

Overall, the policies purportedly sought to reserve land for the greatest good of the community, to manage the reserves for sustained yield, and, in so doing, promote economic development. These worthy objectives were, however, contradictory because, in effect, the policies barred the indigenous people from the age-old practice of freely utilizing the resources of the forests. At the same time, the policies sought to promote the success of forest-destroying British commercial enterprises.

Implementation of Colonial Forest Policies in Gold Coast

In the discussion of the structure of the colonial policy system and the actors involved, references were made to the immense authority vested in the governor, and the enormous power and responsibility of the provincial and district officers. It was within this context that forest policies were made and implemented. Although the indigenous people, through the ARPS, did make an effort, and succeeded in some instances, at influencing forest policy implementation, overall colonial forest policies reflected very minimal input from the outside the government.

Given the hostility of the traditional rulers and elites to policies they deemed unacceptable, the colonial authorities saw the necessity to pursue those policies that were enacted by forceful means. Governor W. B. Griffith's response to the objections raised by C. J. Bannerman (counsel to the traditional rulers of the colony) concerning the provisions of the Lands Bill of 1894, laid out the governor's position, which effectively classified the rights of the chiefs as "inferior rights."[287] As far as Governor Griffith was concerned, the colonial government had concurrent rights to stool lands[288], which, in his opinion, were public lands. He even laid claim, as governor, to the "Right of the Paramount Power" to exercise any and every right which may be exercised by any chief," and called the rights of the chiefs "vague claims," and their actions concerning land "really illegal."[289] This position of the colonial authority rendered the issue of African land ownership highly contentious. It also set the tone of future colonial land and forest edicts, and established the grounds for continued resistance by the traditional rulers and their subjects to colonial authority.

Implementation of colonial forest policies, under the circumstances, took the form of enforcement. The process was as follows: the governor constituted forest reserves, acquired lands, and terminated all rights to lands that were earmarked for reservation. The Governor-in-Council introduced orders and rules that prohibited certain activities in forests.[290] He then appointed the highest officials in the forestry sector, including the conservator of forests, the reserve settlement commissioner, and any other officials for functions he deemed necessary for the achievement of colonial policy goals.

In order to pursue these policies, itinerant courts were established, to rule in cases related to the establishment of forest reserves and infringements of the series of rules and regulations involved in the exercise. Forestry officers had the judicial authority to impose fines on persons who broke forest laws and regulations. What follows are descriptions of the origins, purpose, and activities of two organizations that helped shape deforestation policies in the colonial regime.

The Colonial Department of Forestry: Following the recommendations of H. N. Thompson, a Forestry Department was established in 1909 to serve as the principal agency for implementing colonial forest policies. Although its initial priority was to reduce opposition of the indigenous people to forest reservation, its principal tasks included the conservation and protection of forests, advising the government on forest policy and legislation, and enforcement of forestry legislation.

The Department was organized hierarchically, with the conservator of forests at the top, the provincial forestry officers in the middle, and the district forestry officers at the bottom. All of the top and professional posts were filled by Europeans, and as late as 1952 when the first African officer was appointed, he was the only one among a total of twenty-three.

The hierarchical structure of this department reflected the hierarchical character of the colonial administration. Policies were handed down from the top hierarchies to the lower levels for implementation. The district forestry officers, the officers "on the beat," had a highly limited policy-making scope, their job being mainly to follow instructions that were handed down, and to report back to the superiors. Given the poor communications system that existed, this system faced serious obstacles as it was impossible to monitor the activities of the local officers, neither was it easy for them to reach their superiors who were located at the colonial and provincial headquarters.

The Department of Forestry functioned in an ambiguous situation because even though the existing policies prescribed the colonial government's aims, in most cases procedures did not include the means of achieving those goals. Policy objectives and the means of achieving them were apparently considered to be the same. Considering that the policies were largely in the form of rules about the use of forests, the personnel were pre-occupied with policing these rules. Effective policing in the large area of forest reserves - given the objection of the indigenous population to the colonial government's policies - could not have been possible with the limited personnel, the lack of communications, and the limited means of transportation to cover the reserves.

Activities of the Aborigines Rights Protection Society

The Aborigines Rights Protection Society was the sole African interest group that had some impact on the forest policy process of the colonial era. Its origins can be traced to 1898 after its successful opposition to the Lands Bill of 1897. According to Conway Belfield's account,[291] the society was composed of chiefs of the Central Province and a number of educated native traders and lawyers resident in Cape Coast. Its objective, in Belfield's words, was "opposing and blocking any action by the Government or by any persons which may, in the opinion of the members, be subversive of their interests or likely to be prejudicial to their native customs or their canons of land tenure."[292]

Although Belfield's report suggests that activities of the society were confined to the Central Province, and that the views of its members were not widespread in the other parts of the colony, the society, from every indication, was capable of influencing policies on lands (and forests) as the colonial authorities were mindful of its strength as a watchdog in matters concerning the lands. Belfield, for instance, referred to their "strong opposition ... to the assumption by Government of power to take over any portion of their tribal lands..."[293] In fact, the society was strong enough to send representatives to London to lodge a protest to the king himself against the Land Bill.[294]

In spite of the efforts of the society, the colonial government was determined to proceed with certain policies on lands and forests in line with the suggestions made by Thompson, Chipp, and Belfield, who insisted that forest reservation and the strict enforcement of laws were the appropriate means of managing the forests of Gold Coast. Opposition from the society did not stop the colonial government from increasing the area of forest reserves from 100.6 square miles in 1923 to 2,431 square miles in 1934, and up to 5,791.5 square miles in 1939[295]. It is important to note, however, that the colonial government was compelled to amend the Forest Ordinance of 1911 so as to address the concerns of the society before its re-introduction as the Forest Ordinance of 1927.

Outcomes of the Colonial Forestry Policies in Gold Coast

The limited availability of statistical data on the size of the forest zone and the rate of deforestation in Gold Coast in the late nineteenth and early twentieth centuries, coupled with the differences between the data produced by Thompson, Chipp, and others, renders the use of such data difficult for describing the extent of the deforestation problem. Thomas F. Chipp, probably one of the earliest to provide estimates on the extent of forest cover, estimated in 1922 that 28,000 square miles of Gold Coast were forests.[296] In 1923, N. C. McLeod, then Gold Coast Conservator of Forests, estimated it at 14,000 square miles![297]

Reference was made earlier in this chapter to the government's own estimate of 16,336 square miles in 1950.[298] A more recent estimate agrees with this particular estimate, suggesting that at the turn of the century, there were 33,976 square miles of forest, but by 1950 it had reduced to 16,216 square miles.[299] Regardless of the differences, all these estimates imply a consistently serious problem of deforestation. The authorities may have been aware of this problem, but, as has been mentioned, their priority was not controlling deforestation but managing lands and forests in order to cater to the needs of Britain.

It is also possible to gain an appreciation of the problem from various statements made on the subject by Thompson[300] and Chipp.[301] Thompson's exact words in his 1910 report help to portray the problem as it existed then. He decried the "haphazard methods of exploiting" timber, and proposed measures that were necessary for the preservation of the forests against "excessive exploitation." He also referred to the "damage done to the forests by burning," and "the destruction of the forests clothing the hills," and cautioned that under existing agricultural practices, "there is nothing whatever to stop the gradual spread of arid country into the very heart of the forest region."

In 1923 Chipp reported about Gold Coast forests being "heavily attacked by agriculturists all along their northern edge." He concluded, on the basis of "historical evidence obtained from reports and chronicles of Europeans of long residence in the country, and from the testimony of the natives themselves," that a "rapid regression" of the forests was occurring.[302] Again it is important to recall the government's own admission in 1950 that, given the manner in which they were being exploited, Gold Coast forests were doomed to be destroyed unless measures were taken to replant them.[303] These remarks support the inferences from the statistical evidence that the forestlands of Gold Coast over time were shrinking. The implication was that the policies that had been in place for combating deforestation had failed to have the desired effect.

Conclusions

The discussions in this chapter have revealed the real intentions of British colonial administrations concerning the forest resources of Gold Coast. Evidence has been advanced to show that British colonial policy in Gold Coast was hinged on trade. This is demonstrated by the direct and prominent role British merchants played in policy-making either by themselves or as members of the colonial executive and legislative council. Because the fundamental purpose of British colonial rule in Gold Coast was exploitation of resources, business interests commanded a strong political influence both in the colony and in England.

Given this status of British merchants, it becomes clear why the local administrations that were established in the colony turned out to be instruments by which their economic interests were advanced.

Although the concept of "dual mandate" has been advanced to describe British colonial objectives, it is clear from the facts that British economic objectives far outweighed the development of Gold Coast. The forest policies that were adopted on recommendation of Thompson and Chipp, advocated reservation and strict enforcement of forest laws as means of conservation. But it has been shown that, overall, the British colonial forest conservation drive was not meant to conserve the land and forests for future Ghanaian generations, but rather, to preserve them for future British mercantile exploitation, and also maintain reliable supplies of tropical woods and other forest resources for export to British industries. Central to British colonial forest policy therefore were land tenure policies designed to deny the indigenous people access to land and the forests. The objective was to promote an environment within which British merchants would be enabled to operate without any competition or interference from the indigenous population.

Because the forest policies that were developed during that era were fundamentally grounded in British economic and imperialist concerns, there is little wonder that the forest policies of the colonial era, officially designated as anti-deforestation strategies, in practice turned out to be purely extractive policies, resulting in the promotion of commercial exploitation and export of timber.

The colonial authorities attempted to pursue two contradictory objectives concurrently: the preservation of forests on one hand, and the exploitation of the same forest, on the other. But the need to promote the exploitation of forest resources to cater to the British economy and the interests of British merchants undermined any genuine interest there might have been in conservation. Evidently, the forces behind the latter objective were stronger, and as such it was difficult, if not impossible, to achieve success in the former objective.

Given that the interests of the indigenous population were not taken into account in the formulation of forest policies, the colonial policy apparatus produced policies that bore no regards to the historical, social, cultural and economic realities of the colony. In a situation where secretaries of state for the colonies as well as politicians and bureaucrats in London had little interest in Gold Coast, or, were simply ignorant about it, the task of formulating and implementing forest policies was assigned to the local officials in the colony. Such officials, especially the governor, therefore commanded immense authority and remained virtually free from any supervision from the colonial office.

Under the circumstances, the approach used by such local authorities to protect the forests from, the "careless, ignorant and destructive natives" involved adopting land tenure policies whereby the land and forests would be secured to be exploited, largely unhindered, by British commercial interests. Utilizing his immense authority and power, the governor achieved this by imposing arbitrary laws and regulations that restricted the rights of the indigenous people to use forest resources. Such laws and regulations were enforced in the strictest way possible, without much consideration for the traditions, land tenure practices, and needs of the indigenous people.

The colonial forest policies were therefore formulated without any regards to certain significant factors of the time: factors such as population growth and its associated increasing demand for farmlands, firewood, building materials, bush meat, etc.; issues that were basic to the sustenance of the indigenous people of Gold Coast. Consequently, throughout the colonial era resistance from the indigenous people against the government's policies on land and forests never ceased.

Another important development that undermined the colonial government's efforts was the expansion of cash crop (particularly cocoa) production. Substantial cash rewards from cocoa farming encouraged immigration into the forest region and the clearance of increasing areas of forest for cocoa farms at the time when efforts were being made to preserve the forests. Even more importantly, only a small fraction of the forest area of the colony was earmarked as forest reserves, the large majority remaining open and accessible to farmers and timber merchants. Deforestation therefore proceeded unimpeded in most of the colony.

The strategy whereby laws and regulations were imposed on an uncooperative indigenous population in order to allow a politically powerful, profit-seeking, expatriate merchant class easy access to resources required more political clout, personnel, and accessibility to the forest area than what was available to the Department of Forestry. As such, in spite of strict policing, the imposition of fines, and other punishments, the Department could not cope with the assignment.

The circumstances described in this chapter portray the political, economic and institutional legacies that were left behind at the end of colonial rule. As will be observed from the succeeding chapters, these colonial legacies and their associated defects have remained enduring aspects of the forest policy process in post-independence Ghana. It is important to bear these colonial legacies in mind as explanations for the disconnection between policies to address deforestation in Ghana and their outcomes are sought.

The following chapter contains an examination of the contextual settings within which formulation and implementation of deforestation policies in post-independence Ghana have occurred. In addition, there are analyses of the declared deforestation policy goals of the government, and the policies that have been adopted for achieving those goals. The objective of these analyses is to determine the relevance of the various identified factors in explaining the disconnection between deforestation policies and their outcomes in Ghana in the post-independence era.

Chapter 4

The Contextual Setting of the Deforestation Policy Process in Ghana: Discussion of the Explanatory Model

This chapter deals with the external environment of the forest policy process in Ghana as portrayed in Fig 1 (page 14). The purpose is to analyze political, economic, social, and cultural factors that help to explain the disconnection between deforestation policies and their outcomes in Ghana.

The analysis is undertaken with the objective of verifying the validity of the hypotheses of this research, which are:

1. Deforestation has continued to occur in Ghana because the absence of a political environment that is stable, peaceful and involves predictable transitions of authority has rendered it impossible to formulate and implement long-term policies to address the problems;

2. The policy process in Ghana had been dominated by the executive and bureaucracy because the country lacks a legislative tradition of policy-making; and,

3. In the Ghanaian forestry policy environment, two sets of bureaucratic institutions have been operating at cross-purposes -- one set promoting exploitation, and the other, protecting the forests. Given the economic circumstances of the country, the priority given to the policy outputs of these bureaucratic institutions will reflect the decisions of the heads of state and high-level politicians, which will, in turn, reflect the demands that have been made on the state.

The following factors will be discussed here:

- Limited legitimacy of the state, and deriving from it, the lack of citizen support and compliance with forest policy requirements;
- The political atmosphere of the public policy-making process in Ghana;

- Political instability and the lack of consistency in deforestation policies;
- The structure of Ghana's economy, and in connection with that, the prominence of primary commodities as sources of external revenue;
- The need to generate revenue for providing social amenities and infrastructure, and for external debt-servicing;
- Population growth and its associated increasing demand for land and forest resources;
- Market-driven external demand for Ghanaian timber; and,
- The political economy of stabilization and structural adjustment in Ghana and its implications to deforestation.

Limited Legitimacy of Ghanaian Governments: Consequences on the Outcomes of Deforestation Policies

In addition to the already discussed historical, political, and economic factors, another factor that provides additional explanation for the problem is the limited legitimacy of government. Closely connected to this issue of legitimacy are the attitudes and responses of the citizenry to policies on forests and toward the government agents assigned to implement those policies. The attitudes of Ghanaians, especially those residing in the rural areas, who derive their livelihood from the land and forest resources, are particularly significant in this respect. This is because, given their occupations and lifestyles, and the fact that they live in settlements that are widely dispersed in the forest region; it would be impossible to implement effective deforestation policies without their support and cooperation.

The question about legitimacy is as relevant today as it was during the colonial era. The primary objective of the British in the Gold Coast was to extract resources from what was then a colony for commercial gain. The primary beneficiaries of this exploitative political economy were British nationals in both the public and private sectors. The colonial authorities sought to achieve this objective by establishing an autocratic government whose modus operandi was the use of laws and regulations as well as coercion and punishment to implement policies. The undemocratic and authoritarian nature of colonial administrations in the Gold Coast have been mentioned as a contributing cause of subsequent political and social conflict and instability in the post-colonial era.[304]

The tradition that was established in the colonial era did not die out with the advent of self-rule.[305] There is little doubt that an enduring legacy of the colonial era has been the "Crown Colony bureaucratic and coercive apparatus"[306] that operates in Ghana today. The colonial authoritative style under which the top political leaders, bureaucrats and elites have dominated policy-making, giving little or no consideration to the wishes and opinions of the grassroots citizens, has been perpetuated in post-independence Ghana. A result is that, forty years after independence, the question of legitimacy remains highly relevant in explaining state-society relations.

The first indigenous government under Dr. Kwame Nkrumah effected this form of rule through a one-party system, within which a single national party, the Convention Peoples Party (CPP), served as the supreme institution of power and control, an equivalent to the state.[307] All the diverse indigenous groups were compelled to submit to the dictates of this party and to the government, regardless of socio-political leanings. It is important to note that most of the ethnic groups that occupied the forest area of Ghana, in particular, the Asantes, the Akyems, and their affiliate ethnic groups, owed allegiance to other political parties that were banned under the one-party system. Most of them therefore, persistently refused to endorse the CPP or to support this regime. In any case, when economic conditions in Ghana deteriorated in the early 1960s, not even the charisma Nkrumah possessed was enough to mitigate the legitimacy crisis that confronted the regime.[308]

Although successive governments in Ghana, both civilian and military, have differed considerably from the one led by Nkrumah, particularly in terms of the extent to which the ruling party occupied center stage in government, and the level of autocracy that prevailed, the country has been traditionally ruled by a succession of highly centralized and powerful governments which exercise almost total control over the available resources. A consequence is that there has existed a paternalistic relationship between the state and the citizens, with the state determining and imposing policies that it deems appropriate, and the citizens expected to comply with the dictates of those policies regardless of their opinions.[309] Within this framework, the state has been expected to convince the various social classes of its ability to meet their economic and political needs and to secure for them what they perceive to be their rights. So far as the peasants and rural population are concerned, the state has been unable to do this.[310] Hence, the legitimacy crisis has endured in post-colonial Ghana.

During the era of the Peoples National Defense Council (PNDC), Flt. Lt. Rawlings sought to enhance the legitimacy of his government through various anti-urban, pro-rural pronouncements. In practical terms, his government instituted certain benefits for farmers as an integral part of the World Bank-recommended Economic Restructuring Program (ERP). Producer prices of cocoa, for example, were raised under the scheme. But the producers discovered that apart from those benefits being tentative, only the large scale farmers benefited from those increases.[311] Overall, the ERP, contrary to the intentions of the Rawlings government, had adverse effects on the material conditions of the rural population.[312]

Other economic factors that also undermined Rawlings' chances of achieving increased support from the rural classes included the increased taxation associated with some of the reform measures, and the increased financial responsibilities parents were required to bear for the education of children. As a result, the PNDC government fared no better in the area of legitimacy with the rural population.[313]

The catalogue of literature that treats the question of legitimacy in Ghana is long indeed. Naomi Chazan,[314] Tapaan Biswal,[315] Jeffrey Herbst,[316] and E. Gyimah-Boadi,[317] have advanced various arguments all implying that the state in Ghana is afflicted by a weakness that derives from its lack of legitimacy. Chazan makes the point that governmental structures in Ghana have remained separated from the citizens because such structures have been institutionalized in their "judicial administrative" as opposed to their "political participatory" roles. She adds that because political power is concentrated in the hands of a few politicians, the development of local level structures for accentuating the felt needs of the population has been thwarted. She alludes to the continued relevance of local authority figures such as chiefs, lineage heads, elders, religious leaders, teachers, etc., in Ghanaian society. Because these leaders are held accountable and compelled to reflect public opinion, they serve to accentuate the needs of the citizens better that the government. This helps explain why political integration between Accra (the capital) and the local level has taken long to be realized even though the constitution of the Fourth Republic instituted mechanisms for promoting decentralization and grassroots participation in public affairs.

Chazan concludes that the existence of traditional and local community institutions has resulted in the emergence of a dual set of institutions in Ghana - state and non-formal. The relationships between these two institutions, according to Chazan, are "fluid." Therefore, it has not been possible for the state to permeate the society, with the corollary that the operational capacity of the state has been severely curtailed.

In a study two decades ago, Chazan concluded that the anti-government stance, which was adopted during the colonial era in Ghana, was not abandoned when indigenous Ghanaians assumed power in the early independence years.[318] She showed that there existed an extremely sophisticated awareness of politics among Ghanaians, and that a gap prevailed between the values of certain key segments of the population and the regimes that purported to reflect their attitudes. A consequence of this gap had been the prevalence of "non-support and non-identification"[319] with the early regimes of post-independence Ghana. She indicated that such non-support and non-identification did not derive from a lack of political information, but rather from political awareness, realistic expectations, and critical judgement."[320]

Other findings made by Chazan in this study are even more significant for explaining state-citizen relationships in Ghana. They indicate that traditional local authority figures continue to command a great deal of political power and stature in the eyes of the people, even though those leaders have been superseded at the state level by soldiers and politicians.[321] Her research has revealed that among Ghanaian leaders, only chiefs rated consistently high in terms of both power and respect. She therefore concluded that traditional authorities are by no means de-legitimized by the prominence of national politicians. One of her explanations was that interaction between the central government and the grassroots population has largely been in the form of laws that imposed limitations on the freedoms the people (freedoms they traditionally enjoyed under traditional rule), taxation of various kinds, and different coercive actions designed to force them to comply with the government's requests.

A key reason for political instability in Ghana, she concluded, was a pervasive dissatisfaction, on the part of the citizens, with the performance and structural inadequacies of the regimes. The lasting allegiance Ghanaians owe to their indigenous rulers, and the common opinion that national political institutions are alien impositions that do not command as much legitimacy as the chiefs and elders, are realities that undermine the ability of the government to implement policies effectively. Added to this, the centralized nature of the government has rendered it rather remote and too foreign for the citizens to develop the necessary connection to it.

Chazan goes to the extent of suggesting that, empirically, in the context of "Weberian legitimacy," the Ghanaian state has collapsed.[322] This, in her opinion, explains why some Ghanaians have disengaged themselves from the state by conspicuously engaging in illegal or corrupt activities that are contrary to the demands of the government. She attributes this disengagement to the way sections of the society are excluded from the political and the decision-making processes.[323]

Crawford Young's contribution to this topic deals with the perpetually poor performance of the state in the areas of economics and political governance, and the result that various socio-economic groups have become disillusioned, apathetic, and often reactionary towards the government.[324]

Information obtained from the district forestry officer of Kyebi affirms the state of affairs portrayed in the foregoing analysis.[325] According to the officer, the most serious obstacle facing the Department of Forestry at the local level is the non-cooperation; sometimes utter hostility, of the local population towards employees of the department. These attitudes on the part of the citizens are so intense that the employees, who are perceived to be agents of the government, have operated under very unsafe circumstances.

Biswal, on the other hand, traces the problem of legitimacy to the high level of distrust that existed between the CPP government and the opposition during the first republic, and the "forced compromise" nature of the independence constitution of 1957.[326] Strong differences between the political parties, not only concerning the content of the Constitution, but also the manner in which Dr. Nkrumah and his supporters manipulated it to advance partisan objectives, meant that right from the dawn of Ghana's self-government, opposition to the CPP government was strong, sectional, and ethnic-based. Significant sections of the citizenry considered the central government as unacceptable and non-legitimate. Biswal contends that the trend that was set under the first Ghanaian regime, whereby an executive-dominated government refused to allow opposing views to influence policies, has endured. Successive governments have therefore remained unresponsive to the people.

Jeffrey Herbst has assigned the failure of Ghanaian governments to the "hopelessly weak states."[327] His argument encompasses all those presented above. It consists of three dimensions. He takes the positions that:

1. Ghanaians do not support their governments because of the governments' limited relevance to the citizens in terms of their needs and concerns.

2. The over-concentration of state power in the hands of individuals or a few people has marginalized the citizens, depriving them of avenues for making inputs into the policy process or influencing its outcomes. As a result, Ghanaian citizens do not identify with the state or recognize its leaders as their own representatives.

3. The inability of the Ghanaian state to meet the expectations of the citizens through the delivery of amenities and benefits has undermined the legitimacy of the state. Herbst sees a strong link between the weakness of the state on one hand, and the persistent absence of democracy, and concludes that Ghanaian governments have been "frequently authoritarian because they are so markedly authoritative."[328]

Gyimah-Boadi approaches the issue of legitimacy from the context of the strength and endurance of Ghanaian civil society. He highlights the traditional role of civil societies in Ghana, and concludes, on the basis of their demonstrated capabilities and disposition, that state and regime recognition and acceptability have been severely diminished because of the exclusion of civil society from the policy arena.[329] An effect of this is that it has undermined democracy and policy effectiveness.[330]

In advancing the same argument as Herbst, Robert Pinkney points to the prevalence of a domineering state which has attempted to control every aspect of political life, but, at the same time, has been a weak state because it has not been able to convert popular demands into policy outputs.[331] He suggests, as Rothchild and Lawson had done earlier, that there has been a "societal disengagement" from the government.[332] Pinkney concludes that limited state legitimacy in Ghana is due to the existence of a gap between the government and the governed, and the absence of adequate autonomous institutions in the society that could bridge this gap. Military regimes are not exempt from these criticisms. If anything, the situation described is more applicable to these types of governments.

Emmanuel Hansen and Paul Collins, in their study of the military and politics in Ghana, have indicated that the most serious task faced by the military after it seizes power is to establish a basis for its legitimacy.[333] Like their civilian counterparts, military governments in Ghana have been largely perceived to be "foreign" entities by the majority local population who are more traditional, and whose scope is limited to their immediate socio-cultural and economic realities.[334]

The conclusions drawn from the above discussions fit into Joel Migdal's concepts on state-society relations in the third world.[335] According to Migdal, a sophisticated political and administrative system existed in traditional Ghanaian societies prior to the introduction of colonial rule and the western-style political establishment of the independence era. An important aspect of this traditional Ghanaian society was the operation of institutions through which members expressed their aspirations, goals, and concerns. But such avenues of expression have been subdued by the succession of regimes, which have imposed state control over the society to such an extent that the hitherto autonomous institutions have been subdued. Thus the enduring perception of the state in Ghana is that it is an alien, authoritative establishment. This negative image has been strengthened by the inability of the state to deliver in the areas of social needs and amenities because of a persistent severe economic deterioration. The legitimacy of the state in Ghana has therefore been consistently undermined.

These realities help to explain the circumstances under which deforestation policies have been implemented. They imply that the lack of support and cooperation of the citizens during implementation of policies for addressing deforestation is an important explanation for the disconnection between those policies and their outcomes.

The Political Atmosphere of the Public Policy-Making Process in Ghana
Political Instability

Since 1957 when Ghana gained political independence, the policy landscape has undergone a series of frequent changes in terms of the political environment and the principal actors. Underlying these changes is the fact that Ghana's post-independence political history has, until 1992, been characterized by erratic changes between constitutional regimes and military dictatorships. (See Table 4.1).

TABLE 4.1
GHANA: POST-COLONIAL GOVERNMENTS (1957 - 2000)

YEAR	HEAD OF STATE	FORM OF GOVERNMENT
1957-1966	Dr. Kwame Nkrumah	Constitutional
1966-1969	General Ankrah/General Afrifah	Military Dictatorship
1969-1972	Dr. K. A. Busia	Constitutional
1972-1979	General Akyeampong/General Akuffo	Military Dictatorship
1979-1980	Fl. Lt. Jerry Rawlings	Military Dictatorship
1980-1981	Dr. Hilla Limann	Constitutional
1981-1992	Fl. Lt. Jerry Rawlings	Military Dictatorship
1992-1996	Fl. Lt. Jerry Rawlings	Constitutional
1996-2000	Fl. Lt. Jerry Rawlings	Constitutional

During thirty-nine years of independence, Ghana has been ruled by eight different governments, four of them military dictatorships, which have ruled for a total of twenty-two years. The remaining seventeen years have been under constitutional governments. In reality, the tenure of constitutional governments could be pegged at thirteen years, considering that the four-year (1992-1996) regime of Jerry Rawlings was nothing less than an extension of his preceding military regime.

Policy-Making Under Constitutional Regimes

Constitutions in Ghana have been typically fashioned in line with the principles of democratic rule.[336] They contain clearly defined roles and powers of the three arms of government: the executive, the legislature, and the judiciary. They also recognize and affirm the central position of citizens as the source of all political power. As a consequence of the political instability engendered by recurrent *coups d'etat*, there have been as many as five constitutions in Ghana Since 1957. Nevertheless, a common feature of all the different constitutions has been the principles of democracy and rule of law.

Affirmation of the central position of the citizens is manifest in constitutional provisions such as free and fair elections of public officials: the head of state, members of the legislature, and members of local administrations. Each of the four constitutions contemplated that government policies and actions would be established and pursued, with the consent of, and for the good of all the citizens. They also contain mechanisms by which individual citizens and interest groups could directly influence the public policy-making process. Viewed at their face value, therefore, the kind of political environment that these documents envisaged has been similar to the one assumed by Ripley in his discussions on the policy process.[337]

In practice however, the Ghanaian case differs from what prevails in typical democratic settings. In spite of provisions contained in the constitutions, and the consistent affirmation of those ideals by the political leaders, the policy process has been a closed one, dominated by high level politicians (presidents, prime ministers, ministers and their deputies, and high political party operatives), bureaucrats, and, to a limited extent, a small class of business owners and elites.[338] Together, this group appears to wield what Oliver Saasa describes as the "unchallengeable power and influence on the policy making process."[339] The prominent role played by legislators, committees and sub-committees of the legislature, and interest groups in the liberal democratic nations has been non-existent in Ghana.[340] The erratic and short-lived existence of the legislature in Ghana implies that few public officials in Ghana have been popularly elected.[341] Hence, the notion of electoral accountability to mass-based constituency groups has little relevance in the Ghanaian system.

The largest section of the society; the poor, the less educated and largely rural-dwelling peasants, have played very little, if any role at all, in politics or the policy process. Their participation has been limited to the occasional vote casting during elections and to rare protests by workers' unions.

The Busia and Limann regimes showed some signs of increased liberalization of the public policy process. Contrary to the prevalent tradition, there was some accommodation of the opposing views and other forms of citizen inputs. But in both cases, such political behavior was rather short-lived, as those civilian governments were removed through military *coups d'etat* in 1972 and 1981.

Policy-Making Under Military Regimes

Military governments in Ghana have simply been dictatorships. On the assumption of power, the soldiers have typically suspended the constitutions, banned all political activity, and usurped all privileges of policy decision-making. The ruling juntas, usually comprising service commanders and a few senior officers, assume the role of the ultimate policy-making organs. Ranking officers, who are usually appointed to other high public offices in government agencies and in the administrative regions, remain answerable only to the executive-cum-legislative arm of government (their commanders). Openness and accountability of democratic governments have typically been absent.

Impact of the Media, Consumer and Interest Groups

Consumer and interest groups in Ghana have not demonstrated any significant influence over the public policy process. It appears that lack of organization has deprived the citizens of the political clout, the forums for advancing their interests, and the means for effectively attracting the attention of other important actors in the policy arena. Thus far in this research, no evidence of any consumer advocacy activity in Ghana has been uncovered. At the same time, the few currently existing environmental groups such as The Landlife Group, Friends of the Earth, and the Ghana Wildlife Society are in their infancy, not yet well established or strong enough to exert any significant impact on the policy process.

Until the mid-1990s the media in Ghana was completely owned and controlled by the government. The main newspapers, radio and television studios were managed by government appointed boards. These sources of information therefore functioned largely as mouthpieces of the government in power, used to propagate news items that were favorable to the government and promote its approved policies and ideas. In the areas of constructive criticism, analysis of public issues, information and education, and the generation of public debates on public policy matters, the constructive role of critically analyzing issues, informing and educating the public, and generating public debates on public policy matters, the media in Ghana had been extremely wanting.[342]

Conclusions

Four conclusions emerge from the foregoing overview of various aspects of Ghanaian political history and political culture about the unique circumstances within which the Ghanaian policy process has occurred. They are: i) the policy process is dominated by heads of state, high level politicians and bureaucrats, and to a limited extent a small class of elites; ii) transitions in Ghanaian governments usually do not take place through the electoral process. Instead, military *coups d'etat* have been the major mechanisms through which shifts in governmental authority have occurred; iii) non-governmental organizations and interest groups are weak and have barely made any significant impact on the policy process; and, iv) the existing mechanisms for citizen input into the policy process are inadequate.

Under the circumstances, citizen feedback and citizen input, key ingredients of effective public policy-making, have been missing in Ghana. Given the isolation of the state from the society, policy-making has been simplified thereby creating three important outcomes: i) the policies have not given due account to the hopes, fears, aspirations, and experiences of the citizens; ii) the institutions responsible for implementing policies have been designed in such a way that their principal approach for realizing the policy goals has been authoritarian; iii) the institutions responsible for realizing policy objectives have not been capable of performing their tasks because they have not been able, using their coercive approach, to prevent citizens from exploiting land and forest resources, activities that are basic to their livelihood.

Political Instability and its Effects on Deforestation Policies

The outcome of erratic changes in governments in Ghana since independence has been a succession of eight different governments within a span of forty years; four of them established by means of *coups d'etat*, and two lasting less than two years. It would be expected that these frequent changes in government would also be accompanied by a rapid turnover of the key policy-makers, and consequently, frequent changes in the content of public policies. The large number of policies in the forestry sector of Ghana might be presumed to be result of such political instability.

Leaders of military coups have typically called for the removal of corrupt and inept politicians. Their agenda has invariably included the cleaning-up of the presumed political and economic mess created by their predecessors, the replacement of certain unacceptable policies, and the eventual transfer of power to newly elected politicians. Even though military governments in Ghana have, without exception, created the impression that they are temporary, overall, their average lifespan has been far longer than that of civilian constitutional ones. The Akyeampong/Akuffo regime and the Rawlings regime lasted 7 years and 11 years respectively. But incessant coup attempts and rumors of subversion rendered them unstable. It can be presumed that regimes that considered themselves temporary and which were constantly under the threat of forceful overthrow would not consider long-term policies.

On the other hand, constitutional regimes have been short-lived, their tenures terminated by *coups d'etat*. With the exception of the Nkrumah government, which lasted nine years, and the current Rawlings regime, the other two were very brief; the Busia regime lasting three years, and that headed by Limann, one year. Constitutional regimes in Ghana therefore have not had the opportunity to formulate and implement long-term policies.

An examination of the declared goals and content of forest policies in Ghana, has however, rendered the expectation that political instability would result in rapid changes in the content of forestry policies invalid. Although changes in regimes have resulted in the emergence of new individuals at the top echelons of government, irrespective of regime type, there has been a consistency in overall policy goals and the institutions responsible for the implementation of forestry policies. The occasional policy declarations that suggest various reforms and change have had no significant impact on the content of forest policies; neither have they had any impact on the implementation and outcomes.

Lack of success at achieving declared policy goals under successive Ghanaian governments has also been consistent. As has been pointed out by Ire Omo-Bare, this consistency prevails in all areas of public policies in Ghana.[343] Unchanging factors such as the structure of the economy, the importance of external trade and finance, Ghana's protracted external debt crises, external influences over the content of deforestation policies, and the process by which policies have been formulated help to explain the consistency of forest policies. Regardless of their declared priorities, the various governments have operated under similar circumstances, confronted with similar problems, and used the same instruments to function.

Overall, regimes in Ghana have pursued sets of economic and political priorities that have been considered to be far more important than conserving natural resources.[344] In the absence of stakeholder advocacy about forest conservation, the often-spoken rhetoric about protecting the environment has had little support. Therefore, they have remained exactly that - rhetoric.

Certain characteristics of the bureaucracy in Ghana also help to explain the content and consistency of forest policies. As has been pointed out, the bureaucracy in Ghana fits Graham Allison's description of large organizations in his discussion of the organizational process theory. They function "according to standard patterns of behavior,"[345] and rules of thumb that ensure concerted action. Because the way the Ghanaian bureaucracies function does allow only marginal and incremental change, political instability has not fostered any inconsistencies in the content or outcomes of deforestation policies.

Another important explanation of the consistency of forest policies lies in the stability and indispensability of the Ghanaian bureaucracy. In addition to its central role in the policy process, the bureaucracy in Ghana has become the only stable government institution within the domestic policy arena.[346] In post-independence Ghana, the expertise and experience of civil servants have enabled the bureaucracy to constantly play an indispensable role as formulators and implementers of policies under successive regimes. As such, despite political instability, the bureaucracy has facilitated an element of stability.

Because of their knowledge and expertise, bureaucrats in Ghana have served as a major source of policy ideas. They have also been responsible for framing such ideas into official public policies, and for the administration of their implementation. The permanence of the bureaucracy, and its adherence to standard processes, procedures and established routines, has been a factor in the level of consistency in the content in forest policies.[347]

Based on the foregoing, it is clear that the stability of the bureaucracy and its central role in the policy process explains why, in spite of political instability in Ghana, forest policies have remained largely consistent and changed only incrementally. Such consistency has rendered the policy apparatus less responsive to changing circumstances such as the worsening deforestation problem, the need to discard the old ineffective strategies for forest protection, and the increasing need to reduce the dominance of politicians and bureaucrats and allow stakeholders a role in the policy process that is commensurate to their significance in the forestry sector. An overall result has been a failure to achieve the objectives of policies for combating deforestation.

Structure of the Ghanaian Economy: Prominence of Land and Forest Resources as Sources of Sustenance

Prominent among the contemporary factors that affect Ghana's forest policy process is the consistent decline of the economy,[348] and consequently, the severe economic hardships that the citizens have had to endure for the past three decades.[349] In this connection, there has been an urgent need for social and economic transformation of the country. Given the structure of Ghana's economy, especially the prominence of farming as the means of livelihood for a fast-growing population, the role of forests as sources of building materials, medicines, game, domestic fuel, etc., and the high dependence on the export of primary produce for external earnings, solving the problem of deforestation turns out to be a highly complex undertaking.

The importance of timber and cocoa as sources of foreign revenues, and the position of agriculture as the source of a huge portion of Ghana's GDP, denote an economy that has primary production at its foundation. (See Tables 4.2 and 4.3)

This foundation was laid in the late nineteenth and early twentieth centuries by the colonial administration that emphasized the production and export of primary products such as timber, cocoa, and minerals. Although the first government in post-independent Ghana embarked on an aggressive industrialization scheme with the objective of changing the basic agricultural and extractive structure of the economy, that effort failed to achieve the desired long-term impact.[350]

Table 4. 2
GHANA: EXPORTS OF COCOA AND TIMBER (1980-1993)
(Millions US$)

	1980	1985	1991	1992	1993	1994	1995
Total Exports	1104	633	998	986	1051	n/a	n/a
Cocoa	793	412	347	303	280	320	365
Timber	34	28	124	123	127	165	190

Source: The World Bank, Trends in Developing Economies: Extracts, Volume 3, Sub-Saharan Africa, (Washington, DC, The World Bank, 1994), p.81. International Cocoa Organization, Quarterly Bulletin of Cocoa Statistics, Bank of Ghana, Bulletin of Statistics

Consequently, the extractive sector has remained disproportionately large, and the economic prospects of Ghana continue to be critically linked to the performance of agriculture, mining, timber, and other primary activities. The position of agriculture and the primary sector as a whole is evident from statistics on the ratios of the three major sectors of the economy. (Table 4.3).

Table 4. 3
GHANA: SHARES OF GDP BY SECTOR (1981-1993)
(in %)

SECTOR	1980	1985	1991	1992	1993
Agriculture	57.9	44.9	48.6	48.6	47.3
Industry	11.9	16.7	16.0	16.2	16.0
Services	30.2	38.4	35.4	35.3	36.7
TOTAL	100	100	100	100	100

Source: The World Bank, Trends in Developing Economies: Extracts, Volume 3, Sub-Saharan Africa, (Washington, DC: The World Bank, 1994), Page 80.

Although over time the proportion of Ghana's GDP that is derived from agriculture has declined, it still remains the largest revenue-producing sector in the economy. The World Bank continues to designate cocoa as "central to Ghana's economy both for its contribution to export performance and tax revenues and its generation of rural income and employment."[351] This fact is supported by the data in Table 4.2.

The data in Table 4.2 also indicate a combined decline in export earnings from cocoa and timber from 75% to 39% (as a percentage of total exports)

between 1980 and 1993, probably an outcome of the drive to diversify Ghana's export base. This decline notwithstanding, the two items continue to be very important sources of Ghana's external earnings.

The data further show an impressive increase in the importance of timber as a source of revenue. In the period covered (1980-1995), earnings from cocoa steadily declined by about 65% from $793 million to $280 million, while earnings from timber increased almost three-fold from $34 million to $127 million. This means that even though consistently more revenue has accrued from cocoa than from timber, the importance of cocoa has steadily dropped while timber has emerged as a major commodity. This evidence clarifies developments in the deforestation policy scenario, and helps to show that in spite of the enactment and implementation of policies to address the deforestation problem, timber exploitation and expansion in production of cash crops have emerged as principal means of generating external revenue. Hence, exploitation of timber and clearance of forests for cash crop production have increased.

In addition to the above information about the structure of the economy, evidence of Ghana's fragile economic situation, as indicated by various World Bank data,[352] provides additional information on the contextual setting within which the forest policy process has occurred. Ghana is among the poorest nations in sub-Saharan Africa. GNP per capita is about $390.[353] In contrast, the GNP per capita of Great Britain, Ghana's ex-colonial ruler, is about $16,100! Ghana's balance of trade has consistently been negative. (Appendix 4 portrays Ghana's economic performance since 1957.) For example, the trade deficit increased from -$112 million in 1988 to -$470 million in 1992. Current accounts balances also worsened from -$134 million in 1985 to -$572 million in 1993, and external debt as ratio of GDP increased from 31.6% to 72% between 1980 and 1993. The total outstanding external debt amounting to $5.4 billion at the end of 1994, almost 76% of the GDP, is growing. Even though agriculture remains the largest sector of the economy, Ghana still depends on imported food, spending an average of about $40 million each year between 1980 and 1993. This implies a prevalent need to expand agriculture even further. In the absence of more efficient agricultural practices, the only means to achieve this remains clearing more forests in order to increase the acreage of farmlands.

Poverty, indebtedness,[354] food shortages, and a dependence on a limited range of exports are central factors that explain the disconnection between deforestation policies and their outcome. There appears to be a structural contradiction between the economic realities of this country on one hand, especially the prominence of agriculture and timber as sources of GDP, and the need to prevent the potentially disastrous consequences of the incessant clearance of forests on the other hand. The makeup of the economy suggests that Ghana needs to grow more food locally and export more so as to reduce dependence on imported food, meet foreign debt obligations, and generate critically needed capital for development. Given the limited sources from which badly needed foreign exchange can be generated, however, the only solution available at the present is to increase the amount of tillable land and boost the export of primary resources, among which timber is an important item. This structural contradiction appears to be an important contextual factor for explaining why protective regulatory deforestation policies have not had their desired impact.

The Need to Generate Revenues for Social and Economic Development Programs in Post-Independent Ghana

The practice during the colonial era whereby the government was solely responsible for providing social amenities and infrastructural facilities in the country has been sustained after independence, and prevails today. In the earliest years of Ghana's independence, the government, under Prime Minister Kwame Nkrumah, made it a priority to develop Ghana's infrastructure, services, and industries as quickly as possible so as to bring them to par with those of more developed countries. Such an ambitious objective, and the determination to pursue it, placed an enormous strain on the country's finances.

The strategy for achieving this objective was development planning. Since Ghana was, and still is, dependent on the export of primary resources and agricultural produce for revenue, there has been a corresponding need to intensify the exploitation of such resources as the need to expand and maintain such facilities increased over the years. A series of development plans, all based on financing to be derived from natural resources and cocoa, have been implemented in Ghana since independence.

A close examination of the objectives, content, and sources of funding for these development plans reveals that the pursuit of economic development objectives in post-independence Ghana has been associated with the increased exploitation of timber and other resources, as well as expansion in cash crop production.

The earliest development plan in post-independence Ghana was the Consolidated Development Plan of 1958/59.[355] In this plan, a total of $36,935,356 (38.6% of the grand total expenditure) was allocated to public infrastructure (including roads, electricity, rural and urban water), communications, education, and health. In addition, $29,565,904 (30.9%) was allocated for the development of the new township of Tema and its harbor. In all, these two allocations - infrastructure and Tema Township - accounted for 69.5% of the total budget. It is important to note that funding for these programs was taken for granted as it was not given the necessary attention in the plan.

The ambitious scale of the 1958/59 Plan, and its emphasis on infrastructure and amenities was maintained under the Second Development Plan of 1959-1964.[356] Out of the total budget of $700 million, $200 million was allocated for construction of the Volta hydroelectric project, a dam and power plant that were intended to generate large amounts of cheap electric power for domestic use as well as for an anticipated industrial development. Two hundred and eighty-thee million US dollars (80% of the total budget) was allocated to communications, education, housing, health, sanitation and water supplies. On the question of funding, the plan simply stated that revenues were to be "determined by the Government's reserves, taxable capacity, and by borrowing capacity."[357]

Such a lack of specificity was the first indication that the central government was not concerned with undertaking projects based on availability of resources, and that it was willing to exceed the available funds in order to achieve its development goals. This Second Development Plan also marked the start of the trend towards Ghana's indebtedness, a trend that has continued to the present. As will be discussed later on in this chapter, Ghana's external indebtedness has been a key factor in the necessary decisions to continue the exploitation and export of her natural resources.

The Seven-Year Development Plan of 1963/64-1969/70 was described as "a program of social and economic development based on the use of science and technology to revolutionize Ghana's agriculture and industry..."[358] In accordance with this, most emphasis was placed on the modernization of agriculture and "the most rapid expansion of industrial activity."[359] Furthermore, the central government sought to use this plan as an instrument to advance its goal of establishing the grounds for a socialist society in Ghana.

President Nkrumah set the ambitious goal of creating "a strong and progressive society in which no one will have any anxiety about the basic means of life, about work, food and shelter; where poverty and illiteracy no longer exist and disease is brought under control; and where our educational facilities provide all the children of Ghana with the best possible opportunities for the development of their potentialities."[360] Pursuant to these objectives, the central government instituted free education and health care for all Ghanaians, as well as highly subsidized supplies of electricity, water, and other amenities. Such programs, without a doubt, required large amounts of revenue to undertake.

While maintaining the unprecedented development of Ghana's infrastructure and services, (social services and infrastructure receiving $43 million and $25.6 million respectively as against $12.4 million and $13.2 million in the previous plan) the central government also undertook huge investments in the productive sectors, particularly in the establishment of manufacturing industries, under the Seven-Year Plan. This sector was given a boost: allocations of $50.3 million per year as against $3 million per year under the Second Development Plan. This plan was adopted in spite of the fact that Ghana's balance of payments and budget account balance in the preceding seven years had been, for the most, negative and not improving.[361] (See Appendices 4.1 and 4.2) Projections of the central government's finances for the plan period (1963/64 - 1969/70) also showed an annual financial gap that would amount to $108 million by 1970. It was expected that funding for the plan would be procured mainly from exports, from loans and from grants.

As can be observed from Table 4.4, exports from Ghana were projected to increase during the plan period, fetching a total of $2,180 million. The value of exported timber and timber products was estimated to double, increasing from a yearly average of $30 million in 1960-62 to $58 million in 1969/70. Given that

TABLE 4.4
GHANA: ESTIMATED EXPORTS 1963/64 - 1969/70
($ Million)

ITEM	YEARLY AVERAGE	PROJECTED EXPORTS	PROJECTED EXPORTS	TOTAL
	1960-62	1966/67	1969/70	1963/64-1969/70
COCOA PRODUCTS	140	172	200	1,210
TIMBER PRODUCTS	30	42	58	306
GOLD	22	26	28	178
MANGANESE	10	10	14	76
DIAMONDS	16	20	122	134
ALUMINUM	-	-	28	50
RE-EXPORTS	5	8	10	60
SERVICES & OTHERS	20	24	24	168
TOTAL	244	302	390	2,180

Source: Ghana, Seven-Year Development Plan 1963/64 - 1969/70, (Accra: Office of the Planning Commission, 1964), page 234.

most of Ghana's timber exports were in the form of logs, the only means of increasing the value of exports was through increased felling of trees.

Although Nkrumah's socialist ideology was discarded after his overthrow in 1966, the practice whereby the central government of Ghana bore responsibility for providing infrastructure and services, and undertaking industrial development was not discarded. As a result, government deficits continued to increase. In the face of this deteriorating financial situation there has been an urgent need to generate more revenues. Under the circumstances, the only means of doing this has been through increasing exports. Projections on the balance of payments during the Five-Year Development Plan of 1975/76 to 1979/80 (Table 4.5) showed a decline in the deficit for the first three years, but a consistent increase in the last three as the rate of increase in government payments exceeded that of its receipts. This was in spite of the projected growth in exports. The value of exports was projected to increase by 51% from $817.3 million in 1974-75 to $1235.8 million over the course of the plan period. Exports of timber were projected to increase by 74.8% in that five-year period. While there is no indication of whether these targets were achieved, the projections were extremely optimistic.

The main objectives of the 1983-86 Five-Year Development Plan included increasing import capacity. To achieve this, various measures were to be taken to revitalize the export sector, especially cocoa, minerals, and timber in order to increase foreign exchange earnings.[362] It is important to note that among the objectives of this plan was increasing output of the forestry sector by 2.5% in

1981/82 and 3% in 1982/83, and importing more machinery and equipment to facilitate the achievement of an increase of 5.5% over the 1983/84 output.[363]

Another objective was to boost the production of cocoa; an action that would require, among other things, clearing forests to make way for more farms.[364] In accordance with these projections, earnings from the export of timber and timber products were projected to increase by a total of 116.7% between 1981/82 and 1985/86.[365]

TABLE 4.5
GHANA: PROJECTED BALANCE OF PAYMENTS 1974/75 - 1979/80
($ Million approx.)

	1974-75	1975-76	1976-77	1977-78	1978-79	1979-80
TOTAL RECEIPTS	902.7	102.5	1,134.30	1,192.00	1,252.20	1,304.10
EXPORTS	817.3	912.3	1,000.20	1,072.00	1,161.20	1,235.80
TOTAL PAYMENTS	1,086.10	1,051.30	1,136.40	1,232.10	1,313.90	1,407.50
DEFICIT	183.4	26.3	2.10	40.1	61.70	103.4

Source: Republic of Ghana, Five-Year Development Plan 1975/76 - 1979/80 Part 1, (Accra: Ministry of Economic Planning, 1977), p. 72.

These projections and the underlying pressure to boost exports from Ghana can be explained if one considers the projected government accounts balances for the period. The overall government deficit was projected to average approximately $28.75 million. Faced with this scenario, it was critical for the government to generate more revenue, and the only means available for such short-term increase in revenue were resources such as timber.

The facts contained in the above discussions point to another explanation for the disconnection between policies for combating deforestation in Ghana and their outcomes both in the early independence years and even today. At the same time that policy statements and actions of government leaders suggested a determination to curb the rate of deforestation, the government's development objectives and the means of funding them have required that production of cocoa and exploitation of timber and other natural resources are intensified. In the final analysis, the result of these has been an increased elimination of forests.

Population Growth: Implications of Increasing Demand for Land and Forest Resources
The population of Ghana has been growing at a consistently high rate, with certain adverse ramifications for the deforestation problem. Table 4.6 contains data that denote this high rate of population growth between 1960 and 1995, and the resulting high densities in Ghana.

TABLE 4.6
GHANA: POPULATION GROWTH (1960 - 1994)

YEAR	POPULATION	INCREASE FROM PREVIOUS CENSUS	GROWTH RATE % OVER PREVIOUS YEARS	AVERAGE DENSITY (per sq. ml.)
1960	6,726,816	-	-	57
1970	8,559,313	21.2	3.1	73
1984	12,296,681	43.7	2.7	93
1991	15,400,000	25.2	4.3	133
1995	17,200,000 (est.)	11.7	3.4	162

Source: Irvin Kaplan et al., Area Handbook of Ghana, Foreign Area Studies Series, (Washington, DC.: American University, 1971). LeVerde Berry (Ed.), Ghana: A Country Study, Area Handbook Series, Federal Research Division, (Washington, DC.: Library of Congress, 1994). Europa Publications: Africa South of the Sahara, (London: Europa, 1995).

On the average, the rate of population growth in Ghana between 1960 and 1995 was 3.4%, among the highest in sub-Saharan Africa. The 0.4% drop in the rate between 1970 and 1984 was only temporary, as, by 1991, it had increased by 1.6% to 4.3%. Associated with such high rates of growth have been increases in the average population density in the country from 57 people per square mile in 1960 to 162 people per square mile in 1995. Projections for the year 2025 indicate there will be almost 38 million Ghanaians.[366] These increases reflect high average annual rates of 3.6% for the period 1980-1985, 3.0% for 1990-1995, and a projected 2.8% for 2000-2025.[367]

A significant aspect of Ghana's population growth has been the rapid increase in the proportions of the population that live in urban centers (See table 4.7). Over a span of 13 years, this proportion increased from 23% to 37%, an alarming increase of about 14 percentage points.

TABLE 4.7
GHANA: URBAN POPULATION (1960 - 1992)

YEAR	1960	1970	1984	1989	1992
% OF URBAN POPULATION	23.1	28	32	34.5	37

Sources: Ghana Statistical Service, Quarterly Digest of Statistics, Tables 94, 95 and 96, Accra, December 1991. Ghana Statistical Service, Living Standards Survey, First Year Report, Accra, August, 1989.

Among the consequences of such a high rate of population growth have been increased clearance of forests for foodstuffs and cash crop production, increased demand for building materials such as lumber, bamboo, vines, and rattan for the construction of housing and other amenities, increased consumption of fuel in the form of firewood and charcoal, and increased consumption of important components of Ghanaian diets such as bush meat, snails, and mushrooms. The forests are also a source of herbs and plant medicines for many Ghanaians. Undoubtedly, these are developments that undermine government policies to combat deforestation.

Population growth has also engendered an increased need for infrastructure, especially inter-city roads, highways and feeder roads, the provision of which require the removal of trees and other vegetation. The increased demand for forest products, and the spread of human activities into hitherto forest lands, as settlements expand and development of infrastructural services proceed, are among the factors of the environment within which deforestation policies have been administered.

Another outcome of infrastructural development, especially expansion of the road network, is the opening up of formerly less accessible forest areas. The increased accessibility created when roads are constructed through forest areas has served as an incentive for timber contractors and farmers to move in, their activities helping to intensify the removal of the forest. A 1989 World Bank study suggested that in sub-Saharan Africa, the two phenomena: rapid population growth, and environmental degradation are mutually reinforcing.[368]

Statistics on the types of fuel used by Ghanaians and trends in the production and consumption of the various sources of energy show that there has been an increase in the exploitation of forests for fuel in the country as the population increased.

The Ghana Living Standards Survey, 1989,[369] contains information that substantiates the consequences of Ghana's fast population growth on its forests. In 1989, 65.5% of Ghanaians resided in rural areas. 85% of households in the forest zone of Ghana were engaged in agriculture; 84% of them as crop-growers, and 43% as livestock producers. The average farm size in the forest zone was 21.3 acres. By 1991-92, the population of Ghanaians who were employed as farmers remained high, at 42.8% overall, 79% of them operating in the forest zone.[370] Given the limited use of fertilizers and high yielding crops, it is inevitable that as a result of population growth, increased acreage of forests would have to be cleared by the increasing number of farmers as they endeavor to feed the growing population and produce cash crops.[371]

The 1989 Living Standards Survey reported that 94.3% of Ghanaian households most frequently used wood and charcoal for cooking.[372] (See Table 4.8). The only variation between rural and urban areas, was the fact that charcoal-use was predominant in the urban areas. For example, in Accra, the capital city, 81% of households most frequently used charcoal. In other urban localities, 49.7% used charcoal and 42.1% wood. In rural localities, 92% of households used wood most frequently for cooking. Although the 1991-92 Ghana Living Standard Survey indicated a slight reduction (1.35%) in the dependence on wood and charcoal between 1989 and 1991/92, 92.3% of Ghanaian households still used the two as the main fuels for cooking (67.4%

using wood, and 24.9% using charcoal).   Although in Accra, the capital city, the number of households that used firewood had increased by 1.9% in the period, those who used charcoal had decreased by 11.6%. Yet, there were barely any changes in the other urban localities.   In the rural localities, on the other hand, wood and charcoal use remained high, at 95.4%.   There was some increase in the use of natural gas and kerosene, especially in Accra, between 1989 and 1991/92, but those two sources of fuel remained insignificant overall.

TABLE 4.8
GHANA: TYPES OF COOKING FUEL USED BY HOUSEHOLDS,
1989 AND 1991/92
(in % of households)

	ACCRA		OTHER URBAN AREAS		RURAL AREAS		TOTALS	
TYPE OF FUEL	1989	1991/92	1989	1991/92	1989	1991/92	1989	1991/92
WOOD	1.1	3	42.1	42.1	92	87.2	68.7	67.4
CHARCOAL	81	69.4	49.7	50.4	5.4	8.2	25.6	24.9
GAS	4.8	14.1	0.8	2.3	-	0.3	0.8	2.2
ELECTRIC	1.7	4.6	1.1	1	0.1	0.1	0.5	0.8
KEROSENE	10.8	8.07	5	2.9	0.8	0.5	3	1.9
OTHER	0.6	0.2	1.3	1.2	1.7	3.6	1.4	2.7
TOTALS	100.9	100.9	100	99.9	100	99.99	100	99.9

Source: Ghana Statistical Service, "Ghana Living Standards Survey," 1989 and 1991/92.

Additional data from the Energy Information Center of the Ghana Ministry of Energy (contained in Appendices 4.3, 4.4, and 4.5), show the relative importance of wood as a source of fuel in Ghana   The statistics, which show trends in the production and consumption of energy by source between 1974 and 1994, reveal a consistent increase in the production of fire-wood from 2.41 million tons of oil equivalent (TOE) to 4.61 million TOE, a 47.67% increase over the twenty years.   The increase in production of the second major fuel, hydro-electricity, over the same period was 32.89% (from 438.38 TOE to 653.32 TOE). The increase in production of firewood corresponded to increases in consumption; by 42.76% from 1879.21 TOE to 3282.96 TOE. Overall, fuel-wood accounted for 65.53% of the total consumption of energy in Ghana during the period in question. As Appendix 8 shows, wood-fuels are not for domestic use only, but also for commercial and industrial use as well.

To sum up, data on fuel production and consumption in Ghana show that wood and charcoal remain the most common cooking fuels; a situation that, from every indication, will not change in the foreseeable future. This implies that the exploitation of the forests for domestic fuel has been a factor in deforestation in Ghana.   It also implies that deforestation resulted from an increasingly intensive exploitation for firewood and wood for charcoal production to cater to the needs of an increasing population. The problem is bound to remain inevitable until significant and effective policies are introduced to replenish the trees harvested for fuel.[373]

External Debt and Market-Driven External Demand for Ghanaian Timber

The importance of timber as a source of external revenue has been previously mentioned as one of the features of the Ghanaian economy. However, as the following analysis will show, there is an external element that foments this situation, and in so doing augments the forces that generate increased removal of forests. Events in the international timber market have had major ramifications for the volume and composition of Ghana's exports, earnings from the timber trade, and on the content of forest policies.

For well over a century, trade in forest products worldwide has consistently increased. Available data show that there was almost a 114% increase in the value of total world round wood exports ('round wood' being wood that is in the actual state in which it was felled), from $46.6 billion in 1982 to $99.6 billion in 1993[374]. Historically, Ghana has been an active participant in this trade. Ghana's earnings from timber exports have grown in consonance with worldwide demands. Data compiled by Barbara Ingham show a pattern of rapid increases in the volume and the corresponding value of timber exports from Ghana, from 90,000 logs (about $136,000) in 1900 to 29 million logs and 8,300 cubic feet of sawn timber (totaling about $32.5 million) in 1960.[375] Between 1982 and 1993, the value of Ghana's exports of forest products increased by a multiple of about 14, from $11.2 million to $154.2 million.[376] In 1994, cash-strapped Ghana resorted to an unprecedented sale of timber on the world market, probably the easiest and quickest way to generate foreign exchange. Two hundred and twenty-two million US dollars was generated from the export of 34.7 million cubic feet of wood, a 23% increase over 1993 exports.[377] The amount realized from timber exports in 1997 was $164.6 million, a 5.6% increase over 1996 revenues.[378]

These increases in exports over the years, and in particular, the fact that a world market existed to support a 23% increase in Ghana's exports within one year, confirm the existence of an expanding world market for timber products. For a poor nation such as Ghana, with a consistently worsening balance of payments (-$571.7 million in 1993 from -$38.8 million in 1984),[379] and a total external debt that ballooned from $861 million in 1967 to $5,463 million in 1994, the huge potential of the forests as an avenue for partial economic relief features prominently among the factors that condition the policy process regarding deforestation.

Effects of the New International Economic Order

Another dimension of the contextual setting of the Ghanaian forest policy process is the emerging international economic order that emphasizes the law of comparative advantage and trade liberalization. This "new" order is making it much more difficult for developing countries to effectively initiate and sustain an industrialization process and compete with the industrialized west and the newly industrialized nations of Asia in the sale of manufactured goods on the world market. Ghana has been no exception to this. Handicaps such as the lack of capital, lack of technical know-how, limited local markets, etc., appear to be undermining efforts at expanding the economic base to include other sectors apart from the agricultural and extractive sectors. Whereas numerous enterprises in the industrial sector have failed in the past, those still in operation have been largely unprofitable, surviving because of financial subsidies and protection from the government.

Ghana's inability to engage effectively in international trading in manufactured goods and services, and the fact that it makes more economic sense to import needed manufactured goods instead of producing them locally at higher cost, seems to imply that, given the prevailing circumstances, the options open to Ghanaian policy-makers are extremely limited to the intensified exploitation and export of primary produce.[380] This is part of the explanation why the volumes of timber, and mineral exports have considerably increased in the past 15 years. Developments in international trade and their effects on Ghana's export sector therefore need to be given ample attention in order to understand the forces that have been at work to cause the disconnection between Ghana's forest policies and their outcome.

Thus far, the information contained in this chapter has provided answers to different aspects of the central research question of this research: why the forests of Ghana have been consistently been depleting in spite of the existence of a series of policies to address the problem. It has been shown that the development objectives of post-independence Ghanaian governments and the means by which they have sought to achieve those objectives are of particular significance as an explanation. This discussion has also dealt with the financial crisis that has become a dominant and enduring feature of the Ghanaian political economy in the past four decades, and the pressure it has placed on the government to seek relief through exploitation of Ghana's resources. Given the realities of the Ghanaian situation, especially the level of poverty of the citizens, the extremely low standard of living, and the ambitious goals of past and present development plans that have been adopted by the government, it is apparent that the continued and intensified exploitation of natural resources, including forests, is inevitable, even though Ghanaian governments have consistently declared the importance of combating deforestation.

The Political Economy of Stabilization and Structural Adjustment in Ghana: Implications to Deforestation Policies

A stabilization and structural adjustment program was adopted in Ghana in 1983. It is a comprehensive economic package intended to terminate the downward slide of Ghana's economy and restructure it so as to set it on a course towards stability and sustained growth.

A great deal of documentation exists on the economic crises that prompted the adoption of the SAP in Ghana.[381] Aspects of the crises included runaway inflation, scarcity of basic necessities, negative per capita growth, declines in the producer prices and total production of cocoa, declines in the terms of trade, declines in the production of minerals and timber, the two other leading export commodities, and scarcity of imports. (Appendix 4 shows the trends in the economic conditions of Ghana before and after the structural adjustment program.) The currency (the Cedi) was so overvalued that the production of exports was rendered increasingly uneconomic. As the years went by, there were increasingly massive budget deficits, and a runaway inflation that averaged over 50% per year, creating extremely hard living conditions for Ghanaians. In addition to the general economy, infrastructure had suffered an extensive and prolonged collapse in an international environment that was "hostile, politically and economically."[382]

In the face of these problems, the government's influence over the economy had drastically diminished, and its fiscal and institutional capabilities were devastated.[383] Jon Kraus has suggested that there were no feasible political or economic alternatives to a drastic reform.[384] Beginning in 1982, Ghana, with the advice and guidance of the World Bank, the IMF, and the major aid donor countries, adopted a stabilization and structural adjustment program (SAP).

There are indications, however, that the structural adjustment program has prompted the increased exploitation of timber as well as other resources for external revenues. Although the program was designed as a short-term process intended to fix the problems and redirect the economy on a path towards sustained growth, it has remained in effect for fifteen years, with no indication as to when it might be terminated. Without a doubt the policies and conditionalities of SAP have become long-term features of Ghana's economy. As such, they will probably remain key aspects of the environment within which deforestation policies in Ghana will be formulated and implemented in the foreseeable future.

The main goal of Ghana's SAP is to reduce the balance of payments deficits and arrears by stimulating exports and restraining demand for imports. In connection with this, the policy measures taken have included: i) repeated massive devaluations of the overvalued currency in order to maximize incentives to exporters, ii) producer price increases for cocoa and foodstuffs, iii) control of government budget deficits in order to arrest inflation, iv) removal of price controls, and, v) removal of subsidies on certain goods and services.

The IMF and World Bank have, since the beginning of the program, guaranteed large amounts of loans and grants from donor countries. Those institutions have, in addition, advanced credits and grants to Ghana thus enabling it to repay external loan arrears.[385] These funds were also intended for procuring the required capital and essential goods as the program got under way.

Table 4.9 shows that over the four years prior to the launching of the SAP, IDA commitments and disbursements to Ghana totaled about $100 million. During the four years, fiscal year (FY) 1983-1986, IDA commitments increased by nearly $500 million. Disbursements exceeded $200 million. Thereafter, the lending program was further built up to commitments averaging about $250 million annually and disbursements of close to $200 million. Of the total commitments of $2.4 billion during FY1983-1994, adjustment lending amounted to about $1 billion (roughly 40%). In contrast with the limited aid flows to Ghana in the years prior to the SAP, aid to Ghana was increased after 1983. Official development assistance commitments averaged about $800 million per year between 1987 and 1993.[386]

TABLE 4.9
IDA COMMITMENTS AND DISBURSEMENTS IN GHANA, FISCAL YEAR 1979-1994
($ Million)

SECTOR		1979-82	1983-86	1987-90	1991-94	TOTAL 1983-94
Agriculture	Loan Credit	30	25	116	217	358
	Disbursement	34	22	43	158	223
Industry	Loan Credit	19	60	177	141	378
	Disbursement	4	29	128	160	317
Infrastructure	Loan Credit	54	114	160	307	518
	Disbursement	80	55	148	145	348
Social	Loan Credit	0	50	190	230	470
	Disbursement	2	14	66	132	212
Public Sector Manufacturing	Loan Credit	0	220	285	148	653
	Disbursement	0	105	344	220	669
Grand Total	Loan Credit	103	469	929	1,042	2,439
	Disbursement	120	226	730	814	1,769

Source: Robert Armstrong, "Ghana Country Assistance Review: A Study in Development Effectiveness," (Washington, D.C.: The World Bank, 1996), p. 36.

There has been a continuing debate over the success of this structural adjustment program.[387] That issue, however, is not a major concern of this research. Our interest lies in the possible effects of the program on the contents and outcomes of deforestation policies.

The trends in production and exports of timber products since 1984 (see Appendix 9) suggest that policies that have been pursued under the adjustment program - devaluations of the currency, coupled with the deliberate policy of shifting resources to the export sectors, rehabilitation and repair of the roads and railway networks and supplies of spare parts and inputs - have resulted in a revival of industry.[388] The International Trade Statistics Yearbook for 1994 reported an increase in earnings from Ghana's timber exports from $88 million in 1989 to $230 million in 1994. In 1991 revenue from the forestry sector accounted for 60% of Gross Domestic Product, and 8% of total export earnings.[389] Although the production of log and sawn timber had declined by over two-thirds during 1970-1982 resulting in a fall in revenues from exports from $130 million in 1973 to $15 million in 1983 (See Appendix 10), the series of devaluations resulted in an over a hundred-fold nominal increase in the payments log and lumber exporters received between 1981 to 1990.[390] This was incentive enough to increase production. Consequently, the total annual volumes of log and lumber production tripled in that period. Under structural adjustment, there was almost a four-fold increase in the capacity of the equipment used by firms in the forestry sector, from an average of about 16% in 1983 to an average of about 60% in 1989. A $157 million World Bank soft loan advanced to Ghana allowed the acquisition of equipment used for extraction, and helped to expand production very quickly. A result of this was a substantial increase in the production and export of timber products.[391] Between 1981 and 1990, log production increased by 31,802,120 cubic feet while mill production increased also by 14,132,000 cubic feet.[392] Overall, there was a 65% increase in the two areas. Export of logs grew from 1,907,820 cubic feet in 1981 (valued at $3.7 million), to 11,976,870 cubic feet (valued at $4.3 million) in 1988. In all, total earnings from the export of wood products increased by 800% from $15.3 million in 1982 to $125.3 million in 1990.

An increase in the percentage of the labor force in agriculture, forestry and fishing, (from 57.2% in 1970 to 61.1% in 1984, and to 66.1% in 1987) has been attributed to the deterioration in urban job opportunities under the SAP.[393] Losses in secondary and tertiary sector jobs were caused in part by the mandated reduction in the civil service work force, and the closure of several money-losing public-owned industries. There is evidence that improved prices for farm produce (another aspect of the SAP), and various government projects that re-integrated the victims of job losses into agriculture, established agricultural projects and farm service centers, and supplied inputs to farmers have had an impact on the acreage of farmlands as well as the production of foodstuffs and cocoa.[394]

The foregoing provide enough grounds for concluding that Ghana's SAP has borne some serious consequences for the forests in the form of increased exploitation of timber and increased conversion of forests to farmlands. A cause for concern is that, in spite of the increases in exports and the revenues that have been earned from this exploitation thus far, Ghana's debt service, and current account deficits have continued to increase.[395] The increases in external loans under the SAP have boosted Ghana's external debt (including IMF and World Bank loans) from $1.9 billion in 1984 to $5.4 billion in 1994.[396] A consequence of this became evident in 1988 when about 70% of all revenues derived from exports was needed to service Ghana's debt. This situation, without a doubt, aggravated the deforestation problem because it intensified the need on the part of the government to promote forest destroying economic activities.

Summary and Conclusions

In the above discussions about the external environment within which policies to combat deforestation in Ghana have been conceived, formulated, and implemented in the post-independence era of Ghana, various explanations have been advanced to show why forests in Ghana have continued to be depleted in spite of the existence of policies to address the problem. The information also indicate that the incidence of deforestation in Ghana should not be perceived in simple terms; the mere removal of trees. They reveal that the continued incidence of deforestation in Ghana is the result of the operation of a complex of factors with historical, social, political, international, and economic dimensions.

Compounding the economic factors underlying the problem is the all-important issue of limited legitimacy of Ghanaian governments. Public policies have usually been dictated by the extremely powerful heads of state and a few individuals at the highest echelons of the government. Overall, avenues for channeling popular inputs and demands into the public policy process have been restricted. These, and the fact that the post-colonial governments of Ghana have not been able to meet the expectations of the citizens, have undermined these governments' legitimacy. Consequently, Ghanaian citizens, in large part, do not accord their government the necessary acknowledgement as an institution through which they can express their concerns and needs. The support and cooperation that are necessary for successful realization of the goal of addressing the problem of deforestation have been lacking.

Over-ambitious development strategies in the early post-independence years and the continuing role of the government as the sole provider of amenities and facilities in Ghana have been shown as having placed a great deal of financial stress on Ghanaian governments. The need to intensify exploitation of resources such as timber in order to generate revenues to pay mounting outstanding debts and embark on development projects has been very strong. As such, at the same time that the government has been adopting policies and expending resources on curbing deforestation, it has engaged in the contradictory activity of promoting increased exploitation and export of timber, one of the few export commodities. The drive to reduce deforestation has therefore been undermined by the reality that Ghana critically needs external revenue.

The population of Ghana has consistently increased at a high rate in the past half century. Accompanying this population increase has been a growing demand for farmlands, lumber, firewood, and other forest resources. More and more forests are being eliminated as Ghanaians endeavor to meet their food, fuel, housing, and other needs. Lastly, the structural adjustment program, which Ghana has been executed since 1983, has required the intensified exploitation of Ghana's natural resources in order to honor its mounting external debt obligations. As has been mentioned, timber is one of the few resources available to Ghana for a short-term boost in exports.

The gist of this chapter is that the above factors are central to explaining the failure to achieve the desired outcomes from the policies to combat deforestation in Ghana. This chapter serves as the framework within which the internal workings of the deforestation policy process in post-independence Ghana will be examined in chapters six and seven.

This chapter has also helped to verify two of the central hypotheses of this research. Whereas the first hypothesis has been rejected, the second has been shown to be valid. The first hypothesis: that the disconnection between policies to combat deforestation and their outcomes is a result inconsistencies in policies due to political instability has been shown to be invalid. It has been shown that the policies themselves, the government institutions that deal with them, and the processes of formulation and implementation have been consistent in Ghana irrespective of the rapid changes in government.

The second hypothesis: that the lack of legislative tradition in Ghana has fostered a domination of the deforestation policy process by politicians and bureaucrats, has been shown to be valid. Policy ideas do not originate from the citizens or their elected representatives, even though they, the citizens, bear the brunt of the effects of the policies and the requirements of their implementation. The result is that the non-governmental stakeholders, who have been excluded from the process, have been uncooperative, even hostile to the government and its agents. This has thwarted the efforts of the government to pursue its chosen courses of action that would resolve the deforestation problem.

Policy outputs have also reflected the external demands that have been made on the state; especially, demands to honor Ghana's external debt obligations, and at the same time, provide amenities and services to Ghanaian citizens.

The discussions in the next chapter will be focused on the content of policies intended to address deforestation in Ghana. Policy statements made by high level government officials and politicians will be analyzed so as to shed some light on their perceptions about the nature of the Ghanaian forestry problem as well as the kinds of policy actions they have taken to address it.

Chapter 5

A Review of the Content of Deforestation Policies in Post-Independence Ghana

The objective of this chapter is to examine policies on deforestation in post-independence Ghana in terms of their content and the mechanism for their implementation. The purpose is to identify the intended goals of the policies, and seek answers as to why the depletion of forests in Ghana has continued in spite of such policies.   Information will be presented to confirm that, historically, extraction of forest resources has been a priority of governments in Ghana.   Therefore, in spite of the frequently expressed commitment to forest conservation, and in spite of the series of conservation policies that have been adopted, the drive to generate revenues from the forests has perpetually outweighed the motivation to preserve the resource.   Given these, it will be shown that, in practice, the actions of the government of Ghana have not matched the rhetoric about forest conservation.

In order to achieve the above purpose, the discussion will be focused on declared deforestation policy goals of the government.   In addition, the formulation process and contents of three of the most recent policy documents will be analyzed. They are:

1.   The Ghana Environmental Action Plan of 1988,[397]
2.   Ghana Environmental Action Plan of 1994, and[398]
3.   The Ghana Forest and Wildlife Policy also of 1994.[399]

The legal and administrative instruments by which these policies have been implemented will also be examined. In addition to these, past evaluations and critiques of Ghana's deforestation policy process will be reviewed so as to deduce any additional explanations they may advance for the disconnection between deforestation policies and their outcomes.

Declared Deforestation Policy Goals of Ghanaian Governments

As was the case with the colonial governments, leaders of post-independence Ghanaian governments have, without exception, consistently expressed the need to combat deforestation.   It was stated in chapter one that politicians and bureaucrats have on several occasions cited evidence of deforestation and its consequences, and affirmed the need for the government to take the necessary remedial action.

Reference was also made to a series of actions that have been taken for the purpose of dealing with the problem of deforestation.[400]   These actions are testimony to the level of attention Ghanaian governments have given to this problem.   The inclusion in the 1992 constitution of provisions [under section 269(1)] for the establishment of a number of commissions, including one on forestry, within six months after the first meeting of the parliament, is an indicator of the importance of forests and forestry matters in Ghana.

One of the earliest acts passed by parliament was the Forestry Commission Act 453 of July 1993, which reconstituted the agency responsible for coordination, regulation, management, and utilization of forest and wildlife resources.[401] The scope of responsibilities of the Forestry Commission was reduced, limited to national forestry policy formulation. It was also assigned to advise the government on forestry matters.   The functions and role of the commission in the policy process will be discussed in greater detail in chapter seven.   However, the fact that prompt action was taken by parliament to reconstitute this commission and redefine its functions appears to establish that the political leaders of Ghana attached some importance to forests and the problems associated with them.

For the five years beginning in 1993, concerns about deforestation in Ghana and the need to combat it have not been merely verbally expressed.[402]   The government has gone beyond words and taken specific actions reflecting the government's concern about forestry interests. Prominent among them are the institution of an annual National Forestry Week,[403] and the establishment of a number of agencies to deal with the forestry sector. Publications from various public institutions[404] have been used to re-affirm a determination on the part of the government to gather information, promote and maintain an awareness among Ghanaians of the threat posed by deforestation, and a resolve to pursue policies that would help preserve Ghana's forests.   The two environmental action plans and the forest and wildlife policy referred to earlier are major actions taken for purposes that include conservation of forests.[405] These plans and policies are examined in the following section.

The Content of Deforestation Policies in Ghana

A notable feature of the forest policies and environmental action plans that have been introduced by governments in Ghana in the past half-century is that subsequent ones have not been designed to terminate existing ones. Rather, new policies and plans have been introduced as complements to old ones. Consequently, aspects of colonial forest policies, in particular, the Forest Policy of 1948,[406] which was intended to achieve colonial mercantile objectives, have been maintained and continue to be an important part of contemporary forest policy in Ghana.

In the following sections, the three most recent policies, referred to above, will be analyzed in terms of their objectives, formulation process, and contents. Table 5.1 shows a categorization of the policies.

TABLE 5.1
CATEGORIES OF DEFORESTATION POLICIES IN POST-INDEPENDENCE GHANA

POLICY	CATEGORY OF FOREST POLICY	PRINCIPAL PURPOSE	PRINCIPAL ACTORS IN THE FORMULATION PROCESS
Ghana Environmental Action Plan, 1988	Extractive	Forest Conservation for Present and Future Extraction	The Bureaucracy
Ghana Environmental Action Plan, 1994	Extractive	Forest Conservation for Present and Future Extraction	The Bureaucracy
Ghana Forest and Wildlife Policy, 1994	Extractive	Sustainable Utilization of Forest Resources	The Bureaucracy and Other Stakeholders

The Ghana Environmental Action Plan of 1988

It is important to note that for thirty years after the end of colonial rule in Ghana, the Gold Coast Forest Policy of 1948 remained the principal instrument guiding the administration of forests in the country, even though, for all intents and purposes, political, social, economic, and other developments had rendered that policy outmoded.

According to the Ghana Environmental Protection Council, the agency that coordinated the formulation of the 1988 Ghana Environmental Action Plan, the need for a comprehensive plan arose from the recognition that efforts at addressing environmental problems in the country had been largely "ad-hoc, cosmetic, ... and limited in scope," and that existing legislation had been "inadequate and unimplemented, ... with no bearing on present day realities as well as the aspirations of Ghanaians."[407]

The declared main objective of the plan was "to ensure a reconciliation between economic development and natural resource conservation," based on the principle of "optimum sustainable yield in the use of resources and ecosystems."[408]

The idea to prepare this plan originated from the government. The Ghana Environmental Protection Council (E.P.C) functioned as facilitator, planning and organizing the plan. Accounts from the plan indicate that in March 1988 the government established a task force of handpicked experts in forestry, environmental, and other related areas. This task force was given the assignment of reviewing existing policies related to environmental protection in Ghana, and proposing a strategy for addressing the key issues including deforestation, deterioration in soil quality, and better management of renewable resources.[409] The result of this task force's deliberations was the Environmental Action Plan of 1988.

The task force comprised bureaucrats and experts from the Environmental Protection Council, Department of Forestry, The Forestry Commission, Ministry of Agriculture, Ministry of Industries, Water Resources Research Institute, Ministry of Lands, Department of Mines, Department of Town Planning, Meteorological Services Department, and the Institute of Renewable Natural Resources.

There were two phases in the preparation of the plan. First, the experts were organized into six groups under the following sectors: land management; forestry and wildlife; water management; marine and coastal ecosystems; mining, manufacturing industries and hazardous chemicals; and, human settlements. A seventh group, made up of the leaders of the six sectoral groups, addressed legal, institutional, cross-sectoral, environmental education, environmental data systems, and monitoring issues.

The main tasks given the groups included:
1. Identifying inadequacies of information and, in connection with that, additional research needs;
2. Reviewing existing legislation and policy recommendations;
3. Proposing a system for monitoring the effects of development on the environment; and,
4. Reviewing institutional arrangements for implementing the recommendations of the task force.

Reports on the deliberations of the working groups were compiled into a draft strategy on the environment of Ghana. After a two-day review of this draft by the whole task force in January 1989, the working groups reconvened to revise them in light of the comments and suggestions advanced.

The second phase of the process was a national conference held in June 1989 to discuss the draft proposals and to seek wider public participation in the plan-preparation process. The 200 participants in this conference represented interests such as district assemblies, non-governmental organizations, and government functionaries. This conference adopted the plan in principle, and assigned the E.P.C. to finalize the document, taking into account the ideas that emerged during the sessions.

Because this plan was an integral part of a wider strategy for the sustainable development of Ghana,[410] the E.P.C. had to undertake the task of incorporating economic factors into the plan, with particular regards to the overall and sectoral economic development strategies of the government. In addition, the E.P.C. was responsible for assigning specific administrative functions required for implementing the plan to specific institutions, and also for drafting the legislation for implementing of the plan.

Certain facts emerge from the policy-formulation process described above:

1. The idea to formulate a policy on the environment originated from the government.
2. The plan was perceived as an integral part of an economic development strategy for Ghana - sustainable development. Environmental protection was dealt with, not in terms of conservation per se, but rather in terms of meeting Ghana's the economic needs, which was a priority. The purpose of the Plan was to devise a means of exploiting Ghana's resources and minimizing the harmful effects of such exploitation at the same time. As such, in spite of expressed concerns about the environment, economic development needs of the country remained a prime factor in the preparation, and consequently the contents of the plan.
3. The government appointed participants in the process.
4. Government bureaucrats, and to a lesser extent, experts from the various sectors dominated the process.
5. Groups of stakeholders, such as farmers, timber contractors, charcoal manufacturers, and traditional rulers did not participate in the deliberations leading to the plan.

The 1988 plan was intended to address the principal causes of deforestation, such as, the increasing scale of timber extraction, the demand for more agricultural land to feed the growing population, the increasing incidence of bush fires, and the extraction of wood fuel to meet energy demands of households and cottage industries.[411] In line with this, a large amount of information on these factors is discussed by authors of the plan in preparing the grounds for the proposed actions for solving environmental problems in Ghana.

Apart from the physical disappearance of forests, the degradation of existing forests through selective logging, both within reserved and non-reserved forest areas, was also identified as a major problem in this government document. Compounding these problems, according to the document, was the lack of an adequate system for monitoring the exact rate of deforestation.[412].

Because this plan was considered to be an improvement over the Forest Policy of 1948, an effort was made by the authors to justify replacing the old plan. This was done through a criticism of the old policy, citing, in particular, the absence of a permanent role for trees in land use outside the reserved forests. The plan also criticized the Ghanaian central government for tolerating the progressive exploitation of forest resources in non-reserved areas without encouraging replacement. This exploitative practice was deemed to have led to the unchecked destruction of forestlands through their conversion into other uses.

The plan contained the following principles for combating deforestation:

1. A commitment to environmentally sound use of resources, both renewable and non-renewable;
2. The creation of awareness among the community of the significance of the environment to socio-economic development, and in lieu of that, the necessity for rational resource use;

3. Institution of an environmental quality control program that would require environmental impact assessments of all ventures that would be deemed to affect the quality of the environment;
4. Development and maintenance of a professional cadre to administer legislation and procedures necessary for safeguarding the environment.
5. Promotion and support of research programs to expedite environmentally sound management of resources;
6. Establishment of an adequate legislative and institutional framework for monitoring, coordinating, and enforcing environmental matters;
7. Restructuring the agencies involved in the environmental policy process, especially the Environmental Protection Council, and strengthening inter-agency coordination;
8. Education and encouragement of District Assemblies (Local Governments) to establish and monitor protected areas and control wood cutting;
9. Promotion of community involvement in environmental conservation through the establishment of community environmental committees, provision of environmental education for local community groups, and support for tree planting and agro-forestry initiatives; and,
10. Sustenance and enforcement of legislation on the control of bush burning.

It is evident from these principles that the forests of Ghana were perceived primarily as a resource. Consequently, the plan was designed to be part of a broad national environmental policy framework whose aim, as stated, was to "ensure a sound management of resources, ... and to avoid exploitation of these resources in a manner that might cause irreparable damage to the environment."[413]

The strategies contained therein are therefore based on the premise that exploitation of forests is an on-going process. The need to control deforestation co-existed with the reality that, to solve her economic problems and cater to the basic needs of the citizens, Ghana had no alternatives to exploitation of the forests and other natural resources. At issue, therefore, was not how to preserve the forests, but rather, how to minimize the adverse effects of exploitation activities. Consequently, the 1988 Environmental Action Plan was, in principle and in content, an extractive policy.

Collectively, the principles of the plan formed an all-embracing wish list, the realization of which would, in all probability, have addressed Ghana's deforestation problem. However, the plan had a serious handicap in the sense that it was too generalized. In addition to the fact that it lacked the innovative actions required for solving the problem, given its increasing magnitude, the plan contained no specifics about the actions required for realizing these principles. From every indication, makers of the plan took interpretation and implementation for granted.[414] This is an important explanation why the desired outcomes from those policies were not realized.

The Ghana Environmental Action Plan of 1994

Although the title of this plan creates the impression that it was a replacement for the 1988 plan, it was essentially a review of the 1988 plan. The Environmental Protection Agency (formerly Council) once again played the role of facilitator, organizing and coordinating the process that resulted in the formulation of this plan. In every respect, the process was similar to what occurred in 1988-89 during the preparation of the 1988 plan.

A task force comprising of experts and bureaucrats in environmental-related sectors (mining, marine and coastal ecosystems, water resources, land management, and forestry) was formed and assigned to prepare a new Ghana Environment Action Plan. This time there was an existing plan (the 1988 plan) to serve as a guide.

Working groups were formed, each concentrating on a specific aspect of the environment. The report of each group was reviewed and revised by the whole task force at a work-session that was attended by representatives of NGOs, local governments, and other experts. The E.P.A. was responsible for preparing the final draft of the plan. Just as was the case in 1988, several important groups of stakeholders; including farmers, timber contractors, traditional rulers, and industrialists) did not participate in the process. The main actors therefore were bureaucrats from the E.P.A., Department of Forestry, Forestry Commission, research institutions, universities, Ministry of Agriculture, Ministry of Mines, and other government agencies.

The 1994 plan was largely a reiteration of the principles and goals of the Environmental Action Plan of 1988. The declared aim for the forestry sector was to prevent exploitative uses "that cause significant or irreparable damage to ecological balance" and to protect nature and habitat, landscape, flora and fauna from the threat of further degradation and depletion."[415] The broad purpose was to "ensure a reconciliation between the satisfaction of people's needs and economic development on one hand, and forest/wildlife conservation and environmental protection on the other hand."[416] Thus the underlying objective was no different from that of the previous plan: protection of the forest so as to ensure its long-term availability as a resource.

The 1994 plan included a review of the then existing forest policy framework; a review that was, in most part, a recount of selected legislation, such as: a) the Forest Ordinance (Cap 157); the law that established forest reserves, b) the Forest Protection Decree, 1974 (NRCD 243), which was largely a catalogue of offenses and their associated punishments, c) the Trees and Timber Decree, 1974 (NRCD 273), which dealt with the protection of certain timber-carrying lands outside reserves, d) the Trees and Timber (Control of Cutting) Regulations, 1950, that contained specifications of the sizes of trees that may be legally felled, e) the Concessions Act, 1962 (Act 124), designed to stipulate the conditions under which the right to exploit timber can be granted, and, f) the Peoples National Defense Council (PNDC) Decree 42 S.34, which dealt with the functions of the various forestry institutions.

In some instances, such as the 1994 Trees and Timber Decree, existing deficiencies of the policy process were pointed out. In others, for example, Cap 157, the relevance of the laws was re-stated and emphasized. Changes effected by new legislation, such as the Concessions Act, 1962 and its follow-up PNDC Decree 42 S.34, were pointed out and discussed.

The 1994 plan also contained a review of the status of previous policy recommendations. On the creation of forest plantations, it was indicated that although in the 1960s the Ghana Land Use Planning Committee accepted a proposal from the United Nations Food and Agricultural Organization for the establishment of a 1.5 million acre national forest plantation and for replanting forests at a rate of 12,000 acres per year, (a proposal that was reviewed and endorsed in 1979), the lack of necessary funding and resources had prevented the achievement of the targets. However, the establishment of forest plantations was re-affirmed as part of Ghana's forest policy.

The architects of the 1994 Plan applauded certain measures, such as, the formation of a National Agro-forestry Committee, the establishment of an agro-forestry unit within the Ministry of Agriculture, and the introduction of various courses in the universities and the Sunyani School of Forestry, as appropriate steps towards promoting agro-forestry, a practice that was considered by experts as useful for maintaining and replenishing the tree cover of lands outside forest reserves.[417]

It was acknowledged in the plan that the 1979 government ban on the export of fourteen species of logs had resulted in the introduction of lesser known species of timber to the export market and allowed Ghana to utilize her forest resources more efficiently. Yet, according to the plan document, the World Bank had proposed a study to review the ban and to explore alternative strategies for conserving the forests.[418] Although the reason behind this World Bank proposal is not clear to this author, the idea seems to confirm the prevalent notion that a primary interest of the World Bank and its affiliates lies in the ability of indebted countries, such as Ghana, to meet their debt obligations. Any validity in this notion would help explain why the Bank would harbor reservations about banning the exploitation of some species of timber, if such a ban would limit the volume of exports from the particular country.[419]

In the tradition of the 1988 plan, the 1994 plan included a review of existing projects in the forestry sector. Also included were proposals for additional projects in such areas as renewable energy, extension of the existing agro-forestry/rural forestry projects, and increased research on forest management.

The chapter that dealt with institutional issues was a mere catalogue of the institutions within the forestry sector and their current responsibilities, followed by a proposal for re-allocating responsibilities to those institutions. These were capped with a brief expression of the need to increase funding so as to alleviate the problems confronting the institutions.

In spite of its title, the 1994 Ghana Environmental Action Plan contained little in terms of new substantive policy provisions. Chapter twenty-three which dealt with the "policy framework," was simply a review of past and existing policies and legislation. Although there were a few instances where very generalized proposals were made about forestry, the plan did not call for any specific action to deal with deforestation.

As already mentioned, the stated objective of the plan, however, portrayed the intent to reconcile the necessity to exploit forest resources so as to cater to the needs of Ghanaian citizens on the one hand, with conservation and environmental protection on the other hand. Based on this alone, the plan can be categorized as primarily exploitative. Policies for protecting of forests and trees and regulating the activities of users of the resource were designed for the key purpose of ensuring the sustained supply of timber.

The Ghana Forest and Wildlife Policy, 1994

This policy marks the first time that bureaucratic domination of the process of formulating forest sector policies in Ghana was tempered by the participation of other categories of actors. The lengthy process through which the policy was drafted suggests a resolve on the part of the Forestry Commission to ensure that the new forest policy of Ghana benefited from the knowledge and concerns of the population at large and therefore stood a better chance of being effective.

The formulation process, which ultimately resulted in this policy, was set in motion in April 1989, and took five years to complete. As part of the preliminary activities for formulating this policy, the Forestry Commission organized two national consultative symposia. The main purposes of these symposia were: first, to review the first national forest policy (the 1948 policy); second, to facilitate input from all sections of the Ghanaian society and international institutions and individuals; and third, to generate public debate on the circumstances surrounding Ghana's forests.[420] The objective of the commission was to provide channels for voicing policy concerns, and establishing a frame of reference for the proposed policies.

Participants from thirty-five institutions attended the first symposium, held in April 1989, including foresters, researchers, scientists, bankers, university faculty, administrators, policy-makers, politicians, traditional rulers, landowners, farmers, representatives from the timber industry and the grassroots of the Ghanaian population.[421] The ideas that emerged from the deliberations were collated by the Forestry Commission and used to prepare a draft forest policy. This draft formed the working document for revising the forest policy of Ghana.

In May 1989, a draft forest policy, written by a technical committee of seven local experts, was circulated among local and international experts and institutions for comments. Recipients of the draft included regional secretaries (administrators), 110 district secretaries (administrators), 110 district assemblies, ten regional houses of chiefs (representatives of the traditional rulers), universities and research institutions, local and international non-governmental organizations (such as the World Bank, the Oxford Forestry Institute, and International Timber Trade Organization), and government institutions that deal with forests, agriculture, and land. There is every indication that great efforts were made to solicit the reactions of a wide range of stakeholders and interest groups.[422]

A second seminar was organized in December 1991 at which forty participants from various forestry institutions studied the draft forest policy. Following this seminar, the Forestry Commission arranged a series of meetings at which personnel from the forestry sector ministries re-examined the draft. The Forestry Commission recommended that the proposals that resulted from this protracted exercise should be adopted by the Ministry of Lands and Forestry.

This draft was subjected to further scrutiny to ensure that, apart from being consistent with national and other sectoral policies, it also reflected the social and economic circumstances of the country. Sub-groups were formed within the ministry to review different aspects of the draft. The Ministry of Land and Forestry also held consultations with relevant sector ministries such as agriculture and environment, the Environmental Protection Agency, donor agencies, and non-governmental organizations to ensure coherence of the contents of the policy. After the draft policy had been made available to activists and interest groups in the environmental and forestry sectors for a final review, it was sent to the cabinet, which gave it approval in December 1994.

Contents of the foreword to this document shed light on the context within which the policy was formulated. There was evidence of a determination on the part of the government to advance new, effective measures for addressing deforestation within the context of the contemporary political, social, and economic environment of Ghana. An emphasis was placed on the "need for specific government guidance and control of forestry activities ......because of changes that had occurred in the nature of Ghana's forests since the adoption of the 1948 Forest Policy."[423] This validates the earlier assertion that, as of 1994, the 1948 Forest Policy was still in effect in Ghana.

The reasons offered for the new policy remained the same as those for preceding policies with three additions: advances in science and technology, institutional changes, and the increasing need for popular participation in resource management. The stated causes of forest depletion and degradation were no different from those listed in earlier plans either. They were: increasing pressure from rapid population growth, leading to the clearing of forests for farming; expansion of logging and surface mining; uncontrolled bush fires; and, growing demand for fuel-wood and charcoal. Given these factors, a new policy was deemed necessary because "it had become obvious that most of the provisions of the old policy could not adequately deal with the totality of emerging issues."[424] In essence, the decision to formulate a new forest policy in Ghana implied an admission on the part of the Forestry Commission that the goals of existing policies had not been realized, even though efforts had been made to make the forest policy process more comprehensive by introducing a series of donor-assisted projects, such as the Forest Resource Management Project and the Forestry Planning Project.

This new policy was intended to provide an "additional basis to develop a national forest estate and a timber industry that would provide the full range of benefits required by the society in a manner that is ecologically sustainable and that conserves Ghana's environmental and cultural heritage."[425] The new emphasis on sustainability, the benefits of the society, and conservation of the cultural heritage of Ghanaians is notable.

The guiding principles for this policy were derived from a variety of sources: the position of the government concerning the need to protect the environment for the benefit of present as well as future generations, provisions of the 1992 Constitution of the Fourth Republic of Ghana (specifically Section 269(1); the new Forestry Commission Act 453 passed in July, 1993); the 1994 Environment Action Plan; the Forest Resources Management Project; international guidelines and conventions such as the Guidelines for Tropical Forest Management;[426] and, the Rio Declaration on Forest Principles.[427]

Contents of the 1994 Forest and Wildlife Policy Act show that, for the first time, the Ghanaian government made the rights of Ghanaians to have access to natural resources for maintaining their livelihoods, and their concomitant responsibility for ensuring the sustainable use of such resources part of the central theme of its forest policy. In line with this, there was an emphasis in this plan on the concept of participatory management; the protection of forests through the development of effective capability of the citizens at all levels for sustainable management of forests. It is apparent that the government had come to terms with the fact that land and forest resources are basic needs from which majority of the citizens derived their livelihoods. Accordingly, the government was attempting to devise a new approach towards dealing with the forces behind deforestation (population growth and its accompanying increasing demand for farmlands and domestic fuels, the need to service Ghana's growing external debts, and the need to generate revenues for development).

In contrast to the previous instances where farmers, timber contractors, and charcoal burners were considered the villains whom the government had to police and threaten with sanctions in order to protect the forests and trees, there appeared to be a shift towards facing the reality of the socio-economic circumstances of Ghanaians, and an attempt to deal with deforestation in a pragmatic way. Instead of emphasizing the government's authority and devising policies for controlling the activities of the citizens over land and forests, there was a new approach that focused on the participation of the stakeholders in order to foster the sustainable utilization and management of the forests.[428] The 1994 Ghana Forest and Wildlife Policy therefore, was clearly an extractive policy, the key object being a collaborative approach to exploiting forest resources.

The strategy proposed for achieving the plan's objectives involved allowing market mechanisms to determine realistic product prices, and stimulating specialization and efficiency in resource utilization.[429] There was a proposal to incorporate the operational plans of all the respective institutions involved in the forest policy process into a national plan for achieving the objectives.

The objectives of this plan were wide-ranging. They included:

1. Expansion of forest reserves;
2. Inclusion of unreserved forests under the management of the Department of Forestry, the lead agency responsible for implementing Ghana's forest policies;
3. Revision of resource management standards;
4. Enforcement of resource management plans;
5. Periodic auditing of forest utilization operations to ensure compliance with forest management specifications;
6. Promotion of rehabilitation and reforestation of degraded forest areas;
7. Introduction of environmental impact assessment as a prerequisite for resource management and utilization projects;
8. Creation of incentives for investors to modernize and innovate their plants so as to rejuvenate the timber industry;
9. Deregulation and streamlining of the wood export sector;
10. Encouragement of value-added process and optimum utilization of wood, and the eventual phasing-out of exports of logs and sawn lumber;
11. Development of markets for lesser-used timber species;
12. Training schemes for wood process operators and produce graders;
13. Development of a well-structured local market in order to maximize the utilization of harvested timber;
14. Emphasis on research and the adaptation of research findings to the realities of the local environment;
15. Promotion of public awareness and involvement in conservation of forests through education programs, promotion of agro-forestry, dissemination of research information, and the organization of fairs, seminars and trade promotion events;
16. Development of consultative and participatory mechanisms to enhance land and tree tenure rights of the local populations;
17. Promotion of tree planting programs;
18. Strengthening the institutions dealing with forestry matters, for example, through reorganizing the Forestry Department into an autonomous agency, promoting inter-agency cooperation and coordination, and developing a long-term master plan to guide implementation of the policy and strategies;
19. Cooperation with international entities, trade associations, private interest groups, and non-governmental organization in order to forge a concerted effort towards achieving sustainable utilization of forest resources;
20. Review of existing legislative instruments;
21. Provision of adequate funding to ensure continuity in forest resource management activities;
22. Implementation of human resource development programs to improve capability in the sector institutions; and,

23. Establishment of suitable database systems and information linkages to facilitate decision-making and policy analysis.[430]

A clear omission was the usual emphasis on legislative and institutional frameworks for monitoring the activities of would-be violators of forestry laws. Instead the policy was focused on collaboration between the government, its institutions, and the private parties concerned. The comprehensive nature of the objectives suggests that the policy-makers took into account all aspects of the deforestation problem. In terms of the approach for implementing this plan however, this policy conforms to earlier policies and plans. Even though the principle of participatory management is upheld in this policy, and the equitable distribution of costs and benefits among the principal stakeholders - the Department of Forestry, landowners, local communities, and concessionaires - is advocated, an emphasis was still placed on the actions of the government and the activities of the bureaucracies in realizing solutions to the deforestation problem, a clear contradiction. In fact, the first statement in the foreword of this policy document alluded to the necessity for "specific government guidance and control of forestry activities in Ghana."[431] Evidently, the government was not in the position to relinquish its control over the lands, forests, and the wealth it has historically derived from them.

Furthermore, this plan was documented simply in terms of objectives with no indication of the specific strategies or means by which those objectives could be realized.[432] In addition, there was no assignment of specific responsibilities for realizing the various objectives to any specific agency. It is apparent from these facts that the modalities for interpretation and implementation of the plan were to be determined by the bureaucratic establishment.

No specific information about the rate of deforestation in Ghana since 1994 is presently available, and four years may be too short a period of time for a reliable assessment of the results achieved by the 1994 plan. Yet, the fact that government leaders and environmentalists continue to sound the alarm concerning increasing deforestation suggests that there has been no abatement in the problem since the 1994 policy was adopted.[433]

Strategies for Implementing Deforestation Policies in Ghana:
The Use of Acts, Decrees and Regulations
It was indicated in the introduction that acts, decrees, and regulations have been the main instruments for pursuing forest policies in Ghana. Policing of forest reserves and non-reserved forests remains the principal activity of the Department of Forestry, the lead agency responsible for implementing the government's forest policies. Some of the public policies have been used to define forest-related crimes and offenses, as well as procedures for obtaining permission for usage of forest resources. Others, such as, the Environmental Protection Council Decree 1974 (NRCD 239), The Ghana Forestry Commission Act, 1980, and The Forestry Commission Act, 1993, have been used to establish

new commissions and agencies, and to re-organize existing ones in the forestry sector.

Overall, the tone of these edicts suggests that, over time, Ghanaian governments have resorted to the use of threats of punishment and the use of force to enforce deforestation policies. The Trees and Timber Decree serves as a good illustration of this. Article 2 of this Decree states; "No person shall cut or fell any growing tree for export in log form or for conversion in a mill unless he has first registered a property mark at the office of the Chief Conservator of Forests...." Article 8 states: "No person shall buy, sell, export, or be in possession of any log which is not duly marked in accordance with the provisions of this Decree," and Article 11, a provision that stipulates punishment for contravention, states that "Any person who contravenes or fails to comply with any of the foregoing provisions of this Decree shall be guilty of an offense and liable on summary conviction to a fine not exceeding C5,000 or to imprisonment not exceeding five years or to both."[434]

The Forest Protection (Amendment) Law, 1986 which amends the Forest Protection Decree, 1974 is also a catalogue of "forest offenses" and their related punishments. Article a of this law states that any person who:

1. Fells, uproots, lops, girdles, taps, injures by fire or otherwise damages any tree or timber;
2. Makes or cultivates any farm or erects a building;
3. Causes any damage by negligence in felling any tree or cutting or removing any timber;
4. In any way obstructs the channel of any river, stream, canal, or creek;
5. Hunts, shoots, fishes, poisons water, or sets traps or snares;
6. Subjects to any manufacturing process, collects, conveys, removes any forest produce;
7. Pastures cattle or permits any cattle to trespass; shall be guilty of an offense and liable on summary conviction to a fine not exceeding C10,000.00 or to imprisonment not exceeding five years or both.....[435]

The philosophy behind implementation is evident from the contents of the series of laws and regulations, especially their authoritarian tone that suggests that Ghanaian deforestation policy-makers have acted on the premise that the citizens would object to the policy goals and the means of achieving them.[436] As such, the sole effective means of achieving those goals is the use of threats and force. An important responsibility of the Department of Forestry therefore has been to arrest offenders and, in cooperation with the police, prosecute them in the court of law.

It is important to note that this approach, especially, the stern tone of the edicts and their format of rules and prescribed punishments for infringements, are a legacy of the colonial era. The large number of edicts suggests that the threat of punishment has remained a key means of maintaining the compliance of citizens with the prerequisite conditions for realizing the goals of deforestation policies.

Criticisms of the Deforestation Policy Process in Ghana

A common conclusion that has been drawn by critics of Ghana's deforestation policy process is that, given the overall historical, cultural, economic, and political environment of Ghana, the problem will remain unsolved unless the strategy for addressing it changes. Such criticisms have touched on subjects such as the content of the policies and the implementation process, viz., enforcement of the laws, the procedure for establishing forest reserves, etc. These issues will be examined forthwith beginning with colonial era policies. Colonial era policies are revisited because they remain relevant at the present, being the foundation upon which future policies have been built.

Overall, the earliest colonial authorities made a false start when the Crown Lands Bill of 1894 was enacted. This bill was conceived and designed with a total disregard for traditional indigenous forestry conventions and customary land tenure practices. It was intended to vest what was considered by the colonial rulers as "waste and uncultivated forest lands" within the Colony in the British Crown.[437] Strong opposition from the indigenous people on the grounds that there was no such thing as waste or unoccupied lands in any part of the colony, forced the authorities to withdraw this bill.

A successor to the Crowns Lands Bill, the Lands Bills of 1897, was also abandoned following an equally strong protest by the indigenous people who viewed it as a means by which the colonial government was going to appropriate their land. Considering the tone and contents of future forest policies in Ghana, it is clear that these earliest forest laws set the standard for future forest policy formulation and implementation. Early colonial forest policies also set the tone for the position taken by the future traditional rulers and the citizens of Ghana concerning government policies on lands.

The interpretation that the indigenous people gave to these early laws and the successes they achieved in opposing them, led the colonial government to abandon them. A legacy of the colonial era, however, was that it helped to establish a culture of suspicion and a determination on the part of Ghanaian citizens to be on the guard so as to resist any government actions that appeared to interfere with their rights to land and forests.

History, therefore, helps to explain the present disconnection between forest policies and their outcomes in Ghana, because, overall, subsequent policies have retained, to varying extent, the restrictive and punitive tone of the earlier ones.[438] The tradition whereby the government has maintained an exclusive authority over forests, and assumed the right to administer the exploitation of the resources therein, while all other stakeholders (landowners, farmers, communities that reside in forest areas or near forest reserves, concessionaires, operators of timber industries, etc) played a marginal role has proven ineffective and "unworkable."[439]

In the face of objections and resistance of citizens who are affected by Ghana's forest policies, the content of past policies shows that over the years it has become increasingly necessary for the government to resort to more laws and more severe punishments in its efforts at enforcing its policies. This, however, has proven unsuccessful because it has not been possible for the government to allocate the resources required - personnel, equipment, finance, etc. - for the policing work required.[440]

Other criticisms have targeted the obsolescence of forest laws, particularly, the Forestry Ordinance of 1948 which still remains the core of forest laws in Ghana even though the fact that it is outdated has been well documented.[441] This 1948 Ordinance was based on the Indian Forest Act and ideas borrowed from other British colonies.[442] In spite of various amendments to it, and the number of new acts and decrees that have been enacted over the years to complement it, it remains the gist of forest laws in Ghana. The Forest Protection Decree, 1974 (NRCD 243), for example, clearly, was framed in consonance with the old edicts that were introduced in the colonial era. Its contents suggest that an offense is committed only if a forbidden act is committed within a forest reserve. This perception conveyed by the 1974 Decree has been deemed the reason why non-reserved forests have been so wantonly destroyed.[443] Some critics have suggested that until new laws that would drastically revise existing ones and take cognizance of social, economic, and political realities are introduced, the goal of conserving Ghana's forests will remain unattainable.[444]

Another critique of the contents of forestry policies in Ghana deals with the actual intentions of the policies.[445] As was mentioned earlier, forestry policies in Ghana have been in the form of rather generalized declarations of intents. But the specific actions for pursuing the declared policy objectives have been seldom explicitly declared.[446] In addition, the arbitrary manner in which land rights have been established, the procedure by which forest reserves have been established, the process by which rights to exploit timber have been assigned, and the method of enforcing forest laws all suggest that the motive of the government for pursuing forest policies has been simply to control the timber industry for two purposes: to ensure that the government remained a principal beneficiary of the revenue generated, and to ensure that adequate supplies of timber existed for future exploitation. These are the grounds for classifying forest policies in Ghana as extractive. From every indication, the government's actions have not been for promoting the quality of the environment or the interest of the citizens who depend on the forests. Forest policies in Ghana therefore cannot be called protective regulatory policies.

K. Tufuor provides a perspective on the organizational structural dimension of the problem.[447] In his opinion, the main defect of the existing forest policies is excessive centralization that has strengthened the hand of the central government and vested all rights with respect to timber or trees on any lands outside forest reserves in the office of the President. This policy, according to Tufuor, has rendered the traditional rulers, who, prior to colonization, were the custodians and administrators of lands, mere nominal owners whose rights to shares of land revenues are more or less *ex-gratia* from the national government. He further submits that the non-consideration of the local economy and the non-involvement of private citizens and other stakeholders in the formulation and implementation of forest policies has fostered "confrontation, bitterness, and resentment"[448] on the part of those who have been affected by the policies.

Other reasons advanced by Tufuor for the failure of deforestation policies relates to the lead agency responsible for administering the government's forest policies: the relative low status of the Department among other government agencies, handicaps it has faced over the years, and the functional procedures it has followed in its operations. Evidence has been provided in this dissertation to indicate that for a long time, forestry was treated as a "residual appendage" of the Ministry of Agriculture of which it was a part. There was no improvement when it was transferred to the Ministry of Lands. Furthermore, the greatest emphasis has been placed by this agency on management of reserves as a source of timber. Hence, extraction has had a historical priority.

Given the fact cocoa has been a major source of external earnings for Ghana, and that increased production of this crop as well as foodstuffs to feed the growing Ghanaian population generally occurred at the expense of forests, conservation of forests has, for a long time, not been considered a priority, even though deforestation had been recognized as a serious problem.[449] Instead, in spite of government policies that state otherwise, in practical terms, forests have been regarded simply as a source timber, game, and vegetation cover that ought to be cleared when land was needed for farms. Tufuor arrives at a similar conclusion when he states that "forestry in Ghana has been adversely affected by the economic considerations that favored the export-oriented timber industry and also by the low competitive position of forestry versus other forms of land-use - especially cocoa farming ...."[450]

An important conclusion that emerges therefore is that most forest degradation "is caused directly or indirectly by the effects of policies outside the forestry sector rather than by forestry policy itself."[451] Such a conclusion means that deforestation should not be perceived to be a problem that is strictly confined to the forestry sector. Rather, it is a multi-dimensional problem, the scope of which extends beyond forestry into the domains of population growth, urbanization, agriculture, external trade, infrastructure, supply of fuel for both domestic and industrial purposes, etc. This reality, in practical terms, has not been given due consideration in the formulation and implementation of forestry policies in Ghana.

Problems that arise in the enforcement of the laws intended to curtail deforestation are another basis for criticizing the deforestation policy process in Ghana. It has been suggested that the protracted procedure for constituting forest reserves under the Forest Ordinance has rendered decisions to establish new reserves a clarion call for farmers to invade the proposed reserve lands and establish farms before the reservation is effected, thus defeating the purpose of the exercise.[452] In the area of enforcement, the Ghanaian police and judiciary have been cited as partly responsible for the ineffectiveness of deforestation policies. The assertion has been made that because of their ignorance about ecology, the extra-economic value of trees, and the laws that regulate access to forest resources, the police and judiciary have, in most cases, either ignored the provisions of existing forestry laws or failed to impose the appropriate punishments that would serve as deterrents to those who break forestry laws.[453] This issue will be discussed further in chapter eight as part of the reason why the Department of Forestry in Ghana has not succeeded at achieving its deforestation policy objective.

Other criticisms have centered on the inadequacy of well-trained personnel, facilities and equipment in the Department of Forestry;[454] the multiplicity of agencies and institutions dealing with the forestry sector (a factor that often creates conflicts and confusion),[455] and the lack of commitment of traditional rulers and their subjects to the goal of forest conservation.[456] A closer look will be taken of these problems in subsequent chapters.

The outcome of these deficiencies is that several factors that account for the depletion of the forests in Ghana have not been given due attention by the national leaders and policy-makers, citizens, law enforcement authorities, and the judiciary. A consequence of this confluence of factors is that individuals and businesses engaged in forest-depleting activities have not been confronted with the types of constraints and incentives that would compel or encourage them to give adequate consideration to forestry conservation.

Conclusion

The above discussions have pointed to the fact that the policies that have been introduced for addressing the problem of deforestation in Ghana, apart from being too simplistic in terms of treating forestry in virtual isolation from cultural, economic and political realities of the Ghanaian environment, have also been autocratic, placing excessive emphasis on rules and regulations.

Until 1983 when the first of two environmental action plans were adopted, there had been no attempts at approaching forest policies from a comprehensive perspective. The continued application of old laws and edicts in spite of the political and economic changes that have been occurring in Ghana, and in spite of the well-known fact that the problem of deforestation is getting worse, implies that political leaders and the bureaucracies (the two groups of actors who have dominated the policy process) have failed to change their attitudes towards the forestry sector. Given the forestry scenario, this would be a necessary step towards an innovative approach that would generate effective policies.

The following three chapters will deal with the two groups of key actors in the forestry policy arena. Chapter six will focus on the heads of government and their aides, chapter seven will focus on bureaucracies that deal with the forestry sector, and chapter eight, the Department of Forestry, the lead agency for implementing deforestation policies in Ghana. The objective is to examine the motives, relationships, and the manner in which actions of the individuals concerned shape forestry policies and influence their outcomes. It is anticipated that the analyses will reveal additional reasons for the disconnection between policies for combating deforestation and their outcomes.

Chapter 6

The Power and Dominance of Heads of Government and Politicians Over the Ghanaian Forest Policy Process

.

It was indicated in chapter four that factors prevailing in the external environment (the contextual setting) of the forest policy process in Ghana have had significant impact on decisions and actions of the key actors involved in the process. Consequently, it was argued that in addition to the internal environment, the external environment of the policy process (comprising of historical, political, economic, and other factors, both of local and foreign origins) is equally significant as it conditions the internal environment of the policy process. In so doing, the external environment influences the outputs of the Ghanaian policy process. It was argued that the external environment helps to explain the disconnection between policies to combat deforestation and their outcomes in Ghana.

This chapter is devoted to an important component of the internal environment of the deforestation policy process in post-colonial Ghana: heads of governments and their closest aides (See the explanatory model, Fig 1, in Chapter one). The objective here is to examine the politics of the public policy process for the purpose of characterizing the executive-centered structure of formal-legal authority (power) in the post-colonial era. In connection with this, and in line with the hypotheses of this research, the discussion in this chapter covers the status, roles, and activities of Ghanaian politicians. It deals particularly with the extent to which government officials and their closest advisors have been able to dominate the forest policy process and influence the content and outcomes of forestry policies since independence, with the effect that the policies have reflected their preferences. The information and analyses provide additional insight into the outputs of the deforestation policy process as well as some explanations for the failure of those policies to achieve their desired effects.

The external environment of the policy process will be referred to, where necessary, in order to clarify the workings of the internal dimensions of the policy process.

Ghanaian Heads of State: Their Status and Role in the Policy Process

The attitudes of Ghanaians towards politicians, especially, their expectations regarding the authority and functions of their heads of state, help to explain the status and role of the executive branch of government in post-independence Ghana in the public policy process. Seeds of separation between the rulers and the ruled were sown during the colonial era. As was shown in chapter three, the colonial governor and his European aides dominated the political landscape, freely executing their will without any significant restraints, or any input from the indigenous people.

Chiefs and individuals who cooperated with the rulers were "rewarded" at the rulers' own discretion, and those who resisted, or failed to win the rulers' favor, were punished. The government was appointed without the consent of the indigenous people, and it was therefore not accountable to them. It was shown how the colonial authorities consolidated their hold on the Gold Coast through the establishment of a highly centralized administrative and bureaucratic apparatus, located at the colonial capital, and controlled by foreigners. The policy process began and ended with the government.

This colonial government created an atmosphere that caused Ghanaians to develop a particular mind-set concerning the power of government leaders. Their concept of the government was an all-powerful institution with absolute authority to rule.[457] Since the colonial government was not installed by the free will of the indigenous people, nor required their mandate to rule, the indigenous people, overall, did not have much power to influence its decisions or actions. The colonial government acted in such a way that suggested it was endowed with resources and the power to provide modern amenities, jobs, and favors or penalize those considered to be uncooperative or "enemies" of the government.

Most Ghanaians, citizens and political leaders alike, have not discarded this prevalent notion about government cultivated at the time power was handed over to the new Ghanaian leaders at independence. As Naomi Chazan has stated, at independence the political apparatus in Ghana was "Ghanaianized but not democratized."[458] An effect of this colonial legacy is that local creativity and initiatives in the areas of politics and public policy have, to a large extent, been blunted.[459] This colonial legacy was coupled with the fact that Ghana experienced a mere six years of internal self-rule (from 1951 to 1957) prior to the granting of independence. A consequence of this has been that, four decades after independence, a large number of Ghanaian citizens regard the constitution of their country as something in the abstract, the concern only of the prime minister or president. Many of them do not know that it is they who must exercise control over the government and see to it that their rights to life, security and liberty are protected.[460]

In her analysis of the sources of political power in Ghana, Chazan makes an observation in connection with this situation by corroborating A. K. Ocran's position that, to Ghanaians, "government means the head of state and his cabinet." Individuals holding high public offices are viewed as the "focal point of policy formulation and implementation, and hence, directly representative of, and responsible for, the performance of the state."[461] This perception of government differs from that held by the citizens of western democracies where interest groups, lobbies, and sometimes private individuals play direct and significant roles in shaping public policy.

Paul Nugent also advances this "social contract" explanation of the Ghanaian policy situation in his explication of the centralization of power, and the resulting huge amount of power wielded by Ghanaian heads of government.[462] (A "social contract" notion of government assumes reciprocity between a government and its citizens.) Nugent explains that Ghanaian attitudes towards the government have been based on the assumption that state intervention would further the interests of the whole community. A point of view that emerges from the literature is that most citizens have considered it prudent to allow those in power to command enough authority so that they can operate without much hindrance.

Results of the exploratory survey conducted by this researcher, however, indicate otherwise. Overall, the opinions about the government's land and forest policies and its approach towards managing those resources were mixed. For example, even though all the employees of the Department of Forestry expressed the opinion that, that department, the lead agency for implementing the government's forestry policy, was doing a good job in the area of forestry policies, only 50% of those within the private timber industry felt that way. That view was held by as little as 7% of the farmer respondents. Furthermore, although overall over 70% of respondents in the survey felt that it is necessary for the government to do much more to protect the forests of Ghana, at the same time, 33% felt that government regulations concerning forests were excessive. These findings show that opinions concerning the government's forestry policies are mixed and not necessarily supportive of the government.

In advancing the same arguments that had been previously made by Pinkney,[463] Nugent[464] uses Ghanaian cultural constructions of hierarchy and authority to explain why the dominance of the national political leadership has endured. Both Pinkney and Nugent explain that there exists a Ghanaian tradition of trust and respect for authority, with the consequence that politicians have been able to assume enormous power. These scholars conclude that the nature of relationships between the state and the society in Ghana derives from the culture of the people. These writers, as well as Chazan, suggest that culture holds the key in an explanation of why the holders of power at the state level in Ghana have dominated the policy process to the exclusion of civil society, rendering politics in Ghana undemocratic.

There are however grounds to dispute such conjecture. On the face of it, the traditional Ghanaian political leaders (chiefs of various categories) command enormous authority and deference, their status embracing both the physical and the spiritual. Yet, these rulers have not been autocratic or domineering. The traditional Ghanaian political system comprises a sophisticated hierarchical arrangement that accommodates all families and clans (even non-indigenes). It includes structures that facilitate access of all citizens to the policy-making process. The chief's court includes sub-chiefs and elders from the various clans and families who serve as the de facto representatives and spokespersons of all the people at those high levels of political authority. Chiefs never make important decisions independent of their elders.[465]

This arrangement guarantees that policies that are advanced by the leadership reflect the fears, wishes, and concerns of the grassroots citizens, irrespective of status. Traditional Ghanaian rulers are accountable to their subjects. Because leaders who fail to perform according to the popular wish can be dethroned, they value the counsel and opinions of the elders and subjects. In fact, the traditional systems render the rulers obligated to grant audience to all subjects who wish to register their grievances.[466]

The foregoing demonstrates that the traditional Ghanaian political system is democratic, albeit patrimonial in some respects. The notion that the dominance of contemporary Ghanaian political leaders derives from the indigenous concept of authority is erroneous. To the contrary, decision-making is democratic, both directly and indirectly. Evidence abounds of Ghanaians registering their objection to and resisting colonial government policies that did not give due consideration to the concerns of the people.[467] The indigenous system of democracy contrasts with the type being practiced by the post-colonial constitutional regimes that merely allows the citizens the opportunity to make periodic choices of government leaders, but it does not really enable them to have any impact on the public policy process.[468] The conflict between the policy-making approach of national leaders and that of the indigenous system is one of the reasons for the disconnection between policies for combating deforestation and their outcomes. (This issue, raised in chapter four during the discussion on legitimacy of the government, will re-emerge at various points later as a basis for the lack of support for the government's forestry policies.)

The gist of this chapter is that there has been a disconnection between policies for addressing the problem of deforestation and the outcomes of such policies because of one important reason: the post-colonial political leaders in Ghana have maintained the colonial legacy of authoritarianism and an approach towards public policy-making that has marginalized the citizens. Consequently, contrary to the practice under Ghanaian traditions, where there exist channels of communication to facilitate access by all members of the community to the highest levels of political authority, and enable them to express their opinions about policies, citizens in post-colonial Ghana have been denied the means of making inputs into the government policy-making process. As such, the policies and the means of their implementation have not reflected the values, traditions and concerns of the citizens, but the preferences of the authoritative president or prime minister (whatever the case may be) and his closest political collaborators and advisors.

In this regard, the political system in post-colonial Ghana has maintained the colonial era subjugation of the traditional institutions. Political power has been concentrated in the hands of the head of state and a few individuals. These new leaders have sought to impose policies that are rife with laws and regulations, which, for all intents and purposes, are designed to deprive the citizens of their perceived traditional rights to land and forest resources. The more the population grows resulting in increasing scarcity of land and forest resources, the more the restrictive forest policies become threats to the means of livelihood of the citizens. The dissociation of the grassroots citizens from the forestry public policy machinery, together with the content of the policies that have been introduced, and the mechanisms for implementing them have alienated the citizens from the government. These, in addition to the failure of Ghanaian governments to deliver services and amenities and fulfill the expectations of the citizens, have undermined the legitimacy of the governments and diminished its ability to execute policies.

The following sections provide an historical account and analysis of how the heads of government in Ghana and individuals occupying the highest echelons of power have been able to dominate the public policy-making process. The account will substantiate the hypothesis proposed in this research, as well as the argument advanced in the preceding pages that executive dominance of the policy-making process in Ghana is one of the most important features of the internal environment of the policy process.

Executive Dominance of the Policy Process During The Nkrumah Regime
The Ghana independence constitution of 1957 provided for the separation of powers between the three arms of government: the executive, the legislature, and the judiciary.[469] The power to make appointments to various public offices (including those to the cabinet), and administer the government was assigned to the prime minister. Parliament (the legislature) was given the role of lawmaking, appropriations, and, review and authorization of public policies. Because of this tripartite division of power, the constitutional arrangement appeared to be capable of checking possible excesses on the part of the three institutions.

In spite of this, the first prime minister, Dr. Kwame Nkrumah, and the ruling Convention Peoples' Party (C.P.P.) were able to manipulate the constitution in such a way that, by 1966, when that government was overthrown, political power had become over-centralized in the hands of Nkrumah and an inner circle of party operatives.[470]

In the first place, this development was possible because of the substantial majority of the C.P.P. in the parliament, and the ability of the prime minister to take advantage of this majority to promote policies he personally preferred. It was also possible for the government to exploit loopholes in the constitution in order to advance the leaders' wishes. Secondly, Dr. Nkrumah was able, using the massive propaganda machinery of the C.P.P., as well as the government-controlled Ghanaian media, to promote a personal charisma, and ultimately, by 1960, to institute a one-party state. In the absence of other parties, or any form of significant opposition, the head of state and the ruling party increasingly dominated politics and public policy.

Dr. Nkrumah's personality has often been cited as the main reason for the immense power he was able to acquire, and the dominance he was able to exercise over Ghanaian politics and policy-making.[471] He did not entertain any opposition or individuals who sought to compete with him for power. Under the circumstances, by 1960, his personal socialist ideals and vision had become the C. P. P.'s ideology. "Consciencism,"[472] his unique type of socialist ideology, was meant to be total, embracing the whole life of Ghanaian citizens. In pursuit of this ideology, he set up political machinery that was intended to encompass every facet of Ghanaian society.

Nkrumah's dream and ambition was for Ghana to be transformed into an industrialized nation within the shortest time possible; a nation where the social and economic needs of all citizens would be fully catered for.[473] In the foreword to the Seven Year Plan for National Reconstruction and Development, for example, Nkrumah defined the aim of the plan as:

> to establish... a strong and progressive society in which no one will have any anxiety about the basic means of life, about work, food and shelter; where poverty and illiteracy will no longer exist and disease is brought under control; and where our educational facilities provide al the children of Ghana with the best possible opportunities for the development of their potentialities.

Such a declaration helped to reinforce the Ghanaian perceptions about the functions and abilities of government as had been fostered during the colonial era.

The strategy Nkrumah chose for realizing these objectives was to establish a comprehensive centralized administrative machinery that permeated all sectors of the Ghanaian economy.[474] The political and administrative set-up that was established during this regime ultimately reverted Ghana to a situation resembling the colonial system. Policy decision-making was over-centralized at the political top, where Nkrumah personally commanded virtual absolute authority.[475] As Colonel A. A. Afrifah recounted after the 1966 overthrow of the Nkrumah government, "...Nkrumah combined the functions of supreme legislator, supreme administrator, and supreme judge.... His was the sole power to approve or to abrogate legislation,..."[476] Because the C.P.P. held no congresses and had no independent decision-making leadership apart from Nkrumah himself or his chosen officials, the party remained a mere instrument that was used only to advance the leader's will.[477]

It is important to note that the almost limitless power acquired by Nkrumah during Ghana's first republic was also facilitated by the structure of the 1960 Republican Constitution.[478]   This constitution was written by a C.P.P.-dominated legislature, which had been convened as a constitutional drafting committee. The 1960 constitution literally solidified the highly centralized state that had been initiated after independence.[479] It became an instrument by which Nkrumah was able to translate his belief that Ghana needed emergency measures under a totalitarian kind of leadership[480] into reality.

Parts of that document serve to illustrate the constitutional basis of Nkrumah's power. Article 9 conferred the executive power of the state in the office of the president. The president's extreme independence was assured by a clause that stated that: "....in the exercise of his functions, the President shall act in his own discretion and shall not be obliged to follow advice tendered by any other person."[481]   Article 15 also illustrates the high status conferred on the president in relation to his cabinet. It gave the president power to appoint ministers "to take charge, under his direction, of ministries and departments he would assign to them. Under Article 15 (6), the president could at any time revoke the appointment of a minister. Although provisions of the 1960 constitution assigned legislative power to both the national assembly (legislature) and the presidency, each with clearly defined functions, in practice, the legislature was subordinate to the president. The president, through the C.P.P., could personally appoint legislators for the constituencies (electoral districts). He also had the power to veto bills and give directions by legislative instrument, with or without the assent of the national assembly.

Simply put, in reality, "there were no substantive limits"[482] to what Nkrumah could personally do in Ghana. A radio broadcast at the dawn of February 24, 1966, the day Nkrumah's government was overthrown in a *coup d'etat*, affirmed this state of affairs.[483] The broadcast referred to "the concentration of power in the hands of one man" who had been running the country as his "own personal property."[484]   In essence, by 1966 the colonial system had been replaced with an even more centralized personal rule with power over the state residing in one man.

Political Power at the Regional Level
The Ghana independence constitution of 1957 contained a provision for Regional Constitutional Commissions assigned to design administrative structures for the then five regions in the country. However, using the power he had acquired, and the support of a weak legislature, Dr. Nkrumah, as prime minister, personally appointed individuals to the post of Regional Commissioners. This was done amid protests from the opposition that it was in conflict with the constitution. Through the regional commissioners, who all belonged to Dr. Nkrumah's inner circle of supporters, and whose tenure of office was at his discretion, Nkrumah secured personal control of political and economic developments in the whole country.

Contrary to the spirit of the constitutional provision that called for a decentralized government and the appointment of heads for the regions with some authority to administer the regions,[485] heads of the regions were appointed on the basis of political considerations with the objective of bringing rebellious regions firmly under control of the central government.[486] The result was that the C.P.P. and the regional governments had become fused together. The regional heads of the party occupied the offices of the former colonial provincial commissioners, and presided over the administrative hierarchy just as was the practice during the colonial era.

According to an account by Biswal,[487] the reports of the Regional Constitutional Commissions that were formed to make recommendations on the membership of regional administrative institutions were amended by the ruling party in such a way that the proposed regional assemblies were diminished, becoming mere advisory bodies. Opposition boycott of the regional assembly elections, instead of putting pressure on Dr. Nkrumah to abide by the constitution, rather enabled the C.P.P. to take control of all five assemblies, and paved the way for the government to revise the 1957 constitution to suit the wishes of Dr. Nkrumah. Control over the assemblies also eventually allowed the C.P.P. to abolish the regional assemblies and vest legislative power over the whole country in the Nkrumah-controlled national assembly.[488]

Power and the Policy Process at the Grassroots Level

The C.P.P. implemented an elaborate scheme by which it established branches at most of the local levels in Ghana. By 1966, the party had evolved into an enormous hierarchy with the president at the top and local executives at the lowest levels. The party displaced local institutions such as farmers', workers', youth, and women's organizations as the most dominant political institution throughout the country. Fuelled by government resources and facilities, local branches of the C.P.P., under the leadership of "a new class of poorly educated commoners,"[489] were able to maintain a high profile and mobilize the leadership of traditional institutions. Ultimately the president succeeded at establishing his power base in majority of the localities in Ghana. His power as leader of the massive C.P.P. super structure, and as head of the national government, gave him utmost control and a dictatorial capacity over public policies throughout the country. The public policy process in Ghana under the Nkrumah regime therefore became highly simplified, politicized, and exclusive, dominated by he himself and, to the extent he allowed, by the national, regional and local operatives of the C.P.P..

The result of this deliberate centralization of power was that the state was isolated from the traditional participatory processes. Because of the absence of institutional structures that were meaningful, and to which the local population could identify, it was impossible to incorporate the needs, knowledge and opinions of the local population into policies and programs.

The State Lands Act, 1962 (Act 125) is an example of a government policy during the reign of Dr. Nkrumah that diminished the import of local customs and needs concerning land and forests. This law commuted the customary tenure of land and allowed "foreign" individuals and businesses, who could afford it, to acquire lands and utilize them for maximum economic gain. Apart from the fact that the citizens at the grassroots considered the policy as to be an abrogation of their rights to land, it also enabled the new "owners" to exploit the lands according to their own wishes, with little concern for their future utility.[490]

Inevitably, hostility towards the government intensified at the grassroots level, especially among those who claimed customary rights to lands, which, to them, had been sold by the government. Whatever level of legitimacy existed for the regime prior to this act, was even further diminished after its implementation, because to most Ghanaians, the government posed a threat, not only to their traditions, but also to their livelihoods. As has been discussed earlier, so far as grassroots citizen support and cooperation were concerned, limited legitimacy of the regime doomed to failure the policies and programs originating from the president's office.[491]

The foregoing denotes the environment in which forest policies were adopted and implemented during the early years of Ghana's independence. Over-concentration of political power in the hands of Dr. Nkrumah and his closest confidants, and the domination of this centralized authority rendered the national government as the sole source of public policies. The national government also commanded the authority to implement the policies. In an environment where opposing views had been subdued, and where an important section of the stakeholders of forest policies, the rural population, had been alienated from the government, there existed enormous obstacles toward realizing the objectives of those policies. This issue will be examined further in chapter eight.

Significance of the Ghanaian Bureaucracy Under Dr. Nkrumah

The authority of Dr. Nkrumah and his associates nevertheless, the Ghanaian bureaucracy remained an important factor in the public policy process, playing a significant, albeit low profile role in the formulation and implementation of policies. As will be discussed further in the next chapters which deal with the roles and activities of bureaucracies in the forestry sector, the skills and knowledge possessed by Ghanaian civil servants, coupled with the need on the part of the government for advice and for an administrative machinery for interpreting and implementing policies, have helped this institution to secure a lasting role for itself in the policy process.[492]

Public Policy-Making Under the National Liberation Council (1966-1969)

The Ghanaian military in 1966 has been described as "singularly ill-equipped to govern."[493] Accounts of the early days of National Liberation Council (N.L.C.) rule indicate that members of that junta had very hazy ideas about the demands of government and their responsibility as rulers.[494] Remarks made by Colonel Afrifah, a member of the Council, almost a year after that government had assumed power, depicted the mind-set of the new rulers. According to him, members of the new government were aware that, as soldiers, they were not cut out to govern. Therefore, they simply thought they could stand in briefly and put things right as quickly as possible. They had no other program other than that of removing the Nkrumah government, securing themselves in power, and eventually, handing over authority to a new civilian regime.[495]

Under the circumstances, although the N.L.C. had ultimate authority over policy-making, it relied on the civilian bureaucracy and the intelligentsia as the principal instruments for policy-making and implementation.[496] For the first few months after the 1966 coup, Ghana was virtually administered by civil servants. Over time, this role was expanded. Although senior military officers were appointed to head government departments and the administrative regions, and the N.L.C. remained the *de jure* executive and legislative authority,[497] in practice, bureaucrats were the sources of policy ideas. Bureaucrats were also responsible for translating such ideas into official policies, and for their implementation. In reacting to the suggestion that the N.L.C. was a government of civil servants, Major General Ocran, another member of the junta, observed: "I have yet to see a government in any part of the world which does not rely on civil servants for advice or even for initiating policies."[498] He went on to admit that a government becomes one that is run by civil servants "if those at the helm have no clear-cut policies."[499] This, in effect, was a reiteration of Afrifah's acknowledgement of the military's inadequacy in the area of government, and the prominent role civil servants were called upon to play.

Reports that no strong bonds ever developed among members of the N.L.C., and that relationships among them were, in fact, cold, suggest that the atmosphere required for a concerted action to formulate effective policies did not exist.[500] Other factors that undermined effective policy-making under the N.L.C. emerge from Ocran's report that some of the leading military officers had no enthusiasm for the political positions they occupied, and that members of the military government could not cope with the task of combining military with government responsibilities. An overall lack of political leadership qualities, knowledge, dedication, patriotism and planning skills, tribal differences, and disagreements over methods of implementing policies compromised the policy-making ability of the N.L.C.

The absence of a strong leadership that enjoyed the recognition and support of the members was another aspect of the N.L.C.'s policy-making impairment. Because its chairman, Lieutenant General J. A. Ankrah, was not the original planner of the coup, his rank and official status did not count for much. He could not command obedience from his colleagues. Under the circumstances, the government was not able to perform independently of the indispensable civil servants who filled in the vacuum, assumed positions of influence, and "virtually ran the ministries."[501]

Dominance by the executive arm of government over policy-making in Ghana was not altered under the N.L.C. in spite of the prominence and expanded role of bureaucrats and some members of the elite class in the policy process. Policies were issued in the name of the N.L.C., bearing the signature of its Chairman. In spite of their lack of expertise or interest in policy matters, it was clear who was in charge of the government. There was little question about the power the council members had either to reject or alter policies they did not favor. The appointment of subordinate military officers to head the administrative regions (as Regional Commissioners) and government corporations (as Managing Directors) demonstrated the level of control the N.L.C. had over the country.

Although civilians were retained as District Administrative Officers, their role in the policy process was restricted to implementation. They took their directives from their superiors at the national and regional levels, and reported back on all aspects of their activities. In conformity with the tradition established by the colonial administrations and the preceding Nkrumah regime, the grassroots population played an extremely limited role in the policy process. The N.L.C. recognized the status of traditional political authorities and accorded chiefs a greater amount of prestige than had the Nkrumah regime. Farmer organizations, timber merchants associations, and all other institutions were allowed increased freedom to operate. Even though it became easier for chiefs and other citizens to express opinions about public policy matters, direct participation in the land and forestry policy process was restricted to the government and to the bureaucracy.

Power and Policy-Making During the Second Republic (1969-1972)

The constitution of the second republic of Ghana provided for a prime minister as head of the executive branch of government, and a cabinet to be chosen by the prime minister, subject to the approval of parliament.[502] In effect, this constitution was intended to restore power to the legislature to the extent that it could influence the composition of the executive branch. This, apparently, was designed to prevent a replay of the structure of authority under Nkrumah, during which he was able to assume virtually limitless power because of his control over the cabinet. There was a provision in the second constitution for elected regional councils and regional administrations presided over by central government-nominated chairpersons. The second constitution also categorically called for a decentralization of public administration and public decision-making.

Events during this short-lived regime, however, were contrary to the intentions of the constitution. The actions of the Prime Minister, Dr. Kofi Busia, denoted his own perceptions concerning the levels of power vested in his office. Decision-making, which was intended to be consultative, became increasingly centralized.[503] The presidency was a purely ceremonial office, and in the absence of another institution or office that would challenge the executive branch, the prime minister quickly consolidated decision-making powers in his office and in his advisors.

Contrary to the spirit of the constitution, the Local Administration Bill, prepared by the Progress Party which dominated the legislature, gave the Busia government control over both regional and district administrations. The power scenario of the Nkrumah era was replayed, and the bill assigned to the prime minister the authority to appoint chairpersons of regional and district councils. In addition, the instruments of appointment based the tenure in office of such appointees upon "such terms and conditions as may be specified by the prime minister."[504]   Consequently, regional and district administrations were effectively placed under the control of the executive.   The historically hierarchical nature of Ghanaian public policy apparatus was therefore perpetuated, with politicians occupying the top level of government with bureaucrats at the national and local levels, advising the politicians and undertaking the intricate and technical tasks involved in policy formulation and implementation.

The opposition parties were rendered largely irrelevant in the area of public policy-making.   Because of the Busia government's demonstrated excessive intolerance for opposition, legislators from the minority parties, especially the National Alliance of Liberals (NAL), the main opposition party, were effectively shut out from the policy-making process.   The comfortable majority enjoyed by the Progress Party facilitated this exclusion of members from other parties, and enabled Dr. Busia to pursue policies that expedited his position, and that of his top party colleagues, as the dominant actors in the policy arena.[505]

Even though the Busia government appeared to have taken charge of public policy-making and diminished the status of the bureaucracy, the entrenched position and level of influence of the bureaucracy in Ghana was demonstrated, even reinforced, during this regime when the firing of the manager of Ghana National Trading Corporation (GNTC), a state-owned commercial enterprise, was overturned by the Ghanaian Court of Appeal.[506] In fact, it is widely held that, the dismissal of 568 bureaucrats and public servants by the Busia government eroded much of its popularity among the citizens and helped to trigger the *coup d'etat* that terminated its tenure.

Although the Busia regime professed to be a genuine democracy, and declared the majority rural population to be the focus of its political and economic policy, no significant forestry policy initiatives were taken during its tenure. But as has been shown, there was no significant change in the character of the Ghanaian policy process during this time.

Political Power and the Policy Process Under the National Redemption Council/Supreme Military Council (NRC/SMC) Regime, (1972-1979)

The prevailing penchant for centralized decision-making in previous regimes of Ghana was further enhanced during the NRC/SMC regime. Because of this government's plans for long-term rule, military officers were appointed to administrative and managerial posts in almost every sphere of the political and economic activity.[507] Military participation and control of the policy process extended to all levels of the government, far beyond what prevailed under the NLC, the first military regime.

In spite of this inordinate permeation of the country's policy and administrative institutions, the style and the tools with which the NRC government set about the task of administration were no different from those used by previous governments. Ghana continued to have a highly centralized administration, with all major policies originating from the central government. The NRC/SMC held ultimate power and took credit for all public policies. The relatively junior officers appointed to head the regions and public corporations did not possess much policy-making authority, but simply took orders from the government authorities in Accra and reported back to them.

Because of their lack of expertise in running the government, the NRC/SMC members, like their NLC predecessors, were heavily dependent on the civil service. Bureaucrats were again called upon to take charge of the highest-level government functions. Just as was the case under the previous military government, the bureaucrats were very important to this government, because they remained indispensable for running the country. Yet, because the NRC/SMC yearned to take fuller control of the country, its chairman, General Ignatius Akyeampong as well as other high-ranking military officers, actively interfered in the work of the bureaucrats, overruling them and imposing their preferred policies.

From the beginning of its tenure, the NRC/SMC appeared to possess a united front. To the outside observer, it appeared the members of the government made policy decisions as a group. But, before long, it had become obvious that the chairman wanted to take a leading, more authoritative role. The reshuffles that occurred between 1972 and 1975 caused this junta-like appearance to dissolve. More and more, power became consolidated in the hands of the chairman. His authority in decision-making was enhanced in an October 1975 purge during which the NRC was dissolved and replaced with an SMC. The original members of the government were retired, dismissed or arrested, and the then Colonel Akyeampong assumed a new, higher rank of General. These events assured that members of the new government were subordinated to the chairman. The overall outcome was that it became clear who was the head, and in control of policies.[508] From then on, General Akyeampong became the principal decision-making authority.[509]

It is on record that General Akyeampong was intellectually less endowed than his military contemporaries. He is reported to have had no time or inclination for hard facts or administrative details,[510] and because he was not capable of undertaking the task of running the government, he relied even more critically on civil servants and intelligence aides. This was in spite of his lust for power, and his desire to take control of the public policy machinery.

General F. W. K. Akuffo, vice chairman of the SMC, offered an insider's account of the extent to which General Akyeampong wielded power soon after the latter's overthrow. He stated, *inter alia*, that the channel of communication between Akyeampong and the rest of the government had virtually broken down, and the whole of the governmental activity had become a "one-man show."[511] Furthermore, according to Akuffo's account, Akyeampong had unilaterally varied decisions that had been made collectively at SMC meetings, and made certain important decisions without consulting or informing his colleagues.   These revelations portray the level of concentration of policy-making, and the extent to which an individual dominated the process between 1972 and 1979.

The Armed Forces Revolutionary Committee (AFRC) Era –1979

The SMC was overthrown in a military *coup d'etat* in December 1979 and replaced by the Armed Forces Revolutionary Council (AFRC).   This new government, comprising relatively young and junior soldiers, quickly declared that its intention was to remove what they referred to as the corrupt, inept, and dictatorial SMC regime and save Ghana from further political, economic, and social deterioration.   Fulfilling their promise to return Ghana to constitutional rule quickly, they organized elections and installed a new constitutional government, led by Dr. Hilla Limann, within a year.

Because of the brief tenure of the AFRC, and the fact that this government made no major policies or took any actions concerning forestry and deforestation, very little commentary is devoted to this military regime.   It is worth noting, however, that in overall policy-making, the AFRC maintained the pattern that had been set by the previous military regimes.   Policies were introduced in the form of decrees issued on behalf of the committee by Flight Lieutenant J. J. Rawlings, the chairman, who, from every indication, occupied a commanding position relative to his colleagues in the government.   The bureaucracy retained its role as facilitator of government policies while the citizens as a whole remained outside the fringes of the policy process.

Political Power and Policy-Making Under the Third Republic (1980-1981)

As the foregoing accounts indicate, the public policy apparatus that has been inherited by successive regimes in Ghana has been designed or re-shaped to allow the executive to dominate the policy process.   Although the constitution of the Third Republic, like preceding ones, had been designed to promote the active participation of the legislature and the citizens at large in public affairs, under the regime of Dr. Hilla Limann, it was manipulated in such a way that the status of the executive became enhanced.[512]   The absence of a formal set of decision-making rules in Ghana had fomented the propensity towards centralization of decision-making under every regime.

President Limann's government, though short-lived, quickly emerged as a pure repetition of the past trend.   Constitutional devices for participation were neglected or circumvented, and where they appeared to operate, it was sporadic at best.   No major forest policies were adopted under this regime, but this government also upheld a Ghanaian tradition, under which the central government remained disproportionately strong, and state decision-making remained exclusively in the hands of the head of state.[513]

The People's National Defense Committee (PNDC) Era: 1981-1992

Within less than two years the Limann government was overthrown in coup led once again by then retired Flight Lieutenant Jerry Rawlings.   One of the main grievances of Rawlings and his associates in the new regime was that the Limann government had performed in a manner that was no different from its predecessors, in the sense that in addition to the prevalence of rampant corruption by public officials, the grassroots Ghanaian population had remained marginalized from the public policy process. They found the dominance of Ghanaian politics and public policy making by the politicians, bureaucrats and other elites to the exclusion of the other classes; especially the workers and farmers unacceptable.

Consequently, one of the declared objectives of the PNDC regime was to give the military and the grassroots citizens of Ghana a more direct role in the government. In this regard, it represented a break with the established trend of central government control. Flight Lieutenant Rawlings revealed this on the day of his take-over by declaring: "The military is not to take over. We simply want to be part of the decision-making process."[514] He maintained that only a revolution would include the masses, the farmers, the police, the military, and a cross-section of Ghanaians in the public policy-making process.

However, after a brief period in which there appeared to be moves towards dismantling the existing policy apparatus and replacing it with one that included a wider range of stakeholders, the PNDC quickly emerged as the supreme political authority. In conformity with the tradition of military regimes, the PNDC became the exclusive policy body, ruling by decrees.

The encouragement given by this government to the formation of "People's Defense Committees" and "Workers' Defense Committees" at all levels (in towns and villages, educational institutions, offices, factories and military and police barracks, etc.) initially appeared to be a genuine attempt to promote popular grassroots participation of Ghanaians in the public policy process. Rawlings' vision for these committees was that they would become vehicles for mass participation. The idea was to provide ordinary Ghanaians with forums for debating national and local issues and taking collective decisions; an alternative to parliament. To Rawlings, this was a better option than the concentration of power at the top of Ghanaian governments. But it turned out that these committees did not have any policy-making role under the PNDC. They were simply charged with 'defending the revolution' and exposing corruption and sabotage. Before long, they had lost their revolutionary fervor as well as their relevance in the area of public policy-making.[515]

The PNDC government was plagued by political instability and ideological differences.[516] Its members had strong differences over policy matters, and by 1982, three ideological factions could be identified within the government. A series of reshuffles and terminations culminated in Rawlings eventually emerging as the leader of the most powerful faction. Between 1982 and the end of the PNDC rule, his dominance of public policy-making was unquestioned.

Rawlings' power and influence were not confined to national level policies alone; it extended to the local levels as well. The establishment of Regional and District Assemblies to serve as instruments for decentralizing the government and enabling local policy-making and administration did little to curtail the reach of the authority of the head of state. All regional secretaries (chief executives) were appointed directly by Rawlings. In addition, a third of the district assembly members as well as all district secretaries (chief executives) were government appointees. It was therefore possible for Rawlings to control policies at the local level.[517]

Although the status and role of the Ghanaian bureaucracy was threatened during the early days of the PNDC when Workers' Defense Committees challenged the authority and legitimacy of top civil servants and other elites, before long, the indispensability of bureaucrats and skilled individuals was evident. In spite of revolutionary rhetoric of the government that suggested the role of bureaucrats had been diminished, before long, bureaucrats had reverted to their previous status as advisors to government leaders, and implementers of policies.[518]

Political Power and Policy-Making in the Fourth Republic of Ghana

Just as was the case under the three previous republican constitutions, the constitution of the Fourth Republic of Ghana, inaugurated in 1992, endows the presidency with substantial executive powers. The president has the prerogative of appointing ministers, and hence, his cabinet who are assigned a mere advisory role under this constitution.[519] The NDC government was the first to rule Ghana under this constitution. It was the party formed by Rawlings in 1991 in his bid to retain political power as his PNDC government implemented a plan to hand over power to a constitutional government. The NDC therefore was purely an offshoot of the PNDC; a coalition of the workers, youth, farmers, women, and other movements that had emerged during PNDC era. This party took office in 1992 after winning both the presidential and paliarmentary elections.

Using the powers of his office, as dictated by the constitution, the first president to assume office under this constitution, Flt. Lt. Rawlings, was able to appoint fifty-four of his eighty-one ministers and deputies, as well as twelve of his sixteen cabinet ministers from outside the parliament.[520] Provisions of the constitution that enable the president to appoint non-members of parliament as ministers, essentially, have allowed policy decision-making to take place outside of a democratic framework. It is widely held that confidants of the president wielded considerable political influence, even though they held no public offices.[521] President Rawlings' reputation and stature from the AFRC and PNDC eras have made him an even more authoritative figure.

The boycott of the 1991 elections by the minority parties to protest against rulings and policies of the Electoral Commission helped to enhance Rawlings' power by creating a virtual absence of an opposition in the parliament. The result was that during the first term of his constitutional rule (1992-1996), it became possible for the government to make decisions without the traditional pressure and involvement of the opposition parties. This situation remained largely unchanged through the second term of that government.

Concentration of power in the hands of Rawlings and those at the top echelons of the government was to such an extent that even the ruling National Democratic Congress (NDC) party apparatus played a highly limited role in the articulation of public interests.[522] Pinkney has suggested the party's "lack of the means, and possibly the will"[523] to generate policy ideas as the reason for this.

Rawlings' charisma, and deriving from it, the trust his followers and numerous Ghanaians held that he would pursue the best policies for the country were two other reasons why opposition to his government's policies has remained weak.

The NDC government, up to its second term of office, had been pronounced "unaccountable"[524] to the citizens of Ghana.   Decision-making has been restricted to the president and few confidants.   Pinkney maintains that even though some ministers made claims concerning their influential roles in policy decision-making, either directly or through consultation, the were lingering suspicions that they occupied the peripheries of the policy arena, their participation limited to thier reactions to already formulated policies.[525]

It is important to note that in spite of President Rawlings' dominance of the public policy-making process, the status of the Ghanaian bureaucracy did not diminish as an important actor in this process. Although the size of the civil service has been consistently reduced under Ghana's Structural Adjustment Program,[526] bureaucrats continue to occupy their traditionally critical place as experts, advising the government leaders and implementing public policies.

Conclusion

Throughout the preceding discussion about political power and the role of the heads of state in policy-making in Ghana since independence, it has been emphasized that heads of state (the executive branch) in the succession of governments, have dominated the public policy-making process. The conditions necessary for individual citizens and groups within the Ghanaian civic society to actively participate in or have an input into the public policy process have not been realized.   Whereas the four military governments ruled by decrees that were issued from the offices of authoritative leaders, under constitutional regimes, legislatures have been under the control of more powerful executive branches, and manipulated to an extent that they have merely played an ancillary role. Therefore, overall, legislatures in Ghana have been ineffective as public policy making institutions.

By implication, in the area of policy-making, centralization of power and of the process by which polices have been made, have caused the state to become isolated from the larger society. The failure of popular participatory structures to develop into forms that are meaningful and accessible to the citizens, even where they have been sanctioned by constitutions, means that, on the whole, Ghanaian citizens have had very limited influence over the policy process. They have therefore not been able to make the necessary inputs into the content of public policies, nor have they been able to shape the outcomes of the policy process.   Under the circumstances, there are grounds to argue that policy decisions in Ghana palpably lack legitimacy, as this concept is known in the West.

The bureaucracy in Ghana, on the other hand, has endured, and maintained its importance and indispensability in the policy process.   In spite of severe political instability that has characterized much of post-colonial Ghana, the excessive power of political leaders, and occasional threats to their status, the Ghanaian bureaucracy has survived and established itself as a key institution in the public policy process.

Significance of the Scenario
There is no apparent reason to think that deforestation policies are exempt from the policy scenario described above.   On the contrary, there are adequate grounds, given the questions that have been raised in chapter four about the legitimacy of Ghanaian governments, for suggesting that deforestation policies in post-independence Ghana have not necessarily reflected what the citizens would consider to be their wishes and the needs.

Given the political circumstances that have been described in this chapter, the approach taken by the Ghanaian government in the post-colonial era to implement policies for addressing deforestation, has been the imposition of laws and regulations, and the use of threats, fines and other punishments to enforce them. (See chapter 5) The overall outcome has been a general non-compliance on the part of the citizens and, consequently, a failure to realize the goal of combating deforestation.

The following chapters focus on the bureaucratic institutions that are directly involved in the administration of the deforestation policy process in Ghana. The objective is to analyze their mandates, functions, and deficiencies, and determine how these attributes help to explain the disconnection between policies for combating deforestation and their outcomes.

Chapter 7

The Roles of Bureaucratic and Non-Governmental Institutions in Determining the Outcome of the Forestry Policy Process

In the following two chapters attention will be devoted to the bureaucracies that are involved in the forestry sector of Ghana. As has been shown, bureaucracies have been important components of the internal environment of the forestry policy process. It was hypothesized that the multiplicity of bureaucracies within the forestry sector is one of the reasons for the Ghanaian government's inability to realize its deforestation policy objectives. Another speculation of this researcher was that the competing, often conflictive and contradictory mandates and missions of these bureaucracies have thwarted the achievement of the goals of those policies that have been instituted. An analysis of the mandates, functional characteristics, activities, and the impact of these institutions on the deforestation policy process will help to verify the above hypotheses.

Bureaucratic Institutions Within the Forestry Sector of Ghana

There are six bureaucratic institutions within the forestry sector of Ghana: the Forestry Commission, the Lands Commission, the Timber Exports Development Board, the Forest Products Inspection Bureau, the Department of Game and Wildlife, and the Department of Forestry. (See Figure 3, Page 138). The first five will be addressed in this chapter. The Department of Forestry, the lead agency responsible for implementation of Ghana's deforestation policies, is set aside for exclusive attention in Chapter Eight. Another institution that will be examined to determine its impact on the forestry policy process is the Environmental Protection Agency (E.P.A.). The name E.P.A. suggests an institution dealing with policies and actions to safeguard the environment of Ghana. The analysis will therefore be geared towards assessing its protective regulatory role in the deforestation policy crisis.

The missions of the institutions considered in this chapter support the inference made in chapter five that there are two contradictory and conflictive categories of forestry policies in Ghana: those promoting exploitation and sale of forest resources; and, those assigned to address deforestation. In accordance

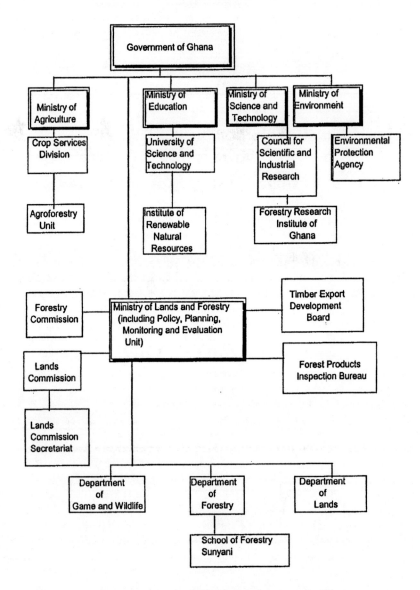

Source: IIED, <u>Study of Incentives for the Sustainable Management of the</u>
<u>Tropical High Forest of Ghana</u>, (London: IIED, 1994), p. 34.

Fig. 3

Government Agencies Operating in Ghana's Forestry Sector

with this, the bureaucracies have been placed into two groups: those promoting the extraction of timber resources (the extractive bureaucracies), and those assigned with protecting the forests and regulating activities within them (the protective regulatory bureaucracies). The discussion in this chapter will be organized according to this categorization.[527]

This chapter also contains a review of the roles, and assessment of the relevance of institutions that are not part of the government establishment. Entities such as business interests, traditional rulers, local governments (district assemblies), and non-governmental organizations (NGOs) are examined so as to assess their relevance in the policy formulation and implementation process.

Extractive Bureaucracies Within the Forestry Sector of Ghana
The Lands Commission
The Lands Commission is the principal institution responsible for managing lands in Ghana. A subsidiary of the Ministry of Lands and Forestry, it is a semi-autonomous body whose mission is to implement the government's land policies. Its functions include the administration of deeds, registration of records on lands, and, until 1991, the granting of logging concessions. The last function, authorization of timber extraction, and determination of the conditions for such exploitation, accorded this commission a strategic role in the timber industry. Considering that timber extraction has been identified as a leading cause of deforestation, the membership and activities of this commission deserve close attention.

The Lands Commission includes seven representatives from various land-related bureaucracies. Notably excluded, however, is a representation from the Department of Forestry, the lead agency responsible for implementing the government's deforestation policies. The justification for this policy is not clear. However, the exclusion of the Department of Forestry probably deprived the commission of information and ideas that might influence the members' attitudes about deforestation and what could be done to address it.

Until 1991, the Lands Commission played a central role in the forestry policy process; determination of how much of the forests in Ghana had been eliminated through tree felling. Its function involved accepting applications, evaluating them, and awarding concessions to timber contractors. The commission performed this function even though it did not have adequate field staff for monitoring the activities of concessionaires, nor staff who possessed the requisite expertise in forestry.[528]

Since 1991 the granting of timber concessions has been the responsibility of the Timber Lease Committee appointed by the Minister of Lands and Forestry. The committee, chaired by the head of the Concessions Unit in the Department of Forestry, makes recommendations to the Minister on the allocation of concessions. Other members include:

- Two representatives of the Ministry of Lands and Forestry;
- A representative each from the Forest Products Inspection Bureau and the Timber Exports Development Board;

- A representative of the timber industry;
- The Executive Secretary of the Lands Commission;
- Regional Forestry Officers in charge of regions within the forest zone;
- The Working Plans Officer of the Department of Forestry;
- The Financial Controller of the Department of Forestry; and
- The computer analyst of the Department of Forestry.

Although the transfer of the function of concession granting from the Lands Commission appeared to have deprived it of a high-profile role in a crucial and lucrative sector of the economy, that action did not necessarily eliminate the influence of the commission in that area. The Lands Commission, through its representation on the Timber Lease Committee, and its status as the principal agency responsible for land management in Ghana, has remained highly influential in the timber concession matters.[529]

The activities of the Lands Commission need to be seen from the context that timber has been a leading source of revenue for a succession of financial-strapped Ghanaian governments. As was indicated in chapter four, the governments have historically been under immense pressure to generate revenues for debt servicing, government operations, and development programs. With this background, and given the fact that the tenure of the commission's members was determined by the government, one can deduce that a leading objective of the Lands Commission has been to award more concessions so as to boost the government's revenues.

Another basis for the Land Commission's interest in promoting the timber industry can be found in the direct benefit the commission itself stands to gain from the industry. The commission keeps 10% of the total revenues it helps to generate from royalties and rents paid by the timber industry.[530] This arrangement serves as an incentive for the commission to award more concessions in order to increase exploitation of timber and thereby boost its own financial resources.

The Lands Commission Act of 1993 required that the commission follow directions given by the Minister of Lands and Forestry.[531] Given this arrangement and the means by which the members are appointed, there is little doubt as to the amount of political influence it has been subjected to from the highest levels of government. There is also little doubt that, under the circumstances the threat of deforestation and the need to address it has not been a significant concern of the commission.

The above conjectures can be substantiated with statistics on the trends in Ghana's timber trade (discussed in chapter four), which suggest that in spite of the statements by heads of state and leading politicians concerning the need to address deforestation, the exploitation and export of timber and forest produce has continued, even increased, in Ghana over the years. The Lands Commission has remained an instrument for controlling access to timber resources and facilitating commercial exploitation. Thus, an important outcome of its activities, as it helps generate revenue for the government, has been the elimination of forests.

Although the Timber Lease Committee has been responsible for the award of concessions since 1991, the Lands Commission retains considerable influence over the process. On account of its involvement in record keeping of all land transactions and management of all lands in Ghana, the commission plays a prominent role in decisions on authorization of access to forests. A high-ranking officer of the commission, the executive secretary, sits on the Timber Lease Committee.

Even though the Department of Forestry has a strong representation on the Timber Lease Committee, there is no indication that the Department has been able to adequately sway the government's policy of limiting timber exploitation so as to preserve forests.

Three factors appear to account for this. First, just as is the case of the Lands Commission, individuals appointed to the Timber Lease Committee owe their tenure to the Minister of Lands and Forestry. It is important to emphasize that, being a politician, the minister's decisions and actions stand to be politically motivated. Hence, the committee, in all likelihood, is filled with those who are inclined to endorse the government's objectives.

Secondly, the committee does not have the final decision-making authority. It only makes recommendations to the minister with who rests the decisions for the allocation of concessions. The ultimate decision-making authority on the matter therefore rests with the politicians, who, as has been mentioned, are more inclined towards generating revenue than preserving the forests.

Thirdly, the interests of the timber industry, as well as the two institutions devoted to the promotion of the timber industry (the Timber Exports Development Board and the Forest Products Inspection Bureau), are represented on the committee. Hence, there is pressure from within the commission to promote exploitation of timber. Statistics showing increases in Ghana's timber exports (See Table 4.2 and Appendix 4.7) suggest that commercial interests and the politicians through the Timber Lease Committee and the Lands Commission have achieved their objective of promoting the timber industry at the expense of the forests.

Timber Exports Development Board (TEDB)

The Timber Exports Development Board is a government-appointed corporate body comprising seven members: three from the timber industry, one each from the Forestry Commission and the Forestry Department, and, the executive heads of the Forest Products Inspection Bureau and the TEDB. As is the case with the Forestry Commission and the Timber Lease Committee, representation of the timber industry on the TEDB is politically very significant. Through such representatives, private timber interests have been able to exact some influence on the Ghanaian policy process as it affects the exploitation of timber. A member of this board is selected by the government to serve as the Managing Director.

As its name implies, the TEDB is responsible for promoting sales and exports of timber and timber products from Ghana. It was established in 1985 under P.N.D.C. Law 123 after the Ghana Timber Marketing Board, which previously performed those same functions, had been dissolved amidst allegations of rampant fraudulent practices in the industry.[532] Establishment of the TEDB was part of efforts by the government to revamp the timber industry. Consequently, one of its statutory functions is to promote "the rapid development and servicing of export markets."[533]

The board operates directly under the direction of the Minister of Lands and Forestry. It conducts business directly or through agents, as it pursues its mission of exploring and developing foreign markets for Ghanaian timber and thereby generating revenues for the government.

The TEDB is funded through a levy of 1% of the value of timber and timber product exports. This method of funding serves as an additional incentive to the board to promote timber exports. Under the arrangement, the board is placed in a position where it would be inclined to endorse policies and actions that would boost exploitation of forest resources.

No specific statistical trade information that directly links the activities of this board with the rate of timber exploitation, and as such, the board's contribution toward the loss of forests in Ghana was available to this researcher. Neither was there any information that specifically shows the extent to which exports of timber and forest produce, nor, in connection with them, the revenues realized by the Ghana government in recent years, have been affected by the TEDB. The non-availability of such information makes it difficult to directly and categorically stipulate the effects of this board's activities on Ghana's deforestation problem. Evidence of increased exports of timber and wood products from Ghana in recent years (See Table 4.2 and Appendix 4.7) however, suggests that the government's drive to increase the export of forest products has yielded results. In addition, three factors: the mandate of the TEDB; the fact that three out of seven members of the board represent the timber industry; and, the source of the board's funding, suggest that the board has a vested interest in increasing the exploitation and export of timber and forest products.

In the absence of any significant reforestation in Ghana, the existence of the TEDB, an agency that promotes the exploitation and sale of timber through its mission of developing foreign markets, is a direct contradiction of the government's own declared policy of controlling deforestation. This is because the only way by which the board can achieve its mission is to directly undermine the drive to address deforestation in Ghana by promoting the felling of trees.

Forest Products Inspection Bureau (FPIB)

The Forest Products Inspection Bureau (FPIB) was first inaugurated in 1934 as the Timber Service under the Department of Agriculture, then responsible for forestry. For a period of five years (1954 to 1959), it operated under the Ministry of Trade. The terms of reference of the Timber Service, and its location, albeit briefly, within the Ministry of Trade, imply that it was intended to regulate the timber industry. It was part of a mechanism used by the colonial government to maintain control over the exploitation and sale of timber.

As part of the measures taken in 1985 by the PNDC government to eliminate corruption and revamp the timber industry, P.N.D.C. Law 123 was passed to establish the FPIB.[534] It is a regulatory institution administered by a government-appointed chief executive officer who operates under the terms of policies made by a six-person government-appointed board of directors. In 1994, four out of the six board members came from the private timber industry.[535] The presence of timber business interests on the board implies a direct influence by private sector.

It is difficult to rationalize the appointment of individuals with personal and business interests in timber to sit on a board that is assigned the responsibility for regulating that same industry. The influence of private timber interests on the FPIB implies that, for all intents and purposes, the board has been a "captive agency", a "bureaucratic clientele" of forces that stand to reap political and economic benefits through the continued elimination of Ghana's forests.

The government's role in making appointments, and the business background of the majority of the board's membership are indicators of the extent of political and business domination of this board. Because of this domination, the FPIB has served as an instrument used by the government to help achieve its economic objective of generating revenues from timber. In playing this role, it has been a vehicle for promoting the timber industry and hence exacerbating the deforestation problem.

In addition to establishing and implementing rules for grading and handling export-bound timber, the FPIB recommends regulations and procedures for establishing the sources of such logs and timber products. In performing these, the role of the bureau reaches beyond regulating the timber industry, extending to the granting of timber concessions. It is important to note that the executive head of the FPIB sits on the Timber Lease Committee as well as the Timber Exports Development Board, two agencies that have been shown to be involved in promoting and developing the timber industry.

This FPIB plays no direct role in the deforestation policy process per se. But in performing its functions, it attempts to maintain control of the industry and eliminate black marketeering, theft, and corruption. To achieve these objectives, the bureau has focused on two objectives: ensuring that only authorized persons get involved in the industry; and, verifying the sources and destinations of timber and wood products. This focus does not justify the claim by the bureau that it helps to control deforestation.[536] Rather, all the facts indicate that it is part of the machinery used by the government to ensure that the timber that generates much needed revenue for Ghana is properly accounted for.

Three criticisms have been leveled against the FPIB.[537] First among them is that the bureau does not adequately investigate the background of applicants for timber business registration as is required. As such, the FPIB process "has been reduced to automatic registration upon the payment of a fee."[538] Consequently, there is an over-proliferation of registered timber enterprises in Ghana, with firms that are incapable of making efficient use of forest resources being are allowed to operate.

The second criticism concerns its system for inspecting transit forest products. It has been reported that because the inspection coverage is inadequate, the activities of unlicensed chain-saw operators and traffickers of illegally cut timber have not been controlled.[539] As such, a large number of trees are routinely felled and sold illegally in Ghana and abroad.

The third criticism is that loopholes in the issuance of log measurement certificates have allowed timber merchants to illegally cut underage trees in forest reserves and mark them as if they originated from off-reserve areas where it is legal to cut them.[540]

These criticisms point to the real mission of the FPIB. Contrary to the claim made by this agency, the manner by which licenses have been issued to non-qualified merchants, and the inadequacy of the inspection process, support the contention that the FPIB has been an instrument for promoting the exploitation and trading in timber. Its activities have not regulated the industry. Rather, FPIB system is rife with loopholes and flaws that have helped to create access to timber, thereby directly contradicting the government's declared policy to pursue deforestation as a policy objective.

Department of Forestry

The Department of Forestry will be discussed in greater detail in chapter eight. Nevertheless, it is necessary to comment on its functions as they promote the exploitation of forest resources and hence, augment the deforestation problem.

Historically, the Department of Forestry had been assigned the responsibility for protecting the forests of Ghana. However, a review of its mandates as well as its functions indicate that, in large measure, it has been a part of the machinery for exploitation and export of timber. An important aspect of the functions of the department is to police forest reserves and protect them from encroachment by unauthorized persons. The department has also sought to prevent farmers and unauthorized persons from felling commercial trees on farmlands. The objective of these activities is to enable concessionaires to have exclusive access to the trees. By implication, the department does not protect the forests and trees for the sake of conservation per se. Throughout its existence, its ultimate purpose has been to support the timber industry by facilitating their exclusive access to trees.

It has been shown earlier in this chapter that, the Department of Forestry, through its representation on various boards, is directly involved, in extractive policy-making at the Lands Department and the Timber Lease Committee. Therefore, because it functions as an active part of the mechanism for promoting the exploitation of timber for export, this agency performs the contradictory role of promoting deforestation through extraction.

It is important to note a point that has been reiterated throughout the foregoing discussions. That is; through promoting the commercial exploitation of timber in Ghana, the activities of the extractive bureaucracies have contradicted the Ghanaian government's declared objective of addressing the problem of deforestation.   The existence of those bureaucracies, therefore, helps to explain why government policies on deforestation have failed to achieve their intended outcomes.

Institutions Involved in the Management of Ghana's Forests

The agencies within this category are the Forestry Commission, the Environmental Protection Agency, and the Department of Game and Wildlife.

Forestry Commission

In accordance with Article 191 of the constitution of the Third Republic of Ghana the Forestry Commission was established under Act 405 of 1980. The Forestry Commission is a corporate body assigned the broad responsibility of regulating and managing "the utilization of all forestry and wildlife resources of Ghana and co-ordination of the policies in relation thereto."[541]   The functions assigned to the commission under the act were wide-ranging, and included:

1.   Management, maintenance, and protection of forests;
2.   Establishment of forest reserves;
3.   Management of all forest lands;
4.   Control of deforestation;
5.   Coordination and conduct of research on conservation of forests;
6.   Manpower-training;
7.   Regulation of the timber industry;
8.   Collection of royalties and revenues in respect to forests; and,
9.   Promotion and marketing of timber and other wood products.

The potential conflict between the ninth function, promotion and marketing of timber and other wood products, and the other eight, which are geared towards conserving the forests, is notable. Given the functions as they stand, the commission was required to perform contradictory activities.

The commission was also made responsible for administering all laws relating to forestry in Ghana. By implication, it was mandated to monitor the institutions within the forestry sector so as to ensure that they comply with existing legislation.   The enormous and wide-ranging nature of these responsibilities clearly rendered the commission incapable of functioning effectively.[542]   In addition, some of its responsibilities overlapped those of other agencies within the forestry sector, a situation that fomented confusion and competition. It is understandable that the new constitutional provision on the Forestry Commission trimmed down its functions.[543]

Section 269(1) of the 1992 constitution of the Fourth Republic of Ghana embodied explicit provisions for the establishment of a forestry commission within six months of the first meeting of the parliament. Subsequently, a new Forestry Commission Act 453 was passed in July 1993 to supersede Act 405 of 1980.[544] Unlike its predecessor, the responsibilities assigned to the new commission under this act were considerably reduced. They can be summed up by the second clause of the act which states: the Commission shall "advise on national policy and practices related to forests.....; and ensure a comprehensive data base on forests and wild life resources for decision-making by related agencies."[545] Overall, the main functions of the commission under the 1993 act are: to formulate national policy, advise the government and other agencies, co-ordinate and monitor the activities of agencies in charge of implementing policies, recommend research priorities, and educate the public. Hitherto included activities such as the management of forests and lands, control of deforestation, regulation of timber production, control of the number of timber mills and factories, promotion of timber on the world market, etc., were excluded.

The mandate of this "new" commission implies that it was conceived as a policy and advisory body that would function at a level higher and above the other institutions within the forestry sector. It is intended to formulate policies, advise the government, and coordinate and monitor the activities of the other agencies.

Composition, Appointment, and Qualifications of Members Of the Forestry Commission

The Forestry Commission Act of 1993 stipulates membership of the commission to include a representative of each of the following institutions: the Ministry of Lands and Forestry; the Ministry of Environment; the National Council for Women and Development; the Lands Commission; the Timber Trade and Industries Association; the Ghana Institute of Professional Foresters; and non-governmental organizations involved in renewable natural resources. The heads of the following agencies are also members: Department of Forestry; Department of Game and Wildlife; Timber Export Development Board; Forest Products Inspection Bureau; Institute of Renewable Natural Resources; Agro-Forestry Unit of the Ministry of Food and Agriculture; and the Forestry Research Institute. One seat is set aside for a representative of the National House of Chiefs.

The political clout of the head of state over this commission is evident from the proviso that he dictates the terms and conditions of appointment of its members. The presence of the Ministry of Lands and Forestry also denotes the influence of that minister, a politician. Added to this political influence is the membership reserved for the Timber Trade and Industries Association, an interest group of businesspersons and corporations whose singular goal is to reap profits through increased exploitation of the resource. Furthermore, two institutions charged with promoting the exploitation and sale of timber products (the Forest Products Inspection Bureau and the Timber Exports Development Board) are represented on the commission. The Department of Forestry, also represented on the commission, has been mentioned earlier as a part of the machinery for promoting the timber industry.

Given this membership, it is clear that overall, this commission includes strong forces that are inclined to promote the exploitation and export of timber. This is a contradiction that signifies the lack of a genuine commitment towards achieving the forest conservation aspects of the tasks given to the commission. This may explain why, in spite of the host of information available to the commission and the number of recommendations staff have made concerning the causes of deforestation and the means of addressing it,[546] the commission has not made any significant impact on the deforestation problem in Ghana.

Functions of the Forestry Commission

Under the auspices of the Forestry Commission, several research reports have been compiled and disseminated about the forests of Ghana. The commission has also been actively involved in policy formulation. As was shown in chapter five, it was this commission that initiated and organized the series of seminars and forums that resulted in the production of the Ghana Forest Policy of 1988. The policy process is designed such that policy recommendations from the commission must be forwarded to the minister of Lands and Forestry for transmission to the highest political levels of the government

This has been the fate of the Ghana Forest Policies of 1988, 1991, and 1994. There is no indication that those policies lacked the support of the head of state or other leading politicians. To the contrary, public comments by President Rawlings suggested that he fully endorsed the recommendations contained in the plans. There is also evidence that the government adopted the forestry-related principles contained in the Ghana Environmental Action Plans of 1988 and 1994. The Policy Planning Monitoring and Evaluation Division of the Ministry of Lands and Forestry proceeded to prepare an impressive Forestry Development Master Plan in 1996 as a strategy for guiding implementation of the 1994 Forest and Wildlife Policy.

Other specific actions that have been taken include:
1. Those designed to curb bush fires;[547]
2. Requirement of "certificates of sustainability" to accompany all timber and forest product exports;
3. The regulation requiring environmental impact assessments before the commencement of all development projects and activities that could affect the quality of the environment;
4. Promotion of agro-forestry;[548]

5.   Encouraging private businesses and communities to grow and manage forest plantations;[549] and,

6.   Introduction of environmental education.[550]

Based on a recommendation made after a review of the forestry sector in 1985, the government proceeded to initiate a $64 million Forest Resources Management Project in 1989.[551] In addition, an F.A.O. Forestry Planning Project was introduced in 1990. The purposes of both programs include reforming the forestry sector, improving the management of the forest resources, and promoting rural forestry. Under these programs, steps were taken to re-organize the Department of Forestry, the lead institution for protecting the forests so as to make it more effective at managing Ghana's forests.[552] In spite of all these activities, the expected outcomes have not been realized.

The leading explanation for this, deriving from information presented thus far, is the existence of powerful forces that promote the destruction of forests. Such forces include: i) an economically and politically strong timber industry which has succeeded at influencing policies and thereby promoting the continued extraction of timber; ii) a dominant government that, in spite of its declared goal of preserving forests, has encouraged and participated in timber extraction for the purpose of generating revenue;[553] iii) a growing demand for firewood and charcoal to meet the fuel needs of a rapidly increasing population; and, iv) the expansion of farmlands.

Environmental Protection Agency (EPA)

The name of this agency conveys the impression that it is concerned with all aspects of the environment in Ghana. But to the contrary, throughout its almost thirty years of existence, its involvement in the forestry sector has been minimal.

The EPA (originally called the Environmental Protection Council, until the E.P.A. Act 490 of 1994) is a government-appointed institution. The act assigns the agency an advisory role. Its policy-making council comprises representatives from government agencies whose areas of responsibilities relate to the environment. Regarding its main responsibilities, the decree that originally established it, emphasized advising, coordination, and ensuring that environmental safeguards are observed during the execution of development projects.[554]

The responsibilities of the agency were broadened under Act 490 to include the following: ensuring compliance with environmental impact assessment procedures in the planning and execution of development projects; liaising with other agencies and local administrations to control pollution and protect the environment; advising the Minister of Environment on environmental issues; promoting research for the maintenance of sound ecological systems; and promoting effective planning in the management of the environment. Deforestation has been listed in the EPA Act as one of the environmental problems the agency should deal with. The 1988 and 1991 Environmental

Action Plans of Ghana, prepared under the direction of the EPA, contain sections that deal with the forestry sector. Yet, beyond these, there is little evidence of any actions that the agency has taken concerning that sector. Instead, the agency has concentrated on industrial and urban pollution.[555] The focus of its activities has been on monitoring the activities of industrialists, requesting environmental impact assessments of projects, where necessary, enforcing the rules necessary to prevent threats to the environment that arise from development projects, and abatement of health hazards.

Therefore, in the area of forestry policy, the EPA has had very limited involvement and impact. Consequently, this agency has done little to protect the forest environment.

Department of Game and Wildlife (DGW)

This Department was established in 1965 to manage areas that had been earmarked for the protection of animals and the promotion of animal diversity. Its principal responsibility therefore has been to protect and manage lands that have been designated as national parks. Specifically, these functions entail protecting those parks from logging, hunting, and other uses. Reports on the present conditions of parks in Ghana, however, indicate that the Department has not succeeded in this regard.[556] Some national parks are reported to have been logged "as if they were normal forest reserves,"[557] and hunters have operated within them without the requisite permits. The key reason advanced for this failure is logistics.[558] Reports suggest that the DGW is over-centralized and ill-equipped in terms of staffing, training, and facilities, and hence unable to cope with its responsibilities.[559]

Because of the ineffectiveness of the DGW illegal hunting, firewood collection, and timber extraction have continued within the game reserves. In this regard, this Department has failed to meet its responsibility towards the forests of Ghana. There is also no evidence of any role this Department has played in the forest policy process.

The Role of Non-Governmental Institutions

Attention is now being turned to a group of institutions that exist outside the government bureaucracy, but have some connections with the deforestation policy process. In the preceding section, references were made to the fact that timber interests, through their representation on the various policy-making bodies of government institutions in the forestry sector, have the means to influence Ghana's forestry policies. The following analyses will shed more light on this position.

The discussion will also show that, in spite of their potential, institutions such as traditional rulers, local governments, and non-governmental organizations, have had a limited impact on the forestry policy process and its outcomes in Ghana.

Impact of Timber Business Interests

Before Ghana gained independence in 1957, four large foreign corporations dominated the forestry sector.[560] Together with one domestic firm, these corporations accounted for about 80% of log exports.[561] Until 1972, foreign enterprises were granted concessions that entitled them to long-term felling rights at extremely nominal fees and royalties.

This policy was terminated in 1973 when the government acquired 55% of the holdings of the multi-national enterprises.[562] By 1978 the multi-national establishments had, but for a few exceptions, withdrawn for the timber exploitation business. They, however, maintained their interests in sawmills and other processing industries. Whereas British multi-nationals, especially the United Africa Company (UAC), controlled and managed large enterprises such as the African Timber and Plywood Company at Samreboi and the Mim Timbers, other foreigners, especially Lebanese entrepreneurs, owned and operated medium and small-scale plants in Kumasi, Oda in the Eastern Region, and other locations in the forest area.

Ghanaianization of the Timber Industry

In the 1970s and 1980s, the government, by means of preferential concession policies, subsidies, soft loans for equipment purchases, and tax incentives, encouraged indigenous participation in the timber sector. As a result, the number of Ghanaian-owned sawmills grew from 43 in 1962 to 61 in 1970.[563] Plywood manufacturing plants also increased from 2 to 5 between the early 1960s and 1970. The deliberate policy to encourage Ghanaian participation in the timber sector transformed it from one dominated by a few large foreign corporations to one in which there are a large number of small-scale enterprises. In addition, the proportion of domestic investment in the sector increased relative to foreign investment.[564] In spite of these changes, the fact remains that economically and politically powerful foreign interests have maintained a long-lasting dominance over the Ghanaian forestry sector. This is an important relevant factor in explaining the contents and outcomes of forestry policies of the colonial and immediate post-independence eras.

Consequences of Business Interest Participation

The presence of representatives of private businesses on various policy-making boards, commissions, and bureaus in Ghana suggests that entrepreneurs in the forestry sector have had an impact on policies at the highest levels of the Ghanaian forest policy process. Trade associations such as the Association of Ghana Timber Industries, Ghana Furniture Manufacturers Association, Ghana Timber Association, and Ghana Timber Millers Association have maintained a high profile in the economic and political spheres of Ghana, regularly releasing statements and comments about the government's forestry policies.

Trends in the timber industry, as revealed by production and export data, together with evidence of increasing deforestation, suggest that the government's restrictive policies designed to conserve Ghana's forests have not deterred the industry from increasing timber exploitation.

In addition to the "recognized" formal enterprises, there are numerous illegal chain-saw operators and contractors.[565] Even though, unlike the larger, legally sanctioned, enterprises, the individuals in these activities do not directly participate in the policy process, their activities have been considered a major factor in explaining why policies to address deforestation have not achieved the intended outcomes.[566]

Business Interest Involvement in the Policy Process – the Contradiction

The representation of the timber industry on policy-making bodies of the protective regulatory institutions such as the F.P.I.B. and the F.C. is particularly contradictory, given the fundamental interests of entrepreneurs: generating the most profits through increased exploitation and export of timber. Their participation in the policy process at those high levels of the government may, therefore, provide an explanation for the growth of the timber industry. There is enough reason to conclude that the involvement of business interests in the forestry policy process has enabled those interests to influence Ghana government policies, steering them towards facilitating the continued exploitation of timber.

Enduring Foreign Influence Over Ghana's Forestry Policies

An important dimension of the leverage of business interests over forestry policies in Ghana is the abiding foreign influence over the timber industry. The historical political economy of the colonial and the early independence eras of Ghana were dominated by multinational corporations. Outstanding among them was Unilever. Through its subsidiary, the United Africa Company (UAC), Unilever had "large-scale timber operations" in Ghana.[567] An account by Charles Wilson also describes a UAC-owned "complete township carved out of the dense forests of the Amanfi Aowin region."[568] By 1961 this enterprise, the African Timber and Plywood at Samreboi, was the largest timber business in Ghana, accounting for "a significant proportion of the country's exports."[569]

The UAC is a classic illustration of the leverage foreign interests had over the policy process in a country whose leaders saw external revenue generation and industrialization as high economic priorities. The prominence of UAC, even after Ghana's independence, has been used as grounds to affirm that foreign business interests remain influential over Ghana's forestry policies.[570] The accounts by Fieldhouse and Wilson indicate that the nationalization of businesses in the immediate post-colonial years in Ghana did not terminate the dominance of foreign interests, such as Unilever; it only alleviated it.[571]

Because of the considerable control of foreign interests over some Ghanaian enterprises, even though the business representatives on present-day boards, commissions, and bureaus within the forestry sector are indigenous Ghanaians, clearly in some cases, those individuals are "front-people," acting as agents of

the external interests such as Unilever.[572]   As such, although indigenous
Ghanaian business people have emerged as important actors in the forestry
policy process in Ghana, external forces still exert some influence over the
process and its outcomes.

Given that the ultimate objective of the foreign interests, and the Ghanaian
entrepreneurs alike, is profit-maximization, and given that the easiest and
fastest means of profiting from their investments is to exploit and export
timber, it becomes clear why, in spite of the expressed intention of the
government to address deforestation, timber exploitation and exports from
Ghana have increased in recent years. The presence of representatives of the
business community on the various government policy bodies has been
contradictory, because their primary interest has not been forest conservation.
Rather, it has been profit-maximization, attainable through increased
exploitation of timber.

Enhanced Role of Private Business Interests Under Ghana's Structural Adjustment Program

The potential of foreigners and local businessmen to influence forestry
policies in Ghana stands to become enhanced under the Ghana's Structural
Adjustment Program. The decision to sell government-owned timber interests
under the program, and the creation of a more favorable atmosphere for
investors, have resulted in an increase in foreign ownership of enterprises.[573]
Based on past experience, this increased foreign ownership implies a boost to
private influence over forestry policies. In the absence of any concerted and
genuine effort at reforestation, the outcome of this will be increased
deforestation.

Lack of Mutual Trust Between the Business Community and the Government

Even though private interests have participated in Ghana's forestry policy
process, the level of mutual trust and dialogue between those interests on one
hand and the government on the other hand has been low.[574] Tufuor suggests
that the government, by tradition, has seldom consulted the industry adequately
on major policy decisions. On the other hand, a skeptical and suspicious
industry has tried to keep its distance from the government.[575] The prevalence
of such mistrust implies that, at the very highest levels of the policy process,
the input of business interests could be discarded or altered to suit the
preferences of the politicians.

Given the above, in spite of the documented lasting and important role
business interests have played in the forestry policy process of Ghana, it is
difficult to determine, categorically, the extent to which such interests have
influenced the content of the policies. In the absence of any facts to the
contrary, the production and export statistics indicate that forestry policies have
favored growth in the sector. Consequently, the activities of timber
contractors, owners of sawmills, and others within the sector, and the outcomes

of those activities have undermined the government's policy objective of addressing deforestation.

An important fact that has emerged from the foregoing discussion on the impact of private business interests over the forestry policy process of Ghana is that there has been a long history of multi-national and indigenous business influence over the process at very high levels. This is a direct contradiction of the government's declared objective of controlling the rate of deforestation, in the sense that, the primary objective of those business interests is to maximize profit through increased exploitation of timber. The presence of business interests on those bodies therefore has undermined the prospects of reducing deforestation through timber extraction.

That, that the governments of Ghana, both colonial and post-independence, have deemed it necessary to include timber merchants on major policy bodies is suggestive that the government considers the forest primarily as a resource that must be exploited to generate business and revenue. In accordance with this, it can be suggested that the government regards timber interests as partners with whom it has collaborated in order to ensure a common goal - the increased exploitation of timber. Consequently, in spite of their names, the boards, commissions, etc., have functioned as instruments for controlling and monitoring the resource and the industry, and not for protecting the forests.

Impact of Traditional Rulers

Under the customary and common laws prevailing in the forest regions of Ghana, chiefs and traditional councils are the landholding authorities from whom members of the communities obtain usufruct rights. Authorities of traditional law in Ghana agree that under this arrangement, the occupants of stools are the customary "owners" of timber trees within their domain.[576] Yet since Ghana's independence, traditional rulers have played a progressively reduced role in land and forest policy-making and implementation.

The enormous authority of the national government, especially the executive, has been accompanied with an almost absolute control over the country's natural resources. The process by which forest and nature reserves have been created has deprived the chiefs and communities of most of their historical inherent rights over lands.[577] After Ghana's independence in 1957, the power to grant concessions in lands outside forest reserves was exercised by traditional rulers, subject to validation by judicial tribunals. This was the single remaining avenue through which the chiefs had some direct impact on forest policies. The privilege was, however, terminated under a series of acts, notable among which was the Protected Timber Lands Act of 1959 that allowed the government to assume those powers. From then until 1991, when the Ministry of Lands and Forestry took over the responsibility for the granting of concessions, the Lands Commission was in charge.

Since the colonial era, traditional authorities and communities have been systematically deprived of their historical rights to lands and forests. The prevailing arrangement grants chiefs representations on government controlled policy-making bodies such as the Lands and Forestry Commissions. (Chiefs were also represented as a singular group in the 1989 Forestry Commission consultative symposia that culminated in the formulation of the new Forest Policy of 1994).

Beyond these nominal roles, traditional authorities have also been able to express their positions concerning forest policies through occasional comments in the media, statements issued on ceremonial occasions (such as festivals), and personal appeals made on the rare occasions when, by chance or by design, they have had audiences with the top politicians.[578] But, overall, these roles fall far short of what is considered commensurate with their historical rights and responsibilities.[579]

The above imply that traditional rulers have had a limited leverage over the content and implementation of forest policies. Even though the traditional rulers possess a prestigious and influential, albeit diminished, status in Ghanaian societies, they continue to maintain significant clout over the citizens. They have been allowed little say in matters concerning land and forests. Increasingly, their potential to make contributions to the content of policies and to promote support and cooperation among their subjects has remained unutilized.

The Role of Local Government Institutions (District Assemblies)

Starting from 1979 when the AFRC initiated a series of moves towards the decentralization of government and the inclusion of grassroots institutions in the public policy process, District Assemblies (local governments) have become a more significant feature of the Ghanaian government. One hundred and ten such assemblies, fifty-eight of them in the forest region of Ghana, were inaugurated in 1988 under PNDC Law 207 to replace the old District Councils. The assemblies comprise elected representatives from the towns and villages within the administrative districts and some executive officials appointed by the national government. The Local Government Law that provided for the establishment of the assemblies mandated them to formulate development policies. In addition, the Rawlings-led AFRC and PNDC governments encouraged district assemblies to play an active role in realizing the government's objectives at the local level. In this regard, in the area of forestry policy, they were given the mandate to enforce bush-fire laws, initiate tree-planting campaigns, regulate chain-saw operators, and monitor the activities of concessionaires and timber contractors.[580]

Under the Prevention of Bushfires Law (PNDCL. 229) of 1990, district assemblies were categorically made responsible for funding and implementing public education programs on forest protection, and the training of firefighters. The Trees and Timber (Chain-saw Operations) Regulations of 1991 also granted district assemblies the authority to register and monitor chain-saw operators.

From these responsibilities, it became clear that the assemblies were not intended to be policy-making institutions. Although representatives of these assemblies participated in the 1989 Forestry Commission Symposia for the new Forest Policy of Ghana,[581] the wording of the laws that established the assemblies implied that in the area of forest policy, they were meant to be instruments for policing the forests so as to check illegal activities within them. There have been instances of actions in that direction by local government-sponsored organizations such as Committees for the Defense of the Revolution, and Civil Defense Committees.[582]   There have also been cases of illegal farmers being ejected and the produce from their farms confiscated.[583]   But such activities by local governments and organizations have been very rare.

The reasons for this are not hard to find. Members of those institutions reside in the same towns and villages.   Invariably, they have personal relationships (either friendships or family relations), with those who would break the laws. Therefore, their ability to play an effective role in pursuing the forestry policy objectives has been undermined by their local allegiances and connections.

The limited legitimacy of the central government implies that those assigned to implement the government's policies through enforcing the law at the local level are not likely to side with the government against their kin.   Their awareness (and probable endorsement) of the historical claims to the land and forests by the chiefs and communities, and the fact that the communities depend on the land and forests for sustenance are most likely to deter them from pursuing the restrictive policies vigorously.

Under the Local Government Law, part of the revenues of district assemblies in the forest region (in some instances as much as 20% to 30% of their development budgets) is acquired from the fees collected from the timber industry.   Hence, the assemblies have had an interest in promoting the exploitation of timber.   Instead of working towards reducing timber exploitation the assemblies have rather collaborated with timber contractors because of their stake in the revenues generated.[584]

Because district assemblies have been required to generate revenues for development projects, some of them have even considered participating directly in the timber industry so as to generate funds.[585]   While some have applied for their own timber concessions, others have entered into bilateral agreements with timber contractors so as to become beneficiaries of timber exploitation.   By implication, district assemblies have been apt to compound the deforestation problem, since they stand to gain, either directly or indirectly, from increased exploitation of timber. In large measure, their expected role as watchdogs advancing the government's objectives at the local level has been abandoned, subverted by the contingencies of their mandates.

The Role of Non-Governmental Organizations

Non-governmental organizations in Ghana have, in recent, years shown considerable growth in terms of increased membership and activities.   By means of campaigns, publications, and seminars, environmental NGOs such as Friends of the Earth Ghana, the Landlife Group, the Ghana Association for the

Conservation of Nature, the Environmental Protection Association of Ghana, the Ghana Wildlife Society, and the Africa 2000 Network have gained increased recognition from the government and the educated elites.[586] But, such organizations are presently rather young and "fragile" when compared with those in other African countries or those in places such as the Amazon basin in South America.[587]

In addition to these largely elite and urban-based, organizations, local "self-help," "development," "progressive," and like-named organizations are ubiquitous in Ghana, rural and urban alike. Such organizations have been a part of the mechanisms by which Ghanaian communities have historically promoted cooperation, mutual support, and community development.

In the 1970s and 1980s a perceived need for increased community and local organization activity was prompted by the severe economic hardships that confronted Ghana at the time. The government's lack of resources and the institutional ability to deal with the economic and developmental problems of the country enhanced the role of local civic and community organizations as important instruments for meeting those needs.

However, environmental advocacy has not yet become popular among these organizations as they gain popularity. Their focus has largely been confined to self-help and local development. Even though evidence (from the responses given in the exploratory survey discussed in chapter eight) suggest that Ghanaians see the need to address deforestation because of the threat it poses to the quality of the environment, only a few reports exist about local community organizations with some interest in forestry.[588]

This situation can be explained from the fact that since most citizens depend on the land for sustenance, the forest is perceived to be a resource that must be utilized to meet their needs.[589] An over-emphasis on conservation is therefore out of place, if not senseless.

Reports in the Ghanaian media about the existence of local-based NGOs involved in tree planting and the establishment of wood lots for firewood production suggest the existence of a potential for local organizations to take steps towards addressing deforestation.[590]

It can be concluded from the above facts that there have been increases in the numbers and membership of local NGOs, (a development that has enabled them to slowly gain some recognition from the government as well as the population at large). Furthermore, even though there is evidence that such organizations have the potential to play an active role in the process for addressing deforestation, there is no evidence, thus far, of any impact they have made on the content and outcome of deforestation policies. Their relevance, as well as the prospects of their emergence as instruments for addressing deforestation, however, continues to increase as the deforestation problem becomes more severe and more tangible to the rural communities.

Conclusion

This chapter has provided additional answers to the central research question of this research, that is, why there is a disconnection between policies enacted to address deforestation and their outcomes. The review of the mandates and functions of the bureaucracies within the forestry sector of Ghana lead to the conclusion that the government's objective of addressing deforestation cannot be met under the prevailing arrangement. The main reason for this is the multiplicity of bureaucracies with competing and conflicting mandates. Consequently, there are two main opposing forces within the government establishment: those that seek to promote the exploitation and sale of timber (extractive bureaucracies) on one hand, and those that are attempting to prevent deforestation (protective regulatory bureaucracies) on the other hand.

Facts about the rate of deforestation and trends in the timber industry indicate that, overall, unlike the protective regulatory bureaucracies, the extractive bureaucracies have been successful. The explanation for this comes from Ghana's economic and political circumstances. Generation of revenue has been high among the priorities of Ghana's political leaders. Under the circumstances, the prestige and political clout of those institutions that help generate revenue stand to become enhanced, unlike those seeking to curtail one of the few options available.

These realities have undermined the prospects for addressing deforestation. Because of the limited avenues for the government to generate revenue, there is a strong incentive for the government to promote the exploitation of timber, one of the few resources available. The information in this chapter substantiate the third hypothesis of this research, which states that: in the policy environment of Ghana, where two sets of bureaucratic institutions operate at cross-purposes around the same resource (that is timber), the priority given to the policy outputs of the bureaucratic institutions will reflect the decisions of heads of state, which, in turn, will reflect the demands that have been made on the state.

At the same time, the dependence of a majority of Ghanaians on farming for sustenance, and the predominance of firewood and charcoal as fuels make it unreasonable, even nonsensical, to seek to preserve the forests without providing alternative means of sustenance.

Consequently, in spite of the government's declared intentions concerning deforestation, the same government has put in place a bureaucratic system for promoting the exploitation of timber and other forest resources. The motivation, on the part of the government, for restricting exploitation of timber is far outweighed by that for promoting exploitation. It is apparent that, within the government establishment, those bureaucracies involved in promoting the timber industry (the extractive bureaucracies) carry greater weight than those assigned to prevent the elimination of forests (the protective regulatory bureaucracies).

Based on the foregoing, it is evident that politics holds the key to explaining the activities and accomplishment of the agencies within the forestry sector of

Ghana.[591] It is also the reason why the elimination of forests has continued in Ghana in spite of policies to address it. Politically, it is more expedient for the Ghanaian government to exploit the forest than to preserve it. Therefore, the extractive bureaucracies have been in a politically advantaged position *vis-a-vis* the protective regulatory ones. They are more likely to enjoy the patronage and support of the politicians than the others. In addition, the benefits those bureaucracies stand to reap from the revenues they help to generate are an incentive for them to succeed. Internal organizational and resource inadequacies apart, politics is an explanation why the Department of Game and Wildlife, the Environmental Protection Agency, and the Forestry Commission have not had the necessary impact on the deforestation problem.

An aspect of the political explanation for the performance of the bureaucracies in forestry sector of Ghana is the power and influence of foreign and local timber interests. Through their connection to the policy process, as is manifest from their representation on all boards, bureaus, etc., timber interests have conditioned the Ghanaian forest policy in such a way that exploitation of timber for export has continued, even increased, in spite of the Ghanaian government's declarations and the efforts have been made at addressing deforestation.

Furthermore, because the content of policies and the activities of the protective regulatory institutions have been focused on the timber industry, two other major causes of deforestation: expansion of farmlands, and collection of wood for charcoal and firewood, have not been given the attention they deserve. Where this attention has existed, regulation of farming activities and fuel-wood collection has not been pursued adequately. Hence, those activities have continued to compound the deforestation problem as the population has grown and the demand for land and fuel has increased.

In spite of the potential of non-governmental organizations, indigenous and local institutions, traditional rulers, and local governments (district assemblies) to help achieve the goal of addressing deforestation, they have not had the necessary involvement in the forestry policy process. In particular, district assemblies, because of their locations throughout the country, could be effective instruments for facilitating the formulation and implementation of forestry policies. Yet, the financial burdens imposed on them under PNDC Law 207 of 1988 and PNDC Law 299 of 1990 have prompted some to collaborate with timber merchants and chain-saw operators in exploiting timber. Instead of becoming a force for controlling timber exploitation, as intended by the government, the assemblies have become part of the force behind the eradication of forests.

The following chapter contains explanations why the Department of Forestry has failed to control the growing problem of deforestation in Ghana.

Chapter 8

An Ineffective Department of Forestry: Explanatory Factors

The focus of this chapter is the Department of Forestry, the lead agency responsible for implementing forestry policies in Ghana. The purpose here is to determine why the government's policy objective of addressing deforestation has not been achieved in spite of the activities of the department. Information obtained from the relevant literature, official government documents, and interviews with bureaucrats from the department will be used to provide answers to the question of why deforestation remains a serious problem in spite of the actions taken with the intention of controlling it. The analyses will cover the origins, mandates, organization, functions, and problems that confront the department. References will be made to the results of an exploratory survey, when necessary, for substantiating or refuting deductions made from the analyses.

To facilitate the objective stated above, it is important to briefly recall the overall historical, social, economic, and political environment within which the forestry policy process has occurred, and within which the department has functioned. It is important to recall the discussion in chapter three about the objectives and functional characteristics of the colonial government of Ghana, in particular, the fact that the original purpose for establishing the Department of Forestry was to prevent encroachment into forests by the indigenous population so as to facilitate the commercial extraction of timber. Hence, the forests have been protected not for the purpose of conservation, but for the purpose of enabling the government to exercise control over timber resources. Particularly important is the autocratic approach used to pursue the colonial forestry policy objectives, and the fact that the process of policy-making and implementation in post-independence Ghana has remained conditioned by the colonial era philosophy and strategy.

The following are formidable factors behind deforestation in Ghana. They are also important components of the context within which the Department of

Forestry has functioned. Hence, it is imperative that they are kept in mind when seeking explanations as to why deforestation has continued to occur in spite of the activities of the department:

1.   A majority of Ghanaians directly derive their livelihoods from the land and forests, and their activities tend to contribute to deforestation.

2.   The importance of forests as sources of external revenue for the government of Ghana has increased since the colonial era. Currently, under the structural adjustment program, timber has emerged as a critical source of the revenue required to service Ghana's growing external debts.

3.   Demand for farmlands, lumber, firewood, charcoal, and other forest resources continue to increase as the population of Ghana grows and becomes more urbanized. The deforestation problem becomes pronounced as those needs are met.

4.   As a result of the legacy of autocratic rule from the colonial era, and the lack of connection between the rulers and the grassroots population, government in Ghana lacks political legitimacy. Consequently, the government has imposed protective regulatory policies intended to address deforestation on an uncooperative population. The forestry policies have taken the form of rules and mechanisms for their enforcement. Overall, they have not reflected the needs and concerns of the citizens. As a result, the support and cooperation necessary for their effective implementation have been lacking.

5.   Forestry policies in Ghana have, by tradition, been grounded in economic concerns of the government. Over time, Ghanaian forestry policies have reflected anti-deforestation rhetoric while the practices of the government have, in reality, displayed a commitment to the commercial exploitation of timber.

Mandate of the Department of Forestry and the Environment of its Operations

As was indicated in the introduction and in chapter three, the Department of Forestry was part of the mechanism instituted by the colonial administration of the Gold Coast for controlling access to forests. The initial mission of the department therefore was gate keeping. It was also shown in chapter five that for the purpose of preserving forests, the Ghanaian government had introduced a catalogue of rules that emphasized its own authority over land and forests. Those rules also spelled out penalties for infringements. The key responsibilities of the Department of Forestry since that era, given the content of the policies and the strategy for their implementation, have been: policing the reserves, enforcing the laws, and supporting timber exploitation.

The approach used by colonial government and succeeding post-independence governments has fostered a hostile environment for the Department of Forestry. Implementation of forestry policies entailed "seizure" of lands from the indigenous people, and the conversion of such lands into forest reserves. In addition, the rights to other trees of commercial value have been reserved for the government. Because of the autocratic stance of the government, edicts and sanctions have been prominent instruments for pursuing forestry policies.   To the citizens who derive their livelihood from the land and forests, the department has historically been perceived as an instrument of an authoritative government that has no regards for their historical rights or their survival needs.

Two factors have increased hostility towards the department: the fact that concessions have been granted to timber merchants (some of them foreign owned) to exploit timber from reserved and unreserved forests; and the fact that the local populations have no direct stake in trees of commercial value on their farms or in their vicinities. These factors are the grounds for citizens to consider themselves as victims of a robbery for the benefit of others. Coupled with the above is the already mentioned contradictory role the department has played as an extractive bureaucracy. As the department has taken steps to protect the forests as sources of timber, and monitor the timber industry, it has been perceived, first and foremost, as a facilitator of commercial exploitation of forests.

The high rate of population growth in Ghana has been associated with increasing demand for farmlands, lumber, charcoal, and firewood. In the light of this and the government's stand on forests, the task of the Department of Forestry has remained increasingly difficult. In playing the contradictory role of facilitator of timber exploitation, the department has undermined its own prospects for success at forest conservation.

As was shown in chapter seven, the Department of Forestry has been represented on the policy-making bodies of all of the extractive bureaucracies. Even if the presumption that the department has played the role of an advocate for forest conservation were true, there can be little doubt that this advocacy has been subdued by the strong forces that have operated to promote the exploitation of timber.

The contradictory mandates of the Department of Forestry, the competing missions of revenue-generating government bureaucracies, and growing demand for land, trees and other forest produce have, collectively, undermined the department's ability to achieve deforestation policy objectives.

For the remainder of this chapter, attention will be focused on the internal organizational structure and problems that hinder the effectiveness of the department. Results of interviews and stakeholder opinions, as reflected from an exploratory survey, will be used to describe the internal and external environmental factors affecting the achievements of the department.

Organization of the Department of Forestry

The hierarchical structure of organization that was established at the inception of the Department of Forestry has been maintained in the post-colonial period. (Figure 4 represents the current organizational chart of this bureaucracy.) At the head of this hierarchy is the chief conservator of forests appointed by the head of state. There are four divisions: administration, development, management and working plans, and rural forestry, each of them administered by a deputy chief conservator of forests.

.

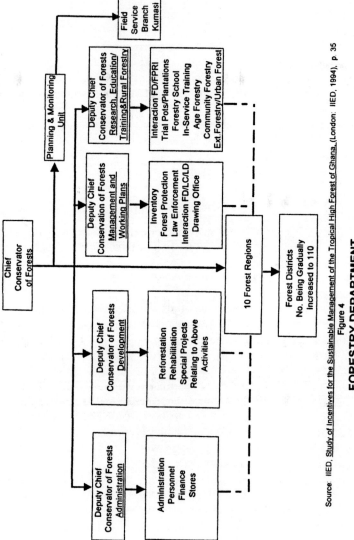

Source: IIED, Study of Incentives for the Sustainable Management of the Tropical High Forest of Ghana, (London: IIED, 1994), p. 35

Figure 4

FORESTRY DEPARTMENT
Organization Chart

The administration division provides organizational support for the headquarters in Accra and in the ten regional offices. Its responsibilities include financial management, procurement, and personnel administration. The development division is in charge of reforestation, plantations, nurseries, and maintenance programs.

The management and working plans division handles forest management and protection; preparation of management plans and inventories. As its name suggests, the rural forestry division handles research, education, and training in rural forestry. This division, in addition, administers the School of Forestry in Sunyani, and coordinates the activities of the department with those of other agencies involved in forestry.

Functional Characteristics and Shortcomings of the Department of Forestry

Recent emphasis on preserving the environment in Ghana as reflected in statements of politicians and the series of new forestry policies and programs for addressing deforestation imply that the Department of Forestry faces new additional responsibilities.[592] They also suggest the need to re-organize the department and re-orientate it towards those new priority objectives.[593] Yet, there has been little, if any, institutional manifestation of the new emphasis on forest preservation in the structure and mission of this unit of government. Not only has the rigid hierarchical structure remained intact, it is in the process of being reinforced and expanded with an on-going program to create district offices in all 110 political-administrative districts in the country.

A dimension of the hierarchical structure of the department is a centralized organization in which policy decisions, regulations, and procedures originate from the top of the bureaucracy at the national headquarters, and to a lesser extent, from the regional offices. These policies, regulations and procedures are transmitted down the hierarchy for implementation at the district level under the supervision of the district forestry officers and technical officers.[594] The authority to make decisions as well as the scope of such decisions diminishes as one moves down the hierarchy. Those operating at the lower levels of the hierarchy are, in turn, required to comply with the handed-down policies, and submit accounts of their activities and developments in their domain through the established channels back to the top of the chain of command.

There are grounds for making the assumption that the employees at the lower echelons of the hierarchy; those "on the beat", directly involved in the activities meant to achieve departmental goals and objectives, are likely to become acquainted with the real nature of the deforestation problem. Consequently, such employees are likely to be in a position to provide valuable information to the policy makers at the top of the hierarchy. However, one might expect the centralized structure and operational process in the department to have stifled the channels for contributing information and ideas, and adequately influencing the content of policies. Employee responses to the exploratory survey, however, suggest that this is not the case. Ninety percent of the employees surveyed disagreed with the suggestion (50% of them strongly) that "top officials of the Department of Forestry do not understand the real causes of deforestation."[595] These respondents supported the position taken by the chief conservator of forests (expressed during the interview with this researcher) that there exist avenues for channeling ideas, concerns, and suggestions to the top hierarchy.

It can be inferred from the above that the lower level employees are in agreement with the top bureaucrats as to the roots of deforestation as well as what needs to be done to address it. The implication is that there is an internal concurrence as to the mission of the department, and the means of achieving that mission. In the light of such an agreement between the top bureaucracy and the lower level employees, there appears to be a very little chance that the changes required for effectively addressing deforestation would originate from within the department.

Responses from the interviews conducted and the exploratory survey indicate that departmental personnel, both high and low in the hierarchy, assign the failings of the institution to problems such as inadequate funding, shortage of personnel and equipment, poor transportation, and non-competitive wages. There was no instance where the organizational structure, and for that matter, over-centralization of authority and decision-making, were included among these problems. It is important to note this fact because of its implication for the idea that personnel of the Department of Forestry embrace the existing practice where policies are imposed from the top.

On the basis of the foregoing, one can identify within the Department of Forestry a corporate culture that sustains established traditions and conventions. This culture is one of the explanations for the ineffectiveness of the department in addressing the problem of deforestation. In this connection, reference should be made to the colonial era "Manual of Procedure,"[596] guidelines on the constitution and organization of the department, which remains in use even to this day. There are several political, economic, institutional and other reasons why this manual is obsolete. For example, even though in the manual, the department was organized with two branches, at the present there are four divisions. Management of the forests of Gold Coast was within the framework of the colonial forest policy. To date, there have been a series of three environmental policies that include forestry policies. The principal function of the department, according to the manual, is maintenance and management of forest reserves. Yet, over the years, there has been an increased emphasis on trees in non-reserved forests. The manual was designed for the framework of colonial rule (under edicts such as the Forest Ordinance [Cap. 122], the Trees and Timber Ordinance, 1949, and the Concessions Ordinance), and a role for traditional rulers ("native administrators") under the Native Authority [Colony] Ordinance. Considering these, the continued use of this manual suggests that a long-standing bureaucratic conservatism to an extent where a transformation in response to changing circumstances has been all but impossible.

Based on the above information, there is reason to conclude that the Department of Forestry is incapable of generating change from within in response to changing needs and priorities.   The unchanging organizational structure and procedures indicate that a series of projects and programs, intended to enhance the department's effectiveness in addressing deforestation, have not succeeded.[597]

Irrespective of past reforms, this institution has maintained its original purposes: policing forests, prosecuting offenders, and facilitating the operations of concessionaires. The change required to trigger a radical transformation of the department in terms of its goals, `organizational structure, and operational procedures would have to originate from an external source

Problems of the Department of Forestry

In addition to the functional shortcomings of the Department of Forestry, there are various operational problems as well.[598] They are:

1.   The political and economic contexts within which the agency has functioned;
2.   Inadequate funding, inadequate equipment, facilities, and manpower;
3.   The contradictions between the functions of the Department of Forestry;
4.   Lack of citizen cooperation; and,
5.   Lack of judicial support.

The Political and Economic Contexts of the Department of Forestry

This theme was treated in detail in chapter four. Of the factors that were discussed however, four are especially relevant due to their implications to the achievement of deforestation policy objectives:

1.   Structure of the Ghanaian economy, and in connection with it, the prominence of timber as a source of external revenue;
2.   Population growth and its associated increasing demand for land and forest resources;
3.   Market-driven demand for Ghanaian timber; and,
4.   The implications of Ghana's structural adjustment and stabilization program to forest resources.

The principal consequence of these factors has been an increasing incidence of deforestation, a trend that points to the inevitable elimination of forests in Ghana in the foreseeable future. These factors remain important elements of the deforestation scenario. Yet, the strategy used by the Department of Forestry to address deforestation has not placed adequate emphasis on them, focusing instead on forest reserves policing and concessionaire monitoring.

Inadequate Funding, Equipment, Facilities, and Manpower

In absolute terms, funding of the Department of Forestry through development plans and annual budgets has been substantial. Yet, compared with other agencies, and considering the size of the department,[599] its changing and expanding role, and the exigencies of forest management in Ghana, those levels of funding have been rather low. (See Table 8.1)

An examination of the trends in this department's funding also reveals a decline in its real value over the years. The magnitude of this decline has been demonstrated in the Silviconsult review[600] which points out that although as of 1984, the department's budgets showed substantial increases over previous years, in stable prices, the budget of that year (1984) was only about 20% of what it had been in 1972.[601] In practical terms, even though the department was being assigned increased responsibilities due to the worsening deforestation situation, it was consistently being deprived of the means to undertake its tasks.

TABLE 8.1
GHANA: 1995 BUDGETARY ALLOCATIONS TO GOVERNMENT
AGENCIES (RECURRENT AND DEVELOPMENT) (in %)

SECTOR	% OF TOTAL
AGRICULTURE	2.24
LANDS AND FORESTRY	**1.37**
MINES AND ENERGY	0.21
TRADE AND INDUSTRY	0.44
TOURISM	0.14
ENVIRONMENT, SCIENCE AND TECHNOLOGY	1.84
WORKS AND HOUSING	2.51
ROADS AND HIGHWAYS	10.47
TRANSPORT AND COMMUNICATION	0.6
EDUCATION	28.79
YOUTH AND SPORTS	0.45
HEALTH	8.11
EMPLOYMENT	0.6
INTERIOR	5.36
LOCAL GOVERNMENT	1.51
GOVERNMENT MACHINERY	5.01
INFORMATION	1.31
JUSTICE	0.36
FOREIGN AFFAIRS	4.17
FINANCE	6.2
DEFENSE	5.28
PARLIARMENTARY AFFAIRS	0.002
EXTRA MINISTERIAL	3.23
OTHERS	9.74

Source: Republic of Ghana, "The Budget Statement and Economic Policy for the Financial Year 1995," Presented to Parliament, February 1, 1995 by Dr. Kwesi Botchway, Minister of Finance.

As Table 8.1 shows, in the 1995/96budget year, an equivalent of $8.3 million (a mere 1.37% of the total budget) was allocated to the Ministry of Lands and Forestry.[602]

Of this amount, the equivalent of $3.1 million, about 37% of the budget of Lands and Forestry, was allocated to the Department of Forestry. The effects of such low funding can be seen in the problems facing the department: poor staffing, lack of equipment, tools and parts, and dilapidated office and residential accommodations.[603]

Poor funding, and the problems emanating from it, were the leading impediments related by the chief conservator of forests as well as the district forestry officer of Kyebi during their interviews in August 1996. At the time of this research, the staff strength of the Kyebi district, one of fifty-three then existing in the country, consisted of one forestry officer, three technical officers, and eighteen forest guards. This, according to the officer, was highly inadequate considering the workload and expectations of the authorities concerning the tasks to be performed. In his opinion, the district needed about three adequately trained forestry officers, ten technical officers, and forty forest guards to function effectively.

The chief conservator confirmed this staffing problem. He added that the personnel shortages that have plagued the department were not simply in terms of numbers, but also in terms of training and skills. Aspects of the personnel problem listed by the chief conservator were: poorly stocked libraries, non-availability of refresher courses, and the lack of facilities for propagating new ideas and information to the personnel. He also referred to the absence of specialists such as sociologists, engineers, anthropologists, plant pathologists, and systems analysts as a serious handicap. In his opinion, the then government policy of downsizing the civil service, sparked by the structural adjustment program, had exacerbated an already tenuous staffing situation.

The constraints inflicted by poor funding on effective implementation of the government's policies have also been demonstrated in various reports on the forestry sector.[604] J. H. Francois, former chief conservator of forests, has, on several occasions, addressed this issue.[605] Edward Prah has suggested that insufficient funding is the primary problem of the department. It is the cause of poor salaries and conditions of service, and the resulting high vacancy rates caused by the loss of professional and technical staff.[606] He reasons that, given the human resource-intensive nature of the department's functions, and the geographical realm it has to cover, the absence of adequate personnel and equipment means that the department cannot function effectively.

A private consulting firm that was assigned to recommend institutional reforms for the department, also identified inadequate personnel and "physical resources" as the most serious of the departments problems.[607] Staffing levels in the department, at the time the firm's report was written, were considered extremely low: 10% of the required professionals, 35% of technical staff, and

55% of laborers. According to the report, compounding the low staffing levels was poor motivation in the form of salaries and allowances.

Overall, the department's endowment of physical resources was considered very poor. For example, fourteen out the sixty-five forest districts that existed at the time had no motor vehicles. Sixty percent of the vehicles available were over six years old. Furthermore, facilities such as computers, stationery supplies, office and residential accommodation, field equipment, and mapping equipment were all rated inadequate in the report.

The prevailing arrangement by which the Department of Forestry is expected to procure part of its funding from royalties paid by concessionaires is part of the reason why inadequate funding has remained a continuing problem.[608] Budgetary allocations to the department have been consistently smaller than the department's requirements because of the expectation, on the part of the government, that the department would acquire additional revenues from royalties, concession fees, and the sale of forest produce.[609] Yet, revenues from those sources have not produced the amounts required to meet the budgetary needs of the department. The reasons for this include:

1. Absence of an accurate register of concessionaires and their holdings;[610]
2. Complications caused by the existence of six different methods of royalty collection;
3. Long delays in royalty payment;[611]
4. Inadequate monitoring of logging activities, and resulting from it, the ease with which concession-holders, third-party loggers, and chain-saw operators perpetuate corrupt activities and thefts.

In 1983, for example, revenues collected by the department aside from government budgetary allocations amounted to only approximately 5% of its total budget, a mere 17% of the cost of management and administration of the forests.[612] It has been estimated that, in order to cover the cost of managing concessions alone, royalties from timber extraction would have to be increased six times.[613]

There is reason to conclude that the department has been in a no-win situation, whereby, its activities are not seen as directly resulting in revenue generation. Its prestige among other agencies has therefore been low. As a result of this perceived low prestige, politicians have not been inclined to award it larger budgetary allocations or avail it the means of acquiring adequate resources. The consequence has been that the department lacks the facilities, amenities, and personnel necessary to improve its effectiveness.

Facts concerning the original purpose for establishing the Department of Forestry help to explain why this agency has routinely been inadequately funded. As was pointed out in chapter three, the colonial government intended that this department would be an instrument of control, meant to protect the forests against encroachment by indigenous Ghanaians, and to ensure that forest resources were exploited only by authorized businesses. The principal goal therefore was to guarantee that timber would be available for exploitation by British businesses for a long time. The department was conceived not in terms of the revenues it would generate itself, but in terms of the benefits of British business interests, and the revenues that would accrue to the colonial government from logging concessions and permits.

This attitude has not changed in the post-independence era. The existence and missions of extractive agencies (such as the Timber Exports Development Board, the Forest Products Inspection Bureau, and the Lands Department) show that the Department of Forestry continues to be seen by the government as an instrument for maintaining favorable conditions under which the exploitation of timber can be controlled and managed. To a large extent, this department is perceived to be a facilitator of the proper conditions for revenue generation and not as an agency that needs to be accorded a high status and funded adequately for the purpose of addressing an urgent environmental problem.

The overall circumstances surrounding the Department of Forestry concerning its resources and the routines involved in its operations have fostered its low status. Historically, because its employees live and work in remote, often poorly accessible forest areas under unattractive conditions, the department has traditionally been among the least prestigious agencies, its funding levels consistently reflecting this comparatively low status. In contrast with other government agencies, this department has been associated with the oldest offices, bungalows, equipment, motor vehicles, etc.[614] Even though additional demands have been made on the department over the years, policy-makers have not seen the need to boost its resources accordingly.

Contradictory Functions of the Department of Forestry

It has been indicated earlier in chapter seven that the Department of Forestry has maintained a dual role within the forestry sector. The agency has commonly been identified with forest protection through the policing of reserved as well as unreserved areas. In so doing, it has been seen to be preventing trespassing, and also monitoring the operations of concessionaires to ensure that they operate within established guidelines. However, as has been shown, the department has had a direct involvement at the policy-making levels of extractive bureaucracies such as the Timber Exports Development Board, the Timber Lease Committee, and the Forest Products Inspection Bureau.

In performing these dual and conflicting functions, the department has been directly undermining the prospects of its own success in addressing deforestation. The economic realities, and the high priority that has been given by the government to boosting external revenues through export of primary produce, have dictated that the department maintains its original mission of supporting the timber industry. Therefore, in spite of the worsening deforestation crisis, the extractive aspect of the department's mission continues to take precedence over conservation. Controlling deforestation has been an important objective of the department, yet it has actively collaborated with other agencies to encourage exploitation of timber, thus helping to aggravate the deforestation problem.

Lack of Citizen Support

It is necessary to again recall the circumstances under which forest reserves were established in Ghana and the strategy by which the government has implemented its forestry policy in order to understand the lack of citizen cooperation with the Department of Forestry.   In connection with this, it is important to recall the protests against the earliest forestry policies of the colonial administration.   From every indication, those protests, started over a century ago, have been sustained because the intent of the governments of the independence era as well as their approach for implementing the policies have remained largely the same as those of the colonial era.

Citizen opposition to autocratic forestry policies and the style of their implementation has been manifested through defiance of the rules and regulations on forests and trees.   In general, and as can be deduced from the results of the exploratory survey, the public considers the government's control over forests to be excessive.[615]   Traditionally, the Department of Forestry has been perceived to be an instrument of oppression used by the government (a "foreign" entity) to deny them their rights to their lands and forests only to hand them over to rich and powerful concessionaires for exploitation.   Overall, in spite of the government's immense authority, the severity of punishments for forest-related offenses, and the work of the Department of Forestry, available evidence indicates that the activities of illegal chain-saw operators, bush millers, charcoal manufacturers, and farmers are very widespread in Ghana, accounting for a significant amount of deforestation both inside and outside forest reserves.[616]

The lack of cooperation from the citizens implies that to implement the government's deforestation policy successfully the Department of Forestry must assign large numbers of foresters, forest rangers and laborers to patrol the forests and to monitor the activities of the citizens.   But this has not been possible due to monetary, personnel, and infrastructural constraints.

Over the past two decades, high unemployment rates and the prominence of land and forests as sources of subsistence in Ghana have compounded the task of the department.   As was mentioned in chapter four, Ghana's structural adjustment program included an on-going reduction in the size of the government.[617]   In a country where the government remains the largest employer, the retrenchment of public servants boosted the ranks of the unemployed.   In the absence of alternative sources of employment, farming, timber contracting, and other land and forest-related occupations emerged as the most feasible and lucrative ways of earning a livelihood for the former civil servants.   The Department of Forestry has not been able to repel the assault launched by this group on the forests. The tone of the forestry laws and the severity punishments they prescribe have not been adequate as deterrents. Clandestine tree felling for lumber and charcoal production have emerged as important parts of the forestry sector. The existence of a growing market for the produce provides an added incentive to defy the government's policies.

The Kyebi District Forestry Officer indicated during an interview that some traditional rulers and farmers, out of concern about uncontrolled destruction of forests, have been cooperating with the department to control the activities of illegal loggers, poachers, and timber contractors.[618] This, however, was the exception rather than the rule. The officer added that a majority of the citizens perceive the department as a hindrance to their endeavors to make a living, and would infringe upon the laws or aid those who do so.

This attitude contradicts the findings from the exploratory survey that indicate that overall, a majority of the respondents (60% of owners of sawmills and other wood processing plants, 53% of farmers, and 53% of those in other occupations) consider deforestation as a very serious problem that deserves the government's attention. According to the survey, 60% of owners of sawmills and other wood processing plants, 87% of farmers, and all those in other occupations agree that it is necessary for the government to do much more to protect the forests of Ghana. By implication, there is a widespread agreement among Ghanaians concerning the need to solve the problem of deforestation. At the same time, the citizens oppose the government's policies and actions in that direction. Under the circumstances, the Department of Forestry does not have benefit of the level of citizen-cooperation required to accomplish its mission.

One of the conclusions of the Silviconsult study was that, overall, farmers would rather have illegal operators fell trees on their plots than licensed loggers, because, in addition to the former doing less damage to crops, they are also paid compensation for the trees felled.[619] This alliance between farmers and illegal operators remains yet another obstacle to the effectiveness of the Department of Forestry in monitoring and regulating illegal timber activities.[620]

The responses of the farmers in the survey reflected their attitudes towards forests and, deriving from that, their behavior with respect to forest conservation and the activities of the Department of Forestry. Even though 53% agreed that deforestation is a serious problem, at the same time, as much as 79% agreed that people worry too much about human activity harming the environment. In addition, as mentioned earlier on, although a majority of farmers and those involved in the timber industry agreed that it is necessary for the government to do much more to protect the environment, respectively, 33% and 60% of them would not endorse actions to protect the forests if such actions would cause job losses. Herein lies another aspect of the obstacles facing the Department of Forestry. The opinions expressed lead one to infer that, to Ghanaian citizens, making a living occupies a higher priority than preserving the forest, hence, their opposition to the Department of Forestry.

Disagreement among the citizens as to the principal causes of deforestation is yet another explanation why the Department of Forestry has been ineffective at addressing the problem. The results of the survey reveal direct contrasts between the opinions of farmers and those of owners of timber-based industries concerning the principal causes of deforestation. Whereas most of the farmers agreed (66.7% of them strongly) that timber exploitation is a major cause of deforestation, only 10% of those within the industry agreed. Thirty percent disagreed, 20% of them strongly, with that statement. To the contrary, 40% of respondents from the timber industry held the opinion that farming was the main cause of deforestation in Ghana. These responses are consistent with those obtained in an earlier study from which executives of the Ghana Timber Association contended that the forests of Ghana are not being over-exploited.[621] Because none of the two key groups whose activities compound the problem recognize or admit their role in causing deforestation, each tends to place the blame on the other, and fail to support the government's moves towards achieving a resolution of the problem.

Opinions about what should be the most important goals of the Department of Forestry also show a pervasive disagreement with the mission and approach used by the department. Sixty percent of the farmers who were surveyed were of the opinion that the most important goals of the department should be tree-planting and regulation of the timber industry. Twenty percent of them felt that the department should open more lands for development. In contrast, although 30% of respondents from the timber industry felt the department should emphasize tree planting, only 20% of them felt that this unit of government should make regulating the industry an important goal. Twenty percent suggested that the department should focus on job-creation and the opening of more forestlands for development.

Other responses from those involved in the timber industry help to clarify their attitude towards the government in terms of its forest policies. Forty percent of this category of respondents disagreed (33% of them strongly) that it is necessary for the government do much more to protect the forests. Also, 50% felt that government regulations concerning forests are excessive.

These responses denote a widespread variation of opinions and the absence of a consensus over the objectives of the department. They help to explain why illegal tree cutting and forest clearance continue to occur in spite of the existence of laws and the activities of the Department of Forestry. The responses obtained from the survey reveal the basis of the lack of citizen cooperation with the Department of Forestry. This lack of cooperation is a serious obstacle facing the department in its endeavors to address deforestation.

Lack of Judicial Support

Two factors have helped to promote the lack of public cooperation with the Department of Forestry: inadequate police and judiciary support in enforcing forest laws.[622] The passive attitude of the police and the Ghanaian judiciary towards forest laws, and their reluctance to investigate and prosecute forest offenses reflect not only the stance taken by those institutions, but also the overall attitude of the governmental establishment towards forest conservation. Whereas the police have shown no enthusiasm about forest-related offenses, the judiciary has failed to impose the prescribed sentences on convicts. Tufuor[623] and Blavo[624] support this argument and confirm that non-enforcement of Ghana's forest laws has been an important factor undermining efforts to halt the unprecedented encroachment into the forest reserves.

Given that by design forest policies in Ghana. are to be realized through the enforcement of laws, the non-imposition of the sanctions prescribed by the laws, arguably, sends a signal to prospective offenders, and undermined the authority of the Department of Forestry.

Directly related to this subversion of forestry policies by the law enforcement and judiciary institutions is the predominant negative perception concerning the effectiveness of the Department of Forestry as conveyed by responses to the exploratory survey. Seventy- three percent of farmers and 40% of respondents from the timber industry disagreed that the department is an effective institution for preserving Ghana's forests. In fact, 66.7% of the farmers and 20% from the industry strongly disagreed with that statement.

Clearly, the department cannot bear total blame for its ineffectiveness. Its internal weaknesses nevertheless, it is clear that other institutions (the police and judiciary, in this case) must remain committed to the cause and support the Department of Forestry by actively applying the forestry laws.

On the basis of the foregoing, it is concluded that the Department of Forestry has been operating in a no-win situation. There is a general agreement on the part of the public about the need to take action to address deforestation. Still, the institutional mechanisms for bolstering the department's authority in the enforcement of the prescribed laws so as to achieve this objective have not received the necessary backing from the governmental institutions concerned. Consequently, the department's effectiveness has been undermined.

Conclusions

Various explanations for the ineffectiveness of the Department of Forestry in addressing deforestation have been highlighted in this chapter. It has been shown that internal organizational problems have prevented from evolving into a dynamic and effective agency that can deal with the problem. Furthermore, inadequate financial resources, and deriving from this, the lack of appropriate personnel, equipment, transportation, and accommodation, have inhibited it from effectively implementing the Ghanaian government's policies for addressing deforestation.

Another explanation for the department's shortcomings is its failure to respond adequately to two realities. First, because the department has upheld and sustained a conservative culture in which old procedures and practices, dating from the colonial era, remain the norm, it has failed to embrace the fact that forests and land resources are critical sources of the livelihood of many Ghanaians. Consequently, even though it is common knowledge that the traditional approach to forest protection has not had the desired effect, policing forests remains the primary function of this department.

Secondly, there has been a sustained emphasis on managing the forest as a commercial source of timber. As a result, not only have the forestry policies in Ghana failed to address environmental conservation, such policies have continued to be formulated primarily with commercial extractive objectives in mind. Their contents have demonstrated insufficient regard for the needs and concerns of the citizens who depend on the land and the forests. The prospects of success for the Department of Forestry have therefore been curtailed because they face the handicap of dealing with an uncooperative population. The effectiveness of the agency has been further eroded because the police and judiciary have failed to render the necessary support of its policing activities.

As the department maintains its contradictory role within the forestry sector, a role in which commercial extraction takes precedence over the protective regulatory policy, it concurrently and effectively undermines its own prospects for making an impact on the deforestation problem.

The closing chapter summarizes the findings and inferences drawn from the research, and recommendations for a more effective approach to formulating and implementing deforestation policies in Ghana.

Chapter 9

Recap and Policy Recommendations

This chapter consists of two parts. Part I is a recap of the major findings and conclusions drawn from this research. It is a summary of the reasons why policies meant to address deforestation in Ghana have not achieved their intended outcomes. The conceptual framework (Fig. 1, page 14) helped to isolate the relevant factors in the deforestation policy process in Ghana. Consequently, it helped to describe and explain the internal and external dimensions of the policy environment.[625] The analyses performed in chapters three through seven led to several conclusions about various aspects of the internal and external environments of the forestry policy process in Ghana. They show that the continued incidence of deforestation in Ghana has been the result of the operation of a complex of factors that have historical, social, political, economic, and international dimensions.

It was shown that, in practical terms, the post-colonial forestry policy regime in Ghana is not different from that of the colonial era. Another inference was that although a great deal of information exists about the various critical factors underlying deforestation in Ghana, these factors have not been adequately taken into account during the formulation and implementation of the policies intended to address deforestation. Consequently, forestry policies have not included the necessary strategies and actions for addressing the problem.

The summary of the findings of this research has been presented according to the explanatory model of the contextual framework within which the forestry policy process has occurred. They are therefore presented in two categories: those related to the internal environment of the process; and those related to the external environment. The second part of this chapter contains policy recommendations for addressing deforestation in Ghana.

Explanations for the Disconnection Between Policies and Outcomes
Factors from the External Environment of the Policy Process

Legacy of the Colonial Forestry Policy Process
Historical accounts of the policy formulation and implementation process in colonial-era Ghana (chapter three) indicate that a clear understanding of the colonial-era forestry policy process is critical for explaining the persistence of the deforestation problem in Ghana. The colonial era forestry policy process has been given increased attention in this research because the precedents that were established in that era concerning policy formulation and implementation have remained an enduring part of the forestry policy process in post-independence Ghana.

The colonial forestry policies were products of a process that was dominated by an extremely powerful colonial governor, assisted by provincial and district officers and highly influential British business interests. The policies of the colonial era were pervaded with conflicts and contradictions. Even though the declared policy objectives suggested a desire to conserve forests, in practical terms, most emphasis was placed on the extraction of timber. Hence, the forestry policy objective of the colonial era was in large measure pseudo-conservation. Protective regulatory policies were combined with extractive policies; a combination that provided the historical basis for the conflictual bureaucratic dichotomy that has characterized the Ghanaian forestry sector.

Leaders of the indigenous population questioned the legitimacy of the colonial government. Beyond that the colonial government was authoritarian. It took control of lands and forests with little regard for the land tenure traditions, and rights of the indigenous people. This scenario demanded that implementation take the form of the deliberate imposition of the policies on an uncooperative population.[626] Most of the efforts of the hierarchical and bureaucratic colonial Department of Forestry were therefore geared towards enforcing forestry legislation. In the final analysis, the colonial era forestry policies not only encouraged the destruction of forests in Ghana, but also established a precedent that set the tone for future government-imposed extractive policies.[627]

The policy routine and guiding principles of the colonial era were not immediately discarded after independence. With the exception of the principal actors being indigenous Ghanaians, the forestry policy process in post-independence Ghana bears a close resemblance to that of the colonial era in terms of:

1. Priority given to extraction and export of timber,
2. Contradiction between the government's economic priorities as they relate to the extraction of forest resources, and its declared goal of reducing the rate at which forests are being destroyed,
3. Dominance of the policy process by politicians and bureaucrats,
4. Content of forestry policies,
5. Strategy by which the policies have been implemented,

6. Failure of policies to address the concerns of stakeholders,
7. Non-cooperation of stakeholders,
8. Functional and organizational characteristics and weaknesses of the Department of Forestry, and,
9. Failure to achieve the government's deforestation policy objectives.

Even though there is evidence of increasing awareness, on the part of Ghanaian government leaders, about the factors behind deforestation,[628] in practical terms, the official actions that have been taken to conserve and regenerate the forests in Ghana, even as they are increasingly exploited to meet the increasing needs of the government and people, have not succeeded in achieving those goals. One of the cardinal conclusions of this research is that in order to effectively address the problem of deforestation, it will be necessary to reconstruct the forestry policy process so that it is radically different from what has been retained from the colonial era.

Structure of the Ghanaian Economy: Prominence of Land and Forest Resources

An important factor behind deforestation in Ghana is that farming remains the principal occupation for the rapidly growing population. The demand for farmlands has increased consistently in response to the increasing demand for foodstuffs associated with the high rate of population growth.[629] Added to this, bush fallowing, the predominant farming practice, requires the clearance of additional forests for new farms as the existing farmlands lose their natural fertility. Thus, there exists a perpetual need to clear more forests every few years. Guaranteed markets, extension services, and other incentives offered by the government to cocoa farmers and, in recent times, to cultivators of "non-traditional export crops" have also encouraged the clearance of more forests to produce those items.

The absence of significant industrial or service sectors is also an explanation of the inclination to clear forests in Ghana. Primary products remain the mainstay of Ghana's external trade; cocoa, minerals, and timber being the leading sources of external revenue. This explains why the cash-deprived government of Ghana has encouraged the exploitation of timber to meet the reliable and growing external demand for tropical woods. The local population has also increasingly exploited the forest for such necessities as building materials, domestic fuel, medicines, and game.

This research has shown that in their efforts at addressing problems such as mounting external debts, shortages in food supplies, and, poor health care delivery, education, infrastructure, housing, etc., Ghanaian policy makers have not seriously considered alternatives to the exploitation of forests for timber, the clearance of more forest lands for foodstuff and cocoa production, and intensification of mineral production. This explains why the government's own declared forest conservation policy objectives have, in practice, ended up being extractive policies.

Under the circumstances described in this research, the fate of Ghana's economy and the sustenance of its people are so closely linked to the land and forest resources that, for the foreseeable future, those resources will continue to be intensively exploited. There exists a structural contradiction between the economic realities in Ghana on the one hand, and the need to prevent the potentially disastrous consequence of the incessant clearance of forests on the other.

As such, in seeking a forestry policy process that would cater to the priorities of the government and the needs of the population and at the same time address deforestation, it is important to reassess the strategic basis of the existing policy process and to devise a more novel approach, centered on sustainability.[630]

The Consequences of Increasing Demand for Fuel

The large amounts of wood extracted for firewood and charcoal in Ghana is yet another reason behind deforestation. Wood remains the sole source of domestic fuel for an overwhelming majority of Ghanaians. As was revealed by the Ghana Living Standards Surveys of 1989 and 1991/92, an overwhelming majority (92.3% in 1991/92) of Ghanaian households used firewood and charcoal for cooking. Data compiled by the Energy Information Center of the Ministry of Energy also reveal a consistent increase in the extraction of firewood (47.7% between 1974 and 1994) corresponding to increases in consumption.

In spite of these facts, government policies have traditionally been focused on measures intended to protect forest resources for the eventual extraction by government-approved commercial enterprises. Those policies have therefore not addressed the growing demand for fuel, a leading root cause of deforestation.

The Effects of Limited Legitimacy of the State and Lack of Citizen Cooperation

Like their colonial counterparts, the governments of post-independence Ghana have been undemocratic and authoritarian. For most of the four decades since the end of colonial rule, governments in Ghana have been either military dictatorships or constitutional regimes that have been dominated by powerful executives and bureaucratic elites. Politics and the public policy process have, therefore been monopolized by these dominant actors, to the exclusion of the grassroots population. As a result, the government has commonly been perceived by Ghanaians to be a "foreign" institution forced upon them only to restrict their freedoms and rights through the imposition of laws, rules, and regulations. This has rendered the implementation of deforestation policies, at best, an uphill task.

In the absence of citizen support and cooperation, and the generous amounts of resources required to maintain compliance with the restrictive laws, the government has not been able to achieve its deforestation policy objective by means of the established strategy. Inadequacies of the Department of Forestry aside, a successful pursuit of policies that will address deforestation cannot be achieved without the support and cooperation of the millions of Ghanaians who live off the land.

The Effects of Ghana's Structural Adjustment Program

There are indications that the Structural Adjustment Program (SAP), implemented in Ghana since 1983, has stimulated the increased exploitation and export of timber and other natural resources for external revenues[631] (See Appendix 9 and 10). Repeated devaluations of the Cedi (the Ghanaian currency), increases in the producer prices of cocoa and other cash crops, and the use of IMF and other donor funds to expand the production capacity of the forestry and mining sectors, have combined to aggravate the deforestation problem. This research also indicates that there have been substantial increases in the production of foodstuffs and cocoa in Ghana since 1983 when the SAP started (See Appendix 9 and 10). Those increases have resulted largely from the clearance of more forests for farmlands.

Requirements of the SAP such as the mandated reduction of the size of the government work force, and closure of several government enterprises, have aggravated the deforestation problem. This is because the affected workers, in some cases encouraged by government incentives, resorted to the land - farming, chain-saw operations, and charcoal manufacturing to make a living. Ironically, the inescapable consequence of IMF and World Bank economic policy prescriptions to Ghana has been the further acceleration of deforestation in that country. The irony lies in the fact that the World Bank categorically endorses sustainability in the utilization of resources.[632] Yet, the prescriptions made by the Bank and its affiliate institutions have demanded that the Ghanaian government pursue aggressive, so far unsustainable, natural resource extraction and export as a solution to that country's economic problems.

Factors Within the Internal Environment of the Forestry Policy Process

Priorities of the Dominant Actors in the Policy Process

It has been reiterated throughout this research that economic and political interests have ranked high among the priorities of the principal actors in the forestry policy process in Ghana. During the colonial era, the principal mission of the administration was to support and promote the extraction of timber for export. Confronted with the mounting external debts, the need to provide health, educational, and infrastructure facilities, and the need to provide jobs and promote economic development, post-independence governments have consistently lacked revenues. The priority of Ghanaian governments has therefore been to promote the extraction of natural resources, including timber, for export, in order to generate the revenue required for their programs.

This priority, coupled with the immense political power wielded by the heads of state, politicians, commercial interests, and the bureaucrats, and their domination of the policy process has caused forestry policies to be dictated by the revenue-generation potential of timber resources. The main objective of the government has been to regulate access to forests and timber resources, not for the purpose of conservation, but rather for the purpose of enabling the government to control extraction - pseudo-conservation.

In practice, addressing deforestation for environmental conservation purposes has not been a priority. In fact, pursuit of that objective, which would entail controlling the rate of timber extraction, or allocating resources for forest regeneration, would amount to the government acting contrary to its mission of generating revenue from forest resources. In accordance with this, politically powerful extractive bureaucracies have effectively contradicted the mission of a weak Department of Forestry, the lead agency for implementing the government's protective regulatory policies. Under the above circumstances, government policies in the forestry sector have overwhelmingly promoted the extraction of timber, a situation that has directly undermined its own programs intended to address deforestation.

The active promotion and support the government gives cash crops (especially cocoa) and foodstuffs production has also encouraged the clearance of forests for new farms thereby adding to the deforestation problem.

Even though the series of public declarations as well as forestry laws and regulations introduced since independence, suggest that Ghanaian governments have been aware of the problem of deforestation and its consequences, due to the facts set forth above, the policies and actions taken to address the problem have proven inadequate. In practice, extractive forestry policies have superseded protective regulatory policies.

Overall the content of forestry policies, the process by which such policies have been implemented, and their outcomes, have not reflected the declared intentions of the principal policy actors to address the problem in Ghana. The Department of Forestry, the lead agency responsible for implementing the government's deforestation policies, has been confronted with six major problems that have hindered it from achieving success.

Obstacles Confronting the Department of Forestry
Historically, the functions and performance of the Ghanaian Department of Forestry have been dictated by economic priorities of the government, the most important being the exploitation of timber resources for revenue generation, and the promotion of cash crop and foodstuff cultivation. As the economic problems of Ghana have continued to mount, as the population has increased, and as access to land and forest resources has become more and more critical, the level of importance attached to controlling deforestation, has in practical terms, diminished. Thus, the major task of the Department of Forestry in the administration of protective regulatory forestry policies has become contradictory and more ominous over time.

The mission of the department has been even more difficult because, in essence, it has been designed to pursue the arduous goal of preventing citizens from making a livelihood by utilizing the few avenues available to them - the land and forests. In contrast to high profile and prestigious agencies such as Finance and Economic Planning, Education, and Defense, Forestry lacks prestige and political clout. Consequently, it has perpetually lacked the necessary funding and resources for successful implementation of restrictive policies that, in the first place, have been actively undermined by the revenue-generating activities of politically more powerful extractive bureaucracies.

Given that traditionally, realization of forestry policies in Ghana depended on effective enforcement of laws, the passive attitude of the Ghanaian police and the judiciary towards forestry laws has diminished the government's ability to maintain control over the forest resources. Internal organizational shortcomings such as an unchanging hierarchical, and over-centralized decision-making and supervisory system have also hindered the department from attempting re-organization and the re-orientation necessary for effectively addressing deforestation.

Finally, because of the negative attitudes of Ghanaian citizens toward the government's protective regulatory forestry policies, the department has not benefited from the popular citizen support and cooperation necessary for implementing the inherently restrictive protective regulatory forestry policies. The results of the exploratory survey (discussed in chapter eight) indicate that there was widespread disagreement among the citizens over the government's policies concerning forest resources. There was also a prevalent objection to the rationale and approach used by the department to implement its policies. A consequence of this is that the main activity of the department has remained the policing of forest reserves and trees in off-reserve areas, using the threat of punishment as a disincentive to would-be trespassers. The department has not performed this function effectively. As a result, illegal farming, extraction of timber, hunting, and other forest destroying activities have continued to occur.

Outcomes of Past Attempts at Forestry Policy Revision in Ghana

Provisions in recent constitutions, the establishment of a series of commissions, periodic reconstitution of existing commissions and agencies, the observation of annual forestry weeks, and the launching of three action plans that contain proposals for addressing deforestation, suggest a determination on the part of government to address deforestation in Ghana.

Yet, analyses of the three environmental action plans (See chapter five) reveal that, in practice, actions taken by the Ghanaian government have not matched its rhetoric and declared policy objectives concerning deforestation. In substance, subsequent policies have not departed significantly from previously ineffective ones. Old extractive policies have therefore survived as key components of contemporary forestry policy, in spite of the emphasis placed on deforestation in recent forestry policies.

The introductions to the Ghana Environmental Action Plan of 1988 and the Forest and Wildlife Policy on 1994 contained reiterations of the intent to ensure sustainability in the utilization of forest resources. Those policies also contained declarations of the intent to maintain stakeholder rights and promote community awareness and involvement in forest conservation. Yet, even though an attempt was made to initiate action in these directions by arranging stakeholder participation in deliberations preceding preparation of the plans, the process remained essentially dominated by the politicians, bureaucrats and business interests. Because of the domination of these actors, their economic interests have remained the primary consideration behind policies. Hence, the policy process has centered on the extraction of timber.

Although it was recognized in various policy documents that the policies and events within other sectors of the Ghanaian economy had inextricable consequences for deforestation, the forestry sector has been largely treated in isolation from other governmental sectors. Instead of comprehensive, rational, and pragmatic prescriptions needed for conserving forests even as they are utilized to meet the economic and sustenance needs of the government and the population, plans have been merely wish lists, generalizations that have not indicated specific innovative actions necessary for addressing deforestation. Therefore, in spite of a series of recent policies, extractive colonial-era policies and legislation from the early post-independence years have remained the principal instruments for defining and implementing forestry policies.

The Problem

Based on the foregoing, the deforestation problem in Ghana can be summed up in terms of an absence of proactive, radical, innovative, and popularly supportable policy mechanisms for balancing the supply and demand of forest resources in order to realize sustainability in their utilization. Going by the past and present trends; consistently increasing demand for timber, non-timber forest products, and farmlands, one can predict, with some certainty, that the forests of Ghana will inevitably be inflicted with the "tragedy of the commons"[633] syndrome, unless timely, effective action is taken to prevent it.

The evidence presented in this research show that the crux of the deforestation problem in Ghana is the expanding gap between the available supply and demand for land and forest resources. Confronted with the fact that for the foreseeable future, the demand for forest resources will continue to increase, the cardinal challenge facing policy analysts who are concerned with this problem is how to devise a policy process that would reconcile two sets of policy outcomes that are at present in conflict.

The first set of policy objectives involves utilizing forest and land resources to generate government revenue and to provide a source of livelihood for the population. It entails making available an adequate supply of timber for domestic use as well as for export; providing an adequate supply of firewood, charcoal, medicines, bush meat; and, dispensing sufficient land for growing foodstuffs and for cash crop cultivation.

The second policy objective is the preservation and regeneration of forests, in spite of the inherently forest-destroying activities involved in pursuing the first policy objective. This is the more difficult objective to accomplish. The contradictory nature of the two desired objectives implies a need to reconcile the demand and supply of farmlands and forest resources so as to establish a balance and forestall the eventual extinction of the forests of Ghana.

The multiple dimensions of the deforestation problem in Ghana, revealed from this research, suggest that a holistic approach is required in order to provide a more complete and effective answer to this policy problem. A forestry policy process is needed that, unlike the past and current ones (which are dictated by the government's economic priorities), will take into account all relevant historical, political, cultural, and economic factors. An important tenet of a new forestry policy process would be that the land and forests of Ghana will, for the foreseeable future, serve as critical sources of sustenance for Ghanaians. A guiding principle in developing an alternative forest policy process should therefore be sustainability.[634] Policy recommendations for achieving this goal are contained in the following section.

Policy Recommendations for Achieving the Sustainable Utilization of Forest Resources in Ghana

Four categories of policy recommendations for addressing deforestation in Ghana have been proposed. Their ultimate goal is to help establish a balance between the supply and demand for forest resources, and ultimately help realize sustainability in their utilization. They are:

1. Policies designed to promote the sustained supply of forest resources;
2. Administrative policies for managing the internal demand for farmlands and forest resources;
3. Economic policies for restructuring the forestry sector for the purpose of augmenting the revenues generated from external markets; and,
4. Political and institutional reforms intended to establish a more effective deforestation policy process in Ghana.

The specific policy recommendations are made from the context of the particular environments of the forestry policy process and the specific explanatory factors they are intended to address. The first set of recommendations therefore deals with the external environment as depicted in the explanatory model (Fig 1).

Policies For Achieving Sustainable Supplies of Forest Resources

Aggressively Undertake Afforestation[635]

Given the extent to which the forests of Ghana have been depleted, critical and immediate action needs to be taken towards their replenishment. Previously forest areas that have been converted to farmlands and other vegetation types need to be replanted. In addition, those forests that are in the process of being degraded should be protected and regenerated.

Under the existing political conditions of Ghana, the government has a direct and facilitating role to play. The fact that budgetary allocations have been made over the years for forest plantations is evidence that the need to replant forests has been recognized for a long time. Nevertheless, so far, the size of those allocations indicates that forest replantation has not been considered a priority.[636]   In any case, although the Department of Forestry reports some action in this area, its performance has fallen short of the level required to replenish the forests of Ghana.[637] Adequate resources need to be allocated for the establishment of plantations commensurate with the past and current rates of deforestation. In connection with this, the pre-eminent task of the Department of Forestry should become the establishment of plantations and tree planting. To facilitate this, the department needs to be reformed organizationally and structurally so as to enable it to effectively undertake this new priority program.

The tree planting activities of the Amansie Tree-Planting and Rural Development Association (referred to in Chapter Seven) and Messrs Bonsuvonberg Farms at Somanya (site of the launching of the 1996 National Forestry Week), are evidence that forestry has the potential to become an attractive activity for local organizations and entrepreneurs. Such ventures need to be supported by the government for the purpose of incorporating private business interests and organizations as major participants in Ghana's reforestation efforts.

In addition to its direct activities in forest replanting, the Department of Forestry must function as a channel for providing extension services. One of its priority activities should be the dissemination of technical information and the education of individuals, businesses, local organizations, and non-governmental organizations within the forestry sector. The department must also be assigned to provide incentives such as long-term technical support and distributing seedlings. In order to make it easy to undertake reforestation and plantation projects, the Lands Department should assist interested individuals and institutions in land acquisition and other facilities.

Modernize Agricultural Practices to Reduce Incidental Damage and Destruction of Trees

It has been established in this research that land clearance for farming, and the practice of itinerant farming (bush fallowing) have been among the leading causes of deforestation in Ghana. Yet, as has been shown, in the forestry policy process, the utmost attention has been focused on the timber industry. Consequently, the destructive side effects of bush burning for land clearance, and bush fallowing have not been addressed in attempts at preserving forests in Ghana. The research institutions and universities in Ghana must be encouraged to intensify studies on permanent (non bush-fallowing) farming techniques and alternative feasible methods of farmland clearance that would not destroy on-site trees or cause the regular wild fires that have destroyed several acres of forests in the past.

There is no gainsaying that the results of research would be useless unless they are publicized among farmers. A system for the effective transfer of information from the labs to the fields needs to be established. Existing channels of communication should be utilized fully to connect researchers, the extension services (of the Ministry of Agriculture and the Department of Forestry), and the intended beneficiaries of the research results.

Create a More Functional Department of Agriculture

The close connection between farming and deforestation implies that the Ministry of Agriculture must assume a central, more dynamic role in forest preservation and regeneration in Ghana. So far, the Agro-Forestry and Extension Units of the Ministry of Agriculture have not assumed the appropriate role considering the need for their services. This is clearly because those areas have not yet been accorded a priority status in Ghana. These two agencies, as well as the Department of Forestry, must be equipped with the tools for effective coordination of programs that will help to halt the use of destructive farming practices such as bush burning and unnecessary tree felling. Adequate propagation of information and the provision of incentives must become new priority activities of the Ministry of Agriculture. Farmers need to be taught how to protect trees on their farms, and how to plant wood lots for firewood, poles, etc.

The primary goals of the agencies within the agriculture sector should be the institution of a novel farming system for Ghana under which the acreage of farmlands and the numbers of destroyed trees would not necessarily have to increase in order to produce enough food and cash crops. To achieve this, the Agro-Forestry unit, in collaboration with the Extension Services Division of the Ministry of Agriculture, should aggressively popularize the practice of agro-forestry with the goal of establishing it as a common farming practice in Ghana. The mission of the Agro-Forestry Unit needs to be re-defined in line with this new, expanded, priority assignment.

Beyond providing the two agencies with the necessary resources, there is a need for structural and organizational changes that will enable them to coordinate their activities and manage their resources effectively. The priority objective should be educating the public, particularly the farmers, about the benefits of agro-forestry, and providing incentives that would encourage its adoption. Facilities of the government-controlled media and the emerging private mass media, as well as traditional institutions and local organizations should be utilized effectively by the agencies concerned, to help them spread information to the widely scattered farming communities. The following policy recommendations have demand-related objectives.

Policies for Managing the Internal Demand for Farmlands and Forest Resources

Control Population Growth

Population growth, the primary factor in the increased demand for farmland, firewood, charcoal, lumber, and other forest resources, deserves critical attention in efforts at curtailing deforestation in Ghana. Until more efficient, land-effective farming practices become the norm, until alternative, more efficient methods of domestic fuel use are discovered and popularized, and, until wood ceases to be a popular construction material, reducing the high rate of births remains one of the most credible approaches in controlling the demand for forest resources in Ghana.[638]   The presently inactive Family Planning Program of the Ministry of Health must be re-activated and expanded in order to educate the grassroots citizens and provide them affordable means of birth control. The mass media, churches, traditional rulers, Ministry of Education, Department of Rural Development, and Department of Social Welfare should also play a collaboratory role in this program.

Improve Currently Under-Utilized But Cultivable Lands
The results of the pilot irrigation projects near Kpong and Afienya in the Accra plains have shown that there exists a potential to boost agriculture in Ghana through irrigation of currently uncultivated lands in areas outside the forest region.[639]   By implication, the forests of Ghana would be spared if the lands north and south of the forest region were improved and efficiently cultivated.   Considering the serious short and long-term consequences of deforestation, irrigation is a worthwhile investment. Therefore the government needs to expand existing programs and provide more lands for farming. This would help reduce the demand for farmlands in the forested areas.

Increase Production of Alternative Sources of Meat
The failure of laws and policing to prevent hunting in reserved forests means that alternatives courses of action are required to reduce the demand for bush meat in Ghana and to help curtail the adverse effects of hunting in forests. Providing affordable alternatives to bush meat would help achieve this. The traditional methods used in poultry, livestock and fish production cannot yield the increased production necessary. Steps need to be taken to improve those methods. Available technical information, funding, land, and other resources required for promoting increased production, preservation and sale of poultry, livestock, and fish have to be disseminated widely with the intent to assist farmers to increase production. The Fisheries, Livestock and Extension Units of the Ministry of Agriculture need to intensify their efforts towards achieving increased productivity as a matter of urgency. Those agencies must utilize the mass media, farmers' organizations, and local institutions to teaching modern, more productive methods.

Reduce Demand for Firewood and Charcoal
It has been estimated that the efficiency of fuel wood usage in the Third World is as low as 7%.[640] This fact, together with the statistics presented in Table 4.8 (Chapter 4) are indicators of the wastage of wood and charcoal that has been taking place in Ghana. It also underlies the need for improved fuel-efficient cooking methods. In this regard, there is no denying that the resources of universities and research institutions in Ghana have not been adequately utilized to find the means to increase efficiency in domestic fuel use. These

institutions, as well as private entrepreneurs, should be made aware of this important research area. However, these institutions need to be given incentives to venture into this research area.

The development of more efficient and affordable kitchen stoves would go a long way to help reduce the quantities of fuel wood taken from the forests. If necessary, the prices of such stoves and gadgets that may be invented should be set low enough in order to render them affordable to all. In addition, research should be initiated (intensified, if already in progress) into ways of boosting the heat generated and prolonging the burning span of firewood and charcoal. The outcomes of such projects would be huge contributions towards the drive to reduce deforestation in Ghana.

Expand Research and Promote Alternative Sources of Inexpensive Energy

The development and extension of hydroelectric power as an alternative source of domestic energy need to be seen in terms of the potential to save the forests from perpetual degradation and eventual extinction. The Volta hydroelectric dams at Akosombo and Kpong are good illustrations of the potential of such sources of energy to cater to the needs of Ghanaians in both rural and urban areas. As part of the effort to reduce dependence on wood-based fuels, it is necessary to explore and develop the full potential of alternative sources of energy in Ghana, especially the potentially limitless supplies of solar energy, to provide affordable energy to Ghanaians. The only way to do this is through the development of simple, affordable electrical and solar-powered appliances for the use of Ghanaians.

Economic Policies for Restructuring the Timber Sector

Transform the Timber Industry to Emphasize Fabrication

One of the practical ways for the sustainable commercial utilization of forest resources in Ghana is to take advantage of advances in industrial technology and restructure the timber sector. Ghana stands to gain a great deal from de-emphasizing log and sawn-wood exports, and, instead, emphasizing fabrication into finished or partially finished goods. This research has shown that an important reason behind deforestation in Ghana has been the increasing rate of timber extraction. Recently, the worsening situation prompted the Department of Forestry to describe the demand for timber in Ghana as "insupportable."[641] The way to change this situation lies in upgrading the timber industry through expanding its manufacturing component.[642] The current World Bank/IMF supported schemes, designed to expand the capacity of sawmills and boost the export of logs and sawn wood under Ghana's Structural Adjustment Program, need to be reconsidered and a new emphasis placed on fabrication of wood into finished products.

Transforming logs and sawn wood into furniture, toys, door frames, wood panels, windows, cabinets, straw-board, plywood, etc., before export would increase the value of the exports, and boost the revenue derived from the resource. Such activity would make it possible for Ghana to generate the increased amounts of external revenues it needs to fulfill its external debt obligations and undertake urgently required development programs without necessarily depleting its forest resources.

In order to achieve the above, the mandates of the extractive bureaucracies within the Ghanaian forestry sector should emphasize manufacturing. Priority needs to be given to identification and utilization of the export potential of non-timber forest products.[643]

A Wood Products Marketing Board (W.P.M.B.) is recommended to replace the Timber Exports Development Board. The first order of this proposed board's business would be to establish connections with existing wood product manufacturers in Ghana for the purpose of supporting them in expanding their enterprises. Besides this, the Board should adjust down the excessive (and still expanding) installed capacity of sawmills and lumber enterprises.[644] Another priority of a proposed W.P.M.B. should be the development of forest based industries - furniture, building frames, handicrafts, toys, wood floorings, wall and ceiling panels, straw boards, plywood, etc. The government should provide this proposed board with adequate incentives and resources, and demand, in return, sustained research into both foreign and domestic markets for those products with the goal of expanding Ghana's share of those markets.

The potential role of private entrepreneurs in this transformation process needs to be recognized and addressed by the forestry sector agencies. This research has shown that, as is typical of private enterprises, the priority of investors in the Ghanaian timber sector is profit generation. It would be problematic to persuade private interests to venture into wood fabrication and non-traditional forest resources unless they are convinced about the benefits of such a move. It is therefore up to the government to provide the necessary information; support and incentives that would encourage businesses to shift into ventures in which they would achieve profits and at the same time help realize the goal of sustainability in the forestry sector.

Price Forest Resources on Economic Basis
An outcome of government control over the forestry sector in Ghana has been that market mechanisms have not been the sole determinant of the price of the resource.[645] Prices paid by timber contractors and sawmill operators for concessions have been much below the economic levels that would justify efficient wood usage or replanting of trees.[646] This prevailing indirect government "subsidy" to private enterprises has been an important reason behind the high levels of timber exploitation.[647] This virtual subsidy must be terminated as a matter of urgency. Royalties, fees, and rents charged extractors must reflect the "full scarcity value"[648] of the resource, reflecting the cost of logging, transportation, renewal, foregone future revenues, and adverse

consequences to the environment. Changing domestic pricing policy to reflect the external market prices for those products would also increase the value of timber and forest resources, encourage efficient utilization of wood,[649] and induce private and public investment in forest replantation.

Promote Exports of Non-Timber Forest Products

Although utilization of non-timber forest products (NTFP) in Ghana has thus far been largely limited to the local economy of Ghana,[650] evidence suggests that they have a large potential for external revenue generation. This potential needs to be explored. The growing interest in alternative medicines, natural remedies, and natural produce in the United States and other western countries, for example, implies an emergent market for plant pharmaceutical, sweeteners, dyes, gums, waxes, and oils. Tropical plants are emerging as critical sources of complex non-synthetic compounds and derivatives for the treatment of cancers, leukemia, Hodgkin's disease, etc.[651]

The ecosystem of the tropical forest in Ghana (a system that contains over 3,600 plant species,[652] 200 mammals,[653] 74 species of bats, 37 rodents,[654] and some 200 species of birds[655]) also has a large potential for eco-tourism. This potential also needs to be explored for eventual development to complement, and eventually replace timber extraction as a source of revenue.

The potential of NTFPs and eco-tourism means that Ghana has less destructive, more lucrative alternatives to timber extraction for external revenue. It is up to the government, and those positioned to influence the forestry policy process, to take the required initiative that will set a trend towards the utilization of those potentials.

The Role of External Forces

Contrary to the World Bank's long-standing assertion that economic development does not necessarily occur at the cost of the environment,[656] and despite the Bank's declared support of the concept of sustainability in the utilization of forest and other natural resources,[657] the position taken by the Bank on Ghana's economic reforms suggest that the Bank cannot be relied upon to help control deforestation in that country. In fact, the current dominant view among environmentalists is that World Bank policies in the forestry sector of Ghana have been "unrealistic and harmful,"[658] and "ecologically unsound."[659] The encouragement and support the Bank has given for the acquisition of more equipment to boost production of logs and sawn wood[660] amount to an endorsement of intensified natural resources extraction for external debt repayment. By accepting the Bank's prescription of extensive cash crop production for export, Ghana has, inadvertently, helped pronounce the deforestation problem.[661] For the above reasons the World Bank and its affiliate institutions are part of the problem of deforestation. It is up to the government of Ghana to ensure that environmental conservation and sustainability become integral dimensions of any deal negotiated with external financiers.

Because the principal objective of external corporate interests for engaging in Ghana's forestry sector has been the generation of maximum profits through increased extraction of timber, they cannot be expected to readily embrace solutions to deforestation except such solutions imply good prospects for profits. Information about the profit potential on NTFPs, eco-tourism, and manufacturing must be circulated as inducements to investors. At the same time, disincentives should be introduced to discourage timber extraction and activities that destroy forests.

Among external forces, non-governmental environmental interest groups, such as Green Peace, Sierra Club, World Wildlife Fund, etc., are among the most well situated to help instigate the changes advocated in this dissertation. Such organizations need to develop increased interest in Ghana's forestry problems. Apart from the information and support they can provide to the government, investors, tourists, etc., they are also situated to apply some pressure on the government to manifest its declared deforestation objectives in practical terms. In addition these groups need to support the young local interest groups and aid them to gain the strength required for long-term impact on forestry policies in Ghana.

The foregoing recommendations amount to a call for a substantial re-orientation of the government's traditional position on forestry. They demand major political changes in the internal environment of the forestry policy process so as to address the root causes of deforestation. The following section contains recommendations on the status, roles, and relationships of the principal actors and institutions involved in the process.

Political and Institutional Policies to Alter the Internal Environment of the Forestry Policy Process

Redefine Forestry Policy Objectives

An important proviso for discarding the colonial era-style forestry policy process and achieving a new system that is more responsive to the deforestation problem in Ghana is for those holding political power to give more prominence to deforestation policy formulation, implementation, and evaluation within political and administrative circles. Such a high profile can only be derived from a strong commitment to discarding the long-lasting colonial legacy of extraction-driven forestry policies thereby forestalling the calamity that looms over Ghana's environment. An equally important stimulus would be a determination, on the part of the principal actors within the policy arena, to make sustainability the focus of Ghana's forestry sector policies. The acknowledged explicit linkage between the economic welfare of Ghanaians and the land and forest requires that the forestry policy process in Ghana should be broader in its focus, giving greater consideration to the wide range of factors that impact the rate of forest resources extraction. In this connection, another objective of the forestry policy process must be to ensure that the forests are preserved in spite of continued extraction of timber and non-timber products, and farming activities.

To ensure that sectoral policies become more integrated and coordinated, the principal actors in the policy process (politicians and bureaucrats) need to reform the existing government machinery and functional processes in the forestry sector in order to establish connections between that sector and other sectors such as agriculture, manufacturing, construction, external trade, etc. What is needed is an overall sustainable economic policy without the conflicts and contradictions between policies and actions of government agencies.[662]

In the formulation of policies, forests in Ghana should not be perceived primarily in terms of their present potential for timber. More importantly, the forests should be perceived in terms of their potential for non-timber-forest-products. [663] The government's new policy objective should be multiple-use management for the purpose of conservation and increased net value for the forests.[664]

Enhance Role of Non-Governmental Stakeholders
The prevailing political and economic circumstances of Ghana indicate that the head of state, other powerful politicians, and the bureaucratic elites will dominate the forestry policy process for the foreseeable future. Nevertheless, the findings of this research have made it clear that in the formulation and implementation of the extraction-oriented forestry policies of Ghana, inattention to the security of tenure and concerns of certain non-governmental stakeholders, has precipitated the non-achievement of the objectives of those policies. Analysis of Ghana's past experiences has shown that protective regulatory forestry policies have been designed to be implemented by means of laws and other restrictions on the citizens and have not been effective.

As such, another important pre-condition for a more effective forestry policy process that will achieve sustainability is the enhanced participation of the hitherto excluded non-governmental stakeholders in the policy process.[665] In order to achieve the support and cooperation of farmers, timber contractors, chain saw operators, hunters and the population at large, it is crucial that the Department of Forestry categorically changes its traditional strategy for operating and embrace the non-governmental stakeholders as partners. Adequate information on sustainable farming practices coupled with an equitable stake in the wealth of the forests will help to establish these stakeholders as beneficiaries and important participants in the drive to combat deforestation. An arrangement whereby farmers, landowners, and the grass roots population as a whole, would directly receive part of the revenue realized from extracted forest resources would provide the necessary incentive to those who are affected, but not directly involved in those activities.

Increase the Role of Local Organizations and NGOs
The widespread incidence of deforestation in Ghana necessitates the emergence of active, influential citizen activist groups to help counter the forces

behind the problem.   The ubiquitous youth associations, development associations, self-help associations, and such similar organizations in Ghana have the potential to evolve into useful instruments for combating deforestation and other environmental problems at the local level.   Given their present strengths and interests, however, the prospects of such local organizations evolving into powerful interest groups that would raise politician and citizen awareness of the threat of deforestation, and make forest conservation (sustainable utilization) an important part of the national political agenda, is a long-term one indeed.

In the interim, it is necessary that a deliberate sustained effort be made by the government agencies to induct the existing organizations, and the population at large, into the forestry policy process.[666] In order to enhance its effectiveness as implementer of Ghana's deforestation policy, the functional regimen of the Department of Forestry needs to be revised so as to include the active participation of local institutions such as traditional rulers, youth associations, development associations, farmers cooperatives, churches, etc., in the management of reserved, as well as non-reserved, forests. There are two pre-conditions for the feasibility of this strategy. First, in view of the level to which the citizens depend on the land and forest resources, the forestry policies should be designed in such a way that they do not pose as threats to the citizens' livelihoods.   Secondly, the citizens need to perceive certain immediate and future benefits from preserving timber and other forest resources. Meeting these requirements would prepare the grounds for an increased citizen effort in forest reserve policing, tree planting, establishment of forest plantations, etc.

Even though environmental interest groups and non-governmental organizations such as Friends of the Earth Ghana, the Ghana Wildlife Society, and the Landlife Group are at present located primarily in the cities, and are not yet significant actors on the policy arena, they all have ambitions toward that goal. Under the prevailing political culture, the Ghanaian government cannot be expected to support and encourage the existing NGOs without necessarily seeking to co-opt them into the government's political control.   Furthermore, even though these young interest groups can continue to advocate change, they stand the risk of imminent confrontation with the government, and end up being labeled as enemies of the state.

Nevertheless, it is up to such non-governmental organizations, if they aspire to play an independent and significant role in helping address deforestation, to take advantage of all available sources of support (including external ones) and initiate a conscious effort to recruit residents of the rural areas and establish local branches.   It is only then that such organizations can become more effective in forest monitoring, public education, and, more importantly, political organization of the grassroots population.

Re-Orientate Institutions For Effective Deforestation Policies
As has been pointed out earlier, some far-reaching institutional changes would be required to implement the policy recommendations contained in this book. It

has been emphasized that sustainability has to be embraced by all government institutions in all decisions and actions. In addition, the prevailing institutional decision-making and implementation processes need to be devolved in order to expand non-governmental stakeholder input and cooperation. Thirdly, the active involvement of non-governmental stakeholders in the policy process would imply that restrictive laws and sanctions would cease to be the main instrument of implementation.

The recommendation has already been made to change the T.E.D.B. into a Wood Products Marketing Board. The current primary task of the Forest Products Inspection Bureau, which is to monitor the transportation of timber across the country for the purpose of controlling unauthorized felling and selling of timber, must be progressively scaled down through a deliberate policy to locate the proposed wood products manufacturing plants in or near the forest regions. Such a policy will reduce, and eventually eliminate, the need to ship volumes of lumber and logs from the forests to sawmills and the harbors.

Transform the Department of Forestry
The Department of Forestry, which, from every indication, has barely deviated from the structure and conventions established during the early colonial era, must be transformed in a way that would bring it on line with the prevailing social, economic, political, and cultural environment of Ghana. To eliminate the disparities between the department's efforts at deforestation control and reforestation, and their outcomes, the concept of sustainability should be translated into specific, measurable criteria that can be meaningfully applied to policy decisions and actions of the department. This would enable the authorities to determine in the future whether meaningful change has taken place or not.[667]

In connection with this, it is necessary to establish explicit directives as to the new mission of the Department of Forestry. In place of its current authoritative stance and methods, the mandate of the department should incorporate the non-governmental stakeholders as partners. The reality that citizens depend on forest resources for their livelihood should guide the content and implementation of the department's policies. Improved working relations between the department and the public would help to create the environment within which the department could effectively perform the advisory and extension role discussed above. Furthermore, increased mutual trust between foresters and citizens would help to establish the grounds for the proposed structural and legal changes in the policy process at the highest levels of the government. Equally important, the department should be given the necessary financial, personnel, and other tools for achieving its mission.

Another requirement for the department's effectiveness is an organizational structure that would decentralize authority and decision-making, and facilitate accommodation of the knowledge, needs, and concerns of grassroots stakeholders. This structure will enable it to become an instrument of technical and administrative support and coordination.

Formulate A New Mandate for the Forestry Commission

The complexity of forestry policy issues in Ghana justifies the existence of the Forestry Commission. However, in order to increase the commission's usefulness as a research and advisory agency, it is necessary to revise its mandate under the 1993 Forestry Commission Act (Act 453) to emphasize the short and long-term sustainability of forests. The links between this commission and the Forestry Research Institute need to be strengthened so as to coordinate their research activities and eliminate possible duplication of efforts. Technical information and research findings generated by this commission must be widely circulated among all relevant agencies, and given adequate media publicity for the sake of the farmers, timber contractors, charcoal producers, and all whose activities impact forests.

As part of its information gathering and publicity program, the series of seminars and forums organized prior to the formulation of the 1988 Ghana Forest Policy should be resurrected as a regular on-going activity of the commission. Such forums must be perceived as a means of assembling popular as well as expert knowledge and ideas for producing comprehensive and effective forestry policies.

Overhaul The Timber Concessions Awarding Process

Even though the Lands Department, because of its function as manager of lands in Ghana, deserves to remain involved in the process of authorizing timber extraction, it is not appropriately equipped to determine the proper conditions for sustainable extraction. So far, the interest of this agency has largely remained in concessions allocation. Furthermore, as was pointed out in chapter seven, the reason for the enduring influence of the Lands Department over the Timber Lease Committee is the direct benefit the department stands to gain from royalties and rents.[668] It is therefore important that this financial incentive to promote increased timber exploitation be eliminated. Appropriations of funds to the Lands Department must come directly from the government just as is the case for other agencies.

The foremost criterion that must guide the Timber Lease Committee is sustainability. To ensure this, the appointment of members to this Committee should be based on their possession of the appropriate knowledge and background for performing the balancing act of managing timber extraction and, at the same time, preserving and regenerating the forests. In order to maintain public trust and confidence in the Committee, its membership needs to be as diverse as possible. In addition to the present representatives from agencies such as the Department of Forestry, the Forestry Commission, the Agro-Forestry Unit, the Timber Products Development Board, the Lands Commission, and the Forestry Research Institute, popularly recognized representatives of traditional rulers, farmers, NGOs, charcoal producers, craftsmen, and the private timber industry must be included in the committee.

For the purpose of streamlining the collection of royalties, taxes, licensing and export fees, rents, etc., that responsibility should be restricted to the Timber Lease Committee. In its capacity as the body that awards contracts and concessions, and therefore possesses up-to-date information on the concessionaires and their activities, this committee is best positioned to stipulate the appropriate fees and to ensure payment.

The Political Implications of Policy Recommendations

It needs to be emphasized again that the policy recommendations contained in this research represent a call for radical transformation of the political and administrative culture and routines that have prevailed in Ghana's forestry sector for many years. These recommendations imply that the Ghanaian state has been an inefficient custodian of the forests. Consequently, the recommendations call for political reforms that would not only alter the power of politicians and bureaucrats, but also modify the priorities of these policy actors. The recommendation that hitherto excluded local organizations, traditional institutions, NGOs, and the grassroots population must be granted increased political and economic empowerment implies that some direct responsibility, and even more importantly, benefits, need to be given to citizens at the local level.

Under the existing Ghanaian political and economic environment, given the power and advantages enjoyed by politicians, bureaucrats, and entrepreneurs, there is a high probability that the fundamental changes called for here will be resisted by those best positioned to initiate them. It is unlikely that those policy actors would be inclined to yield their dominance over the policy process. Neither would they readily forgo the benefits they stand to gain form the existing system, for the sake of what might probably be seen within some circles as idealistic, unattainable objectives. It is also probable that Ghanaian politicians, in the face of the severe economic problems of the country, would lean towards short-term revenue-generation from forest resources extraction instead of the long-term gains that could be derived from actions towards achieving sustainability.

For these reasons, the political dimension of the deforestation problem in Ghana is extremely critical, if not the most critical. The prevalent bias against devolution of power and responsibility to the grassroots population cannot be denied. The immense political power of Ghanaian heads of state, and their vast influence over the content and outcomes of public policies implies that, more than anyone else, they are the ones who could initiate far-reaching policies and actions required for achieving sustainable utilization of forests in Ghana. Hence, the prospects of these difficult, but necessary, actions being taken to forestall the prevailing rate of deforestation, and institute sustainability as the core guiding principle of the forestry policy process, depend on the stance taken by the head of state.

In the final analysis, whether or not the changes advocated take place remains in the hands of the Ghanaian people - the heads of state, influential politicians, bureaucrats and the grassroots population. It is imperative for Ghanaian heads of state, their political associates, and the bureaucratic elites to develop the necessary political will and determination to reach beyond rhetoric and take the necessary steps for addressing deforestation. Those who initiate the above recommendations and succeed in establishing a trend towards the perpetual preservation of forest resources, even as they are utilized to cater to the needs of all Ghanaians in an equitable way, will leave a priceless legacy to future generations of Ghanaians.

Given that the forest is a resource that cannot be quickly replenished, the severe adverse consequences of not taking action to address deforestation should serve as the incentive for those in a position to do so. Chances are that continued deforestation will, at some point in time, eliminate a critical resource on which the citizens depend for their sustenance. It will also deplete a critical source of external revenue for the government. The economic crisis and its associated worsening quality of life that these events would yield, could lead up to political unrest, as, ultimately, it is the government that would be held responsible for the failure to manage the resource effectively.

Areas Requiring Further Research

It has been reiterated in this research that an effective deforestation policy process in Ghana requires the full participation of the grassroots population in the forest region. As was indicated in the introduction, because of various constraints, only a limited survey of the opinions and attitudes of this group was conducted during this research. A large-scale survey needs to be done in this area in order to produce adequate and reliable information on the opinions, attitudes, and the possible roles the individuals and groups at the local level need to play within the policy environment advocated in this research.

For the same reasons, another area that is awaiting more in-depth studies is the objectives, attitudes, and activities of the bureaucratic elites, ministers, and other politicians who have had some influence over the forestry policy process. The information from these studies would shed more light on the problem of deforestation, and help in the design of a framework for implementing the policy recommendations contained in this research.

Conclusion

The deforestation problem in Ghana is the product of a complex of historical, social, cultural, economic, and political factors. This research has shown that the policies intended for addressing the problem have not achieved their intended outcomes because those policies have consistently been conditioned by an over-riding objective, on the part of succeeding governments, to assume control over lands and forests for the purpose of monopolizing the authority over access to forest resources. In addition, the driving force behind the policies has been the commercial benefits of the government and timber interests.

The policy recommendations advanced in this research call for political boldness and a strong commitment to the long-term goal of forestalling an imminent disaster - an environmental disaster that would severely affect the economic and political fortunes of generations of Ghanaians yet to be born. The recommendations also call for a holistic perspective that would engender radical changes in the established political, economic, and administrative traditions.

The changes that have been advocated herein could result in temporary reductions in critically needed external revenues. They would also entail the difficult and risky venture of restructuring Ghana's external trade in forest resources in the interim. The changes in the policy-making and implementation process being advocated herein also literally demand the unusual act, on the part of politicians and bureaucrats, of voluntarily ceding some of their power and privileges.

The justification for such bold actions come from the contention of this researcher that no political or economic price is too high to pay for the purpose of regenerating and preserving the forests of Ghana. Prompt action may make it possible to endow future generations of Ghanaians with an invaluable legacy: a livable and bounteous environment. In the final analysis, the solution to the deforestation problem is fundamentally political.

APPENDIX 1

SCHEDULE OF QUESTIONS FOR THE EXPLORATORY SURVEY

Section A

1. Do you consider deforestation to be a problem in Ghana?
2. If yes, does it merit priority attention from the government?
3. What is the extent of this problem? Provide statistical and other evidence, if possible.
4. What are the main causes of deforestation in Ghana?
5. Which of these do you consider to be the leading cause(s)?
6. What were the policies of past governments in Ghana on this problem?
7. How were these policies formulated?
8. Who were the key participants in the forest policy formulation process?
9. What were the major actions taken under those policies?
10. How do the current policies and actions differ from those of the past?
12. What is your assessment of the effectiveness of those policies and action?
13. What is the present government's policy concerning deforestation?
14. What was the process through which this policy was formulated?
15. Who were the main participants in the formulation process?
16. What actions are currently being taken to combat it?
17. What is your assessment of the effectiveness of the current policy?
18. What are the reasons why deforestation has continued in Ghana?
19. What is the role of the Forestry Department?
20. In your opinion has the Forestry Department been an effective institution?
21. If no, what are the reasons for the ineffectiveness?
21. What can be done to improve the performance of the Forestry Department?
22. What other institutions are involved in the implementation of forest policies?
24 Can you tell me their roles?
25. In your opinion, are these institutions having any impact on the problem?
26. In your opinion, can it be possible to reduce or even halt deforestation in Ghana?
27. What would you recommend for an effective control of deforestation in Ghana?

Section B
To be administered to the Chief Conservator of Forests

28.   What are the goals of Ghana's deforestation policies today?
29.   What strategies has the Department of Forestry used to achieve these goals?
30.   What are the key obstacles to the Department in pursuing its objectives?
31.   Describe the organizational structure of the Department.
32.   Does the Department play any role in formulation of forest policies?
33.   Do political factors influence the content and implementation of policies? Please explain how.
34.   In its present form is the Department adequately equipped to perform its functions? If no, explain.
35.   It has often been suggested that a major reason why policies to combat deforestation have not had the desired effect is because the forestry laws are outmoded. How true is this?
36.   What impact do interest groups have on forest policies in Ghana?
37.   What impact do traditional rulers have on your Department?
38.   In your opinion, do the populations in the forest areas consider deforestation to be a problem?
39.   Do the populations in the forest areas have any input into formulation and implementation of forest policies?
40.   What is the level of cooperation of the local populations with the staff of the Department?
41.   Does the Department have a public education program?
42.   Given Ghana's economic conditions, and dependence on timber and forest products for external earnings, what are the prospects that deforestation can be controlled?

APPENDIX 2

OPERATIONALIZATION OF THE EXPLORATORY SURVEY

An important consideration behind the design of this exploratory survey was in developing procedures that would result in a reasonable level of empiricism, particularly, how to settle on a sampling frame that would enable the collection of adequate information, given the limited resources available for the project. The researcher therefore applied a multi-stage sampling technique to select one of the smallest organizational units in the Forestry Department, a sub-district (referred to within the Department as the Range) to be used as the sampling unit.

At the time of the research, there existed ten forestry regions in Ghana, sub-divided into fifty-three forest districts.[1] Twenty-four of these districts were in the forest area of the country, the other twenty-nine in non-forest areas. Since the principal subject of the survey was the opinions of citizens concerning deforestation and the government's policies to combat it, the districts outside the forest area were eliminated from the survey. The sampling frame was therefore restricted to those districts in forest areas.

Selection of the Sampling Unit: To arrive at the sampling unit, simple random sampling was applied to select one district. Each of the twenty-four districts was assigned a number; then one of them was drawn. The Begoro district, in the Eastern Region, was selected. The same technique was used to select the Kyebi range, one of six within the Begoro district, as the sampling unit. Much as the simple random selection is not the most efficient method possible, it was considered adequate for the purposes of this survey.

The Number and Categories of the Respondents: The survey consisted of fifty respondents, ten from each of the following five categories of respondents: employees of the Department of Forestry, farmers, timber contractors, saw-millers, and others (those involved in other occupations apart from the four listed). The categories were determined with consideration for the intention to focus on the citizens whose livelihoods are directly related to forestry.

The Venue of the Survey: The survey was conducted in three locations within the selected sampling unit. They were Kyebi, Suhum, and Anyinam townships. The selection of these townships was based on the availability of the various categories of respondents. Three out of the five categories of respondents were concentrated in few areas within the sampling unit. Six out of the eight sawmills were located in Suhum, all the Forestry Department employees lived in Kyebi, and fifteen out of the twenty-one timber contractors operated in the Anyinam area. The remaining two categories were widespread in the sampling unit.

---

[1]Plans were being made to increase the number of forestry districts in Ghana to 110 to coincide with the existing political administrative districts.

Selection of Respondents: Convenience sampling was used to contact the target number of respondents. As its name implies, this sampling method involves selecting the respondents who happen to be available. The first ten individuals who met the criteria for each of the established categories of respondents were included in the survey. The questionnaire used can be found in Appendix 3.

Operationalization: Given that this was an opinion survey, it was important to specify concrete empirical procedures that would result in the accurate measurement of variables, and also assist the respondents in giving the answers that closely reflected their thinking. In order to facilitate measurement of the responses, several questions were closed-ended and offered choices of responses. Most of the questions offered a range of variations for the respondent to choose from. In other cases, however, open-ended questions were used in order to avoid restricting the respondents to a few of the possible range of answers.

The gender, age, income, education, and religion of the respondents were recorded because such characteristics are likely to affect opinions on the topic. The questions inquired about their opinions on issues such as rights to exploit nature, the harmful effects of human progress on the environment, the need to control deforestation, the government's regulations pertaining to the forest, and the necessity to conserve forests.

APPENDIX 3

QUESTIONNAIRE FOR AN EXPLORATORY SURVEY OF THE
ATTITUDES OF GHANAIANS TOWARDS DEFORESTATION

(To facilitate utilization of the SPSS statistical system to analyze the responses obtained in this survey, variable names have been assigned to each question. Those names appear in Parenthesis.)

SECTION I

1. Age (*Age*):
2. Sex (*Sex*):   1) Male   2) Female
3. Marital Status (*Marital*):
4. Number of children (*Child*):
5. Occupation (*Occup*):
6. Religion (*Rel*):
7. Education (*Educ*):   1) None   2) Primary
                           3) Middle   4) Secondary
                           5) College   6) Graduate school
8. Total Family Income Per Month (*Income*):
    1)   Less than C10,000 per month
    2)   C10,000   to less than   C50,000
    3)   C50,000   -   -   -   C100,000
    4)   C100,000   -   -   -   C150,000
    5)   C150,000   -   -   -   C200,000
    6)   C200,000   -   -   -   C250,000
    7)   More than C250,000 per month

For each of the following statements please indicate whether you: (1) Agree Strongly, (2) Agree Somewhat, (3) Disagree Somewhat, (4) Disagree Strongly, or (5) Cannot Choose.

9. Nature is sacred because it is created by God (*Sacred*)
    　　　　　1　　　2　　　3　　　4　　　5
10. Man has the right to exploit nature by any means available. (*Right*)
    　　　　　1　　　2　　　3　　　4　　　5
11. People worry too much about human progress harming the environment. (*Worry*)
    　　　　　1　　　2　　　3　　　4　　　5
12. Deforestation in Ghana is a very serious problem. (*Problem*)
    　　　　　1　　　2　　　3　　　4　　　5
13. It is necessary for the government to do much more to protect the forests in Ghana. (*Protect*)
    　　　　　1　　　2　　　3　　　4　　　5
14. There is too much government regulation concerning the forests. (*Excess*)
    　　　　　1　　　2　　　3　　　4　　　5

15.   Forests in Ghana should be protected even if that would cause job
        losses.   (*Jobloss*)

                    1   2   3   4   5

16.   I will be willing to pay higher prices and higher taxes in order to help
        protect the forests.   (*Taxes*)

                    1   2   3   4   5

17.   The Department of Forestry is an effective institution for preserving
        Ghana's forests (*Effect*)

                    1   2   3   4   5

18.   It will be good to scale down the timber industry in order to conserve
        the forests   (*Scale*)

                    1   2   3   4   5

19.   Timber exploitation is a major cause of deforestation. (*Timber*)

                    1   2   3   4   5

20.   It is very important for everyone who cuts a tree to replant. (*Replant*)

                    1   2   3   4   5

21.   Please select from the following what should be the <u>three</u> most
        important goals of the Department of Forestry (*Goals*):

        1)   Tree replanting.
        2)   Protection of forests
        3)   Regulation of the timber industry
        4)   Support of the timber industry
        5)   Collection of revenue
        6)   Creation of jobs
        7)   Opening of more lands for development

11.   Please select from the following the <u>three</u> most serious causes of
        deforestation in Ghana (*Causdef*):

        1)   Growth of settlements
        2)   Charcoal production
        3)   Logging
        4)   Farming
        5)   The legacy of colonialism
        6)   Road construction
        7)   Bush fires
        8)   Not enough regulation
        9)   Government corruption

SECTION II
Questions to be answered by staff of the Department of Forestry

1.   Rank in the Department (*Rank*):
2.   Number of years in the Department (*Yeardep*):

For the following statement please indicate whether you: (1) Agree Strongly, (2) Agree Somewhat, (3) Disagree Somewhat, (4) Disagree Strongly, or (5) Cannot Choose.

3.   "The directors and other top officials of the Department of Forestry do not understand the real causes of deforestation." (*Direct*)

    1   2   3   4   5

4.   What should the government do to preserve the forests? (*Preserve*)
5.   What do you like most about your job? (*Job*)
6.   What do you like least about your job? (*Leasjob*)

SECTION III
Questions to be answered by timber contractors

1.   Number of employees. (*Numemp*)
2.   Where do you fell trees? (*Feltre*)

        1)   Concessions in forest reserves
        2)   Concessions outside forest reserves
        3)   Own land
        4)   Farmlands
        5)   Anywhere
        6)   Other (*please specify*)

For each of the following statements please indicate whether you: (1) Agree Strongly, (2) Agree Somewhat, (3) Disagree Somewhat, (4) Disagree Strongly, or (5) Cannot Choose.

3.   It is easy to find suitable trees to log today (*Suitable*)

    1   2   3   4   5

4.   It easy to obtain concessions (*Concess*)

    1   2   3   4   5

5.   It is easy to obtain permits to fell trees (*Permit*)

    1   2   3   4   5

6.   This business is profitable (*Profit*)

    1   2   3   4   5

7.   What kind of processing plant do you have? (*Plant*)

SECTION IV
Questions to be answered by farmers

1.   Kind of land tenure (*Tenure*):

        1)   own
        2)   rent
        3)   family land
        4)   squatting
        5)   other (specify)

2. Size of farm (in acres) (*SizeFm*)
3. Is your farm permanent? (*FmPerm*)
4. If no, how often do you cultivate a new piece of land? (*Culti*)
5. Where do you obtain firewood? (*Firewd*)
    1) forest reserve   2) farm
    3) unreserved forest   4) fallow land
    5) anywhere   6) no answer

For each of the following statements please indicate whether you: (1) Agree Strongly, (2) Agree Somewhat, (3) Disagree Somewhat, (4) Disagree Strongly, or (5) Cannot Choose.

6. Suitable farmland is easy to obtain (*Obtain*)

         1   2   3   4   5

7. Over the years the sizes of farms are getting smaller. (*FmSize*)

         1   2   3   4   5

8. You would change your method of farming if it will help to preserve the forests   (*Method*)

         1   2   3   4   5

APPENDIX 4

INDICATORS OF GHANA'S ECONOMIC PERFORMANCE: 1957-1996

	BUDGET ACCOUNT BALANCE ($m.)	TRADE BALANCE ($m.)	FOREIGN EXCHANGE RESERVES ($m.)	EXTERNAL DEBT ($m.)	CONSUMER PRICE INDEX
1959	-35.8	-31	299	45.4	82
1961	-59.4	-102	145	152.5	88
1963	-97.2	-92	116	512.3	100
1965	-83.8	-154	125	760.1	144
1967	-59.6	-29	95	861	140
1969	-84.4	-46	70	1040	96
1971	5.5	16	38	1,193.8	105
1973	-110.7	119	163	1,055.1	128
1975	-264	-45	134	1,408.3	230
1977	-623.2	N. A.	143	2,733.9	629
1980	N.A.	N.A.	N.A.	1,398	6.3
1988	-264	-112.4	N.A.	3,128	131.4
1990	-432	-308.2	218.8	3,873	225.8
1992	-592	-470.3	320.3	4,499	293.3
1994	-815	-353.1	583.6	5,463	457.6
1996	-532	N.A.	N.A.	N.A.	N.A.

Source: United Nations Statistical Year Book; 1961, 1974, 1979. , Commodity Year Book; 1964, 1970, World Bank, African Development Indicators, (Washington, D.C.: IBRD, 1997), The Economist Intelligence Unit, London: Ghana Country Profile, 1996/97, and Institute of Statistical, Social and Economic Research (ISSER), "The State of the Ghanaian Economy in 1993", (Legon: ISSER, University of Ghana, 1994), p. 68. For Consumer Price Indexes 1957 to 1977, 1963=100. For Consumer price Indexes 1980 to 1996, 1987=100. N.A : Data unavailable to researcher

APPENDIX 5

GHANA: BALANCE ON CAPITAL AND CURRENT ACCOUNTS, 1955-1962
(US $million)

		TOTAL CURRENT ACCOUNT	TOTAL CAPITAL ACCOUNT	BALANCE ON CURRENT AND CAPITAL ACCOUNTS
1955	Credit	110	12	11
	Debit	108	3	-
1956	Credit	95	-	-
	Debit	107	4	16
1957	Credit	103	3	-
	Debit	116	5	15
1958	Credit	118	5	5
	Debit	105	13	-
1959	Credit	126	14	-
	Debit	135	14	9
1960	Credit	128	11	-
	Debit	155	-	16
1961	Credit	129	11	11
	Debit	182	20	20
1962	Credit	125	27	-
	Debit	153	-	1

Source: Ghana Government, <u>Seven-Year Plan for National Reconstruction and Development,</u> <u>1963/64-1969/70</u>, (Accra: Office of the Planning Commission, 1964), p. 221.

APPENDIX 6

GHANA: PRODUCTION OF ENERGY BY SOURCE, 1974-1994
(toe X 1000)

YEAR	CRUDE OIL	HYDROELECTRIC POWER	WOOD-FUEL	TOTAL
1974	0.00	438.38	2,410.08	2,848.56
1976	0.00	448.67	2,551.09	2,998.76
1978	0.00	400.01	2693.71	3,093.72
1980	0.00	567.17	2,839.76	3,406.93
1982	66.89	531.18	2,989.93	3,588.00
1984	33.43	193.36	3,179.70	3,406.49
1986	0.00	469.99	3,418.41	3,888.40
1988	0.00	516.85	3,578.16	4,195.01
1990	0.00	615.99	3,961.08	4,576.07
1992	0.00	709.72	4,269.50	4,979.21
1994	0.00	653.32	4,606.03	5,259.35

Source: Ministry of Mines & Energy, Energy Information Center, (Accra; National Science & Technology Press, CSIR, 1995).
TOE: Tons of Oil Equivalent
1 metric ton crude oil = 7.33 barrels

APPENDIX 7

GHANA: CONSUMPTION OF ENERGY BY SOURCE, 1974-1994
(toe X 1000)

	PETROLEUM	HYDROELECTRIC POWER	WOOD-FUEL	TOTAL
1974	1,166.37	438.38	1,879.21	3,483.96
1976	1,157.56	448.67	1,984.97	3,591.19
1978	1,160.04	400.01	2,092.44	3,652.49
1980	1,076.56	567.17	2,203.34	3,847.06
1982	1,059.13	531.18	2,320.20	3,910.51
1984	760.18	193.36	2,410.01	3,363.55
1986	899.21	469.99	2,561.05	3,930.25
1988	962.77	516.85	2,722.91	4,202.53
1990	800.15	614.99	2,896.49	4,311.63
1992	957.90	709.72	3,082.81	4,750.43
1994	1,073.67	653.32	3,282.96	5,009.94

Source: Ministry of Mines & Energy, Energy Information Center, (Accra; National Science & Technology Press, CSIR, 1995).
TOE: Tons of Oil Equivalent

APPENDIX 8

GHANA: CONSUMPTION OF WOODFUELS BY SECTORS, 1974-1994
(toe x 1000)

YEAR	RESIDENTIAL & COMMERCIAL	INDUSTRIAL	TOTAL
1974	1,606.86	194.70	1,801.55
1976	1,696.82	205.35	1,902.17
1978	1,788.29	216.22	2,004.51
1980	1,882.77	227.49	2,110.26
1982	1,982.68	239.58	2,222.26
1984	2,061.50	245.00	2,306.50
1986	2167.22	257.91	2,445.22
1988	2,231.81	271.49	2,593.30
1990	2,465.69	285.79	2,751.48
1992	2,619.70	300.85	2,920.55
1994	2,784.70	316.69	3,101.40

Source: Ministry of Mines & Energy, Energy Information Center, (Accra; National Science & Technology Press, CSIR, 1995).
TOE: Tons of Oil Equivalent

APPENDIX 9

GHANA: PRODUCTION AND EXPORT OF TIMBER, FUEL-WOOD AND CHARCOAL, 1982 -1992

	1982	1984	1986	1988	1990	1992
ROUNDWOOD PRODUCTION (CU. FT.)	505,862	579,590	584,499	596,540	618,220	593,644
ROUNDWOOD EXPORT (CU. FT.)	1,872	2,472	6,250	11,970	4,979	5,968
REVENUE FROM ROUNDWOOD EXPORTS ($1,000)	3,4694	5,140	18,440	45,420	34,015	40,972
TOTAL REVENUE FROM FOREST PRODUCT EXPORTS ($1,000)	11,184	17,784	39,522	100,073	109,830	150,117
FUELWOOD AND CHARCOAL PRODN. (CU. FT.)	477,931	544,845	546,716	562,288	567,373	547,740

Source: FAO: "FAO Yearbook Forest Products, 1982 - 1993", (Rome: FAO Forest Policy and Planning Division, 1995).

APPENDIX 10

GHANA: SELECTED PRODUCTION INDICATORS 1970, 1980-1988

	1970	1980	1982	1984	1986	1988
CEREALS ('000 tons)	858	674	544	699	872	995
STARCHY STAPLES ('000 tons)	6,024	4,349	4,431	5,868	6,117	4,500 (Estim)
COCOA ('000 tons)	413	258	178	175	228	305
FORESTRY ('000 m3)	1,920	630	599	801	1,174	n. a.
GOLD (troy ounces)	642	353	331	287	288	383
DIAMONDS ('000 carats)	2,550	1,149	684	346	559	306
MANGANESE ORE (tons)	392	250	160	288	259	282
BAUXITE (tons)	337	225	64	49	204	204

Sources: Ghana, <u>Quarterly Digest of Statistics</u>, various issues; World Bank, 1990.

Endnotes

[1]Protective regulatory policy is one of four domestic policy types advanced by Ripley in his framework for empirical public policy analysis. (The other three are distributive, competitive regulatory, and redistributive policies.) As the name implies, protective regulatory policy is the type intended to protect the interests of the public. It sets conditions under which various private activities can or cannot take place. Usually, it prohibits actions and situations that are thought to be harmful to the general public. Examples of protective regulatory policies and programs in the United States, which Ripley might consider, include the establishment of reserved forests, the declaration of certain lands as national monuments, penalties on manufacturers of cars that do not meet minimum emission standards, bans on harmful food additives, and the requirements for strip miners to restore the land after exploiting it. [See Randall B. Ripley, Policy Analysis in Political Science, (Chicago: Nelson-Hall, 1985), Chapter 3.]

[2]John O. Broader, "Development Alternatives for Tropical Rain Forests," in Environment and the Poor: Development Strategies for a Common Agenda, United States-Third World Policy Perspectives, No. 11, Overseas Development Council, (New Brunswick: Transaction Books, 1989), p. 111.

[3]The United States Congress, Office of Technology Assessment (O.T.A.),Technologies to Sustain Tropical Forest Resources, Publication No. OAT/F/214, (Washington, D.C.: March, 1984), pp. 11-75.

[4]J. Dirk Stryker, "Technology, Human Pressure, and Ecology in the Arid and Semi-Arid Tropics," and John O. Browder, "Development Alternatives for Tropical Rain Forests," in Environment and the Poor: Development Strategies for a Common Agenda, US-Third World Policy Perspectives, No. 11, Overseas Development Council, (New Brunswick: Transaction Books, 1989). See also, Kevin M. Cleaver and Gotz A. Schreiber, Reversing the Spiral: The Population, Agriculture, and Environment Nexus in Sub-Saharan Africa, (Washington, D.C.: The World Bank, 1994).

[5]J. Rile, "Sufferings in Africa: Captain Rile's Narrative" (New York: Clarkson Potter, 1965). In U. S. Congress, Deforestation and Environmental Change in the West African Sahel by J. Gritzner. (Washington, DC: Office of Technology Assessment (O.T.A.) Commissioned Paper, 1982).

[6]Ibid.

[7]The Population Reference Bureau, "World Population Data Sheet 1994," (Washington, D.C., Population Reference Bureau Inc., April, 1994).

[8]Kevin M. Cleaver and Gotz A. Schreiber, Reversing the Spiral: The Population, Agricultural and Environmental Nexus in Sub-Saharan Africa, (Washington, DC: The

World Bank, 1994), p. 179. See also, Jean Paul Lanly, "Tropical Forest Resources," {Rome: United Nations Food and Agricultural Organization (F.A.O.), 1982}, Paper No. 30.

[9]Robert Sutherland Rattray, Ashanti, (Oxford: The Clarendon Press, 1923). See also, Dennis Anderson & Robert Fishwick, "Fuelwood Consumption and Deforestation in African Countries," (Washington, DC: The World Bank, 1984), Staff Working Papers, No. 704, p. 2.

[10]K. Yeboah Daaku, Trade and Politics in the Gold Coast, 1600-1720, (Oxford: Clarendon Press, 1970). See also, A. Adu Boahen, Topics in West African History, (London: Longman, 1966).

[11]James Anquandah. Rediscovering Ghana's Past, (Essex: Longman, 1982), pp. 58- 59.

[12]Ibid.

[13]G. B. Kay, The Political Economy of Colonialism in Ghana, (Cambridge: University Press, 1972).

[14]Ibid.

[15]Mary MaCarthy, Social Change and the Growth of British Power in the Gold Coast: The Fante States, 1807-1874, (Lanham: University Press of America, 1963), page ix.

[16]Anquandah, Op. cit., p. 28.

[17]K. Effah-Gyamfi, "Bono Manso - An Archaeological Investigation Into Early Akan Urbanism," (Ph.D. Thesis, University of Ghana, Legon, 1978). See also, Anquandah, Ibid., page 128.

[18]H. N. Thompson, Gold Coast: Report on Forests, Colonial Reports - Miscellaneous No. 66. London: HMSO, 1910. pp. 97-100.

[19]Ibid., p. 98.

[20]Ibid., p. 97.

[21]Ibid., pp. 100-101.

[22]Thomas Ford Chipp. The Forest Officer's Handbook of the Gold Coast, Ashanti, and the Northern Territories. (London: Crown Agents for the Colonies, 1922), pp. 48 and 67.

[23]Ibid. p. 47.

[24]Gold Coast Colony, Wealth In Wood, (Accra: Public Relations Dept., 1950), p. 9.

[25]Garrett Harding, "The Tragedy of the Commons," Science, vol. 162, 1968, p. 1243. In this article, Harding dealt with the consequence of reckless exploitation of natural resources. He demonstrated this with the example whereby grazers who have a free access to an area of common pasture continually add more livestock to graze the commons, resulting in the commons eventually becoming hopelessly overgrazed and ruined. The key to the tragedy, according to Harding, is the type of usufruct rights, the scale of management responsibility, or lack thereof, and the degree of public trust in the government. Ultimately, all stakeholders stand to lose if the pasture (a common resource) is not managed effectively.

[26]Republic of Ghana, The Constitution of the Third Republic of Ghana, (Accra: Ghana Publishing Corporation, 1980).

[27]Republic of Ghana, The Constitution of the Forth Republic of Ghana, (Accra: Ghana Publishing Corporation, 1992).

[28]Ibid.

[29]See, for example, Alhaji Farouk Brimah, "Statement by the Deputy Minister for Environment, Science and Technology at the Sixth Session of the African Ministers of Environment," Nairobi, Kenya, December 11-15, 1995. See also, Kafui Ameh, "Brief Overview of Ministry of Environment Science and Technology (MEST) Activities," A Paper Presented by the Public Relations Officer of the Ministry of Environment Science

and Technology at the MEST/EPA/UNEP Seminar for Media Practitioners, Cape Coast, Ghana, October 24-26, 1995.

[30]The Environmental Protection Agency was established in 1994 by an Act of Paliarment to replace the Environmental Protection Council which had been in existence since 1974.

[31]Dr. Peter Acquah, "Environmental Issues and Aspects on Their Management in Ghana," (Accra: Environmental Protection Agency (E.P.A.), September 1995), E.P.A. Environmental Management Special Paper 2, p. 4.

[32]Republic of Ghana, Budget Statement for 1975-76, (Accra: Ghana Publishing Corporation, 1975).

[33]Republic of Ghana, Budget Statement for 1976-77, (Accra: Ghana Publishing Corporation, 1976).

[34]Republic of Ghana, Budget Statement for 1980-81, (Accra: Ghana Publishing Corporation, 1980).

[35]Government of Ghana, Five Year Development Plan, Part III, (Accra: Ministry of Economic Planning/Ghana Publishing Corporation, January 1977).

[36]Republic of Ghana, Budget Statement for 1995-96, (Accra: Ghana Publishing Corporation, 1995).

[37]Under the Constitution of the Forth Republic of Ghana (1992) forestry was placed under a new Ministry of Lands and Forestry. Hitherto, the sector had existed under various ministries such as Lands and Natural Resources, and Agriculture.

[38]Ghana Ministry of Lands and Forestry, "Draft National Forest Policy of the Republic of Ghana," (Accra: Ministry of Lands and Forestry, 1993).

The term "sustainability" and the concept of sustainable utilization of forest resources will be dealt with at various points in this book. As such, it is necessary that its definition should be established at the outset. Becky J. Brown et al. ("Global Sustainability: Towards Definition," Environmental Management, vol. 11, No. 6, 1987, pp. 713-719.) performed an in-depth definition and analysis of the concept in all its dimensions. The concise definition offered by Tivy and O'Hare however would serve the purpose of this research. They defined sustainable resource use as the management of that resource "for maximum continuous production, consistent with the maintenance of a constantly renewable stock." {J. Tivy and G O'Hare, Human Impact on the Ecosystem, (Edinburgh: Oliver and Boyd, 1982.)} As shown by Brown et al., "sustainability" is multi-dimensional, including social, economic, and ecological dimensions.

[39]Forestry Department, "Steps Towards Sustainable Forest and Wise Use of Timber Resources," Paper Presented to the 28th Session of the ITTC and the 26th Session of the ITTO Permanent Committees, Accra, Ghana, May 10-18, 1995.

[40]J. B. Hall, "Conservation of Forest in Ghana," Universitas, (Legon: University of Ghana), vol. 8, pp. 33-42. See also, K. Frimpong-Mensah, "Requirement of the Timber Industry," Ghana Forest Inventory Proceedings, (Accra: Ghana Forestry Department/ODA, 1989).

[41]Imperial Institute of London, Journal of the Empire Forestry Association, vol. 1, No. 1, March 1922, p. 12.

[42]Gold Coast Colony, Wealth in Wood, Op. cit., p. 3.

[43]Ibid.

[44]Government of Ghana, "Timber Industry: Report of Fact Finding Committee Appointed by the Minister of Commerce, Land and Mines," (Accra: Government Printing Department, 1951), p. 1.

[45]Ibid.

[46]Henry Gruppe and Waafas Ofosu-Amaah, <u>Legal, Regulatory, and Institutional Aspects of Environmental and Natural Resources Management in Developing Countries; A Country Study of Ghana</u>, (Washington, D.C.: International Institute for Environment and Development, 1984).

[47]United Nations Food and Agricultural Organization (F.A.O.), <u>F.A.O. Yearbook Volume 48, 1994</u>, (Rome: F.A.O., 1995), Statistics Series No. 125, page 4.

[48]United Nations Food and Agricultural Organization (F.A.O.), <u>F.A.O./W.R.I. Production Yearbook, Conservation Table 1001</u>, (Rome: F.A.O., 1992), p. 344.

[49]U.N.F.A.O./United Nations Environment Program (U.N.E.P.), <u>Tropical Forest Resources Assessment Project</u>, (Rome: F.A.O., 1981).   See also, F.A.O., <u>Forest Resources Assessment 1990, Global Synthesis</u>, (Rome: F.A.O., 1990), Forestry Paper 124.

[50]Caroline Sargeant et al., "Incentives for the Sustainable Management of Tropical High Forest in Ghana," <u>Commonwealth Forestry Review</u>, vol. 73(3) 1984, pp. 155-163.

[51]Ibid. p. 157.

[52]Department of Forestry, Op. cit., p. 2.

[53]Ibid.

[54]Ibid. pp. 8 & 10.

[55]Those institutions assigned to protect the forests, and those promoting the exploitation and

[56]Forest produce have featured prominently among Ghana's exports since 1900, earnings from the resource increasing from about $136,000 in that year to $32.5 million in 1960, and to $154.2 million in 1993.

[57]The increase in Ghana's export earnings from timber from 3 percent of the total in 1980 to 12 percent in 1993 denotes this fact. {See The World Bank: <u>Trends in Developing Economies: Extracts, volume 3, Sub-Saharan Africa</u>, (Washington, D.C.: The World Bank, 1994), p. 81.)

[58]Ripley, Op. cit.

[59]Ripley, Op. cit., pp. 37-39.

[60]David Easton, "An Approach to the Analysis of Political Systems," <u>World Politics</u>, v. 9, 1957, pp. 383-400. See also, Easton, <u>A Framework For Political Analysis</u>, (Englewood Cliffs, New Jersey: Prentice Hall, 1965).

[61]Graham Allison, <u>Essence of Decision: Explaining the Cuban Missile Crisis</u>, (Boston: Little Brown & Co., 1971), p. 6.

[62]David B. Truman, <u>The Governmental Process</u>, (New York: Knopf, 1957).

[63]Charles Lindblom, <u>The Policy Making Process</u>, (Englewood Cliffs, N. J.: Prentice Hall, 1968).

[64]Thomas R. Dye, <u>Understanding Public Policy</u>, (Upper Saddle River, N. J.: Prentice Hall, 1988).

[65]Graham Allison, <u>Essence of Decision: Explaining the Cuban Missile Crisis</u>, (Boston: Little Brown & Co., 1971), p. 6.

[66]Robert Presthus, <u>Elites and the Policy Process</u>, (London: Cambridge University Press, 1974).

[67]James Anderson, <u>Public Policy Making</u>, (New York: Holt, Rinehart and Winston, 1984).

[68]Charles Jones, <u>An Introduction to the Study of Public Policy</u>, 3rd Edition, (Monterey, Ca: Brooks/Cole, 1984).

[69]Charles O. Jones, Op. cit.

[70]Randall B. Ripley, <u>Policy Analysis in Political Science</u>, (Chicago: Nelson-Hall, 1987).

[71]Hugh Helco, "Review Article: Policy Analysis," British Journal of Political Science, vol. 2, 1972, p. 105.

[72]Paul Sabatier, "Towards Better Theories of the Policy Process." PS: Political Science and Politics, June 1991, p. 147.

[73]Allison, Op. cit., p.6.

[74]J. A. Egonmwan, Policy Analysis: Concepts and Applications, Benin City, Nigeria: Fiesta Press, 1987), p. 49.

[75]Allison, Op. cit., p. 67.

[76]Incremental decision-making, a process that involves small, marginal changes to existing policy, will be examined in detail later in this chapter when normative theories on policy formulation are treated.

[77] Dye, Op. cit., pp. 26-29.

[78]Earl Lathman, "The Group Basis of Politics", in Heinz Eulau, Samuel J. Eldersveld, and Morris Janowitz (eds), Political Behavior, (New York: Free Press, 1956), p. 239.

[79]Daniel Green, "Structural Adjustment and Politics in Ghana," Trans Africa Forum, v. 8, Summer 1991, pp. 67-89.

[80]Fred M. Hayward, "A Reassessment of Conventional Wisdom About Informed Public: National Political Information in Ghana," American Political Science Review, v. 70, June 1976, pp. 433-451.

[81]Allison, Op. cit., p. 6.

[82]Ibid.

[83]Ibid., p. 67.

[84]Ibid., p. 162.

[85]A. L. Adu, The Civil Service in New African States, (New York: Praeger, 1965). See also A. L. Adu, The Civil Service in Commonwealth Africa: Development and Transition, (London: Allen and Unwin, 1969).

[86]Robert Presthus, Elites and the Policy Process, (London: Cambridge University Press, 1974).

[87]Thomas Dye and Harmon Ziegler, The Irony of Democracy, 5th Ed., (Belmont, Ca.: Wardsworth, 1981).

[88]The term elites refers to politicians and bureaucrats, as well as those who, by birth, better education, and access to opportunity, are in positions of leadership and influence in the professions, academia, the armed forces, the bureaucracy, business, the media, and traditional and political associations. What distinguishes these elites from the rest of the society is their inequitable share of expertise, class, status and wealth.

[89]Presthus, Op. cit. See also Charles Jones, Op. cit., p. 55.

[90]Dye, Op. cit.

[91]Bjorn M. Edsman, Lawyers in Gold Coast Politics, 1900-1945: From Mensah Sarbah to J. B. Danquah, (Upsala: University Press, 1979).

[92]C. L. R. James, Nkrumah and the Ghana Revolution, (London: Allison and Busby, 1977). See also, Kwame Nkrumah, The Autobiography of Kwame Nkrumah, (London: Panaf, 1973).

[93]Daniel Green, "Ghana's Adjusted Democracy," Review of African Political Economy, vol. 22, 1995, pp. 577-586. See also, Jon Kraus, "Ghana's Radical Populist Regime," Current History, vol. 84, April 1985, pp. 164-168, 186-187., Henry Bienen, "Populist Military Regimes in West Africa," Armed Forces and Society, vol. 1, Spring 1985, pp. 357-377, and Donald Rothchild, "Military Regime Performance : An Appraisal of the Ghana Experience, 1972-78," Comparative Politics, vol. 12, July 1980, pp. 459-479.

[94]African Association for Public Administration and Management (A.A.P.A.M.), The Ecology of Public Administration and Management in Africa, (New Delhi: Vickas, 1986), pp. 195-243.

[95]Peter S. Cleaves, "Implementation Amidst Scarcity and Apathy: Political Power and Policy Design," in Merilee S. Grindle (ed), Politics and Policy Implementation in the Third World, (Princeton, N. C.: Princeton Univ. Press, 1980), pp. 281-303. See also Hayward, Op. cit.

[96]The high profile activities and sometimes intense advocacy of "youth", "development", "progressive", cultural", and similarly named associations, which are typically local and often highly political organizations that are invariably led and organized by the better educated and more successful businessmen, suggest that the elites do also possess strong allegiance to their clans, tribes, home-town etc.

[97]James S. Wunsch, "Traditional Authorities, Innovation, and Development Policy," Journal of Developing Areas, vol. 11, April 1977, pp. 357-371.

[98]Charles Lindblom, "The Science of Muddling Through," Public Administration Review, v. 79-89, Spring 1959, p. 19. See also, Lindblom, "Still Muddling, Not Yet Through," Public Administration Review, v. 39, 1979, pp. 517-526.

[99]Disjointed incrementalism is based on the following assumptions:

- Small marginal (incremental) changes to existing policy are made.
- Constraints of time, intelligence, and costs prevent policy-makers from identifying the full range of policy alternatives and their consequences.
- Political factions prevent the establishment of clear-cut societal goals and the accurate calculation of cost-benefit ratios.
- Targeted policy ends are appropriately linked to available means, (against the rational model that takes the view of sequential relationships between ends and means.)
- Problems are not solved at one stroke, but are successively tackled, step-by-step.
- Policy makers do not attempt to produce a future ideal state. Rather, they endeavor to reduce known social ills by trial and error governmental actions.
- Problems are continually being redefined, hence incrementalism allows continuous adjustments so as to make problems manageable.
- The decision-making process is disjointed because diverse individuals and groups have access to it and make inputs into it at different points.
- There is no single right solution to any problem.

[100]A sample of development plans and annual budgets are examined in this research to illustrate this point.

[101]Ira Sharkansky (ed), Public Administration: Public Policy Making in Government, 2nd Ed., (Chicago: Markham, 1972).

[102]Yehezkel Dror, "Muddling Through" – "Science or Inertia?" Public Administration Review, v. 24, 1964, pp. 153.

[103]Yehezkel Dror, Op. cit., p. 155.

[104]Ibid., p. 153.

[105]A. O. Hirshman and Charles Lindblom, "Economic Development Policy Making: Some Converging Views," Behavioral Science, v. 7, 1962, pp. 211-2.

[106]John Dryzek and Brian Ripley, "The Ambitions of Policy Design," Policy Studies Review, v. 7, 1988, pp. 705-719.

[107]Robert Gooding, The Politics of Rational Man, (New York: John Wiley and Sons, 1982), p. 20.

[108]Amitai Etzioni, "Mixed-Scanning: A Third Approach to Decision-Making," Public Administration Review, v. 27, 1967, pp. 387-388.

[109]Amitai Etzioni, Ibid.

[110]Etzioni, Op. cit., pp. 388-390.

[111]The basic assumptions of the rationalist theory are that policy goals are clearly specified, that relevant information is available, and that all possible alternative courses of action are known, examined and evaluated. Therefore, in line with the rationalist tradition, when faced with a problem, the decision-maker clarifies his goals and ranks them. He then lists all possible ways of achieving those goals, investigates and composes their consequences, and chooses the one whose outcome closely matches his goals. Rationalism postulates an ideal process of decision-making that assumes objective rationality. {See Yehezkel Dror, Public Policy-Making Re-Examined, Part IV: An Optimal Model of Public Policy-Making, (San Francisco: Chandler, 1968). See also, William N, Dunn, Public Policy Analysis: An Introduction, (Englewood Cliffs N. J.: Prentice Hall, 1979.)}

[112]Ibid., p. 390.

[113]G. Smith and May D., "The Artificial Debate Between Rationalist and Incrementalist Models of Decision Making," Policy and Politics, v. 8, no. 2, 1980, pp. 147-161.

[114]Egonmwan, Op. cit., p. 76.

[115]Information obtained from interviews with the Deputy Minister of Forestry, the Chief Conservator of Forests, and officials of the Forestry Commission indicate that policy decisions are based on information, derived from scientific research conducted by institutions such as Forestry Institute, Kumasi, Institute for Renewable Natural Resources, University of Science and Technology, Kumasi, and the Planning Division of the Department of Forestry.

[116]The researcher is aware that the treatment of sub-Saharan Africa as an undifferentiated region could be problematic because of historical and present political variations between the countries. There were no less than four colonial powers in the region. Consequently, there have been variations in how the British, the French, the Portuguese, and the Belgians governed. Variations continue to prevail in the administrative structures and processes. Nevertheless, as the literature considered in this review will show, there are enough grounds for treating the region as an analytical unit.

[117]Fred Riggs, Op. cit., p. 2. See also, United Nations Economic Commission for Africa (E. C. A.), "Integrated Approaches to Rural Development in Africa," Proceedings of E. C. A. Conference on Rural Development, Moshi, Tanzania, (New York: UN, 1971), p. 75.

[118]Lucian Pye, Armies in the Process of Political Modernization, (Santa Monica: Rand Corp., 1961), p. 73. See also, Crook, Ibid.

[119]Robert K. Gardiner, "From Colonial Rule to Local Administration," and A. L. Adu, "The Administrator and Change," in A. H. Rweyemanu and Goran Hyden (eds.), A Decade of Public Administration in Africa, (Nairobi: East African Literature Bureau, 1975), pp. 13-20, and 21-29. See also S. N. Eisenstadt, "Problems of Emerging Bureaucracies in Developing Areas and New States," in B. F. Hoselitz and W. Moore (eds.), Industrialization and Society, (Paris: UNESCO-Monton, 1963).

[120]Goran Hyden, "Discovering the Resource Potential of the Ecology of Public Management," in The Ecology of Public Administration...., Op. cit., pp. 122-141.

[121]M. J. Balogun, Public Administration in Nigeria, (London: Macmillan, 1983).

[122]Price, Op. cit., p. 206.

[123]Ibid.

[124]Price, Op. cit., p. 3.

[125]Ibid., p. 3.

[126]Koehn, Op. cit., p. 4.

[127]Ibid., p. 278.

[128]Price, Op. cit., p. 6.

[129]Ibid., p. 215.

[130]Fred Riggs, The Ecology of Public Administration, (Bombay: Asia Publishing House, 1961), p. 2.

[131]J. O. Udoji, "Tenure of Office of Top Civil Servants," in A. H. Rweyemanu and Goran Hyden (eds.), A Decade of Public Administration in Africa, (Nairobi: East African Literature Bureau, 1975), p. 41.

[132]Nelson Kafir, The Shrinking Political Arena, (Berkeley: University of California Press, 1976), p. 232.

[133]Ben Amonoo, Ghana, 1957-1966: The Politics of Institutional Dualism, (London: Allen and Unwin, 1982), pp. 1, 8-9.

[134]Gelase Mutahaba, "Ecology and Public administration in Africa: A Review of their Relationships Since Independence," The Ecology of Public Administration in Africa, Op. cit., pp. 1-17. See also, Robert M Price, Society and Bureaucracy in Ghana, (Berkeley: University of California Press, 1979).

[135]A. H. Rweyemanu, "The Political Environment of Public Administration in Africa," in The Ecology of Public Administration in Africa, (New Delhi: African Association for Public Administration and Management, Vikas Publishers, 1980), pp. 82-98.

[136]W. N. Wamalwa, "The Ecology of Public Administration in Africa," in The Ecology of Public Administration and Management In Africa, Op. cit., p. 62.

[138]Clement Onyemelukwe, Men and Management in Perspective, (Berkeley: University of California Press, 1983).

[138]M. S. Grindle, Politics and Policy Implementation in the Third World, (Princeton: Princeton University Press, 1980).

[140]James S. Larson, Why Government Programs Fail: Improving Policy Implementation, (New York: Praeger, 1980), p. 4.

[142]Mutahaba, Op. cit., p.12.

[142]Riggs, Op. cit.

[143]J. O. Udoji, "Tenure of Office of Top Civil Servants," in Rweyemanu and Hyden, Op. cit., p. 232.

[145]Price, Op. cit.

[145]C. L. R. James, Nkrumah and the Ghana Revolution, (London: Allison and Busby, 1977).

[148]Kwame Nkrumah, An Autobiography of Kwame Nkrumah, (London: Panaf, 1973).

[148]Amonoo, Op. cit., preface.

[148]Ibid.

[148] Donald Rothchild, "Military Regime Performance: An Appraisal of the Ghana Experience," Comparative Politics, vol. 12, July 1980, pp. 459-479. See also, Daniel Green, "Ghana's Adjusted Democracy," Review of African Political Economy, vol. 22, 1995, pp. 577-586, Jon Kraus, "Ghana's Radical Populist Regime," Current History, vol. 84, April 1985, pp. 164-168, and Henry Bienen, "Populist Military Regimes in West Africa," Armed Forces and Society, vol. 1, Spring 1985, pp. 357-377.

[150]Kraus, Ibid.

[150]Peter S. Cleaves, "Implementation Amidst Scarcity and Apathy: Political Power and Policy Design," in Merilee S. Grindle (ed), Politics and Policy Implementation in the Third World, (Princeton, N. J: Princeton University Press, 1980), pp. 281-303.

[151]African Association for Pubic Administration and Management (A.A.P.A.M.), The Ecology of Public Administration and Management in Africa, Op. cit., pp. 195-243.

[152]Peter H. Koehn, Public Policy and Administration in Africa: Lessons from Nigeria, (Boulder: Westview, 1990), p. 77-78.

[155]Gardiner, Op. cit., and Eisenstadt, Op. cit.

[155]Mutahaba, Op. cit.

[155]Mutahaba Gelase, Rweikiza, Baguma and Hatfani, Mohamed, Vitalizing African Public Administration for Recovery and Development, (Hartford: Kumarian, 1993). See also, Price, Op. cit.

[157]Clement Onyemelukwe, Men and Management in Perspective, (Berkeley: University of California Press, 1983).

[158]Tony Killick, Development Economics in Action: A Study of Economic Policies in Ghana, (London: Hienemann, 1978).

[159]Larson, Op. cit.

[159]E. Bardach, The Implementation Game: What Happens After a Bill Becomes Law, (Cambridge: MIT Press, 1977), p. 85.

[160]E. Hargrove, The Missing Link: The Study of Implementation of Social Policy, (Washington, D C.: The Urban Institute, 1975), pp. 22-23.

[161]Gabriel U. Inglesias, "Implementation and the Planning of Development: Notes, Trends, and Issues, Focusing on the Concept of Administrative Capability," in Gabriel Inglesias, Implementation: The Problem of Achieving Results. A Casebook on Asia Experiences: Eastern Regional Organization for Public Administration (E.R.O.P.A.), (Manilla: E.R.O.P.A., 1976), pp. xv - xxxix.

[162]The term "dual mandate" is credited to Lord Laggard, governor of Northern Nigeria (1912-1919). He used it to depict the political and economic objectives of British colonial administrations in West Africa. The concept implied that colonial administrations had a dual objective: promoting the interest of the British economy, and administering the territories. This concept is discussed further in this chapter.

[164]David E. Apter, Ghana in Transition, (Princeton: Princeton University Press, 1972), p. 31.

[165]E. D. Martin, The British West African Settlements, 1750-1821, Imperial Studies No. 2, London, 1927, p. 39.

[166]Francis Agbodeka, African Politics and British Policy in Gold Coast 1868-1900, (London: Longman, 1971), p. 12.

[167]Ibid., p. 12.

[167]A. G. Hopkins, "Economic Imperialism in West Africa: Lagos, 1880-1892," EconHR, vol. x, (1968), pp. 580-606. See also: P. Gifford and W. R. Louis (eds.), Britain and Germany in Africa: Imperial Rivalry and Colonial Rule, (New Haven: Yale University Press, 1967), pp. 47-82.

[168] D. C. M. Platt, "Economic Factors in British Policy During the 'New Imperialism'," P. & P, v. 39, 1968, pp. 120-138. See also: W. G. Hynes, The Economics of Empire: Britain, Africa and the New Imperialism 1870-1895, (London: Longman, 1979), and G. N. Uzogwe, Britain and the Conquest of Africa, (Ann Arbor: University of Michigan Press, 1974).

[169]D. C. M. Platt, Finance, Trade and Politics in British Foreign Policy 1818-1914, (Lodon: Clarendon Press, 1968), pp. 363-364.

[170] W. G. Hynes, "British Mercantile Attitudes Towards Imperial Expansion," HJ, v. xix, (1976), pp. 969-979. See also: Hynes, The Economics of Empire, Op. cit.

[172]A. G. Hopkins, Op. cit. See also: Eldridge, Op. cit., and Platt, Op. cit.

[173]Isichei, Op. cit., p. 239. See also: Metcalfe, Op. cit., p. 121.

[173]G. E. Metcalfe, Great Britain and Ghana: Documents of Ghana History, 1808 - 1957, (London: Thomas Nelson, 1964), p. 213.

[174]Henrika Kuklick, The Imperial Bureaucrat: The Colonial Administrative Service in Gold Coast, 1920-1939, Hoover Colonial Studies Series, Peter Duignan, L. H. Gann and A. H. M. Kirk-Greene (eds.), (Stanford: Hoover Institution Press, 1979), p. xiii.

[177]Rattray, Op. cit.

[177] Elizabeth Isichei, History of West Africa Since 1800, (New York: Africana, 1977), p. 225.

[177]J. B. Webster, A. A. Boahen, and Michael Tidy, The Revolutionary Years: West Africa Since 1800, (Essex: Longman, 1978), p. 199.

[178]Ebere Nwambani, "The British Labor Party, The "Dual Mandate" and Africa, 1945-1951," Transafrican Journal of History, v. 21, No 1, 1992, pp. 93 - 110.

[179]G. B. Kay, The Political Economy of Colonialism in Ghana: A Collection of Documents and Statistics 1900 - 1960, (Cambridge: University Press, 1972), p. 42.

[180]According to statistical data assembled by Kay, transportation accounted for 75% of the total expenditure of the ten-year development plan that was implemented during Guggisburg's tenure as governor. (See Kay, Ibid., p. 42.)

[183]Kuklick, Op. cit., p. 106.

[183]Ibid., p. 121.

[183]G. E. Metcalfe, Great Britain and Ghana: Documents of Ghana History, 1807-1957, (London: Thomas Nelson, 1964), page 3.

[186]Gold Coast Colony, "Wealth in Wood," (Accra: Public Relations Department, 1950), page 7.

[186]Op. cit.

[186]Paul Knaplund, James Stephen and the British Colonial System, 1843 - 1847, (Madison: University of Wisconsin Press, 1953).

[188]Ibid, p. 38.

[189]Brian L. Blakeley, The Colonial Office, 1868 - 1892, (Durham: Duke University Press, 1972), p. vii.

[192]Knaplund, Op. cit., pp. 38 - 45.

[192]Blakeley, Op. cit., pp. 4-16.

[193]Ibid., p. xiii.

[193]Knaplund, Op. cit., p. 41. See also: Blakeley, Op. cit., p. xiii.

[195]Alan Burns (Sir), Colonial Civil Servant, (London: George Allen and Unwin, 1949), page 173.

[198]Ibid., page 175.

[198]Blakeley, Op. cit., page xiii.

[199]Knaplund, Op. cit., p. 45.

[201]Alan Burns, Op. cit., p. 157.

[202]Knaplund, Op. cit., p. 42.

[202]Blakeley, Op. cit., p. xiv.

[202]Burns, Op. cit., p. 155.

[203]Burns, Ibid.

[203]Blakeley, Op. cit., p. xii, 116 and 119. See also: Burns Op. cit., p. 167.

[204]Casely Hayford, Gold Coast Native Institutions, (London: Sweet and Maxwell, 1903), p. 218.

[207]Isichei, Op. cit., p. 214.

[209]Henrika Kuklick , Op. cit., pp. 31, 33, 34, and 35.

[209]Burns, Op. cit., p. 167.

[209]Ibid., p. 162.

[209]Ibid.

[209]C. E. Skeene, writing about H. A. Bonavia in an unofficial diary entry written while Skeene was Acting Commissioner for the Central Province of Gold Coast Colony, October 17, 1932, (Accra: National Archives of Ghana).

[215]Kuklick, Op. cit., pp. 85 - 86.

[216]Ibid., p. 90.

[216]Ibid., p. 95.

[216]Ibid., p. 107.

[216]Blakeley, Op. cit., p. xii.

[216]Ibid.

[216]Martin Wright, The Development of the Legislative Council, 1606 - 1945, Studies in Colonial Legislation, volume 1, London, 1945, p. 148.

[220]Burns, Op. cit.

[220]Burns, Op. cit., p. 158.

[220]Ibid., p. 159 - 160.

[220]Martin Wright, Gold Coast Legislative Council, Studies in Colonial Legislatures Series, Margery Perham (ed.), (London: Faber and Faber, 1946), p. 101.

[222]Ibid., pp. 102 and 141.

[222]Sir James Stephen was Under Secretary of State for the Colonies until 1847. He was a highly regarded official and considered to be an innovator of administrative procedures in the Colonial Office.

[225]Minute, January 18, 1843, Colonial Office, 201:313.

[225]Martin Wright, Op. cit., pp. 142-143.

[225]G. E. Metcalfe, Great Britain and Ghana: Documents of Ghana History 1807 - 1957, (London: Thomas Nelson, 1964), p. 214.

[227]Knaplund, Op. cit., p. 45.

[227]Wright, Op. cit., p. 111. The term "governor-in-council" refers to the governor acting in collaboration with his executive council.

[229]Ibid. See also: Kuklick, Op. cit., p. xiii.

[230]Report, February 25, 1830, on Act # 6, Colonial Office, 323: 47, Folio 274.

[231]Report, July 20, 1820, on Dominica Act # 28, 1820. Colonial Office, 323:41, folio 106.

[232]Knaplund, Op. cit., p. 49.

[233]Colonial Office, Report on Gold Coast, (London: His Majesty's Stationary Office, 1950-51), p. 5.

[236]Knaplund, Op. cit., p. 45.

[236]Minute, April 23, 1841, Colonial Office 201:299.

[237]Blakeley, Op.. cit., p. 67.

[238]Martin Wright, Gold Coast Legislative Council, Op. cit., p. 39.

[238]G. E. Metcalfe, Op. cit., p. 213.

[239]Colonial Office, Report on Gold Coast: 1949, (London: His Majesty's Stationary Office, 1950-51).

[240]Letter from Sir Hugh Clifford to Lewis Harcourt, April 15, 1915, quoted in Metcalfe, Op. cit., pp. 552-553.

[242]Ibid., p. 553.

[242]Ibid., p. 111.

[242]Elizabeth Isichei, Op. cit., p. 214. See also: J. B. Webster, A. A. Boahen and Michael Tidy, The Revolutionary Years: West Africa Since 1800, (Essex: Longman, 1980).

[243]"Constitution of Gold Coast Territory," Introduced by a House of Commons Charter, 1850, Article Two, National Archives of Ghana, Accra.

[246]Metcalfe, Op. cit., p. 213.

[246]Wright, Op. cit., p. 102.

[247]Kuklick, Op. cit., p. xii. See also: Wright, Op. cit., p. 24. and Metcalfe Op. cit., pp. 262-282, and 431-433.

[250]Ibid.

[251]Gold Coast Colony (Legislative Council) Order in Council of 1925.

[252]Wright, Op. cit., p 41.

[252]Ibid., p. 105.

[252]Ibid., p. 148.

[252]Martin Wright, The Development of the Legislative Council, 1606 - 1945, Studies in Colonial Legislatures, volume 1, London, 1945.

[254]Record of Proceedings, Gold Coast legislative Council, March 20, 1934, National Archives of Ghana, Accra, p. 114.

[255]Remarks quoted from Wright, Op. cit., p. 113.

[255]Resolution of the Joint Provincial Council read by Nana Ofori Attah in the Legislative Council, March 20, 1934, Accra: National Archives of Ghana, p. 98.

[256]Resolution of the Joint Provincial Council read by Nana Ofori Attah in the Legislative Council, March 21, 1934, Ibid., p. 145.

[257]Gold Coast Colony, (Legislative Council) Orders in Council, 1925-1939, section 55. Obtained from Wright, Op. cit., Appendices 1 and 2, pp. 208 - 267.

[260]Gold Coast Colony (Legislative Council), Standing Orders and Rules Number 21.

[261]Wright, Op. cit., p. 129.

[261]Kuklick, Op. cit., p. xi.

[263]A. W. Cardinall, In Asante and Beyond, (London: Seeley, Service and Company, 1927), p. 70-71.

[263]Op. cit., p. 71.

[263]Government of Gold Coast, "Select Committee of the Legislative Council on the Africanization of the Public Service: Report," Accra, p. 13.

[264]Personal entries and comments made by G. B. Freeman, District Commissioner, Southern Mamprusi in an unofficial diary, January 8, 1924, (Accra: National Archives of Ghana). See also: S. J. Oliver, Assistant District Commissioner, Navrongo, Unofficial Diary Entry of February 10, 1933, National Archives of Ghana, Accra).

[266]Kuklick, Op. cit., pp. 8 and 68.

[266] A. H. C. Walker Leigh, Chief Commissioner, Wa District, Unofficial Diary Entry, February 10, 1927, (National Archives of Ghana, Accra). See also: K. A. Busia, The Position of the Chief in the Modern Political System of Asante, (London: Oxford University Press, 1951).

[267]G. O. Parker, Assistant District Commissioner, Wa District, Unofficial Diary Entry, February 10, 1927, (National Archives of Ghana, Accra).

[268]Confidential Report by Governor Guggisburg on A. F. L. Wilkinson, 1920, (National Archives of Ghana, Accra). See also: Governor Slater's letter to Wilkinson of January 8, 1929, in Wilkinson's papers {Oxford University Colonial Records Project (OUCRP)}, and Guggisburg's confidential memo about A. W. Norris, District Commissioner, November 17, 1926, (National Archives of Ghana, Accra).

[270]E. K. Lumley, Forgotten Mandate, (London: C. Hurst and Company, 1976), p. 9.

[270]C. H. Hagan, Chief Commissioner for Asante, Unofficial Diary Entry, November 3, 1921, Oxford University Colonial Records Project (OUCRP).

[273]Kuklick, Op. cit., p. 70.

[273]Ibid., p. 74.

[273]J. G. K. Owusu, "Evolution of Forest Legislation in Ghana." (Unpublished), 1980. See also: S. Y. Bennuah, "Development of Forestry in Ghana." B.Sc. Thesis (Unpublished), Institute of Renewable Natural Resources, University of Science and Technology, Kumasi, Ghana, 1987.

[274]J. G. K. Owusu, "Milestones in the Legislative History of Forestry in Ghana." Paper Presented at the RENARSA Forum, 1986.

[275]T. F. Chipp, The Forest Officers Handbook of Gold Coast, Asante, and the Northern Territories, Government of Gold Coast, (London: The Crown Agents for the Colonies, 1922).

[276]Ghana Publishing Corporation, "Forest Ordinance of 30 March 1927, Chapter 157," (Accra, Ghana Publishing Corporation, Printing Division).

[277]H. N. Thompson, Report on Forests, Colonial Reports - Miscellaneous, # 66, (London: His Majesty's Stationary Office, 1910), p. 98.

[279]T. F. Chipp, "Gold Coast Forestry Problem," Empire Forestry Journal, vol. 1, April, 1923, p. 65.

[279]S. Kolade Adeyoju, "A Study on Forest Administration Problems in Six Selected African Countries," Food and Agricultural Organization (FAO), Rome, 1976.

[282]Owusu, Op. cit.

[282]Owusu, Ibid.

[283]Martin Wright, Gold Coast Legislative Council, Op. cit., p. 25-26. See also: Chipp, Op. cit., p. 49.

[284]Thompson, Op. cit., pp. 202-226.

[284]W. A Gordon, "The Law of Forestry," Her Majesty's Stationary Office, London, 1955. See also: C. J. Taylor, Tropical Forestry, (London: Oxford University Press, 1962) and Owusu, Op. cit.

[285]J. Francois, "Timber Resources Development and Management," Paper Presented at the National Conference on Resource Conservation for Ghana's Sustainable Development, Accra, April 28-30, 1987.

[287]Gordon, Op. cit.

[287]Legislative Council Debates on the Lands Bill of 1894, and the Lands Ordinance, June 29, 1897, in G. E. Metcalfe, Great Britain and Ghana: Documents of Ghana History 1807-1957, (London: Thomas Nelson, 1964), pp. 498-500.

[288]Under the customs of the ethnic groups in the forest region of Ghana, the chief is custodian of the land. He is responsible for its defense. His rights to the land coexisted with those of the lineages and individuals within his domain. Certain, usually large areas of land is, however, set aside as "stool lands." Although the occupant of the stool (the king or chief) has the rights to use and profit from such lands, he actually held it in trust for the whole ethnic groups. He could sell it, but not without the consent of his council. The king or chief also has the rights to any treasures found on the land in his domain. [Source: K. A. Busia, The Position of the Chief in the Modern Political System of Ashanti, (London: Oxford University Press, 1951), p. 44.]

[291]G. E. Metcalfe, Op. cit.

[291]Forestry Ordinance of 1901, in Thompson, Report on Forests, Op. cit.

[291]H. Conway Belfield, "Report on the Legislation Governing the Alienation of Native Lands in Gold Coast Colony and Ashanti," (London: Her Majesty's Stationary Office, 1912). Belfield's report was the outcome of his assignment by the Secretary of State for the Colonies to investigate the circumstances surrounding the protests against the Lands Bill.

[294]Belfield, Ibid., p. 38.

[295]Ibid.

[295]Casely Hayford, Gold Coast Native Institutions, (London: Sweat and Maxwell, 1903), pp. 172-181.

[295]S. Kolade Adeyoju, "A Study on Forest Administration Problems in Six Selected African Countries," (Rome: Food and Agricultural Organization (FAO), 1976).

[299]Chipp, Op. cit., p. 25.

[299]Chipp, Op. cit., p. 65.

[299]"Wealth in Wood", Op. cit.

[299]K. Frimpong-Mensah, "Requirement of the Timber Industry," Ghana Forest Inventory Project Seminar Proceedings, Forestry Department, Accra, 1989, pp. 70-79.

[302]Thompson, Op. cit., pp. 5-154.

[302]Chipp, Op. cit., pp. 65-75.

[302]Thomas F. Chipp, "Gold Coast Forestry Problem," Empire Forestry Journal, Journal of the Empire Forestry Association, Imperial Institute, London, vol. 2, No. 1, April 1923, p. 69.

[304]"Wealth in Wood," Ibid.

[304]Kwame Ninsin, "The PNDC and the Problem of Legitimacy," in Ghana: The Political Economy of Recovery, Donald Rothchild (ed.), (Boulder: Lynne Reinner Publishers, 1991), page 49.

[305]Sheldon Gellar, "State-Building and Nation-Building in West Africa," in S. N. Eisenstadt and Stan Rokkon (eds.), Building States and Nations: Analyses by Regions, vol. II, (Beverly Hills, CA.: Sage, 1973), pp. 398-399.

[306]Richard Cook, "Legitimacy, Authority, and the Transfer of Power in Ghana," Political Studies, vol. 35, 1987, p. 572.

[308]Kwame Nkrumah, I Speak of Freedom, (New York: Praeger, 1961), p. 209.

[309]Maxwell Owusu, Uses and Abuses of Political Power, (Chicago: University of Chicago Press, 1970).

[310]Daniel M. Green, "Structural Adjustment and Politics in Ghana," Trans Africa Forum, volume 8, Summer 1991, p. 84.

[311]Ninsin, Op. cit.

[311]As a percentage of FOB (free on board), at the official exchange rate, the nominal producer price of cocoa actually declined from 38.0% in the 1982/83 season to below 20.0% through the 1986/87 season, rising to 33.2% in the 1987/88 season. Source: the World Bank: "Ghana: Structural Adjustment for Growth," Report # 7515-GH (Washington, D. C.: World Bank, 1989), p. 20.

[312]United States Government, "Report of a Staff Study Mission to Great Britain, Ghana, Senegal, Cote d'Ivoire, and France, November 29-December 20, 1988, to the Committee on Foreign Affairs, U.S. House of Representatives," (Washington, D.C., U.S. Government Printing Office, 1989).

[313]Henry Bienen, "Populist Military Regimes in West Africa," Armed Forces and Society, volume 11, # 3, Spring 1985, pp. 368-371.

[314]Naomi Chazan, An Anatomy of Ghanaian Politics: Managing Political Recession, 1969-1982, (Boulder: Westview Press, 1983).

[316]Tapan Prasad Biswal, Ghana: Political and Constitutional Developments, (New Delhi: Book Center, 1992).

[317]Jeffrey Herbst, The Politics of Reform in Ghana: 1982-1991, (Denver: University of Colorado Press, 1993).

[317]E. Gyimah-Boadi, "Associational Life, Civil Society, and Democratization in Ghana," in Civil Society and the State in Africa, John W. Harbeson, Donald Rothchild, and Naomi Chazan (eds.), (Boulder: Lynne Rienner, 1994), pp. 125-148.

[318]Naomi Chazan, "Political Culture and Political Socialization: A Ghanaian Case," The Review of Politics, vol. 40, 1978, pp. 3-31.

[321]Ibid., p. 8.

[321]Ibid.

[321]For example, although 19% of the respondents considered politicians and army officers to be authoritative figures, 93% placed primary power with chiefs.

[324]Naomi Chazan, An Anatomy of Ghanaian Politics: Managing Political Recession, 1969-1982, Op. cit.

[324]Ibid., p. 341.

[324]Crawford Young, "The African Colonial State and Its Ideology," in Donald Rothchild and Naomi Chazan (Eds.), The Precarious Balance: State and Society in Africa, (Boulder: Westview Press, 1988), pp. 25-66.

[327]Interview with the District Forestry Officer at Kyebi, August 5, 1996.

[329]Biswal, Op. cit., pp. vii and 58-60.

[329]Jeffrey Herbst, Op. cit., p. 32.

[329]Ibid., p. 32.

[329]A similar argument is advanced by R. Crook in "State, Society and Political Institution in Cote d'Ivoire and Ghana," IDS Bulletin, Sussex, v. 21, # 4, October 1990, pp. 34.

[330]E. Gyimah-Boadi, "Associational Life, Civil Society, and Democratization in Ghana," in J W. Harbeson, Donald Rothchild, and Naomi Chazan (Eds.) Civil Society and the State in Africa, Op. cit., pp. 125-148.

[331]Robert Pinkney, Democracy and Dictatorship in Ghana and Tanzania, (New York: St. Martins Press, 1997)   Joel Migdal, in Strong Societies and Weak States: State-Society Relations and State Capabilities in the Third World, (Princeton: Princeton University Press, 1988), treats the subject exhaustively.

[332]Donald Rothchild and U. Lawson, "The Interactions Between State and Civil Society in Africa: From Deadlocks to New Routines," in J. W. Harbeson et al., (Eds.) Civil Society and the State in Africa, London: Lynne Rienner, 1994), pp. 255-281.

[333]Emmanuel Hansen and Paul Collins, "The Army, the State, and the Rawlings Revolution in Ghana," African Affairs, vol. 79, January 1980, pp. 3-23. See also: Ninsin, Op. cit., p.50.

[335]Ibid., p. 23.

[335]Joel Migdal, Strong Societies and Weak States: State-Society Relations and State Capabilities in the Third World, (Princeton: Princeton University Press, 1988). See also: Walter Rodney, How Europe Underdeveloped Africa, (Washington, DC.: Howard University Press, 1982), Ch. 2.

[336]Government of Ghana, Independence Constitution of 1957, (Accra: Government Press, 1957).   Republic of Ghana, Constitution of the Second Republic of Ghana, (Accra: Ghana Publishing Corporation, 1969). Republic of Ghana, Constitution of the Third Republic of Ghana, Op. cit. , and, Republic of Ghana, Constitution of the Forth Republic of Ghana, Op. cit.

[338]Ripley, Op. cit., pp. 31-56.

[338]Robert M. Price, Society and Bureaucracy in Contemporary Ghana, (Berkeley: University of California Press, 1979), p. 4.

[339]Oliver S. Saasa, "Public Policy-Making in Developing Countries: The Utility of Contemporary Decision-Making Models," Public Administration and Development, 3 (1983): pp 300-321.

[340]Naomi Chazan, "Political Culture and Socialization to Politics: A Ghanaian Case." Review of Politics, 40, (Jan. 1978): pp. 3-31. See also: C. K. Kumado, "Judicial Review

of Legislation in Ghana Since Independence," <u>Black Law Journal</u>, 5 :2 (1977): pp. 208-230.

[341]Six national elections for legislative seats have been held in Ghana since independence in 1957. With the exception of the Nkrumah era (1957-1966) and the Rawlings era (1994-1998), legislatures in Ghana have not had the opportunity last long and evolve into the prominent law-making institution envisaged by the constitutions.

[342]This situation has began to change however, since the advent of the Fourth Republic. The emergent private broadcast and print media have assumed the role of alternatives to the government-controlled media as sources of information and opinions.

[343]Iren Omo-Bare, "Military and Civilian Regimes in Sub-Saharan Africa: A Comparative Analysis of Public Policy Outputs and Outcomes," Ph.D. Research (Unpublished), The Louisiana State University and Agricultural and Mechanical College, 1990.

The absence of differences in the policy statements and goals of military and civilian regimes has been the subject of discussion by Pirro and Zeff, among others. The explanation offered for this is that these governments face similar problems and settings. Even where new policies have been considered, the governments have been of such short duration that such policies are barely enacted before change occurs. Ellen B. Pirro and Eleanor E. Zeff, "A New Look at Military-Civilian Governments," <u>Journal of Strategic Studies</u>, v. 2, 1979, p. 206-231. See also: R. D. McKinley and A. S. Cohen, "A Comparative Analysis of the Political and Economic Performance of Military and Civilian Regimes: A Cross-National Aggregative Study," <u>Comparative Politics</u>, vol. 8, # 1, October 1975, p. 1-30, and R. Jackman, "Politicians in Uniforms," <u>American Political Science Review</u>, vol. 70, # 1, December 1976, p. 1078-1097.

[344]Yaw Agyeman-Badu and Kwaku Osei-Hwedie, <u>The Political Economy of Instability: Colonial Legacy, Inequality, and Political Instability in Ghana</u>, Third World Monograph Series, (Lawrenceville VA; Brunswick Publishing Co., 1982), pp. 17-24.

[346]Allison, Op. cit., p. 6.

[346]Robert M Price, <u>Society and Bureaucracy in Contemporary Ghana</u>, (Berkeley: University of California Press, 1979). See also: Ben Amonoo, <u>Ghana 1957 - 1966: The Politics of Institutional Dualism</u>, (London: George Allen & Unwin, 1986), and Guillermo O'Donnell, <u>Modernization and Bureaucratic Authoritarianism: Studies in South American Politics</u>, (Berkeley: University of California Institute of International Studies, 1962), p. 62.

[347]Robert E. Dowse, "The Military and Political Development," in Colin Leys (ed.), <u>Politics and Change in Developing Countries</u>, (Cambridge: Cambridge Univ. Press, 1969), p. 240.

[348]Statistics on the Ghanaian economy since 1980 indicate a general decline. For example, Ghana's total debt to Gross Domestic Product (GDP) ratio increased from 31.7 in 1980 to 72.1 in 1993. The long term debt to GDP ratio also increased from 26.3 to 53.8. For the same period, the current account balance after transfers deteriorated from $29 million to -$572 million. {Source: The World Bank, <u>Trends in Developing Economies, Extracts: Volume 3. Sub-Saharan Africa</u>, (Washington, DC: The World Bank, 1994), pp. 80 - 81.)}

[349]Colleen Lowe Morna, "In Ghana, Even a Senior Official Can't Make Ends Meet," <u>Christian Science Monitor</u>, September 1988, p. 8.

[351]Douglas Rimmer, <u>Staying Poor: Ghana's Political Economy, 1950-1990</u>, (Oxford: Pergamon Press, 1992), pp. 215-216.

[351]The World Bank, <u>Trends in Developing Economies: Extracts; Volume 3, Sub-Saharan Africa</u>, (Washington, DC, The World Bank, 1994), p. 77.

[353]The World Bank, Op. cit., p. 79.

[354]The World Bank, World Development Report 1992, (New York: Oxford University Press, 1992), p. 219.

[354]Jeff Haynes, W. Trevor, and Stephen Riley, "Debt in Sub-Saharan Africa: The Local Politics of Stabilization," African Affairs, v. 86, July 1987, pp. 343-366.

[355]Ghana Government, The Consolidated Development Plan, 1958/59, (Accra: Government Printer, 1957, Appendix I, pp. 8-9.

[358]Ghana Government, Second Development Plan, 1959-1964, (Accra: Government Printer, 1958).

[358]Ibid., p. 1.

[358]Government of Ghana, Seven-Year Development Plan For National Reconstruction and Development, (Accra: Office of the Planning Commission, 1976), Foreword.

[361]Ibid.

[361]Ibid.

[361]The statistics in Appendix 5 reveal a deterioration in Ghana's balance in current and capital accounts between 1955 and 1962.

[363]Ghana, Five-Year Development Plan, 1982-86, (Accra: Ministry of Economic Planning, 1981).

[366]Ibid., Table 3.4, p. 35.

[366]Ibid., p. 24.

[366]Ibid., Table 3.8, p. 38.

[366]United Nations/ International Labor Office, World Resources: A Guide to the Global Environment, (New York: Oxford University Press, 1996), p. 190.

[368]Ibid.

[368]H. Binswanger and D. Pingali, "The Evolution of Farming Systems and Agricultural Technology in Sub-Saharan Africa," Discussion Paper 23, Agriculture and Rural Development Department, (Washington, DC: The World Bank, 1989).

[370]Ghana Statistical Service, "Ghana Living Standards Survey, First Year Report," Accra, 1989.

[370]Ghana Statistical Service, "Ghana Living Standards Survey, Report of the Third Round, September 1991 - September 1992," Accra, March 1995.

[371]During the interview with the Chief Conservator of Forests, he identified land clearance for farming as the principal cause of deforestation in Ghana.

[373]Op. cit., Table 45.

[373]Ministry of Energy, Ghana, "The Prospects for Commercial Charcoal Production from Logging Residues in Ghana," Final Report, Accra, January, 1992.

[375]FAO, "Statistics Yearbook: Forestry Production," vol. 48, FAO Statistics Series No. 125, FAO, Rome, 1995, p.350.

[375]Barbara Ingham, Tropical Exports and Economic Development: New Perspectives on Producer Response in the Low Income Countries, (New York: St. Martins Press, 1981), pp. 334-337.

[378]Ibid.

[378]Trade and Environment Database (TED), Op. cit., p. 1.

[378]Republic of Ghana, "The Budget Statement for Financial Year 1998," Presented to Parliament on February 17, 1998 by Mr. Kwabena Peprah, Minister of Finance.

[380]The World Bank, World Tables, 1995, (Baltimore, Johns Hopkins University Press, 1995), pp. 304-307.

[380]Heike Proff, "Structural Adjustment Programmes and Industrialization in Sub-Saharan Africa," Intereconomics, vol. 29, Sept.-Oct., 1994, pp. 225-233.

[381]Herbert Kwesi Acquay, "The Impact of Stabilization and Structural Adjustment Programs Upon Ghana's Forest and Marine Fisheries (Natural Resources) Policy," Ph.D. Research (Unpublished), Cornell University, 1993, Chapter 3.

[382]Donald Rothchild, "Ghana and Structural adjustment: An Overview," in Donald Rothchild, (ed.), Ghana: The Political Economy of Recovery, (Boulder: Lynne Reinner Publishers, 1991).

[384]The World Bank, World Development Report, (Washington, D. C., World Bank, 1983).

[384]Jon Kraus, "The Political Economy of Stabilization and Structural Adjustment in Ghana," in Donald Rothchild (ed.), Ghana: The Political Economy of Recovery, Ibid.

[385]The first grant offered for this purpose was $203 million in 1984. Between then and 1994 a total of $1769 million had been disbursed to Ghana.

[386]Robert Armstrong, "Ghana Country Assistance Review: A Study in Development Effectiveness," (Washington, D.C. : The World Bank, 1996), p. 36. See also: George Aryeetey, Structural Adjustment and Aid in Ghana, (Accra: Frederich Ebert Foundation, 1996), pp. 15 -17.

[387]George Aryeetey, Ibid. See also, Ho-Won Jeong, "The Impact of the World Bank and the IMF on the Structural Adjustment Program in Ghana," Journal of the Third World Spectrum, vol. 2, Spring 1995, pp. 101-119., Heike Proff, "Structural Adjustment Programmes and Industrialization in Sub-Saharan Africa," Intereconomics, vol. 29, Sept. - Oct. 1994, pp. 225-233, and, Ikubolajeh B. Logan and Kidane Mengisteab, "IMF-World Bank Adjustment and Structural Transformation in Sub-Saharan Africa," Economic Geography, vol. 69, Jan. 1993, pp. 1-24.

[388]Between March 1983 and September 1990, a series of severe devaluations had resulted in a reduction in the official value of the Cedi by as much as -12,809% (from $1 ' C2.75 to $1 'C355). By November 1997, $1 exchanged for C2,150.

[389]United Nations, International Trade Statistics Yearbook, 1994, 26th Edition, (New York: UN Publishing Division), Series E/F. 96XVII.2, vol. 2.

[391]Acquay, Op. cit., p 95.

[391]According to a report by the Oxford Forestry Institute and the International Tropical Timber Organization, as at 1991, there were about 100 sawmils, 13 veneer mills, and 9 plymills in Ghana. The report suggested that the sawmills working at even half their potential capacity would inevitably lead to overexploitation of the remaining high forests in Ghana. {Oxford Forestry Institute and ITTO, "Incentives in Producer and Consumer Countries to Promote Sustainable Development of Tropical Forests," (Oxford, 1991), p. 27.}

[393]Ghana Timber Exports Development Board, "Bulletin on Ghana's Timber Trade," 1991.

[393]Donald Rothchild, "Ghana and Structural Adjustment: An Overview," in Donald Rothchild (ed.), Ghana: The Political Economy of Recovery, (Boulder: Lynne Reinner, 1991), p. 11. See also: Jon Kraus, "The Political Economy of Stabilization and Structural Adjustment In Ghana," in Rothchild, Ibid., p. 141.

[394]Gwendolyn Mikell, "The State, Local Resources, and Political Participation in Ghana," paper presented at the African Studies Association meeting, 1989. See also: Ben Ephson, "Mobilization of farmers," West Africa, February 23, 1987, pp. 364-365; Margaret Novicki, "Going for a Green Revolution," Africa Report, (September-October, 1988), pp. 22-23; Kraus, "The Political Economy of Food," pp. 364-365; and, World Bank memoranda on the economy of Ghana, 1987.

[396]Parts of the loans advanced to Ghana under the structural adjustment program were spent on such projects.

[397] Acquay, Op. cit., p. 29.

[397] Ghana Environmental Protection Council, "Ghana Enviroment Action Plan, Volume 2," (Accra, Ghana: Environmental Protection Council, 1988).

[398] Ghana Environmental Protection Council, "Ghana Environment Action Plan, Volume 2," (Accra, Ghana: Environmental Protection Council, 1994).

[400] Ministry of Lands and Forestry, "Forest and Wildlife Policy," (Accra: Ghana Publishing Corporation, May, 1995).

[400] Such actions have included the enactment of a series of Acts and Decrees since 1957, the inclusion of clauses in the Constitutions of the Third and Forth Republics of Ghana that emphasize the need to combat deforestation, the numerous anti-deforestation and re-afforestation projects that have been undertaken, the commissions and agencies that have been established to formulate and execute deforestation policies, and the large sums of money that have been spent on the venture.

[401] As will be shown in chapter seven, Act 453 of 1993 did not create a new institution. It simply reconstituted an already existing commission and modified its mandate.

[402] In his address to Ghana's parliament in April, 1993, President J. J. Rawlings expressed regret that even though timber ranks third as a source of Ghana's foreign exchange, efforts to strengthen the agencies responsible for the rational and sustainable management of forest resources have been thwarted by uncontrolled land clearing, bush fires, and collection of firewood, and wasteful, poorly managed logging by the rapidly growing population. Also during his address at the launching of Forest Week 1995, President Rawlings re-affirmed the Ghanaian government's determination to combat deforestation, and announced measures being taken by the government to curb the current depletion of Ghana's forest resources. In a little over a week (specifically on October 9, 1997), the President issued a warning to Ghanaians against the dangers of uncontrolled forest resources exploitation, citing the conversion of the hitherto high forests areas of the country into savannah grasslands as evidence of the inappropriate farming methods, bush fires, and over-exploitation of forest resources. (Obtained from "Ghana Review International" on the *Internet* at).

[403] Since 1993 an annual National Forestry Week has been observed in Ghana. At this time, government leaders, through the media and other functions, highlight the need to preserve Ghana's forests. An effort is made to generate increased awareness and draw attention to the value of forests and the need to preserve them.

[404] K. Tufuor, "A Review of Forest Sector Policy of Ghana," Ghana Forestry Commission, Accra, (unpublished) December, 1993. Ministry of Lands and Forestry, "Forest and Wildlife Policy," Accra, November 24, 1994. Forestry Commission, "Proposals for the Revision of the National Forest Policy for Ghana," Accra, 1995.

[405] Ghana Forestry Commission, "Revision of Ghana's Forest Policy," Proceedings of a National Conference, Forestry Commission Symposia Series # 3, April 2-8, 1989. See also, Ghana Environmental Protection Agency, "Ghana Environment Action Plan," volume ii, 1988, and, Ghana Environmental Protection Agency, "Ghana Environment Action Plan," volume ii, 1994. The "Ghana Review International" report of August 21, 1997 (obtained from the Internet at "gr@pbs.port.ac.uk) contained a revelation by Mr. Lewis D. Atsiatome, a program officer at the Ghana Environmental Protection Agency, that the Ghana government is in the process of drawing up a ten-year action plan to establish a sustainable environmental protection system for the country, a system that would include specific policy actions on forestry, among other areas.

[406] Government of the Gold Coast, "Forestry Policy for the Gold Coast Colony," (London: His Majesty's Stationary Office, 1948).

[409] Ghana Environmental Protection Council, Op. cit., Chapter 3.

[410] Ibid.

[410] Ghana Environmental Action Plan, 1988, Ibid., p. 2.

[411] E.P.C., Ghana Environmental Action Plan, 1988, Ibid., p ix.

[412] Ghana Environmental Action Plan, 1988, Ibid., pp. 23 and 46.

[414] Ghana Environmental Action Plan, 1988, Ibid., p. 31.

[414] Ibid., p. ix.

[414] For example, the plan includes a list of objectives that should be met so as to develop appropriate instruments for the successful implementation of the policy.   There are objectives relating to environmental education, environmental monitoring, international cooperation, forest policy, legislation, institutional restructuring, and research, among others.   (See chapters three and four)   Yet there is no indication as to specific and explicit actions needed to achieve those objectives.

[417] Ghana Environmental Action Plan, volume 2, 1994, Ibid., p. 152.

[419] Ibid.

[419] "Ghana Environmental Action Plan, 1994, Op. cit., pp. 174-176.

[420] 22Ibid., p. 176.

[420] Yaw Agyeman-Badu et. al., Op. cit., Donald Rothchild, Op. cit., and Jon Kraus, Op. cit.

[420] J. G. K. Owusu, "Revision of Ghana's Forest Policy," Proceedings of a National Conference, April 2-8, 1989, Accra, Forestry Commission Symposium Series.

[421] E. Kofi Smith, Ben Aninakwa, and George Ortsin, "Formulating and Practicing New Forest Policies: Recent Experiences from Ghana," A Paper Presented at a Seminar in Making Forest Policy Work, Oxford Forestry Institute, July 6, 1995.

[423] K. Tufuor, "A Review of Forest Sector Policy of Ghana," Op. cit.

[423] Republic of Ghana, "Forest and Wildlife Policy," Op. cit., p. 1, Foreword by Dr. Kwabena Adjei, Minister of Lands and Forestry.

[426] Ibid.

[426] Ibid.

[426] International Timber Trade Organization (I.T.T.O.), "I.T.T.O. Guidelines for the Establishment and Sustainable Management of Planted Tropical Forests," I.T.T.O. Policy Development 4, International Organizations Center, Yokohama, 1993.

[427] Ranee K. L. Panjabi, The Earth Summit at Rio: Politics, Economics, and the Environment, (Boston: Northeastern University Press, 1997. See also: Iftikhar Ahmed and Jacobus A. Doeleman (eds.), Beyond Rio: The Environmental Crisis and Sustainable Livelihoods in the Third World, (New York: St Martin's Press, 1995).

[428] The concept of sustainable development has gained increasing endorsement by international development institutions such as the World Bank, and by governments of the less developed economies as a prudent approach to pursuing socio-economic growth. It is an approach whereby the present generation will ensure that the environment is not degraded while they utilize resources and enjoy the fruits of economic development today. The objective is to guarantee that future generations are not rendered worse off. Turning sustainability into a cardinal ingredient of development policy remains a major problem. (World Bank, "World Development Report, 1992: Development and the Environment," (New York: Oxford University Press, 1992). See also: Hans Gingersen and Stephen E. McGaughey, "Social Forestry and Sustainable Development," in Douglas D. Southgate and John F. Dsinger (eds.), Sustainable Resource Development in the Third World, Westview Special Studies in Natural Resources and Energy Management, (Boulder: Westview Press, 1987), pp. 7-20.

[431] "Ghana Forest and Wildlife Policy", Op. cit., p. 9.

431 Ibid., pp. 9-16.

432 Republic of Ghana, "Forest and Wildlife Policy," Ministry of Lands and Forestry, Accra, November 24, 1994, p. 1.

433 Ibid., pp. 9-16.

433 On two occasions within a period of one week in October 1997, President Rawlings is reported to have repeated his warning about the threat of deforestation and stressed on the need to combat it. In November 1997, less than one month after the president's warnings, Lambert Okrah, program officer of Green Earth, a Ghanaian environmental organization, expressed fears that it may not be possible to save the forests in Ghana. On January 6, 1999, Dr Joseph R. Cobbinah, Acting Director of the Forestry Research Institute of Ghana, noted that the forests of Ghana had dwindled at a rate of between 0.84% and 1.3% since the beginning of this century. The consequence of this, according to his account, has been the reduction of the forests from 20.3 million acres to a mere 4.9 million acres. (Ghana Review International Newsreel, October 1 and 7, 1997, and January 7, 1999. Downloaded from the Internet at gr@pbs.port.ac.uk).

434 Government of Ghana, Trees and Timber Decree, 1974 (NRCD 273), [Accra: Ghana Publishing Corporation (Printing Division), 1974].

435 Government of Ghana, Forest Protection (Amendment) Law, 1986 (PNDCL 142), [Accra: Ghana Publishing Corporation (Publishing Division), Assembly Press, 1986].

436 Information obtained during the interviews with the Chief Conservator of Forests, the District Forestry Officer of Kyebi, and the employees of the Department of Forestry affirm this fact. In fact, the responses of these individuals reflected their position that strict enforcement of forest laws was necessary to achieve Ghana's deforestation policy goals. These respondents unanimously advocated greater action by the government of Ghana to control activities that caused deforestation. (See Chapter Eight)

438 J. G. K. Owusu, "Evolution of Forest Legislation in Ghana," (Unpublished) 1980.

438 The Forest Protection Decree, NRCD 243 of 1974, for example, was enacted to stem the increases in forest offenses. The strategy was to impose severer penalties since existing laws were not serving as deterrents. See O. K. Kass-Yerenchi, "Operation of the Two Forest Protection Decrees in Ghana," (Unpublished Dissertation), Institute of Renewable Natural Resources, University of Science and Technology, Kumasi, Ghana, 1984.

439 International Institute for Environment and Development (IIED), "Study of Incentives for the Sustainable Management of the Tropical High Forest of Ghana," Final Report, IIED, London, October, 1994, p. 8.

440 In 1995, for example, the annual budget allocation to the Ministry of Lands Forestry was approximately $8.3 million, a mere 1.37% of the total budget. This was far less than what was required to administer and police thousands of acres of forests, and undertake replanting.

442 Tufuor, "A Review of Forest Sector Policy of Ghana," Op. cit.

442 W. A. Gordon, "The Law of Forestry", His majesty's Stationary Office, London, 1955. See also: J. G. K. Owusu, "Evolution of Forest Legislation in Ghana," Op. cit., and M. S. Phillip, "Management of Tropical Moist Forest in Africa," F.A.O. Forestry Paper 88, 1989, pp. 6-18.

444 Ibid.

444 Gertrude Blavo, The State of Forestry Legislation in Ghana," Forestry Commission Symposia Series #3, 1989, p.288. This view was also expressed by R. K. Bamfo, an official of the Forestry Commission during an interview in August, 1996.

[445] Forest Research Institute of Ghana (FORIG), "Incentives and Technologies for Sustainability of Forest Management in Anglophone West Africa," Draft Report, May, 1995.

[446] Ghana Forestry Commission, "Revision of Ghana's Forest Policy," Proceedings of A National Conference, Accra, Forestry Commission Symposia Series # 3, April 2-8, 1989.

[449] K. Tufuor, "A Review of Forestry Sector Policy of Ghana," Op. cit.

[449] Ibid., p. 7.

[449] The various campaigns to promote increased food production; "Grow More Food," "Operation Feed Yourself," "Operation Feed Your Industries," etc., in effect, led to an assault on the forests of Ghana.

[452] Ibid., p. 12.

[453] Ibid.

[453] K. Kesse, "Enforcement of Forest Laws," Forestry Commission Symposia Series #3, Ibid., p. 293.

[453] O. K. Kass-Yerenchi, "The Adequacy of Forest Ordinance and The Forest Protection Decree as Forest Regulatory and Conservation Instruments in Ghana," B.SC. Dissertation (unpublished), Institute of Renewable Natural Resources, University of Science and Technology, Kumasi, Ghana, July, 1991, pp. 45-49. See also: Silviconsult, "The Forestry Department Review," October 1986, p. 61.

[455] Kass-Yerenchi, Op. cit.

[455] Findings of the United Nations Development Program on the Ghana Forestry Planning Project concluded that the weakened state of the institutions and agencies within the sector, in particular, the lack of coordination, inadequate identification of issues that need to be addressed, limited resources for gathering, analyzing, and retrieving information critical to policy formulation and implementation are some of the reasons for the lack of success at reducing the severe forest depletion in the country. (See U.N.D.P., "Assistance to Forestry Planning, Ghana, Project Findings and Recommendations," U.N.D.P./F.A.O., Rome 1993, p. 1-2.)

[458] Ibid.

[458] Wright, Op. cit. See also: Metcalfe, Op. cit., and, Boahen and Tidy, Op cit.

[458] Naomi Chazan, An Anatomy of Ghanaian Politics: Managing Political Recession, 1969-1982, (Boulder: Westview, 1983), p. 45.

[459] Agyemang-Duah, "Ghana, 1982-1986; the Politics of the P.N.D.C.," Journal of Modern African Studies, vol. 25, no. 4, 1987, pp. 614-615.

[462] A. K. Ocran, Politics of the Sword, (London: R. Collins, 1977), p. 9.

[462] Chazan, Op. cit., p. 45.

[462] Paul Nugent, Big Men, Small Boys and Politics in Ghana, (London: Pinter, 1995), p. 23. See also: Ocran, Op. cit., p. 24.

[464] Robert Pinkney, Democracy and Dictatorship in Ghana and Tanzania, (New York: St. Martin's Press, 1977), p. 22.

[465] Nugent, Op. cit.

[465] J. B. Danquah, Akan Laws and Customs, (London: Oxford University Press, 1957). See also: Kwame Arhin, Traditional Rule in Ghana: Past and Present, (Accra: Sedco, 1985), and K. A. Busia, The Position of the Chief in the Modern Political System of Ashanti, Op. cit.

[466] Danquah, Op. cit., Arhin, Op. cit., and Busia, Op. cit. See also: Nii Amaa Ollennu, Principles of Customary Law in Ghana, (London: Ernest and Maxwell, 1962).

[467] The activities of the Aborigines Rights Protection Society during the colonial era have been referred to in Chapter three. (Martin Wright, The Development of the Legislative Council, 1606-1945, Op. cit.) In the post-colonial era the strong opposition posed by the

Asantes and other Akan tribes to the Nkrumah regime have been well documented. (L. H. Ofosu-Appiah, The Life and Times of Dr. J. B. Danquah, (Accra: Waterville Publishing House, 1974), Pater T. Omari, Kwame Nkrumah, The Anatomy of an African Dictatorship, (New York: Africana Publishing Corporation, 1970), and C. E. K. Kumado, Constitutionalism, Civil Liberties, and Development: A Case Study of Ghana Since Independence, (Accra: Ghana Publishing Corporation, 1980).

[470]Op. cit.

[470]Government of Ghana, The Constitution of Ghana, (Accra: Government Printer, 1957).

[470]Tapan Prasad Biswal, Ghana: Political and Constitutional Developments, (New Delhi: Northern Book Center, 1992). See also: Ocran, Op. cit., Pinkney, Op. cit., and A. A. Afrifah, The Ghana Coup, (London: Frank Cass, 1966), pp. 19-21.

[472] See: Ocran, Ibid., Afrifah, Ibid., and Biswal, Ibid.

[472]Kwame Nkrumah, Consciencism: Philosophy and Ideology for Decolonization and Development with Particular Reference to the African Revolution, (New York: Monthly Review Press, 1965). See also: Charles Adom Boateng, Nkrumah's Consciencism, (Dubuque, Iowa: Kendall/Hunt Publishing Company, 1995).

[473]Republic of Ghana, "Seven-Year Plan for National Reconstruction and Development: Financial Years 1963/64 - 1969/70," (Accra: Office of the Planning Commission, 1963).

[476]Ocran, Op. cit., pp. 39-41.

[476]Ocran, Ibid., p. 42. See also: Phillips, Ibid p. 36.

[476]Afrifah, Op. cit., p. 19. See also: Austin Amissah, "Recent Developments in Ghana," The Scandinavian Institute of African Studies, Uppsala, 1973, p. 6.

[478]J. B. Blay, Legend of Kwame Nkrumah, (Accra: Abicom Ltd., 1973).

[479]The Government of Ghana, "The Republican Constitution of Ghana," (Accra: Ghana Government Printers, 1960).

[479]Simon Baynham, The Military and Politics in Nkrumah's Ghana, (Boulder: Westview, 1988), p. 207. See also: Dennis Austin, Politics in Ghana, 1946 - 1960, (London: Oxford University Press, 1970).

[481]Kwame Nkrumah, The Autobiography of Kwame Nkrumah, (London: Panaf, 1973).

[483]The Government of Ghana, "The Republican Constitution...," Op. cit.

[483]Biswal, Op. cit., p. 69.

[483]Dr. Nkrumah's government was overthrown in a *coup d'etat* in February 1966. His regime was replaced by the National Liberation Council, a junta that ruled until 1969 when it handed over power to a new constitutional regime headed by Dr. K. A. Busia. Dr. Nkrumah remained in exile in Guinea until his death in 1972.

[485]Radio broadcast from Ghana Broadcasting Corporation, Accra, February 24, 1966.

[485]Heads of the regions were to be chosen by the House of Chiefs (assemblies of the high ranking traditional rulers) in each region except Asante where the Asantehene (king of Asante) was the automatic head.

[486]K. A Busia, "Parliamentary Debates, June 4, 1957," (Accra: Ghana Government Printers), vol. 457. See also: J. A. Brain, "Parliamentary Debates, June 21, 1957," (Accra: Ghana Government Printers, 1957), volumes 1189-1195.

[490]Biswal, Op. cit. pp. 62-65.

[490]Ibid., p. 65.

[490]Afrifah, Op. cit., p. 24.

[490]Ellen Hosmer, "Paradise Lost: The Ravaged Rainforest," Multinational Monitor, June 1997, pp. 6-8. See also: Friends of the Earth, "Plunder in Ghana's Rainforest for Illegal Profit: An Expose of Corruption, Fraud, and other Malpractice in the International Timber Trade," (London: Friends of the Earth, 1992).

[495]Chazan, Op. cit., p. 57.

[496]Adu, Op. cit.

[496]Baynham, Op. cit., p. 220.

[496]Ibid.

[496]Interview published in the *Legon Observer*, February 17, 1967.

[498]Biswal, Op. cit., p. 98. See also: Baynham, Op. cit., p. 221.

[498]Austin Amissah, Op. cit., p. 12.

[498]A. K. Ocran, Op. cit., p. 88. It needs to be noted that Major General A. K. Ocran was a member of the National Liberation Council. His account of events, as well as observations about the functioning of that regime, are an insider's version of the scenario that existed.

[502]Ibid., p. 89.

[502]Ibid., pp. 89-103.

[502]Ibid., pp. 114-115.

[503]Government of Ghana, Constitution of the Second Republic of Ghana, (Accra: Ghana Publishing Corporation, 1969).

[504]Chazan, Op. cit., p. 46. See also: Ocran, Op. cit., p. 51.

[504]Government of Ghana, "The Local Government Administration Bill (1970)," Government Gazette, (Accra: Ghana Publishing Corporation, 1970).

[505]J. Opare-Abetia (ed.), "Ghana In Search of a Stable Form of Government," Proceedings of the Twenty-Seventh Annual New Year School, December 29, 1977 to January 4, 1978, (Legon: Institute of Adult Education, University of Ghana, 1978-1979), vols. 1 and 2.

[506]*Sallah v. Attorney-General*, discussed in University of Ghana, "Law Journal," (University of Ghana, Legon, 1970), No. 142.

[507]A. Adu Boahen, "The Ghanaian Sphinx: Reflections on the Contemporary History of Ghana 1972-1987," J. B. Danquah Memorial Lectures, Ghana Academy of Arts and Sciences, Series no. 21, February, 1988, p. 12.

[509]Chazan, Op. cit., p. 46. See also:, Adu Boahen, Op. cit., p. 15, and Biswal, Op. cit.

[510]Mike Oquaye, Politics in Ghana, 1972-1979, (Accra: Tornado Press, 1980). See also: Adu Boahen, Op. cit., p. 15.

[510]Kofi Awoonor, The Ghana Revolution: Background Account From a Personal Perspective, (New York; Oasis, 1984), p. 95.

[511]"Akyeampong Ousted," African Research Bulletin, vol. 15, no. 7, August 15, 1978, pp. 4926-8. See also: M. Godwin, "Change in Command at Burma Camp," Africa, No. 84, August 1978, p. 14.

[513]Government of Ghana, Constitution of the Republic of Ghana, (Accra: Government Printer, 1979).

[513]Barbara Callancy, "National-Local Linkages in Ghana," African Review, vol. 4, No. 3, 1974, p. 407. See also: Chazan, An Anatomy of Ghanaian Politics, Op. cit., p. 54.

[514]Ghana Government. "A Revolutionary Journey: Selected Speeches of Flt. Lt. J. J. Rawlings, Chairman of the P.N.D.C., December 31, 1982," (Accra: Information Services Department, 1983), p. 1.

[516]Yaw Akrasi Sarpong, "Role of the Defense Committees," The Mirror, (Accra: Graphic Corporation, January 24, 1983).

[516]Adu Boahen, Op. cit., 46-9. See also: Biswal, Op. cit. As many as seven plots and attempted *coups* occurred between March 1982 and June 1983.

[517] E. Gyimah-Boadi (ed.), Ghana Under PNDC Rule, (Senegal: Codesria, 1993), Emmanuel Hansen, Ghana Under Rawlings: Early Years, (Lagos: Malthouse Press,

1991), and Kevin Shillington, <u>Ghana and the Rawlings Factor</u>, (New York: St. Martinᗏs Press, 1992).

[518]Frank Kwaw Codjoe, <u>Elites, Ideology, and development Problems of Ghana</u>, (Hamburg: Verlag an der Lottbeg, 1988). See also: Aryee: <u>Anatomy of Public Policy Implementation: Case of Decentralization in Ghana</u>, Op. cit., and, Adu, <u>The Civil Service in New African States</u>, Op. cit.

[519]Ghana Government, <u>Constitution of the Republic of Ghana</u>, (Accra: Government Publishing Corporation, 1992), pp. 62-3.

[521]Ghana Information Service, "Fact Sheet,"' Government of Ghana mimeographed paper, *circa* 1993-1995.

[521]For example, statements made by Mr. Kojo Tsikata, chairman of the Ghana National Petroleum Corporation, Mr. P. V. Obeng , and Mrs. Rawlings have been routinely reported by the Ghanaian government-controlled media as if they were official government policy pronouncements.

[524]Pinkney, Op. cit., p. 178.

[524]Ibid.

[524]R. Tangei, "The Politics of Government-Business Relations in Ghana," <u>Journal of Modern African Studies</u>, vol. 20, No. 1, 1992, pp. 108-9.

[526]Pinkney, Op. cit., p. 179.

[526]The effects of policies under Ghana's Structural Adjustment Program were discussed at greater length in Chapter Four as an aspect of the external factors that shape the internal environment of the forest policy process

[527]In this chapter as well as in Chapter Eight, a number of references have been made to information contained in two reports on the forestry sector of Ghana. The first is "Study of Incentives for the Sustainable Management of the Tropical High Forest of Ghana," a report prepared in 1994 by the International Institute for Environment and Development (I.I.E.D.) in collaboration with the Department of Forestry for the International Tropical Timber Organization (I.T.T.O.). The second is "The Forestry Department Review," prepared in 1986 by Silviconsult, a Swedish consulting group, for the government of Ghana. These two documents were, at the time of this research, the most recent comprehensive studies on the forestry sector of Ghana available to this researcher.

[528]Silviconsult, "The Forestry Department Review," Prepared for the Government of Ghana (Accra: Silviconsult, October 1986), p. 29.

[529]International Institute for Environment and Development (I.I.E.D.), "Study of Incentives for the Sustainable Management of the Tropical High Forest of Ghana," Final Report, (London: I.I.E.D. and Forestry Department, October 1994), p. 54.

[531]I.I.E.D., Ibid., pp. 53-54.

[532]Government of Ghana, "The Lands Commission Act, 1993," (Accra: Ghana Publishing Corporation, 1993).

[532]Ghana Timber Exports Development Board, "Ghana Forests, Wood and People," (London: Timber Exports Development Board, 1989).

[535]I.I.E.D., Op. cit., p. 88.

[535]Silviconsult, "The Forestry Department Review," Op. cit., pp. 30-31.

[535]Forest Products Inspection Bureau, "Welcome to Forest Products Inspection Bureau," Third Edition, (Takoradi: Public Relations Unit, 1994), p. 5.

[541]F.P.I.B., "Welcome to F.P.I.B.,"' Op. cit.

[541]I.I.E.D., Op. cit., p. 86.

[541]Ibid., p. 86.

[541]Ibid.

[541]Ibid.

[542]Government of Ghana, "The Ghana Forestry Commission Act, 1980," (Accra: Ghana Publishing Corporation, 1980).

[544]I.I.E.D., Op. cit.

[544]The Republic of Ghana, "Constitution of the Forth Republic," Op. cit.

[545]The Republic of Ghana, "Forestry Commission Act (Act 453), 1993,' (Accra: Ghana Publishing Corporation, 1993).

[546]Ibid.

[546]Instances of such recommendations are contained in K. Tufuor, "A Review of Forest Sector Policy of Ghana," (unpublished) (Accra: Forestry Commission, December 1993), I.I.E.D., "Study of Incentives for the Sustainable Management of the Tropical High Forest of Ghana," Op. cit., and, J. H. Francois, "Overview of Ghana's Forest Policy," Op. cit.

[548]Government of Ghana, "The Control of Bush Fires Law, PNDCL 46, 1983," (Accra: Government Printers, 1983).

[548]Current policies of the government emphasize the incorporation of forestry practices such as tree planting and protection into farming practices. To achieve this, the Agro-Forestry Unit of the Ministry of Agriculture has organized education programs and undertaken extension activities for the purpose of introducing agro-forestry techniques to farmers. (This information was obtained during an interview with Mr. K. B. Ashong, Principal Technical Officer of the Agro-Forestry Unit of the Ministry of Agriculture in August, 1996.)

[549]To demonstrate the government's support of private enterprise in reforestation and forest plantation, President Rawlings launched the Ghana Forestry Week, 1996 at a forestry plantation in Somanya. His address on that occasion (referred to earlier in Chapter One) included expressions of admiration for the owners of the plantation and encouragement to all Ghanaians to follow their example, not only by protecting the existing forests, but by also establishing tree lots.

[550]Since the mid-1980s, environmental science has become a part of the curricula of elementary and high schools in Ghana. The mass media, especially government-controlled radio and television have also run regular programs that are designed to educate the masses about the need to protect the environment, and how they can help achieve it.

[551]This review was conducted under the auspices of the United Nations Food and Agricultural Organization (F.A.O.), Overseas Development Assistance (O.D.A.), and the Canadian International Development Agency (C.I.D.A.)

[552]Deloitte & Touche Consulting, "Forestry Department of Ghana, Institutional Reform Project," (Accra: Deloitte & Touche, 1995).

[553]As at 1994 the government owned, wholly or partially, the largest eight timber enterprises. These enterprises controlled about a third of all forest concessions, and accounted for about a quarter of the total timber and wood product exports. (Source: .I.I.E.D., Op. cit., p. 63.)

[554]Government of Ghana, "Environmental Protection Council Decree, 1974 (NRC Decree 239), Section 2," (Accra: Government Printers, 1974).

[555]Official documents and publications of the E.P.A. include occasional references to deforestation. But, beyond that, the problem has received only minimal attention from the agency. A possible reason for this is the existence of a number of other institutions specifically dealing with forestry.

[560]I.I.E.D., Op. cit., pp. 55-56.

[560]Ibid., p. 55.

[560]Silviconsult, Op. cit.

[560]Ibid.

[560]Robert Repetto and Malcolm Gillis (eds.) Public Policies and the Misuse of Forest Resources, (New York: Cambridge University Press/World Resources Institute, 1988), p. 313. The main activities within the forestry sector of Ghana have been logging, saw milling, and furniture manufacturing.

[561]Malcolm Gillis, "West Africa: Resource Management Policies and the Tropical Forest," in Robert Repetto and Malcolm Gillis (Eds), Ibid., p.313-322.

[562]John Esseks, "The Nationalization of the Ownership of Resources in Ghana." Paper presented for the Colloquim on Ghana. Department of State, Washington, D.C., October 11, 1974.

[563]Ignatius Peprah, "Foreign Investment in the Forest-Based Sector of Ghana," (Unpublished), (Cambridge Mass.: Harvard University, 1982), p. 66.

[564]Figures assembled by Gillis et al. show that in 1991 domestic investment in the forest sector of Ghana was $207.5 million, 54% of the total.

[565]The activities of illegal chain-saw operators and bush millers are known to account for a significant proportion of timber felled both within and outside forest reserves. (I.I.E.D., op cit., p. 65). This fact was also confirmed by Mr. E. O. Nsenkyire, Chief Conservator of Forests during an interview with this researcher in August 1996.

[567]Tufuor, Op. cit. See also: I.I.E.D., Op. cit.

[567]David Kenneth Fieldhouse, Unilever Overseas: The Anatomy of a Multi-national 1895-1965, (London: Croom Helm, 1978), pp. 339 and 448.

[568]Charles Wilson, Unilever 1945-1965: The Challenge and Response in the Post-war Industrial Revolution, (London: Cassell, 1968), p. 218.

[570]Ibid.

[570]George F. Kojo Arthur, "Structural Adjustments, Dependency and Multinational Corporations: United Africa Company - The Unilever Connection in Ghana,"(Unpublished).

[573]Fieldhouse, Op. cit., Wilson, Op. cit.

[573]Arthur, Op. cit.

[573]Acquay, "The Impact of Stabilization..." Op. cit. See also: Donald Rothchild, "Ghana and Structural Adjustment: An Overview," Op. cit.

[576]Tufuor, Op. cit. See also: I.I.E.D., Op cit.

[576]Ibid.

[576]Joseph Boakye Danquah, Akan Laws and Customs, Op. cit., p. 200. See also: Kwame Arhin, Op. cit., K. A. Busia, The Position of the Chief ..... Op. cit., pp. 40-60, and Nii Amaa Ollennu, Principles of Customary Land Law in Ghana, Op. cit., pp. 4-7.

[580]Ibid.

[580]I.I.E.D., Op. cit., p. 58.

[580]Busia, Op. cit., p. 44.

[580]Kwamena Ahwoi, "Address on the Inauguration of District Assemblies by the Secretary of Local Government," August, 1988.

[586]Tufuor, Op. cit., p. 7.

[587]I.I.E.D., Op. cit., p. 57

[588]Ibid.

[588]I.I.E.D., Op. cit. pp. 56-7

[588]Ibid.

[588]Tufuor, Op. cit., p. 10.

[588]I.I.E.D., Op. cit., p. 68.

[588]Clement Dorm-Adjobu, Ampadu-Agyei, Okyeame, and Veit, Peter G., "Community Institutions in Resources Management: Agro-forestry by Mobisquads in Ghana," Edited

by Center for International Development and Environment, World Resources Institute, (Washington, D.C.: World Resources Institute, 1991).

[589]Results of the exploratory survey support this fact. Sixty percent of respondents from the timber industry agreed (40% strongly) with the statement that "Man has the right to exploit nature by any means available." 53% of farmer respondents agreed with that statement, again 40% of them strongly.

[590]An outstanding example of this is the Amansie Tree-Planting and Rural Development Association, which was reported in April 1997 as having been successful at organizing several villages to participate in such programs in the Bekwai district.   Another example concerns farmers of the Juabeso-Bia district of the Western Region who were reported in September, 1997 to have drawn up a five-year afforestation program to address forest depletion.   (Both examples were obtained from the Internet at pbs2.milton.port.ac.uk)

[591]The term 'politics', in the context of this discussion, refers to the realities of the Ghanaian political economy, and deriving from them, the priorities of those holding political power in Ghana. Given the overall economic circumstances of the country, in particular, the urgency to generate external revenue, and the status of land and forest as sources of sustenance for most Ghanaians, politicians have had no choice other than to promote timber exploitation and avoid the strict enforcement of forestry laws. The performance of the bureaucracies and the overall outcome of policies intended to address deforestation reflect these priorities.

[592]A highlight of the 1994 Ghana Forest and Wildlife Policy is the management and enhancement of Ghana's forest estate in order to restore its original properties. This theme featured prominently in the address by the Ghanaian deputy minister for Environment, Science and Technology, Alhaji Farouk Brimah, at the sixth session of the African Ministers of Environment Conference (Op. cit.) and in President Rawlings' address at the launching of the National Forestry Week, 1996. (Op. cit.).

[593]The Chief Conservator of Forests, Mr. Nsenkyire, reiterated this during the interview with this researcher in August, 1996.

[594]International Institute for Environment and Development (IIED), "Study of Incentives for the Sustainable Management of the Tropical High Forest of Ghana," Op. cit., p. 33.

[596]Details about the design of the exploratory survey, and questionnaire used are contained in Appendix 2.

[597]Forestry Department, "Manual of Procedure," circa 1950.

[597]Examples of projects and programs which had policy and institutional reforms as their objective (or part of it) include:

i. The Forest Resource Management Project, begun in November, 1989 and estimated to have cost $64.6 million;

ii. The Forest Inventory and Management Program; and,

iii. The Forestry Planning Project under which the Policy, Planning, Monitoring and Evaluation Division of the Ministry of Lands and Natural Resources was established.

[598]Publications by institutions (such as the International Institute of Environment and Development (IIED), the Ghana Environmental Protection Council, and the Ghana Forestry Commission), and individuals (such as Edward Prah, and K. Tufuor) that address this problem have been relied on extensively in writing this chapter.

[599]As of 1992, the Department of Forestry was the fourth largest agency within the Ghanaian government. (IIED, Op. cit., p. 36.)

[603]Silviconsult, Op. cit., pp. 77-81.

[603]Ibid., p. 45.

[603]Government of Ghana, Budget Statement for 1995/96, Op. cit.

[603] I.I.E.D., Op. cit., p. 47. The problems that result from poor funding are described in great detail in the Silviconsult review of the Department (Op. cit.) For example, the report describes all existing office equipment, typewriters, adding machines, drawing equipment and furniture as "old and in a poor state of repair." Supplies of stationery are described as "irregular." Throughout the seven regions (comprising thirty- three districts), only two utility vehicles were described in the report as fully serviceable (p. 36-37). This situation, according to the report, was not confined to the regions; it applied to all other branches of the Department. Survey, field camp, and nursery equipment had deteriorated and were less than 5% adequate.

[604] Ghana Environmental Protection Council, Ghana Environmental Action Plan 1994, Op. cit., p. 182. See also: Silviconsult, "The Department of Forestry Review," Op. cit.

[605] An instance where Mr. Francois dwelt on this issue was during presentation of "Overview of Ghana's Forest Policy," at the National Conference on the Revision of Ghana's Forest Policy, Ghana Forestry Commission Symposia series # 3, Accra, April 2- 8, 1989.

[606] Edward Prah, Sustainable Management of the Tropical High Forest of Ghana, (London: Commonwealth Secretariat/International Development Research Center, September 1994), pp. 43-44.

[607] Deloitte and Touche Consulting, "Forestry Department of Ghana: Institutional Reform Project, Working Groups Findings," Circa 1992, (Accra, Ghana).

[608] Under Article 267 (6) of the 1992 Constitution, and Section 8 (1) of Act 481, 10% of timber royalties from off-reserve forests is paid to the Department of Forestry to cover administrative expenses.

[611] Silviconsult, Op. cit., p. 78. See also: I.I.E.D., Op. cit., pp. 53-54.

[611] Silviconsult, Op. cit., p. 61.

[611] I.I.E.D., p. 49. This study reported that as at the end of September 1992, concession holders owed $6.7 million in royalties.

[613] Ibid., p. 79.

[613] Ibid. This issue has been treated in other sources as well. (e.g. I.I.E.D. Op. cit., p. 48., and Tufuor, Op. cit.)

[615] Silviconsult, Op. cit., p. 65-66.

[615] Overall, 33% of the respondents agreed with the statement that there is too much government regulation concerning the forests.

[617] IIED., Op. cit., p. 51. See also: Silviconsult, Op. cit., pp. 65-66.

[617] Although it could not be confirmed from other sources, the statement made in the IIED report that the Ghanaian civil service was reduced from 140,000 in 1987 to 93,000 in 1992, gives an idea about the number of workers of who have lost their jobs under the exercise. (IIED, "Study of Incentives for the Sustainable Management of the Tropical High Forest of Ghana," Op. cit., p. 36.)

[618] This information was obtained from the interview conducted with the Kyebi District Forestry Officer in August, 1996.

[620] Ibid., p. 66.

[620] It is estimated in the Silviconsult study that less than 50% of the active chain saw operators are registered in Ghana, and those who pay some royalty and fees routinely fell more than they are authorized.

[621] Forest Resources Management Project, "Protection of the Forest Industry," A Study Prepared for the Ministry of Lands and Natural Resources, Accra, October 1991, pp. 66- 67.

[622]The lack of police and judicial support was listed by the District Forestry Officer of Kyebi, and confirmed by the Chief Conservator of Forests, as one of the incentives for the citizens to flout the laws against forest destruction.

[624]Tufuor, Op. cit., p. 24.

[624]Gertrude Blavo, "The State of Forestry Legislation in Ghana," (Accra: Forestry Commission, 1989), Forestry Commission Symposia Series, #3.

[624]A highlight of the 1994 Ghana Forest and Wildlife Policy is the management and enhancement of Ghana's forest estate in order to restore its original properties. This theme featured prominently in the address by the Ghanaian deputy minister for Environment, Science and Technology, Alhaji Farouk Brimah, at the sixth session of the African Ministers of Environment Conference (Op. cit.) and in President Rawlings' address at the launching of the National Forestry Week, 1996. (Op. cit.)

[624]The Chief Conservator of Forests, Mr. Nsenkyire, reiterated this during the interview with this researcher in August, 1996.

[624]International Institute for Environment and Development (IIED), "Study of Incentives for the Sustainable Management of the Tropical High Forest of Ghana," Op. cit., p. 33.

[624]Details about the design of the exploratory survey, and questionnaire used are contained in Appendix 2.

[624]Forestry Department, "Manual of Procedure," circa 1950.

[624]Examples of projects and programs which had policy and institutional reforms as their objective (or part of it) include:

1) The Forest Resource Management Project, begun in November, 1989 and estimated to have cost $64.6 million;
2) The Forest Inventory and Management Program; and,
3) The Forestry Planning Project under which the Policy, Planning, Monitoring and Evaluation Division of the Ministry of Lands and Natural Resources was established.

[624]Publications by institutions (such as the International Institute of Environment and Development (IIED), the Ghana Environmental Protection Council, and the Ghana Forestry Commission), and individuals (such as Edward Prah, and K. Tufuor) that address this problem have been relied on extensively in writing this chapter.

[624]As of 1992, the Department of Forestry was the fourth largest agency within the Ghanaian government. (IIED, Op. cit., p. 36.)

[624]Silviconsult, Op. cit., pp. 77-81.

[624]Ibid., p. 45.

[624]Government of Ghana, Budget Statement for 1995/96, Op. cit.

[624] I.I.E.D., Op. cit., p. 47. The problems that result from poor funding are described in great detail in the Silviconsult review of the Department (Op. cit.) For example, the report describes all existing office equipment, typewriters, adding machines, drawing equipment and furniture as "old and in a poor state of repair." Supplies of stationery are described as "irregular." Throughout the seven regions (comprising thirty- three districts), only two utility vehicles were described in the report as fully serviceable (p. 36-37). This situation, according to the report, was not confined to the regions; it applied to all other branches of the Department. Survey, field camp, and nursery equipment had deteriorated and were less than 5% adequate.

[624]Ghana Environmental Protection Council, Ghana Environmental Action Plan 1994, Op. cit., p. 182. See also: Silviconsult, "The Department of Forestry Review," Op. cit.

[624]An instance where Mr. Francois dwelt on this issue was during presentation of "Overview of Ghana's Forest Policy," at the National Conference on the Revision of

Ghana's Forest Policy, Ghana Forestry Commission Symposia series # 3, Accra, April 2-8, 1989.

[624]Edward Prah, Sustainable Management of the Tropical High Forest of Ghana, (London: Commonwealth Secretariat/International Development Research Center, September 1994), pp. 43-44.

[624]Deloitte and Touche Consulting, "Forestry Department of Ghana: Institutional Reform Project, Working Groups Findings," Circa 1992, (Accra, Ghana).

[624]Under Article 267 (6) of the 1992 Constitution, and Section 8 (1) of Act 481, 10% of timber royalties from off-reserve forests is paid to the Department of Forestry to cover administrative expenses.

[624]Silviconsult, Op. cit., p. 78. See also: I.I.E.D., Op. cit., pp. 53-54.

[624]Silviconsult, Op. cit., p. 61.

[624]I.I.E.D., p. 49. This study reported that as at the end of September 1992, concession holders owed $6.7 million in royalties.

[624]Ibid., p. 79.

[624]Ibid. This issue has been treated in other sources as well. (E.g. I.I.E.D. Op. cit., p. 48., and Tufuor, Op. cit.)

[624]Silviconsult, Op. cit., p. 65-66.

[624]Overall, 33% of the respondents agreed with the statement that there is too much government regulation concerning the forests.

[624]IIED., Op. cit., p. 51. See also: Silviconsult, Op. cit., pp. 65-66.

[624]Although it could not be confirmed from other sources, the statement made in the IIED report that the Ghanaian civil service was reduced from 140,000 in 1987 to 93,000 in 1992, gives an idea about the number of workers of who have lost their jobs under the exercise. (IIED, "Study of Incentives for the Sustainable Management of the Tropical High Forest of Ghana," Op. cit., p. 36.)

[624]This information was obtained from the interview conducted with the Kyebi District Forestry Officer in August, 1996.

[624]Ibid., p. 66.

[624]It is estimated in the Silviconsult study that less than 50% of the active chain saw operators are registered in Ghana, and those who pay some royalty and fees routinely fell more than they are authorized.

[624]Forest Resources Management Project, "Protection of the Forest Industry," A Study Prepared for the Ministry of Lands and Natural Resources, Accra, October 1991, pp. 66-67.

[624]The lack of police and judicial support was listed by the District Forestry Officer of Kyebi, and confirmed by the Chief Conservator of Forests, as one of the incentives for the citizens to flout the laws against forest destruction.

[624]Tufuor, Op. cit., p. 24.

[624]Gertrude Blavo, "The State of Forestry Legislation in Ghana," (Accra: Forestry Commission, 1989), Forestry Commission Symposia Series, #3.

[625]As was explained in Chapter Four, the internal environment of the forestry policy process in Ghana refers to the measures of political power, motives, and activities of the heads of state and leading politicians. Also included in the internal environment are the influence, missions, and activities of the two categories of government bureaucracies that have been involved in the forestry sector: the protective regulatory bureaucracies, and the extractive bureaucracies. The external environment comprises the historical, social, cultural, political, and economic factors (both domestic and foreign) that have conditioned the goals, priorities, and actions of the principal actors within the internal

environment.   These factors have also influenced the relationships between those principal actors.

[628]Belfield, Op. cit.

[628]Chipp, Op. cit., p. 69. See also: Ghana Government, "Wealth in Wood," Op. cit.

[628]Such evidence has emerged from official rhetoric by President Rawlings which has demonstrated a determination, on his part, to address the problem. Furthermore, a series of published plans and reforms, intended to address deforestation has been introduced in recent years.

[629]According to statistics released by the World Bank, the rate of population growth in Ghana (an average of 3% since 1985) is among the highest in sub-Saharan Africa.

[630]"Sustainability" has been aptly defined as, the management of a resource for maximum continuing production, consistent with the maintenance of a constantly renewable stock. See: Becky J. Brown, Hanson, Mark E., Liverman, Diana M., and Merideth, Robert W., "Global Sustainability: Toward Definition," Environmental Management, Vol. 11, No. 6, 1987, p. 714.

[633]Aryeetey, Op. cit.

[633]The World Bank, "World Development Report, 1996," (Washington, DC: The World Bank, 1997).

[633]Garrett Hardin, "The Tragedy of the Commons," Op. cit. As was discussed in the Introduction, Harding, in "The Tragedy....," dealt with the consequence of reckless exploitation of natural resources.   He demonstrated how the lack of effective management of natural resources ultimately results in over-exploitation and the eventual destruction of the resources. In the final analysis, all stakeholders stand to lose whatever benefits they could have gained from the resource in the long run, if they had exercised some restraint in their utilization of the "common" resource.

[634]"Sustainability," as has been shown, means the management of resources in order to ensure maximum continuing production, consistent with the maintenance of a constantly renewable stock.   With regards to forest resources, sustainable utilization means managing the rate of exploitation in order to maintain the condition as well as the area of the forest.

[635]"Afforestation" is the replacement of hitherto non-forested lands with forests, and the regeneration of degraded forests.

[637]Republic of Ghana, "Budget Statement for 1995/96," Op. cit.

[637]Even though forest plantation as a means of replenishing forests in Ghana was started as long ago as the beginning of the century, by 1992, a mere 193 square miles had been established, of which only a third (64 square miles) was considered successful. (See: I.I.E.D., Op. cit., p. 10.)

[638]After a study covering ninety-eight countries, Bowonder found a correlation (of .578) between the rate of population growth and the growth rate of wood extraction. (See: B. Bowonder, "Forest Depletion: Some Policy Options," Resources Policy, vol. 9, # 3, September 1983, p. 206.) The implication is that, in order to reduce the rate of wood extraction in Ghana, the rate of population growth would have to be reduced.

[639]Ministry of Agriculture, "Operation Feed Yourself;" : Sustained Gains in Ghana's Agrarian Revolution," Information Bulletin, (Accra: Government Printers, 1976).

[640]R. Revelle, "Energy Sources for Rural Development," Energy, vol. 4, 1979, pp. 969 - 989. by J. J. Talbot in "The Fate of Tropical Forests," Science and Public Policy, vol. 6, # 3, 1979, pp. 185-188 corroborated Revelle's estimate. Although these estimates were made over two decades ago, there is no reason to expect the situation at present to be any different, given that the cooking facilities used by a majority of the population at present are the same as those that were in use in 1979.

[641]Planning Branch, Forestry Department, "Ghana: Steps Towards Sustainable Forestry and Wise Use of Timber Resources," Paper Presented at the Eighth Session of the I.T.T.C. and the Sixteenth Session of the I.T.T.O. Permanent Committees, Accra, May 10-18, 1995, p. 10.

[644]Kuffuor, Op. cit., p. 18.

[644]The potential of non-timber forest products is examined in the following section.

[645]Department of Forestry, Op. cit., p. 10. See also: I.T.T.O., Op cit., p. 120.

[645]Sargeant et al., "Incentives for the Sustainability........," Op. cit., pp. 159-161. See also: Department of Forestry, "Steps Towards ....," Op. cit., p. 10, and Kuffuor, Op. cit., pp. 17-18.

[647]I.T.T.O., Op. cit., pp. 99-108. See also: Bowonder, "Forest Depletion: Some Policy Options," Op. cit., p. 209.

[648]Ibid.

[649]Theodore Panayaton, and Peter S. Ashton, Not By Timber Alone, (Washington D.C.: Island Press, 1992), p. 62.

[649]This researcher observed during his visits to sawmills in the Kyebi district that large amounts of saw-dust, small pieces of wood, and other remnants form the plants, material that can be processed into boards, domestic and industrial fuels, etc., were being burnt off or being simply discarded as waste. This observation confirmed the earlier assessment that an average of 45% of trees felled (stem parts, crown wood, and stumps) were not used at all. See: D. Noack et al., "Better Utilization of Tropical Timber Resources in Order to Improve Sustainability and Reduce Negative Ecological Impacts - Wood Waste and Logging Damage in Nkrabia Forest Reserve, Ghana," I.T.T.O. Project PD 74/90, (Hamburg: Federal Research Center for Forestry and Forest Products, February 24, 1992, p. 54.)

[650]Such products include foods (snails, bush meat, mushrooms, fruits, plant beverages, and seeds), spices, chewing sticks, chewing sponge, cola nut, charcoal, medicines, household goods (pestles, mortars, tool handles, sponges, grinders, mats, and baskets), and canes.

[651]It has been estimated that almost half of all prescription drugs dispensed in the United States contain substances of natural origin. See: Mark Plotkin, "Treasures Among the Trees," International Monitor, June, 1997, p. 9. Plotkin further reports that in 1974 the US imported $24.4 million of medicinal plants. In 1985 US consumers purchased over $8 billion worth of prescriptions in which the active ingredients were extracted from plants. The potential of the tropical forest has been documented elsewhere. See: C. M. Peters, et al, "Valuation of an Amazonian Rainforest," Nature, vol. 339, p. 29.

[652]J. P. Lebrum, "Richesses Specifiques dela Flore Vasculaire des Divers Pays ou Regions d'Afrique," Candollea, vol. 31, pp. 11-15.

[653]N. K. Ankudey and B. Y. Ofori-Frimpong, "Ghana," in Antelopes Global Survey and Regional Action Plans. Part 3: West and Central Africa, R. East (ed.) (Gland, Switzerland: I.U.C.N., 1990).

[654]A. Y. Mensah-Ntiamoah, "Pre-feasibility Study on Wildlife Potentials in the Kakum and Assin-Atandanso Forest reserves, Central Region, Ghana," (Unpublished) Department of Game and Wildlife, Accra, Ghana, 1989.

[655]I.U.C.N., "Ghana: Conservation of Biological Diversity," Draft, Tropical Forestry Program. (Cambridge, UK.: World Conservation Monitoring Center).

[657]World Bank, "World Development Report, 1992: Development and the Environment," Op cit.

[657]Peter Hazell and William Magrath, "Summary of World Bank Forestry Policy," in Conservation of West and Central African Rain Forests, World Bank Environment Paper No. 1, (Washington, DC, 1992), pp. 10-17.

[658]"NGOs Criticize World Bank on Harmful Environment Policies," Africa Recovery, vol. 5, no. 1, June 1991, p. 27. See also: Baffour Ankomah, "World Bank Not Friend of the Earth," New African, November, 1996, p. 19.

[659]Sylvian Buyalama, "Environment Degradation, World Bank Projects, and the Right to a Clean Environment," in George Shepherd Jr., and N. M. Karamo (eds.) Economic Justice in Africa, (Westport: Greenwood Press, 1994), p. 70. See also: John Mihevo's treatise on the consequences of structural adjustment to the Ghanaian environment," in The Market Tells Them So, (London: Zed Books, 1995), Chapters Six and Seven.

[660]See: Chapter Four, Section IX; "The Political Economy of Structural Adjustment in Ghana: Its Implications to Deforestation Policies."

[661]According to the F.A.O., the cutting down of trees for agricultural purposes has accounted for 70% of deforestation in Africa. {F.A.O., "Forest Resources Assessment Project," (Rome, F.A.O., 1981), and "Forest Resources Assessment 1990: Global Synthesis," (Rome: F.A.O., 1990), Forestry Paper # 124.}

[662]The particular agencies in mind are those dealing with land administration, agriculture, mining, transportation, manufacturing, game and wildlife.

[663]Panayotou and Ashton have reported a finding from a study conducted in Iquitos, Peru, that showed that fruits and latex products accounted for 82% of the total net present value (N.P.V.) of the forest. This finding may not be typical of all tropical forests, yet, it shows that other products can be economically competitive with timber. See: Theodore Panayotou and Peter S. Ashton, Not By Timber Alone, Op. cit.

[664]M. D. Bowes and J. V. Krutilla, Multiple-Use Management: The Economy of Forest Lands, (Washington, D.C.: Resources for the Future, 1989), chapter 7.

[665]By the admission of the Department of Forestry, this is a well-known, but increasingly neglected, fact. In "Ghana: Steps Towards Sustainable........," for example, the Planning Branch of the Department stresses that allowing non-governmental stakeholders, especially the grassroots population in the forest regions, an active and central role in the formulation and implementation of forestry policies is necessary for achieving the government's policy objectives. See: Planning Branch, Department of Forestry, Op. cit., p. 8.

[666]As indicated in Chapter Five representatives of non-governmental stakeholders were allowed to participate in the series of seminars preceding the formulation of Ghana's Forest Policy of 1988. Much as this indicated a recognition of the relevance of this group in the deforestation policy process, it is necessary to go beyond that essentially symbolic gesture and institute programs whereby such stakeholders will become active facilitators of Ghana's deforestation policy objectives.

[667]Such measurable criteria may include the extent of virgin forest existing, the extent and condition of reserved and non-reserved forests, the quantities of timber and non-timber forest products extracted, the contents of forest product exports, external and domestic revenues generated from the forestry sector, the total area of farmlands, the total area of farmlands, the total area of tree lots and forest plantations, and the amounts of firewood and charcoal used by Ghanaian families.

[668]As was noted in Chapter Seven, the Lands Commission keeps 10% of the total revenues it helps to generate from royalties and rents paid by the timber contractors.

BIBLIOGRAPHY

Books

Adu, A. L. The Civil Service in New African States. New York: Praeger, 1965.

African Association for Public Administration and Management (A.A.P.A.M.). The Ecology of Public Administration and Management in Africa. New Delhi: Vickas, 1986.

Afrifah, A. A. The Ghana Coup. London: Frank Cass, 1966.

Agbodeka, Francis. African Politics and British Policy in the Gold Coast 1868-1900. London: Longman, 1971.

Ahmed, Iftikhar and Jacobus A. Doeleman (eds.). Beyond Rio: The Environmental Crisis and Sustainable Livelihoods in the Third World, New York: St Martin's Press, 1995.

Allison, Graham. Essence of Decision: Explaining the Cuban Missile Crisis. Boston: Little Brown & Co., 1971.

Agyeman-Badu, Yaw. and Kwaku Osei-Hwedie. The Political Economy of Instability: Colonial Legacy, Inequality, and Political Instability in Ghana. Third World Monograph Series. Lawrenceville VA; Brunswick Publishing Co., 1982.

Amonoo, Ben. Ghana, 1957-1966: The Politics of Institutional Dualism. London: Allen and Unwin, 1986.

Anquandah, James Rediscovering Ghana's Past. Essex: Longman, 1982.

Apter, David E. Ghana in Transition. Princeton: Princeton University Press, 1972.

Arhin, Kwame. Traditional Rule in Ghana: Past and Present. Accra: Sedco, 1985.

Aryeetey, Ernest. Structural Adjustment and Aid in Ghana. Accra: Frederich Ebert Foundation, 1996.

Austin, Dennis. Politics in Ghana, 1946 - 1960. London: Oxford University Press, 1970.

Balogun, M. J. Public Administration in Nigeria. London: Macmillan, 1983.

Bardach, E. The Implementation Game: What Happens After a Bill Becomes Law. Cambridge: MIT Press, 1977.

Baynham, Simon. The Military and Politics in Nkrumah's Ghana. Boulder: Westview, 1988.

Biswal, Tapan Prasad. Ghana: Political and Constitutional Developments. New Delhi: Northern Book Center, 1992.

Blakeley, Brian L. The Colonial Office, 1868 - 1892. Durham: Duke University Press, 1972.

Blay, J. B. Legend of Kwame Nkrumah. Accra: Abicom Ltd., 1973.

Boahen, A. Adu. Topics in West African History. London: Longman, 1966.

Boateng, Charles Adom. Nkrumah's Consciencism. Dubuque, Iowa: Kendall/Hunt Publishing Company, 1995.

Bowes, M. D. and J. V. Krutilla. Multiple-Use Management: The Economy of Forest Lands. Washington, D.C.: Resources for the Future, 1989.

Broader, John O. "Development Alternatives for Tropical Rain Forests." Environment and the Poor: Development Strategies for a Common Agenda. United States-Third World Policy Perspectives, No. 11, Overseas Development Council. New Brunswick: Transaction Books, 1989.

Burns, Alan (Sir). Colonial Civil Servant. London: George Allen and Unwin, 1949.

Busia, K. A. The Position of the Chief in the Modern Political System of Asante. London: Oxford University Press, 1968.

Cardinall, A. W. In Asante and Beyond. London: Seeley, Service and Company, 1927.

Chazan, Naomi. An Anatomy of Ghanaian Politics: Managing Political Recession, 1969-1982. Boulder: Westview, 1983.

Chipp, Thomas Ford. The Forest Officer's Handbook of the Gold Coast, Ashanti, and the Northern Territories. London: Crown Agents for the Colonies, 1922.

Cleaver, Kevin M. and Gotz A. Schreiber. Reversing the Spiral: The Population, Agriculture, and Environment Nexus in Sub-Saharan Africa. Washington, D.C.: The World Bank, 1994.

Codjoe, Frank Kwaw. Elites, Ideology, and development Problems of Ghana. Hamburg: Verlag an der Lottbeg, 1988.

Daaku, K. Yeboah. Trade and Politics in the Gold Coast, 1600-1720. Oxford: Clarendon Press, 1970.

Dror, Yehezkel. Public Policy-Making Re-Examined, Part IV: An Optimal Model of Public Policy-Making. San Francisco: Chandler, 1968.

Dunn, William N. Public Policy Analysis: An Introduction. Englewood Cliffs N. J.: Prentice Hall, 1979.

Dye, Thomas R. Understanding Public Policy. Upper Saddle River, N. J.: Prentice Hall, 1988.

Dye, Thomas and Harmon Ziegler. The Irony of Democracy. 5th Ed., Belmont, Ca.: Wardsworth, 1981.

Danquah, J. B. Akan Laws and Customs. London: Oxford University Press, 1957.

Easton, David. A Framework For Political Analysis. Englewood Cliffs, New Jersey: Prentice Hall, 1965.

East, R. (ed). Antelopes Global Survey and Regional Action Plans. Part 3: West and Central Africa. Gland, Switzerland: I.U.C.N., (1990).

Edsman, Bjorn M. Lawyers in Gold Coast Politics, 1900-1945: From Mensah Sarbah to J. B. Danquah. Upsala: University Press, 1979.

Egonmwan, J. A. Policy Analysis: Concepts and Applications. Benin City, Nigeria: Fiesta Press, 1987.

Eisenstadt, S. N. and Stan Rokkon (eds.). Building States and Nations: Analyses by Regions. Vol. II, Berverly Hills, CA.: Sage, 1973.

Eulau, Heinz. Samuel J. Eldersveld, and Morris Janowitz (eds). Political Behavior. New York: Free Press, 1956.

Fieldhouse, David Kenneth. Unilever Overseas: The Anatomy of a Multi-national 1895-1965. London: Croom Helm, 1978.

Gooding, Robert. The Politics of Rational Man. New York: John Wiley and Sons, 1982.

Gifford, P. and W. R. Louis (eds).Britain and Germany in Africa: Imperial Rivalry and Colonial Rule. New Haven: Yale University Press, 1967.

Grindle, Merilee S. (ed). Politics and Policy Implementation in the Third World..Princeton, N J: Princeton University Press, 1980.

Gruppe, Henry and Waafas Ofosu-Amaah. Legal, Regulatory, and Institutional Aspects of Environmental and Natural Resources Management in Developing Countries; A Country Study of Ghana. Washington D.C.: International Institute for Environment and Development, 1984.

Gyimah-Boadi, E. (ed.). Ghana Under PNDC Rule. Senegal: Codesria, 1993.

Hansen, Emmanuel. Ghana Under Rawlings: Early Years. Lagos: Malthouse Press, 1991.

Harbeson, John W., Donald Rothchild, and Naomi Chazan (eds). Civil Society and the State in Africa. Boulder: Lynne Rienner, 1994.

Hargrove, E. The Missing Link: The Study of Implementation of Social Policy. Washington, DC: The Urban Institute, 1975.

Hayford, Casely. Gold Coast Native Institutions. London: Sweet and Maxwell, 1903.

Herbst, Jeffrey. The Politics of Reform in Ghana: 1982-1991. Denver: University of Colorado Press, 1993.

Hoselitz , B. F. Robert and W. Moore (eds.). Industrialization and Society. Paris: UNESCO-Monton, 1963.

Hynes, W. G. The Economics of Empire: Britain, Africa and the New Imperialism 1870-1895. London: Longman, 1979.

Ingham, Barbara. Tropical Exports and Economic Development: New Perspectives on Producer Response in the Low Income Countries. New York: St. Martins Press, 1981.

Inglesias, Gabriel U. Implementation: The Problem of Achieving Results. A Casebook on Asia Experiences: Eastern Regional Organization for Public Administration (E.R.O.P.A.).Manilla: E.R.O.P.A., 1976.

Isichei, Elizabeth. History of West Africa Since 1800. New York: Africana, 1977.

James, C. L. R. Nkrumah and the Ghana Revolution. London: Allison and Busby, 1977.

Jones, Charles. An Introduction to the Study of Public Policy. 3rd Edition, Monterey, Ca: Brooks/Cole, 1984.

Kafir, Nelson. The Shrinking Political Arena. Berkeley: University of California Press, 1976.

Kay, G. B. The Political Economy of Colonialism in Ghana: a Collection of Documents and Statistics 1900 - 1960. Cambridge: University Press, 1972.

Killick, Tony. Development Economics in Action: A study of Economic Policies in Ghana. London: Hienemann, 1978.

Knaplund, Paul. James Stephen and the British Colonial System, 1843 - 1847. Madison: University of Wisconsin Press, 1953.

Koehn, Peter H. Public Policy and Administration in Africa: Lessons from Nigeria. Boulder: Westview, 1990.

Kuklick, Henrika. The Imperial Bureaucrat: The Colonial Administrative Service in the Gold Coast,1920-1939. Stanford: Hoover Institution Press, 1979.

Kumado, C. E. K. Constitutionalism, Civil Liberties, and Development: A Case Study of Ghana Since Independence. Accra: Ghana Publishing Corporation, 1980.

Larson, James S. Why Government Programs Fail: Improving Policy Implementation. New York: Praeger, 1980.

Leys, Colin (ed.).Politics and Change in Developing Countries. Cambridge: Cambridge Univ. Press, 1969.

Lindblom, Charles. The Policy Making Process. Englewood Cliffs, N. J.: Prentice Hall, 1968.

Lumley, E. K. Forgotten Mandate. London: C. Hurst and Company, 1976.

MaCarthy, Mary. Social Change and the Growth of British Power in the Gold Coast: The Fante States, 1807-1874. Lanham, Md.: University Press of America, 1963.

Martin, E. D. The British West African Settlements, 1750-1821. Imperial Studies No. 2, (London, 1927).

Metcalfe, G. E. Great Britain and Ghana: Documents of Ghana History, 1808-1957. London: Thomas Nelson, 1964.

Migdal, Joel. Strong Societies and Weak States: State-Society Relations and State Capabilities in the Third World. Princeton: Princeton University Press, 1988.

Mihevo, John. The Market Tells Them So. London: Zed Books, 1995.

Mutahaba, Gelase, Baguma Rweikiza, and Mohamed Hatfani. Vitalizing African Public Administration for Recovery and Development. Hartford: Kumarian, 1993.

Nkrumah, Kwame. The Autobiography of Kwame Nkrumah. London: Panaf, 1973.

_____. I Speak of Freedom. New York: Praeger, 1961.

_____. Consciencism: Philosophy and Ideology for Decolonization and Development with Particular Reference to the African Revolution. New York: Monthly Review Press, 1965.

Nugent, Paul. Big Men, Small Boys and Politics in Ghana. London: Pinter, 1995.

Ocran, A. K. Politics of the Sword. London: R. Collins, 1977.

O'Donnell, Guillermo. Modernization and Bureaucratic Authoritarianism: Studies in South American Politics. Berkeley, CA.: University of California Institute of International Studies, 1962.

Ofosu-Appiah, L. H. The Life and Times of Dr. J. B. Danquah. Accra: Waterville Publishing House, 1974.

Ollennu, Nii Amaa. Principles of Customary Law in Ghana. London: Ernest and Maxwell, 1962.

Omari, Pater T. Kwame Nkrumah, The Anatomy of an African Dictatorship. New York: Africana Publishing Corporation, 1970.

Onyemelukwe, Clement. Men and Management in Perspective. Berkeley: University of California Press, 1983.

Oquaye, Mike. Politics in Ghana, 1972-1979. Accra: Tornado Press, 1980.

Owusu, Maxwell.. Uses and Abuses of Political Power. Chicago: University of Chicago Press, 1970.

Panayaton,Theodore and Peter S. Ashton. Not By Timber Alone. Washington D.C.: Island Press, 1992.

Panjabi, Ranee K. L. The Earth Summit at Rio: Politics, Economics, and the Environment. Boston: Northeastern University Press, 1997.

Pinkney, Robert. Democracy and Dictatorship in Ghana and Tanzania. New York: St. Martins Press, 1977.

Platt, D. C. M. Finance, Trade and Politics in British Foreign Policy 1818-1914. London: Clarendon Press, 1968.

Prah, Edward. Sustainable Management of the Tropical High Forest of Ghana. London: Commonwealth Secretariat/International Development Research Center, (September 1994).

Presthus, Robert. Elites and the Policy Process. London: Cambridge University Press, 1974.

Price, Robert M. Society and Bureaucracy in Contemporary Ghana. Berkeley: University of California Press, 1979.

Rattray, Robert Sutherland. Ashanti. Oxford: The Clarendon Press, 1923.

Repetto, Robert and Malcolm Gillis (eds), Public Policies and the Misuse of Forest Resources. New York: Cambridge University Press/World Resources Institute, 1988.

Riggs, Fred. The Ecology of Public Administration. Bombay: Asia Publishing House, 1961.

Rile, J. Sufferings in Africa: Captain Rile's Narrative. New York: Clarkson Potter, 1965.

Rimmer, Douglas. Staying Poor: Ghana's Political Economy, 1950-1990. Oxford, Pergamon Press, 1992.

Ripley, Randall B. Policy Analysis in Political Science. Chicago: Nelson-Hall, 1987.

Rodney, Walter. How Europe Underdeveloped Africa. Washington, DC.: Howard University Press, 1982.

Rothchild, Donald (ed.). Ghana: The Political Economy of Recovery. Boulder: Lynne Reinner, 1991.

Rothchild, Donald and Naomi Chazan (eds). The Precarious Balance: State and Society in Africa. Boulder: Westview Press, 1988.

Rweyemanu, A. H. and Goran Hyden (eds.). A Decade of Public Administration in Africa. Nairobi: East African Literature Bureau, 1975.

Sharkansky, Ira. (ed). Public Administration: Public Policy Making in Government. 2nd Ed., Chicago: Markham, 1972.

Shepherd Jr., George. and N. M. Karamo (eds). Economic Justice in Africa. Westport: Greenwood Press, 1994.

Shillington, Kevin. Ghana and the Rawlings Factor. New York: St. Martin=s Press, 1992.

Southgate, Douglas D. and John F. Dsinger (eds.). Sustainable Resource Development in the Third World. Westview, Special Studies in Natural Resources and Energy Management. Boulder: Westview Press, 1987.

Stryker, J. Dirk. A. "Technology, Human Pressure, and Ecology in the Arid and Semi-Arid Tropics," in Environment and the Poor: Development Strategies for a Common Agenda. US-Third World Policy Perspectives, No. 11, Overseas Development Council. New Brunswick: Transaction Books, 1989.

Taylor, C. J. Tropical Forestry. London: Oxford University Press, 1962.

The United States Congress, Office of Technology Assessment (O.T.A.), Technologies to Sustain Tropical Forest Resources. Publication No. OAT/F/214. Washington, D.C.: March, 1984.

Thompson, H. N. Gold Coast: Report on Forests. Colonial Reports - Miscellaneous No. 66. London: HMSO, 1910.

Tivy, J. and G. O'Hare. Human Impact on the Ecosystem. Edinburgh: Oliver and Boyd, 1982.

Truman, David B. The Governmental Process. New York: Knopf, 1957.

United Nations/ International Labor Office. World Resources: A Guide to the Global Environment. New York: Oxford University Press, 1996.

Uzogwe, G. N. Britain and the Conquest of Africa. Ann Arbor Mich.: University of Michigan Press, 1974.

Webster, J. B., A. A. Boahen, and Michael Tidy. The Revolutionary Years: West Africa Since 1800. Essex: Longman, 1978.

Wilson, Charles. Unilever 1945-1965: The Challenge and Response in the Post-war Industrial Revolution. London: Cassell, 1968.

World Bank. World Tables, 1995. Baltimore, Johns Hopkins University Press, 1995.

Wright, Martin. The Development of the Legislative Council, 1606 - 1945. Studies in Colonial Legislation, Volume 1, London: 1945.

_____. The Gold Coast Legislative Council. Studies in Colonial Legislatures Series, Margery Perham (ed), London: Faber and Faber, 1946.

Periodicals

Agyemang-Duah. "Ghana, 1982-1986; the Politics of the P.N.D.C." Journal of Modern African Studies. Vol. 25, No. 4, (1987).

Ankomah, Baffour. "World Bank Not Friend of the Earth." New African. (November, 1996).

Bienen, Henry. "Populist Military Regimes in West Africa." Armed Forces and Society. Vol. 11, No. 3 (Spring 1985), 357-377.

Brown, Becky. J. Mark E. Hanson, Diana M Liverman, and Robert W. Merideth. "Global Sustainability: Toward Definition." Environmental Management. Vol. 11, No. 6, (1987).

Callancy, Barbara. "National-Local Linkages in Ghana," African Review, Vol. 4, No. 3, (1974).

Chazan, Naomi. "Political Culture and Political Socialization: A Ghanaian Case." The Review of Politics. Vol. 40, (1978), 3-31.

Chipp, Thomas F. "The Gold Coast Forestry Problem." Empire Forestry Journal. London: Journal of the Empire Forestry Association, Imperial Institute, Vol. 2, No. 1, (April 1923), 69.

Crook, Richard. "Legitimacy, Authority, and the Transfer of Power in Ghana." <u>Political Studies</u>, Vol. 35, (1987), 572.

_____. " State, Society and Political Institution in Cote d'Ivoire and Ghana." <u>IDS Bulletin</u>, Vol. 21, # 4, Sussex: (October 1990), 34.

Dror, Yehezkel. "Muddling Through - Science or Inertia?" <u>Public Administration Review</u>. Vol. 24, (1964), 153.

Easton, David. "An Approach to the Analysis of Political Systems." <u>World Politics</u>. Vol. 9, (1957), 383-400.

Ephson, Ben. "Mobilization of Farmers." <u>West Africa</u>. (February 23, 1987).

Etzioni, Amitai. "Mixed-Scanning: A Third Approach to Decision-Making." <u>Public Administration Review</u>. Vol. 27, (1967), 387-388.

Green, Daniel. "Ghana's Adjusted Democracy." <u>Review of African Political Economy</u>..Vol. 22, (1995), 577-586.

_____. "Structural Adjustment and Politics in Ghana." <u>Trans Africa Forum</u>. Vol. 8, (Summer 1991), 84.

Hall, J, B. "Conservation of Forest in Ghana." <u>Universitas</u>. Vol. 8, 1987.

Hansen, Emmanuel and Paul Collins. "The Army, the State, and the Rawlings Revolution in Ghana." <u>African Affairs</u>, Vol. 79, (January 1980).

Harding, Garrett. "The Tragedy of the Commons." <u>Science</u> Vol. 162, (1968).

Haynes, Jeff. W. Trevor, and Stephen Riley, "Debt in Sub-Saharan Africa: The Local Politics of Stabilization." <u>African Affairs</u>. Vol. 86, (July, 1987), 343-366.

Hayward, Fred M. "A Reassessment of Conventional Wisdom About Informed Public: National Political Information in Ghana." <u>American Political Science Review</u>. Vol. 70, (June 1976), 433-451.

Hirshman, A. O. and Charles Lindblom. "Economic Development, Research and Development, Policy Making: Some Converging Views." <u>Behavioral Science</u>. Vol. 7, (1962), 211-2.

Hopkins, A. G. "Economic Imperialism in West Africa: Lagos, 1880-1892." <u>EconHR</u>, Vol. x, (1968), 580-606.

Hosmer, Ellen. "Paradise Lost: The Ravaged Rainforest." <u>Multinational Monitor</u>. (June 1997).

Hynes, W. G. "British Mercantile Attitudes Towards Imperial Expansion." <u>HJ</u>, Vol. xix, (1976), 969-979.

Imperial Institute of London. <u>Journal of the Empire Forestry Association</u>. Vol. 1, No. 1 (March 1922), 12.

Jackman, R. "Politicians in Uniforms." <u>American Political Science Review</u>. Vol. 70, # 1, (December 1976), 1078-1097.

Jeong, Ho-Won. "The Impact of the World Bank and the IMF on the Structural Adjustment Program in Ghana." <u>Journal of the Third World Spectrum</u>. Vol. 2, (Spring, 1995).

Kraus, Jon. "Ghana's Radical Populist Regime." <u>Current History</u>..Vol. 84, (April 1985), 164-168, 186-187.

Kumado, C. K. "Judicial Review of Legislation in Ghana Since Independence." <u>Black Law Journal</u>. 5 :2 (1977). 208-230.

Lebrum, J. P. "Richesses Specifiques dela Flore Vasculaire des Divers Pays ou Regions d'Afrique." <u>Candollea</u>. Vol. 31.

Lindblom, Charles. "The Science of Muddling Through." <u>Public Administration Review</u>. Vol. 79-89, (Spring 1959), 19.

_____. "Still Muddling, Not Yet Through." <u>Public Administration Review</u>. Vol. 39, (1979), 517-526.

Logan, Ikubolajeh B. and Kidane Mengisteab. "IMF-World Bank Adjustment and Structural Transformation in Sub-Saharan Africa." Economic Geography, Vol. 69, (Jan. 1993).

McKinley, R. D. and A. S. Cohen. "A Comparative Analysis of the Political and Economic Performance of Military and Civilian Regimes: A Cross-National Aggregative Study." Comparative Politics. Vol. 8, # 1, (October 1975), 1-30.

Morna, Colleen Lowe. "In Ghana, Even a Senior Official Can't Make Ends Meet." Christian Science Monitor. (September, 1988), 8.

"NGOs Criticize World Bank on Harmful Environment Policies." Africa Recovery. Vol. 5, No.1, (June 1991), 27.

Novicki, Margaret. "Going for a Green Revolution." Africa Report. (September-October, 1988).

Nwambani, Ebere. "The British Labor Party, The "Dual Mandate" and Africa, 1945-1951." Transafrican Journal of History. Vol. 21, No 1, (1992), 93 - 110.

Pirro, Ellen B. and Eleanor E. Zeff, "A New Look at Military-Civilian Governments." Journal of Strategic Studies. Vol. 2, (1979), 206-231.

Plotkin, Mark. "Treasures Among the Trees." International Monitor. (June, 1997).

Proff, Heike. "Structural Adjustment Programmes and Industrialization in Sub-Saharan Africa.." Intereconomics, Vol. 29, (Sept.-Oct. 1994).

Revelle, R. "Energy Sources for Rural Development." Energy. Vol. 4, (1979), 969 - 989.

Rothchild, Donald. "Military Regime Performance: An Appraisal of the Ghana Experience, 1972-78." Comparative Politics. Vol. 12, (July 1980), 459-479.

Saasa, Oliver S. "Public Policy-Making in Developing Countries: The Utility of Contemporary Decision-Making Models." Public Administration and Development. 3 (1983) 300-321.

Sabatier, Paul. "Towards Better Theories of the Policy Process." PS: Political Science and Politics. June 1991.

Sargeant, Caroline et al. "Incentives for the Sustainable Management of Tropical High Forest in Ghana." Commonwealth Forestry Review. Vol. 73 No. 3 (1984), 155-163.

Sarpong, Yaw Akrasi. "Role of the Defense Committees." The Mirror. Accra: Graphic Corporation, (January 24, 1983).

Smith, G. and May D. "The Artificial Debate Between Rationalist and Incrementalist Models of Decision Making." Policy and Politics. Vol. 8, No. 2, (1980).

Talbot, J. J. "The Fate of Tropical Forest." Science and Public Policy. Vol. 6, # 3, (1979).

Tangei, R. "The Politics of Government-Business Relations in Ghana." Journal of Modern African Studies. Vol. 20, No. 1, (1992).

Wunsch, James S. "Traditional Authorities, Innovation, and Development Policy." Journal of Developing Areas. Vol. 11, (April 1977), 357-371.

Ghana Government Publications

Belfield, H. Conway "Report on the Legislation Governing the Alienation of Native Lands in the Gold Coast Colony and Ashanti." London: Her Majesty's Stationary Office, 1912.

Blavo, Gertrude. "The State of Forestry Legislation in Ghana." Accra: Forestry Commission Symposia Series, #3.

Colonial Office, Report on the Gold Coast: 1949. London: His Majesty's Stationary Office, 1950-51.

Deloitte & Touche Consulting. "Forestry Department of Ghana, Institutional Reform Project." Accra: Deloitte & Touche, (1995).

_____. "Forestry Department of Ghana: Institutional Reform Project, Working Groups Findings." *Circa* 1992. Accra, Ghana.

Forest Products Inspection Bureau. "Welcome to Forest Products Inspection Bureau." Third Edition. Takoradi: Public Relations Unit, (1994).

Forest Research Institute of Ghana (FORIG). "Incentives and Technologies for Sustainability of Forest Management in Anglophone West Africa." Draft Report, (May, 1995).

Forest Resources Management Project. "Protection of the Forest Industry." A Study Prepared for the Ministry of Lands and Natural Resources, Accra, (October 1991).

Ghana Environmental Protection Council. "Ghana Environment Action Plan, Volume 2." Accra, Ghana: Environmental Protection Council, 1988.

Ghana Environmental Protection Council. "Ghana Environment Action Plan, Volume 2. Accra, Ghana: Environmental Protection Council, 1994.

Ghana Forestry Commission. "Proposals for the Revision of the National Forest Policy for Ghana." Accra, (1995).

Ghana Forestry Commission. "Revision of Ghana's Forest Policy." Proceedings of A National Conference, Accra, Forestry Commission Symposia Series # 3, (April 2-8, 1989).

Ghana Forestry Commission. "Revision of Ghana's Forest Policy." Proceedings of a National Conference, Forestry Commission Symposia Series # 3. Accra, (April 2-8, 1989).

Ghana Government. The Consolidated Development Plan, 1958/59. Accra: Government Printer, 1957.

Ghana Government. Second Development Plan, 1959-1964. Accra: Government Printer, 1958.

Ghana Ministry of Lands and Forestry. "Draft National Forest Policy of the Republic of Ghana." Accra: Ministry of Lands and Forestry, 1993.

Ghana Statistical Service. "Ghana Living Standards Survey, First Year Report." Accra, (1989).

Ghana Statistical Service. "Ghana Living Standards Survey, Report of the Third Round, September 1991 - September 1992." Accra, (March 1995).

Ghana Timber Exports Development Board. "Ghana Forests, Wood and People." London: Timber Exports Development Board, (1989).

Gold Coast Colony, "Wealth in Wood." Accra: Public Relations Department, 1950.

Gordon, W. A. "The Law of Forestry." London: Her Majesty's Stationary Office, 1955.

Government of Ghana. Five Year Development Plan, Part III. Accra: Ministry of Economic Planning/Ghana Publishing Corporation, (January 1977).

Government of Ghana. "Timber Industry: Report of Fact Finding Committee Appointed by the Minister of Commerce, Land and Mines." Accra: Government Printing Department, 1951.

Government of Ghana. Independence Constitution of 1957. Accra: Government Press, 1957.

Government of Ghana. Seven-Year Development Plan For National Reconstruction and Development. Accra: Office of the Planning Commission, 1976.

Government of Ghana. Five-Year Development Plan, 1982-86. Accra: Ministry of Economic Planning, 1981.

Government of Ghana. Constitution of the Second Republic of Ghana. Accra: Ghana Publishing Corporation, (1969).

Ghana Government. "A Revolutionary Journey: Selected Speeches of Flt. Lt. J. J. Rawlings, Chairman of the P.N.D.C., December 31, 1982." Accra: Information Services Department, (1983).

Government of Ghana. The Constitution of Ghana, Accra: Government Printer, 1957.

Ghana Government. Constitution of the Republic of Ghana. Accra: Government Publishing Corporation, 1992.

Government of the Gold Coast. "Forestry Policy for the Gold Coast Colony." London: His Majesty's Stationary Office, 1948.

Mensah-Ntiamoah, A. Y. "Pre-feasibility Study on Wildlife Potentials in the Kakum and Assin-Atandanso Forest Reserves, Central Region, Ghana." (Unpublished) Department of Game and Wildlife, Accra, Ghana, (1989).

Ministry of Agriculture. "Operation Feed Yourself : Sustained Gains in Ghana's Agrarian Revolution." Information Bulletin. Accra: Government Printers, (1976)

Ministry of Energy, Ghana. "The Prospects for Commercial Charcoal Production from Logging Residues in Ghana." Final Report, Accra, (January, 1992).

Ministry of Lands and Forestry. "Forest and Wildlife Policy." Accra, Ghana: Ghana Publishing Corporation, (May, 1995).

Ministry of Lands and Forestry. "Forest and Wildlife Policy." Accra, (November 24, 1994).

Republic of Ghana. The Constitution of the Third Republic of Ghana. Accra: Ghana Publishing Corporation, 1980.

Republic of Ghana. The Constitution of the Forth Republic of Ghana. Accra: Ghana Publishing Corporation, 1992.

Republic of Ghana. Budget Statement for 1975-76. Accra: Ghana Publishing Corporation, 1975.

Republic of Ghana. Budget Statement for 1980-81. Accra: Ghana Publishing Corporation, 1980.

Republic of Ghana. Budget Statement for 1995-96. Accra: Ghana Publishing Corporation, 1995.

Republic of Ghana. Constitution of the Second Republic of Ghana. Accra: Ghana Publishing Corporation, 1969.

Republic of Ghana. "Forest and Wildlife Policy." Ministry of Lands and Forestry, Accra, (November 24, 1994).

Republic of Ghana. "Seven-Year Plan for National Reconstruction and Development: Financial Years 1963/64 - 1969/70." Accra: Office of the Planning Commission, (1963).

Republic of Ghana "The Republican Constitution of Ghana." Accra: Ghana Government Printers, (1960).

Republic of Ghana, Parliamentary Debates, June 21, 1957. Accra: Ghana Government Painters, (1957).

Silviconsult. "The Forestry Department Review." Prepared for the Government of Ghana. Accra: Silviconsult, (October 1986).

Thompson, H. N. Report on Forests. Colonial Reports - Miscellaneous, # 66, London: His Majesty's Stationary Office, 1910.

Tufuor, K. "A Review of Forest Sector Policy of Ghana." Ghana Forestry Commission, Accra, (Unpublished) (December, 1993).

Ghana Government Acts, Decrees, Etc.

"Forest Ordinance of 30 March 1927, Chapter 157." Accra, Ghana Publishing Corporation, Printing Division.

Government of Ghana, Trees and Timber Decree, 1974 (NRCD 273), Accra: Ghana Publishing Corporation (Printing Division), (1974).
Government of Ghana, Forest Protection (Amendment) Law, 1986 (PNDCL 142), Accra: Ghana Publishing Corporation (Publishing Division), Assembly Press, (1986).
Government of Ghana. "The Local Government Administration Bill (1970)." Government Gazette. Accra: Ghana Publishing Corporation, (1970).
Government of Ghana. "The Lands Commission Act, 1993." Accra: Ghana Publishing Corporation, (1993).
Government of Ghana. "The Ghana Forestry Commission Act, 1980." Accra: Ghana Publishing Corporation, (1980).
Government of Ghana. "Environmental Protection Council Decree, 1974 (NRC Decree 239), Section 2.," Accra: Government Printers, (1974).
Government of Ghana. "The Control of Bush Fires Law, PNDCL 46, 1983." Accra: Government Printers, (1983).
Republic of Ghana. "Forestry Commission Act (Act 453), 1993." (Accra: Ghana Publishing Corporation, (1993).

United States Government Publications

Gritzner, J. "Deforestation and Environmental Change in the West African Sahel." Washington, D.C.: Office of Technology Assessment (O.T.A.) Commissioned Paper, 1982.
United States Government. "Report of a Staff Study Mission to Great Britain, Ghana, Senegal, Cote d'Ivoire, and France, November 29-December 20, 1988, to the Committee on Foreign Affairs, U.S. House of Representatives" Washington, D.C., U.S. Government Printing Office, 1989.

United Nations Organization Publications

Adeyoju, S. Kolade "A Study on Forest Administration Problems in Six Selected African Countries." Rome: Food and Agricultural Organization (FAO), 1976.
Lanly, Jean Paul. "Tropical Forest Resources." Rome: United Nations Food and Agricultural Organization (F.A.O.), 1982, Paper No. 30.
Phillip, M. S. "Management of Tropical Moist Forest in Africa." F.A.O. Forestry Paper 88, (1989), 6-18.
U.N.D.P. "Assistance to Forestry Planning, Ghana, Project Findings and Recommendations." Rome: U.N.D.P./F.A.O., (1993).
United Nations Economic Commission for Africa (E. C. A.). "Integrated Approaches to Rural Development in Africa." Proceedings of E.C.A. Conference on Rural Development, Moshi, Tanzania. New York: UN, (1971), 75.
United Nations Food and Agricultural Organization (F.A.O.). F.A.O. Yearbook Volume 48, 1994. Rome: F.A.O. tatistics Series No.125, (1995).
United Nations Food and Agricultural Organization (F.A.O.). F.A.O../W.R.I. Production Yearbook, Conservation Table 1001. Rome: F.A.O., 1992.
U.N.F.A.O../United Nations Environment Program (U.N.E.P.). Tropical Forest Resources Assessment Project. Rome: F.A.O., 1981.
U.N.F.A.O. Forest Resources Assessment 1990, Global Synthesis. Rome: F.A.O., Forestry Paper 124, 1995.
U.N.F.A.O. "Statistics Yearbook: Forestry Production." Vol. 48, FAO Statistics Series # 125. Rome: FAO, (1995).
U.N.F.A.O. "Forest Resources Assessment Project." Rome: F.A.O., (1981).

U.N.F.A.O. "Forest Resources Assessment 1990: Global Synthesis." Forestry Paper # 124. Rome: F.A.O., (1990).

United Nations. International Trade Statistics Yearbook, 1994. 26th Edition, New York: UN Publishing Division, Series E/F. 96XVII.2, Vol. 2.

World Bank Publications

Anderson, Dennis & Robert Fishwick, "Fuelwood Consumption and Deforestation in African Countries." Staff Working Papers, No. 704, Washington, D.C.: The World Bank, 1984.

Armstrong, Robert. "Ghana Country Assistance Review: A Study in Development Effectiveness." Washington, D.C. : The World Bank, (1996).

Hazell, Peter. and William Magrath. "Summary of World Bank Forestry Policy." in Conservation of West and Central African Rain Forests. World Bank Environment Paper #1, Washington, DC, (1992).

World Bank. Trends in Developing Economies: Extracts, volume 3, Sub-Saharan Africa. Washington, D.C.: The World Bank, 1994.

World Bank. "Ghana: Structural Adjustment for Growth." Report # 7515-GH, Washington, DC.: World Bank, (1989).

World Bank. Trends in Developing Economies, Extracts: Volume 3. Sub-Saharan Africa. Washington, DC: The World Bank, 1994.

World Bank. World Development Report 1992. New York: Oxford University Press, 1992.

World Bank. World Development Report. Washington, D. C., World Bank, 1983.

World Bank. "World Development Report, 1992: Development and the Environment." New York: Oxford University Press, 1992.

World Bank. "World Development Report, 1996." Washington, DC: The World Bank, (1997).

Dissertations and Theses

Acquay, Herbert Kwesi. "The Impact of Stabilization and Structural Adjustment Programs Upon Ghana's Forest and Marine Fisheries (Natural Resources) Policy." Ph.D. Dissertation (Unpublished) Cornell University, 1993, Chapter 3.

Bennuah, S. Y. "Development of Forestry in Ghana." B.Sc. Thesis (Unpublished), Institute of Renewable Natural Resources, University of Science and Technology, Kumasi, Ghana, 1987.

Effah-Gyamfi,K. "Bono Manso - An Archaeological Investigation Into Early Akan Urbanism." Ph.D. Thesis, University of Ghana, Legon, 1978.

Kass-Yerenchi, O. K. "Operation of the Two Forest Protection Decrees in Ghana." (Unpublished Dissertation), Institute of Renewable Natural Resources, University of Science and Technology, Kumasi, Ghana, 1984.

_____. "The Adequacy of Forest Ordinance and The Forest Protection Decree as Forest Regulatory and Conservation Instruments in Ghana." B.Sc. Dissertation (unpublished). Institute of Renewable Natural Resources, University of Science and Technology, Kumasi, Ghana, (July, 1991), 45-49.

Omo-Bare, Iren."Military and Civilian Regimes in Sub-Saharan Africa: A Comparative Analysis of Public Policy Outputs and Outcomes." Ph.D. Dissertation (Unpublished), The Louisiana State University and Agricultural and Mechanical College, 1990.

Addresses, Speeches, Etc.

Acquah, Peter. "Environmental Issues and Aspects on Their Management in Ghana." Accra: E.P.A. Environmental Management Special Paper 2 (September 1995).

Ameh, Kafui. "Brief Overview of Ministry of Environment Science and Technology (MEST) Activities." A Paper Presented by the Public Relations Officer of the Ministry of Environment Science and Technology at the MEST/EPA/UNEP Seminar for Media Practitioners. Cape Coast, Ghana, (October 24-26, 1995).

Arthur, George F. Kojo. "Structural Adjustments, Dependency and Multinational Corporations: United Africa Company-The Unilever Connection in Ghana." (Unpublished).

Binswanger, H. and D. Pingali. "The Evolution of Farming Systems and Agricultural Technology in Sub-Saharan Africa." Discussion Paper 23, Agriculture and Rural Development Department, Washington, DC: The World Bank, 1989.

Blavo, Gertrude. "The State of Forestry Legislation in Ghana." Forestry Commission Symposia Series #3, (1989), 288.

Brimah, Alhaji Farouk. "Statement by the Deputy Minister for Environment, Science and Technology at the Sixth Session of the African Ministers of Environment." Nairobi, Kenya, (December 11-15, 1995).

Department of Forestry. "Steps Towards Sustainable Forest and Wise Use of Timber Resources." Paper Presented to the 28th Session of the ITTC and the 26th Session of the ITTO Permanent Committees, Accra, Ghana.

Esseks, John. "The Nationalization of the Ownership of Resources in Ghana." Paper Presented for the Colloquim on Ghana, Department of State, Washington, D.C., October 11, 1974.

Francois, J. "Timber Resources Development and Management." Paper Presented at the National Conference on Resource Conservation for Ghana's Sustainable Development, Accra, April 28-30, 1987.

Frimpong-Mensah, K. "Requirement of the Timber Industry." Ghana Forest Inventory Project Seminar Proceedings, Forestry Department, Accra, 1989.

Opare-Abetia, J. (ed). "Ghana In Search of a Stable Form of Government." Proceedings of the Twenty-Seventh Annual New Year School, December 29, 1977 to January 4, 1978. Legon: Institute of Adult Education, University of Ghana, (1978-1979), vols. 1 and 2.

Owusu, J. G. K. "Milestones in the Legislative History of Forestry in Ghana." Paper Presented at the RENARSA Forum, 1986.

_____."Revision of Ghana's Forest Policy." Proceedings of a National Conference, Accra, Forestry Commission Symposium Series, (April 2-8, 1989).

Planning Branch, Forestry Department. "Ghana: Steps Towards Sustainable Forestry and Wise Use of Timber Resources." Paper Presented at the Eighth Session of the I.T.T.C.and the Sixteenth Session of the I.T.T.O. Permanent Committees, Accra, (May 10-18, 1995).

Smith, E. Kofi. Ben Aninakwa, and George Ortsin. "Formulating and Practicing New Forest Policies: Recent Experiences from Ghana." A Paper Presented at a Seminar in Making Forest Policy Work, Oxford Forestry Institute, (July 6, 1995).

Internet Source
"Ghana Review International - MC4" at gh@ghana.com

Others
Dorm-Adjobu, Clement. Ampadu-Agyei, Okyeame, and Veit, Peter G. "Community Institutions in Resources Management: Agro-forestry by Mobisquads in Ghana." Edited

by Center for International Development and Environment, World Resources Institute. Washington, D.C.: World Resources Institute, (1991).

Friends of the Earth. "Plunder in Ghana's Rainforest for Illegal Profit: An Expose of Corruption, Fraud, and other Malpractice in the International Timber Trade." London: Friends of the Earth, (1992).

International Institute for Environment and Development (IIED). "Study of Incentives for the Sustainable Management of the Tropical High Forest of Ghana." Final Report, London: IIED, (October, 1994).

International Timber Trade Organization (I.T.T.O.). "I.T.T.O. Guidelines for the Establishment and Sustainable Management of Planted Tropical Forests." I.T.T.O. Policy Development 4, International Organizations Center, Yokohama, (1993).

I.U.C.N. "Ghana: Conservation of Biological Diversity." Draft, Tropical Forestry Program. Cambridge, UK.: World Conservation Monitoring Center.

Noack, D. et. al. "Better Utilization of Tropical Timber Resources in Order to Improve Sustainability and Reduce Negative Ecological Impacts - Wood Waste and Logging Damage in Nkrabia Forest Reserve, Ghana." I.T.T.O. Project PD 74/90. Hamburg: Federal Research Center for Forestry and Forest Products, (February 24, 1992).

Owusu, J. G. K. "Evolution of Forest Legislation in Ghana." (Unpublished) 1980.

Oxford Forestry Institute and ITTO. "Incentives in Producer and Consumer Countries to Promote Sustainable Development of Tropical Forests." Oxford, (1991).

Peprah, Ignatius. "Foreign Investment in the Forest-Based sector of Ghana." (Unpublished), Cambridge Mass.: Harvard University, 1982.

The Population Reference Bureau, "World Population Data Sheet 1994." Washington, D.C., Population Reference Bureau Inc., April 1994.

Index